Moon Astrology for Lovers

By the same author:
Panchang Moon Astrology (Thorsons, 2001)

Moon Astrology for Lovers

Michael Geary

Thorsons
An Imprint of HarperCollins*Publishers*
77–85 Fulham Palace Road
Hammersmith, London W6 8JB

The Thorsons website address is: www.thorsons.com

and *Thorsons*
are trademarks of HarperCollins*Publishers* Limited

Published by Thorsons 2002

10 9 8 7 6 5 4 3 2 1

A catalogue record for this book is
available from the British Library

ISBN 0 00 714310 9

Printed and bound in Great Britain by
Clays Ltd, St Ives plc

This book is dedicated to Sri Gopiswara Mahadeva, my mentor, friend and guide, and to the many people he has led me to consult over the years. Each of us has a story to tell about our quest to realize happiness and the love that lies at the heart of our soul. I have learned a great deal from all of you and wish you well on your journey.

'If you want to write a song about the heart,
Think about the Moon before you start.'

Paul Simon, Song about the Moon

Contents

Acknowledgements ix
How to Use this Book xi
Introduction xiii

Chapter 1: The Moon 1
The importance of the Moon in astrology

Chapter 2: The Language of the Heart 6
How the symbolism of the Moon reveals our deeper emotional nature and how it can help create mutual understanding in relationships

Chapter 3: The Moon in Signs 12
A detailed description of the Moon in the 12 zodiac signs
- Aries Moon 14
- Taurus Moon 26
- Gemini Moon 36
- Cancer Moon 48
- Leo Moon 61
- Virgo Moon 73
- Libra Moon 87
- Scorpio Moon 98
- Sagittarius Moon 111
- Capricorn Moon 122
- Aquarius Moon 134
- Pisces Moon 146

Chapter 4: The Spice of Life ... and Love 157
A comparison of how any two Moon signs will interact in a relationship with each other
Aries and... 158
Taurus and... 168
Gemini and... 178
Cancer and... 187
Leo and... 196
Virgo and... 203
Libra and... 210
Scorpio and... 215
Sagittarius and... 220
Capricorn and... 223
Aquarius and... 226
Pisces and... 228

Epilogue 231
Appendix: Find your Moon Sign 233
Index 263

Acknowledgements

It has been my good fortune to study the *Vedas* under the guidance of Srila Bhaktivedanta Swami Prabhupada and Sripad B.V. Narayana Maharaja. Their tutelage helped me understand that astrology is but a tool on a deeper path of self-discovery, mutual understanding and divine service. I am eternally grateful to them both.

Many thanks to Belinda Budge, who offered inspiration, guidance and a deft hand in taking this book from conception to reality. My editor, Susanna Abbott, has been a great sounding-board, helping me to keep the needs of my readers at the forefront of my efforts. Lizzie Hutchins, my copy-editor, has been instrumental in fine-tuning the content and offering well-timed, kind words of encouragement along the way.

Thanks to Marcel Landman, my friend and business partner at Panchang.com, and Joe Mills, who has offered patient, friendly support to all my efforts in the last few years. Crispian Mills has been a good sounding-board and offered valued creative input. Thank you to Peter Gabriel for his album *Passion*, which often became the background music for the writing of this book. Paul Simon Music has graciously given permission to quote Mr Simon's *Song about the Moon.* And a thank you to Lorraine Fitzgerald, an old friend whose infectious laughter often lifted my spirits – especially when the joke was at my expense.

Countless thanks to my wife and life partner Pandita, from whom I have learned and shared so much. My daughters Rasa, Sudevi and Larli have supported me along the way. Thank you all. Last but not least, thank you to my mother, Pauline Theoret.

A final word of gratitude to my friend and father-in-law, Don Julio Sprockel, who offered me quiet encouragement from afar. Thanks for being there when I needed you.

How to Use this Book

This book introduces you to Vedic Moon astrology and gives you the basic dictionary you need to understand and speak the heart language of your friend or lover. It will also help you to understand your own emotional nature and will reveal how any two people will interact to create the energy and dynamic of a relationship. If you are not currently in a relationship but want to know more about someone who has caught your eye, get their birth date and look up their Moon sign in the tables starting on page 235. Read the appropriate section in Chapter 3 and you will have an early understanding of their hidden emotional nature and a better chance of mutual understanding and a happy relationship. Each section has detailed descriptions, Top Tips and practical advice on how to make more of any existing or potential love, including a Troubleshooting section for when the path of love gets a little bumpy. As you become familiar with the effects of the Moon in the various zodiac signs you will become more fluent in the often elusive heart language symbolized by the Moon.

Introduction

Astrology is an ancient language of self-understanding and although very few of us speak it fluently, most of us speak enough of it to know our Sun sign or the Sun sign of a friend or lover. Yet for an experienced astrologer, describing someone by just their Sun sign is like trying to speak a language with only one verb. While even a limited astrological vocabulary lets us see a little of the zodiac in someone, an experienced astrologer uses a larger lexicon to express the depth and breadth of a personality. Essential to this deeper view is the Moon, especially when it comes to intimate relationships. The Moon is the magic key to unlocking the heart. The unique language of the heart is concealed within the symbolism of Moon astrology, especially the accurate system from ancient India popularly known as Vedic astrology.

☾

History tells us that our familiar Western zodiac language has developed over great spans of time and has, like most languages, changed as it has moved through ages and cultures to the present day. The Sun takes centre stage in our modern astrological language, but adherents of Vedic astrology contend that the Moon was originally at the heart of ancient astrology (both Western and Eastern), and that the astrology most of us know is in fact a dialect of the original astrological language written in the *sutras*, or codes, of the *Vedas*.

The central importance of the Moon was described in the Vedic texts which pre-date the Judaeo-Christian–Buddhist cultures by many centuries. The father of Vedic astrology, sage Parashara, in his astrological treatise *Parashara Hora Shastra*, describes the Moon as the 'pivot on which all astrological interpretation is successfully based'. He goes on to say that the strength and influence of any other heavenly body must be interpreted and evaluated using the Moon 'as the centre or ascendant of the chart'. Of course, it may be argued that an ascetic sage living thousands of years ago would place the Moon at the centre, if only for its obvious proximity and recognizable effects. But as modern studies of ancient cultures demonstrate, venerable societies were advanced in many subjects – not least the Vedic civilization, which has a special pedigree all its own in the form of the *Vedas*, written by the sage Vyasadeva, and corollary Vedic subtexts and commentaries.

The *Vedas* are a comprehensive body of knowledge covering a wide range of disciplines including medicine, architecture, political and military arts, astronomy, logic, poetry, art, semiotics and astrology, to name but a few. Examples of how the sophistication of the *Vedas* contrasts with their antiquity abound and include for example the discovery of Pi in sixth century BC by Budhayana and his explanation of the Pythagorean Theorem; the discovery of zero; the discovery of algebra, trigonometry, calculus and quadratic equations; the naming and use of large numbers (10^{53}); the calculation of the Earth's orbit of the Sun as 365.258756484 days by Bhaskaracharya in the fifth century BC; the invention of chess (Shataranja); the use of the oldest form of medicine (Ayurveda), navigation, reservoirs and dams; and the establishment of the world's first recorded university, at Takshila in 700 BC, attended by over 10,000 students. Einstein himself commented that the Vedic culture taught us 'how to count, without which no worthwhile scientific discovery could have been made'. Vedic knowledge is thus at the root of much of our current knowledge and many of our systems, not least of which is our own English language, as Sanskrit is considered the origin of all Indo-European languages.

There are obvious reasons why early wisdom traditions like the *Vedas* considered the Moon to be the most important planet in astrology. As the nearest heavenly body to the Earth, its physical effects are easy to observe. It moves the tides, affects the weather and is a known catalyst for growth and fertility cycles. Its effects are also well documented in research and statistical patterns related to finance, mental health and the emergency services. One curious example is the Russians' use of the effects of lunar phases on gauging the psycho-physical suitability of officers manning their nuclear warheads. It is thus easy to demonstrate that if there is a heavenly body whose gravitational pull or magnetic energy influences us, it is without doubt the Moon.

What does the Moon tell us in the language of astrology? We know that astrologically the Sun represents the vitality of our ego and the essence of our soul and its expression into the outer world. The Sun signifies *dharma* or life purpose, the path of our destiny and the nature of our conscious being. The strength of our ego and how it is expressed are coloured by the Sun's placement in the zodiac signs, which symbolize the nature and quality of our experience. The Sun thus has an 'external' expression and is about who we are on the outside. The Sun is bright light, hard shadows and strong heat, where things are definite and clear. In the sunlight we advance, confident, righteous and positive, because we can see where we are going and know the steps. The Sun is self-justifying rationale – a chain of well-defined, well-rehearsed affirmations. It is clarity, even when we are not clear. Its strength is its authority, the will that lends form to the formless and destination to that which needs direction. It is easy to see how the Sun has assumed this symbolism, for all its luminosity, grandeur and pride of place as the most visible and energizing of heavenly bodies.

The Moon is less definite. It is changeable, shadowy and uncertain. In moonlight we feel our way forward, rely on our intuition. Our steps are less planned, less obvious. Moonlight is more ethereal, blending with shadows, bending and creating tenuous feathery patterns. Its cool light projects our momentary dreams onto the screen of our waking state. It is reveries mingling with silvery beams, daydreams that whisper how we really feel and visions that free us from the hard scripts of our ego. Moonlight is the magical shifting forms of our unconscious which tell us stories in riddles that change in shape and meaning the more closely we look at them. Moonlight is gentle thought, creative glimpses and romantic impulses that inspire us if we treat them subtly, sensing them with our heart rather than applying too much hard-headed scrutiny.

The Moon is more 'internal' and hints at who we are beneath the surface – our inner self, our emotional being. Do you know if the Moon is full tonight? Is it waning or waxing? The Moon is full for less than a day, is most often only partially visible and is sometimes completely obscured. It is less 'aggressive' than sunlight and symbolically is thought of as feminine, cool, sensitive and elusive. Its soothing rays are stimulating and stirring, giving the Moon its emotional, romantic associations. As it expands and contracts in its waxing and waning cycles it embodies the changeability of nature, the flux of feelings and emotions in our lives. Sensitive people often claim that they are influenced by the Moon. It embodies the subtle undercurrents of our lives, those we sense but often cannot easily put into words. It is who we are behind the mask we show the world, the reflection we see at our most private, intimate moments. Astrologically, the Moon therefore lights a pathway to deep self-discovery.

Self-understanding and enlightenment are the essence of Vedic knowledge. One of the first Vedic Sanskrit aphorisms says *Tamasi ma jyotir gama* – 'Leave the darkness and come into the light' – while another is *Atato brahma jijnasa* – 'I am conscious spirit' – the idea being that the better we know ourselves, the happier, more self-fulfilled and powerful we become. The *Vedas* offer many ways to achieve this, including yoga and meditation, which are considered helpful to anyone. But specific to the individual is their *Rasi*, or astrological chart, which offers, if you will, a personalized manual for living, a map or objective reference point for self-understanding. It is a most useful tool for understanding an individual's strengths, weaknesses, opportunities and challenges. It is not proscriptive or limiting, but rather helps a person understand their real nature, thereby leading to self-acceptance and contentment.

In practical terms there may be no better use of Vedic astrology than understanding the dynamic of relationships. Even a little knowledge of your Moon sign will help you understand yourself better, as well as how others see you. It is fair to say that your Moon sign will reveal more secrets about you or your lover than your Sun sign, if only because the Moon represents what we don't normally see in a person.

So do you need to learn a whole new system of astrology to take advantage of Vedic Moon astrology? The answer is, no, you don't. There are many differences between modern Sun-sign astrology and Vedic astrology, but the understanding you may have about the various zodiac signs applies to Vedic astrology. You will not be in totally unfamiliar territory in reading this book and, with a little practice, you will begin to recognize familiar zodiac traits in yourself and your lover.

If the Moon does reveal more about our emotional being, why do we see Sun-sign astrology in all our newspapers and magazines? Sun-sign astrology as we know it began with the birth of Princess Margaret. In August 1930, the *Sunday Express* published an interpretation of her astrological chart written by R. H. Naylor, a British astrologer, who described in some detail the finer aspects of her character to the great pleasure of the *Express* readership. The editor was inundated with letters of appreciation and recognized a unique chance to increase his reader base. He approached Naylor, who was also successful in predicting an air disaster at the time, and asked if it was possible to offer a similar astrological interpretation for the masses. While we don't know the details of the conversation, Naylor probably would have informed the editor that each chart is unique and has thousands of factors that must be analysed before an accurate interpretation is possible. This didn't dissuade the persistent editor. To make things easy, Naylor proposed that they use just one factor – the Sun – to describe the events of the day for one-twelfth of the population.

The reason they chose the Sun is because it's the only heavenly body whose place in the zodiac can be accurately – and conveniently – determined by reference to the calendar day. With this, Naylor and the *Sunday Express* gave birth to Sun-sign astrology – at once the dumbing down of a complex system and the creation of a hopelessly simplistic view of the world, arguably deserving criticism from those who fail to observe one-twelfth of us dancing to the same tune on any given day.

Nevertheless, our need to know ourselves and to understand others helped to make the astrological column a success, earning the *Express* more readers while giving a backhanded compliment to astrology by popularizing an awareness of some of its basic elements. Even a novice astrologer will tell you it's possible to understand something of a person by knowing their Sun sign, but they will also tell you that it is only one part of their being.

The service Naylor did for astrology has been a mixed blessing at best. Astrologers are now trying to re-educate the public about the depth of the astrological language and, gradually, some progress is being made, especially with the recent appearance in the West of Vedic astrology and Panchang Moon astrology. This book may help in that cause by introducing the importance of the Moon and its ability to reveal our inner emotional world – and how compatible we are with another person.

'How well will we get along?' 'Will they understand me?' 'Do I understand them?' 'Are we compatible?' Just a few of the perennial questions in the game of love, ones that often come up after more basic ones are answered, like 'Are they attracted to me?' Once we get beyond the physical attraction stage, our need to know the deeper personality of a prospective lover is paramount. Mostly, this is a matter of time, of getting to know each other through the trial and error, trial and success process. While it can sometimes be painful, the 'learn as we go' approach can help us and our partner grow together. Still, wouldn't it be so much easier if we had inside knowledge beforehand?

Moon-sign astrology gives you a glimpse into how your partner feels. It gives you the insider knowledge you need to come to a better understanding of them and of how the two of you will get along. While the Moon is only part of the astrological story of your lover, it is the most important element in understanding their essential emotional nature and how that is expressed in their relationships. It gives you a clue as to how they will strive to express their feelings and find emotional fulfilment with you. The Moon gives you a point of departure on your journey to relate to your lover. It reveals the heart language of your lover and highlights important aspects of their 'emotional ego' rather than their external ego, the mask they display to the world as their outward character.

Observing the effects of your lover's Moon will, in time, create understanding and acceptance, which will help you make more of your relationship. It will let you accept your partner for who they really are. This will open the door for an honest, genuine and satisfying partnership based on emotional reality. It will identify where you are similar and where you are different, letting you celebrate the one and accept the other. A better understanding of your lover will help you keep the relationship fresh, fun and progressive.

Moon-sign astrology will also give you access to your own deeper emotional nature and subtle inner world. It will thus give you a chance to explore your own needs and can offer a reference point for understanding not only your own emotional dynamic, but also, maybe more importantly, how your partner experiences your emotional being.

'The heart has reasons that reason does not understand.'

Blaise Pascal

One final note on the symbolism of the Sun and Moon. It seems logical that our astrological language has been dominated by the Sun for the last 70 years, a time that was notably influenced by male archetypes – power, will, domination, conquest, social and political urges and an insistence on linear progress – often at the expense of anything natural, nurturing or rhythmically cyclical. Ego and machines mix symbiotically to give the appearance of rapid progress, but appear to be sending us in uncertain directions, a symptom, it seems, of the counter-intuitive *in-extremis*.

For every action there is an equal and opposite reaction – and inevitably the pendulum must swing the other way to safeguard the infinitely fine balance of nature. The early symptoms of a trend away from purely solar-masculine thinking are beginning to become apparent. Collectively, we are starting to recognize that nature is cyclical and that what goes around comes around. The sorry state of our environment and the message it is sending us may be the best example of this.

As we move towards a recognition of natural cycles and the need to nurture and protect the resources of our world, the symbolism of the Moon will begin to rise in the collective mind. It is already doing so, with the power of *Shakti* feminine energy becoming more evident in our collective thinking, in the growing awareness of the need to respect and reconnect with a more natural way of life.

The Sun represents the rational side of our being, the Moon our emotional side. Astrology can play a small role in helping to reconcile the rational and emotional that simultaneously exist in everyone as male (Sun) and female (Moon) archetypes. Their union is considered magical and represents the two halves of our individual and collective consciousness working harmoniously with each other. In alchemy, this harmonious relationship is called *coniunctio*, the union or conjunction of the Sun and the Moon. It is also called the 'chymical' wedding and symbolizes the perfect interdependent complementary joining of body and soul, male and female, conscious and unconscious, Yin and Yang, the cosmic principles whose reciprocity creates the conditions and events of this world.

Their union also emphasizes an important paradox of self-awareness. Emotions often defy description. They are fluid, changeable, 'irrational', subtle. We experience them, we do not think them. For many of us, emotions are the part of our being which seem somehow disconnected from the other parts. Our minds cannot understand them. Equally, can our emotional being understand the logic of our minds and intellect? Symbolically, our Sun and Moon are not on speaking terms. In this conflict, the strength of emotions is often more powerful, or subtly more influential than the logical side of our nature. Our tendency to rationalize our emotions is nevertheless symptomatic of our innate need to bring both sides of our being into harmony with each other – difficult as that may be.

To allow our rational mind to appreciate our emotional being, and understand it to some extent, and for our emotional being to benefit from the mind requires an equal acceptance and validation of both. Einstein, not lacking in the rational department, summed it up nicely by saying, 'The intuitive mind is a sacred gift and the rational mind is a faithful servant. We have created a society that honours the servant and has forgotten the gift.' One aim of astrology is to harmonize both principles, to put the rational mind at the service of the heart and create a happy working whole.

The knowledge (Sun) of emotions (Moon) and our inner nature is what this book is about. It aims to put our rational ability to know and understand at the service of our hearts, helping us all live powerfully as individuals, loving each other in happy interdependence.

'The only real valuable thing is intuition.'

Albert Einstein

Chapter 1

The Moon

'The enamoured Moon blushes with love.'

Edgar Allan Poe

The poet in you knows that the Moon and the heart are one. The Moon has long been associated with emotions, feelings and romance. The ancient *Vedas* describe Gaylord Krishna, the scion of Moon dynasty, and his moonlit dalliances with the cowherd damsels of Vrindavana as the essence of amorous divinity. Poets have described the enchanting effects of the Moon's reflection on the Taj Mahal, the most famous monument to lost love, while nowadays almost all Americans are able to hum the tune to *Moonlight in Vermont*. There are countless examples of how every culture in every age has seen the Moon as the symbol of love, gentle gestures and clandestine meetings in the garden of the heart.

When full, the Moon evokes wonder, anticipation and a restless mind. It stirs the heart and churns our emotions. It is a shining symbol of our inner soul projected onto the heavens. It's magical and it's magic. It heightens our yearning yet soothes our mind. The medieval poets of India wrote that it consoles the hearts of separated lovers who watch it glide through clouds, thinking of their distant love gazing at that same Moon. It offers them an embrace with its light, easing the pain of their separation.

The romantic nature of the Moon is inescapable and the astrological sages of India described it as the impetus for love and the symbol of our hopes and inner emotions. Like our feelings and moods, it too waxes and wanes in cycles that remind us of the stream of our desires and romantic needs.

Be True to Your Heart

In Vedic astrology, the Moon is thus the centre, the pivot, the sensitive heart of an astrological chart. It represents the inner person, the core being, the tenor of the emotions and the nature of the mind. It symbolizes what a person needs and what is important to them, and hints at the way in which they will try to satisfy their wants and nurture their growth.

The Moon represents our inner self, which is rarely the person that we project in our dealings with the outer world. The Moon is our fundamental being, the real person around which all the other character traits are layered. There are times when the outer layer is very different from what is underneath. It can be argued that this contradiction is one reason why it takes so long to really get to know someone. We have to penetrate their external ego to catch even a glimpse of what is happening inside. To really know someone is to know their Moon sign, which gives us insight into their private, hidden world.

Our current culture tends to emphasize the externals – how we appear, rather than who we are. The social psychologist Erich Fromm (Sagittarius Moon) philosophized that our modern world is more about 'having' than 'being'. The expectations that modern society throws our way can, if we are not careful, be hurdles to finding a genuine self-expression. Keeping up appearances can make us too outward-looking, causing us to neglect our more important inner life. Attempting to find acceptance by pleasing others and compromising ourselves in the process is a certain path to personal failure. Yet finding the balance can be difficult because we all have a need to be accepted. Getting it right takes time and effort – and requires a good measure of self-knowledge.

It sometimes takes a lonely commitment to be yourself and wait patiently for the right company to find its way to you, so to speak.

Most of us know that the discovery of self takes time. It rarely happens in Hollywood hyper-time, where a lifetime is neatly packed into 125 minutes. Rather, life has a way of presenting us with gradual, imperceptible challenges, which can mean a small forfeiture or an important gain of self. Sometimes it's the smallest decision, taken with the best of intentions, that results in the biggest change. A one-time friend of mine once said that our soul is rarely sold off wholesale, but in small parcels with lots of self-assured justification.

Getting it right, or wrong, is a lot less dramatic than the cinematic clash of good and evil. But losing, or never finding, our authentic self is our greatest loss and is often at the core of our serious discontents. Of all life's choices, the one we have the greatest influence over is whether we will be the person we really are or the person circumstance dictates. If you know a genuinely happy person, it's a sure bet that at some important juncture in their life they chose to be themselves, regardless of the price or the consequences.

Anything that can help us in our quest for self-fulfilment is welcome. Anything that confirms the best of our nature, helps us to reconcile our contradictions, gives us a way to understand ourselves and maybe helps us manage our difficulties, in part or in whole, is a boon. Wherever we get it – from a friend, lover, book or experience, in big bits or small bits – getting it bolsters our confidence and helps us achieve our authentic potential. Vedic Moon astrology is a gift from the ancient sages. The deeper you go in understanding what they have given, the more you will discover of yourself and your partnerships. Reading this book and meditating on its symbolism will help you recognize patterns of behaviour that may otherwise go unnoticed or be misunderstood. It will help you become conscious of tendencies in your emotional being in a way that will help you unravel, accept and manage them. Whether you are in a helpful or challenging time of your life, a Moon astrology map is handy to have along the way.

The Scent of a Rose

There are only 26 letters in our alphabet, but the range of possible expression is limitless. In astrology there are thousands of factors and hundreds of thousands of possible permutations of them in any astrological chart. While the Moon is only one of those factors, it plays a powerful role as the lens through which the rest of the chart takes shape. As the symbol of our 'emotional ego', it represents the personality behind the mask, while the Sun and the Ascendant (the zodiac sign rising on the eastern horizon at the time of our birth, also known as the 'rising sign') signify the masks and the roles we play in life. The Moon tells us about our essential emotional nature. It tells us how we feel – not at any particular moment, but the way in which we feel, the style, experience and quality of our inner experience.

The various Moon-sign chapters in this book describe the essential quality of that experience, giving you a way to explore how they will manifest in the people you know or love. The descriptions are thus indicative rather than proscriptive. Try not to take them in a pedantic or overly literal way, but rather as suggestive of mutable patterns of an emotional being that shift, change and express themselves according to time and circumstance. Moon-sign language in a sense has the same nature as moonlight – looking too closely at the detail may cause you to miss the patterns that emerge as you stand back and experience the ebb and flow over time. Experimenting with this will give good results, as will an open, curious mind that takes the descriptions of each sign more as metaphors than rigid, absolute generalizations. Taking this approach will, in fact, offer you the chance to deepen your knowledge of astrology and its rich language.

An example may help illustrate this point. Blindfold, most of us will know the difference between the scent of a rose, gardenia or carnation. And while a rose is a rose, each rose has its own unique scent, stronger or weaker, its own expression as a rose. The Moon in the various signs works something like this, where the respective qualities scent the emotional character of the individual. In strongly-scented cases, the qualities will be very evident in many areas of the person's emotional character. In other cases, the scent of the Moon in a particular sign may manifest more subtly. And in some cases it will manifest so strongly that it is the pollen transformed to honey, condensed so strongly that its flavour is inescapable.

So the Moon sign gives you a starting-point to observe, explore, discover and understand the deeper character of both yourself and your partner, which, in turn, can help you strengthen any partnership through tolerance, acceptance and love.

Chapter 2

The Language of the Heart

'The best and most beautiful things in the world cannot be seen or even touched. They must be felt with the heart.'

Helen Keller

What could be better than falling in love? The prospects of real love fill us with expectation, excitement, wonder and abundant energy. When we are swept away by passion, it is hard to concentrate on anything other than the next kiss or embrace. It brings out the best in us. We become generous and thoughtful and pay attention to little details and courtesies we would normally find tedious or troublesome. It can make us ache, but in such a hopeful, happy way that the pain seems pleasurable – a mixing of opposites, of heat and cold, sweet and sour. Love is the discovery of treasure and of coming home to a lost but not forgotten refuge. It renews us, uplifts us and inspires us. As the barmaid in the movie *Amélie* said, 'Love is the best beautician.'

The start of a new relationship can be heady, intense – even distorting. Desires are often so strong that they can blur, even obliterate, the differences that exist between two people. The excitement of a new love makes differences something to celebrate, not something that creates distance or keeps you apart. As a relationship deepens and you get to know your new partner

better, it is almost certain that what you first saw in them will change. When things begin to settle down, some of the differences that were ornaments to the early relationship can become familiar traits you 'learn to live with', become contentedly accustomed to, or, at best, continue to celebrate. In most functional relationships it's usually a mixture of all these.

Every relationship develops at its own speed. Some go quickly while others take time. In any case, time reveals the real nature of a relationship – which of course for the new lover has no meaning, because a one-minute separation can feel like a day and an intimate day pass in the blink of an eye. But, objectively speaking, time and experience will reveal the deeper character of any love.

Of course, exploring your partner's mysteries is part of the fun of any new relationship. Anticipation, tension and curiosity are helpful ingredients to love, driving you on to get to know your lover better. While discovery is important, an element of mystery helps keep any relationship fresh and alive. Nevertheless, the challenges in a relationship often arise from what we don't know or understand. How many times have you said, 'If only I had known!' A little bit of knowledge can be a great advantage when making a relationship work.

Prince or Frog?

Having an insight into the emotional nature of your lover can help you test your view of a relationship. Are things really what they seem? It is no secret that we tend to see the world through our own eyes and this subjective view sometimes creates a mirage. This very human trait can be especially pronounced in relationships. It's not uncommon to find that the person we are first attracted to is not the person they turn out to be.

First impressions *can* be correct, it's just that we don't always remember them as they get covered over by our own emotional needs, hopes and desires, all of which are projected onto a new relationship. This sets the stage for either partner to have to live up to the other's ideals for a perfect romance, potentially setting both parties up for extra work or future disappointment. To some extent this is inevitable and is part of the process of working through a relationship. But where it can lessened, it should be. If we have a good knowledge of our own expectations and some understanding of whom we are getting involved with early on, we stand a much better chance of creating a balanced, happy relationship.

Getting the balance between hopes and expectations and acceptance and compromise usually comes later, as the relationship matures. The basic ingredient for this is a clear, honest assessment of yourself and your potential partner. Fairy-tales and Hollywood reinforce our innate desire for a picture-perfect partnership, but the perfect partner doesn't really exist. The perfect *relationship* may exist, but only on the basis of living with each other's imperfections, at least to some extent. Of course it is essential that any relationship is based on as many common interests, values and ambitions as possible. But there is always the need to take a little bad with the good. While thinking like this may take the blush off the giddy mood of early love, in fact this balance and realism is what love is about.

Love is an action word, a state of being in which we reach beyond ourselves to nurture and give to another person. In its ideal sense, love is really about the other person, and in its most mature stage is conspicuously absent of any narcissism that expects our partner to be at our beck and call. From this point of view, love is when two people make each other the object of giving, concern and nurturing. With this as the central theme, love is sure to work despite the faults of either partner, if only because it is *active* and not indulgently *passive*. Love celebrates itself as the object of love is fulfilled. It is therefore sensible to acknowledge that no one person can be all things at all times to us. If we keep this in the back of our minds, we stand a better chance of nurturing the early bud of a new love into a healthy, balanced relationship.

Moon astrology is helpful in cultivating that bud into full bloom. It helps us understand our own nature and expectations, and potentially those of our lover. This doesn't mean we have to sacrifice our vision of them as an ideal partner, if only because that ideal is an important part of the loving process. But not to worry, as nature herself helps with this, frequently overdoing it. Who has not, or will not, at some point in their lives fall for a Prince or Princess Charming? And having fallen, who will not inevitably be surprised when that prince or princess wakes up one day and exerts their free will to be who they really are? This is the point where relationships often get interesting, especially in terms of the response of both parties. The degree of surprise, excitement or disappointment depends on how much understanding was there in the first place. Millions of pounds and millions of tears are spent every year recovering from the shock of disillusion.

Experience helps a lot with this. As we grow older and wiser, we come to know ourselves more, know what we want and what is good for us and learn to recognize the same in another person. One of life's rules is that we pay a price for these lessons, sometimes a high one. Luckily, there are always less costly ways to learn – one of the many being through Vedic Moon astrology.

Moon astrology gives us a way to look beyond appearances. If applied correctly, it can help us learn about one another more easily and more quickly. It takes time and some tedium to learn that our new lover appears confident but inside feels insecure, or vice versa. We have to accumulate a good many experiences before we recognize a pattern in their behaviour, but even a little knowledge of Moon astrology gives direct access to their inner emotional world. Your partner's Moon sign will tell you how they experience their own emotions and how they grow from the experience of loving or being loved by another person. It will give you an idea of what's behind the 'protective' mask of their external ego and helps you get to the bottom of why they think, feel and act as they do.

Mind the Gap

Moon astrology also helps you 'mind the gap' in a relationship by highlighting the differences and similarities between the two of you. It gives you the opportunity to step into their shoes, to take a peek at how they feel things. Looking at your own Moon sign also helps you stand back from yourself, giving you a chance to see how your partner may see you. Looking at yourself, and your partner, in this way helps you explore the real being in both of you and gives you a chance to understand where the differences and similarities work and where they don't.

In a deeper sense, Moon astrology also helps you understand the similarity-in-difference and difference-in-similarity in your relationship. For example, in the latter case, while both of you may be shy there may be different causes for your shyness. In the former case, one partner may try for a better self-understanding by relating with people, whereas the other partner may want to do it quietly on their own and alone with just their own self. Both are interested in self-awareness but have chosen different means. Knowing how this works in a relationship can help both partners accept the different approach and the similar purpose. In Chapter 4, 'The Spice of Life ... and Love', we look at some of the similarities and differences between two Moon signs and how they relate.

Learning the Language

As you explore the Moon signs you will gradually start to recognize patterns in the emotional character of your relationships – lovers, friends, family and colleagues. You will perceive similar nuances of attitude and emotional expression, common to two or three people but expressed differently by each. Language is a good example in this regard. While everyone in a room may speak the same language, each person will speak in a fashion unique to them. Inflection, tone, dialect, accent, volume and unique personality traits, such as frequent word choice, grammar and colloquial expressions, tell you who is talking, even when the lights go out. Sharing the same language doesn't limit our originality.

You may not be fluent in the heart language of your lover, but you have a much better chance of understanding and being understood if you know a few words. Your only access to French may be your Linguaphone™ quick guide, but it's usually enough when the heart demands a chat with an attractive French-someone. In a similar way, knowing your lover's Moon sign helps you understand the cultural orientation of their heart. Are they outgoing outside, but shy inside (Pisces, Scorpio)? Or the reverse (Leo, Sagittarius)? Are they emotionally picky, particular and reserved (Virgo, Aquarius)? Or are they gregarious and energetic (Aries)? These are not limiting labels, though, any more than 'French' is for someone from Brittany.

With practice, this book will help you speak the heart language of your lover more fluently. It will give you a sense of their emotional experience and outlook. There is no substitute for experience, and relationships take time and challenge to grow and deepen. But knowledge of your partner's heart language will help you communicate not just in words but in feelings, gestures and moods. It can help you reduce the pain and frustration in a relationship by knowing when to take something personally and when it is just part of your partner's nature. It can help you develop an intuition about your partner and help your sense of timing – is it a good time to discuss something? What is the best way to confront a new partner with a problem? The simple answer is the way that is comfortable for you – but will your approach also be comfortable for your partner? What inspires or stifles your partner? What turns them on or off? What makes them need you? What makes you seem too needy? All these questions and more are answered by the symbolism of your partner's Moon sign.

Getting acquainted may take time and the challenges may be part of the natural process of relationships, but speaking the heart language of your lover helps the poetry in your relationship. Moon-sign astrology can help you unravel, and keep secret, the mystery of your relationship, creating mutual understanding and empowering you both to be at ease and at one with each other.

'The consciousness of loving and being loved brings a warmth and a richness to life that nothing else can bring.'

Oscar Wilde

Chapter 3

The Moon in Signs

'Love is life. All, everything that I understand, I understand only because I love. Everything is, everything exists, only because I love. Everything is united by it alone. Love is God, and to die means that I, a particle of love, shall return to the general and eternal source.'

Leo Tolstoy

Most of us take great care when revealing our feelings – not only because it makes us emotionally vulnerable, but because we may feel that it gives our confidant access to the deeper recesses of our being. To avoid this we sometimes talk in riddles, play word games, drop hints or find some way to share ourselves with the other person in a way that makes them prove their worth, their sensitivity and their genuine perception of our true feelings. We cloak our secrets to test the tenderness and insight of our confidant.

It is therefore no surprise that life's bigger mysteries are guarded by sphinxes and oracles who test our mettle and our worthiness. Will we respect and use the knowledge they guard responsibly and for the greater good? Or will we use it selfishly and thoughtlessly?

Regardless of whether secrets are large or small, generational or humbly personal, the use of symbols helps guard their deeper meaning and real value. Symbols act as both signposts and barriers to what is ever-fresh, sacred, life-giving and loving. Just as wordplay can hide a heart full of feeling, so a symbol keeps many things secret, and is simultaneously inviting to the sincere and foreboding to the hypocrite.

The ancient symbols of astrology are deep wells of collective meaning. Like the folk and fairy-tales that disguise generations of wisdom and experience with fanciful characters and unlikely plots, astrological symbols are deceptively simple. But, like legends and fairy-tales, they are complex repositories of meaning ready to unfold their secrets. Folk-tales entertain, and even when taken at face value their subtle message tickles our curiosity and awakens us to the magic in the most ordinary of days. Legends are beautiful for their simplicity, mystery and paradox – and whether folk-tale or astrological symbol they defy easy explanation while inviting us to listen carefully to the story, to observe it within us and discover what secrets it has to unfold in our heart of hearts.

You will encounter legendary characters in the descriptions that follow – figures that symbolize the nature and meaning of the zodiac signs. These are the esoteric characters of the zodiac court – princes, knights, queens, jesters, kings, sages, spies and hermits to name but a few. Each embodies a deep symbolism of how the Moon adopts a particular nature in each zodiac sign and suggests the deeper character of each one of us. These royal persons are the archetypes that exist in each of us. Understanding even a fraction of their symbolism lets us discover their meaning in ourselves and our lover. Do we have the quiet, retiring and gentle emotional nature of the Hermit, or are we gregarious, bold and adventurous like the young Knight? And if we are one, and our lover the other, how can we find agreement despite our differences?

Within each of these symbols lies the key to reconciliation and harmony – the accommodation of different natures and the understanding that the combination of differences and similarities are what makes life, and love, rich and rewarding. Remembering their symbolism will help you understand yourself and your partner, and give you a way to celebrate what is larger than life in the both of you.

The Moon in Aries ♈

Aries is the first sign of the zodiac and is associated with the rejuvenation of spring and the joy of new life. In essence, Aries is a celebration of life, because it represents not only new life, but more importantly the first view of life through the eyes of the newborn. This view imbues everything with a sense of wonder, discovery, revelry and excitement. Aries is urge itself – a strong desire for new experience, spontaneity and the thrill of adventure.

In the court of the cosmic zodiac, the Aries Moon represents the young prince or knight champion. It is the archetype of vigour, bravery, adventure and youthful dignity. Aries is ruled by the planet Mars and is symbolized in the Tarot as the Knight of Wands – eager, charging, impassioned by a sense of mission and emboldened by a rush of adrenaline.

The Passionate Pioneer

Passion, vitality and enthusiasm are the hallmarks of those whose Moon is in Aries. A sportive, playful spirit drives an Aries Moon to embrace the unexpected and to venture into unknown territory, often with no regard for the consequences. Close calls with danger only bring a sense of living life to the fullest, and the spirit of Aries brings a belief that intrinsic innocence – which more staid impartial observers call naïveté – will serve as protection from pitfalls and damage.

The will to go on, despite the pain of experience, is one of the great survival traits of an Aries Moon. Invariably after a disappointment they will pick themselves up, dust themselves off and strike out again. To Aries, what does not destroy them makes them stronger, and the journey is definitely more important than the destination. If they are not sure exactly what their destination is, they are certain they will know it once they find it. The downside of this is that they can be so quick to move on from a fall that they sometimes fail to learn important lessons and set themselves up for another cycle of learning the hard way. They easily forget the painful past because they are so forward-looking, so absorbed in the future – what's next, what new thing will unfold in their life to give them the thrill of living that affirms their sense of being, the cosmic approval that echoes 'yes' everywhere they turn.

The vivacious nature of an Aries Moon is not always immediately evident to others, as the Moon represents our inner feelings and desires, which are often hidden. However, even the concealed Aries Moon will feel an abundance of emotional energy which will be revealed in due course to others, especially those with whom they are in close or intimate relationships. In general, an Aries Moon is abundantly expressive, its spirit colouring most areas of a person's life in one way or another. Aries has its own *joie de vivre* and the Moon offers a special field of play, one that gives the heart great latitude for emotional exchange. Meryl Streep, Ingrid Bergman and Lauren Bacall are good examples of actresses whose range of expression is powered by their passionate, sometimes tempestuous Aries Moons.

The Aries Moon is born with a deep sense of purpose, but usually needs time to find the mature expression of that purpose. For them, having purpose is itself satisfying enough, but their real strength develops as life deepens their mission through wisdom, a little patience and acceptance of life's inevitable limits.

'Being yourself' is very important to the Aries Moon and most often comes easily to them. Their sense of being drives them on and gives their emotional bearing importance, singularity and not infrequently a touch of drama. In relating to an Aries Moon it is important to enjoy this and, where possible, be fed by it. This is not easy for everyone and at times people will think the Aries Moon too forceful or driven. An Aries Moon likes to press through the crowd to take a position of prominence. They have something to say, and in relationships something to feel. Their feelings are urgent, central and important – not just for them, but for us – and we should know it. Often their disappointments come from others not recognizing this or the good intentions they have in imposing their needs. This is not usually too much of a problem, as their emotional resilience moves them on to find others who are ready to play and validate the importance of their feeling. A relationship that fails to affirm them is sure to bore them, creating a desire to look elsewhere. No one likes being taken for granted, but they find it especially irksome.

The Chivalrous Romantic

Aries Moons have strong desires, especially when it comes to finding happiness in relationships. They bring a kind of youthful exuberance to relationships that can be quite captivating and intoxicating. There is an excitement to an Aries courtship and the early part of a relationship can be quite moving, almost disorienting. Being swept away by an Aries Moon is not uncommon, due to their chivalrous nature that likes grand entrances, theatrical gestures and the delivery of surprises – mixed with the right amount of humour and frivolity. An intoxicating mix!

Aries Moons are in fact great romantics and enjoy their dealings with the opposite sex. They love the idea of being with a soul-mate (playmate) who understands and accepts them, while at the same time challenging them. Despite this, they tend to dislike limits and feel claustrophobic when faced with them. Getting them to commit is not always that easy. In time they usually realize that discipline creates the best freedom, but if confronted suddenly by limits they will run the other way. Probably the best way to attract them is through excitement and recognition of their good traits. Letting them take the lead is also not a bad idea. It will help you establish a rapport.

Once in a relationship, Aries Moons can be tender, affectionate lovers and enjoy sharing their love of life and fun with their partners. Yet the challenge for them is to reach a level of emotional maturity where they value their partner's experience as much as their own – and let them know it. To do this they consciously need to reach beyond their sense of 'youthful self-importance'. All astro*logical* qualities have a plus and a minus, and the quality that gives Aries Moons a lust for life can power them forward, leaving others behind in their wake. If they are not careful, this can cause their partners to feel neglected. It is not difficult for them to balance this out – it only requires a little conscious effort to stop and consider the needs of their partner.

They also love the excitement of a new romance, and in some cases this can create the urge to wander in search of the perfect mate. Although they are loyal and reliable, they can, in their romantic idealism, be perpetually in pursuit of ever-fresh love. This means that they can be demanding and expect that their lover will help them realize the perfect and elusive love. This search for the ever-fresh is part of their emotional evolution, especially in coming to terms with the limits of human love and the reconciliation and compromise needed to make it work – for real.

An Aries Moon may be inclined to keep things lively, moving to newer and newer experiences in which they play a central role, accompanied by an inspired playmate who shares the experience and adds spice to the exchange. However, the realization of an Aries Moon's deeper emotional nature comes by meeting the needs of their partner as much as their own, playing a game of tag where both take turns playing the leading role. The trick here is to acknowledge when they have moved aside to play a supporting role. This will help deepen the relationship and inspire them to think in terms of the partnership as a whole. It will also demonstrate your appreciation of the giving, caring side of their nature. A heart has two halves, and happy monologues are rare in the theatre of life. The trick for an Aries Moon is to realize that there is plenty of room at centre stage.

People are important to Aries Moons, however, and they tend to be socially adaptable. They have a special ability to understand others and what is needed to make them grow and thrive. They can be outgoing when it comes to sharing their good ideas about your life, and have a knack of sensing when you are down or low in energy. Their energy will lift your spirits. They love to spark life into another, stimulate and get things moving.

An Aries Moon likes to feel that a relationship is 'going somewhere' and the worst thing that can happen for them is that things feel stagnant. Movement is definitely more important than direction, and thus some partners will think that their tendency to deal with problems by doing things seems like avoidance – but for them activity is a way of getting things moving again. If you have a problem to work out with them, then take a ride in the country or on a Ferris wheel, a walk in the park or a turn on the dance floor.

In emotional matters, it is a good idea to remember that the Aries Moon can be strong yet sensitive, chivalrous yet slightly self-centred – and at times competitive. The picture is one of the young prince entering the court with a sense of robust self-importance. It is this sense of 'I am here' that colours the emotional fabric of the Aries Moon, and to be in partnership with them means being willing to celebrate their presence and involvement. If you are their partner, you can encourage their finer qualities by subtly appealing to their sense of strength, purpose, dignity and chivalry. In matters of conflict, a direct challenge demands their direct response, as they rarely shrink from an emotional dare.

Going for the Ride

Being in a relationship with an Aries Moon means being ready to keep things fresh and new. Symbolized by the ram, an Aries Moon is the 'rebel with a cause', or causes, one of which is to throw out anything old and boring. If you are looking for predictability (is your Moon in Virgo?), then look elsewhere. Being in a relationship with an Aries Moon means agreeing to 'go for the ride', wherever it takes you, and that is often to the cutting edge of fashion and attitudes. Jackie Onassis, the fashion standard-bearer for the early 1960s generation, had her Moon in Aries. If you want to know what's radical, creative or expressive, ask an Aries Moon like Elton John. Having a sense of adventure and a willingness to explore with your Aries playmate will keep the relationship fresh, while exceeding the pace will ensure that your Aries partner feels motivated, fulfilled and challenged.

A good partner for Aries lends a hand in directing their energies productively towards a desired end and is ready to remind them when they are getting off course, or losing interest, which is easy for them. This should be done with care, though, as Aries Moons don't always take criticism easily. In fact, they can react quite strongly if they feel under threat or unjustly accused. Aries is ruled by the energetic planet Mars and has all the connotations of martial inclination. Ironically, while Aries Moons can appear full of themselves, they can be quite aware of their own foibles and shortcomings. They need to take a healthy approach to this and try not to overcompensate for their perceived failings. Helping them with this takes tact, gentle handling and a non-confrontational approach. Remind them that personal faults need to be managed, not magically disappeared. The paradox of the Aries Moon is that while they seem strong on the surface, they can get very tender when scrutinised too closely by others – a trait shared by the other astrological Fire signs of Leo and Sagittarius.

An Aries Moon needs a partner who is understanding, who enjoys a youthful emotional experience; someone who is not too staid or restrictive. In many cases they need help in reining in their impetuous nature, help that is tactful and that doesn't judge them or hinder their free spirit. They are loyal but sometimes fickle. They usually bring a high level of commitment and involvement early on, but may lose the intensity of feeling once the relationship has been established. This can leave you feeling that they have lost interest. This is not necessarily the case and it may simply be that they now feel secure enough to pursue their many interests. They can be accused of not sustaining their own level of intensity in a relationship, but if you confront them with this, it will hurt their feelings and trigger a defensive response. If this happens, the best way to address the issue is to create new efforts that involve both of you, bringing you together for yet another adventure or discovery.

At all times in a relationship with Aries, it is a good idea to remember that they have a royal-like nature – although they are shy to admit it. Their need for understanding and acceptance, even unqualified acceptance, is the key to their heart. Remembering that they feel deeply, passionately, even physically to the point where heartache is a physical pain, will help you make the right approach when dealing with difficult situations.

Because they are passionate, they are quick to be hurt, but with the right apology are also quick to forget, as long as the approach is sincere. An Aries Moon also has an intrinsic trust in others' capacity to forgive, and when for some reason they are disappointed in this, they are more hurt than if they had had a good argument. Dealing with those who are inclined to hold on to hurt feelings can be very difficult for them. They tend to think fully towards the future, whereas other Moon signs, such as Cancer, tend to look at the future through the lens of the past. As well as being forward-thinking, don't forget that Aries Moons are martial, and a good argument for them can just be an overture, the prelude to love-making and playful exchange. It's the ride that's important and the destination is just the intermezzo to the next departure.

Locking Horns

Aries Moons can be competitive and combative, and it is not always easy for them to restrain this. In the best case, this is part of their sportive nature. They enjoy the stimulation of meeting an obstacle or challenge head on (again the ram). At times they can get carried away in the rush of this emotional energy, which can cause misunderstandings. 'Why are you attacking me?' you may ask, to receive the somewhat surprised reply that they are not attacking you. The challenge for an Aries Moon is when and how to apply this powerful side of their character in the right measure to get the right result. An extra focus can help them achieve that – and a little reminder now and then from their patient partner. Otherwise, a thoughtless moment can erupt into hurt feelings and sharp words, especially if they are under pressure. The tendency for Aries is to have something of a temper, especially if cornered. So, a good partner will know when to leave it or when to get on the wrestling mat, lock horns and work things out with a little confrontation. The worst slight to an Aries is to leave the arena with things unresolved, even though they may be guilty of that themselves from time to time.

If things aren't going their way, their first reaction is to take control. They are capable of taking charge and getting good results through sheer will-power. But this doesn't always work out in relationships. So life teaches them that going head-to-head is not always the most effective way of solving a problem. Their fiery, forceful nature can be disturbing, and while it is not desirable to even suggest that this be extinguished, a little forethought or self-restraint will bring more constructive and agreeable outcomes.

Aries Moons don't take well to life thwarting their cherished aims, of course. Their natural impatience and passion lead them to expect that life will turn out results as quickly as they desire it. If this is not the case and they fail to bring order to their often frenetic, high-energy approach to life, they can, for short periods, succumb to moodiness or despondency. The best way to help them is through encouragement, to which they tend to respond quickly and well. Speaking to the angel in them will bring out the better side of their natures, soothe their feelings and give them peace of mind. Helping them regain their focus is also very useful to them, especially given their tendency to get distracted and lose interest. With their abundance of energy, which can sometimes get trapped, they will find meditation, prayer or other forms of relaxation especially beneficial. They give them the chance to soften their pace and direct their energy more consciously and productively.

The most important aspect of an Aries Moon is the ideals that inspire them. Lose them, and lose much of what they are as vital souls. As all our lives move in cycles large and small, there is a need to realign and modify our ideals. In the case of an Aries Moon, this is the well-spring of their evergreen youthfulness and the power of their ability to affect and attract those around them. Their energetic personality makes them fun-loving and enjoyable to be with and as long as they are with someone who offers the right mix of challenge, acceptance, excitement and down-to-earth grounding, they can be a wonderful, giving partner.

Aries Top Tips

- Aries Moons expect a lot from life and even more from relationships. They like to be involved, at the centre, where things are happening. They thrive on reciprocation so, to make the most of a relationship with them, be proactive and try, if you can, to be even more energetic than they are. Be adventurous and a willing playmate.
- In seduction, appeal to their sense of theatre, emotional dignity and right to centre stage. Making them feel important will earn the response you are looking for.
- Be ready to reassure them. They are not always as confident as they like to appear, so tell them you understand them, but in a subtle way that lets them keep their pride.
- Get their attention with a touch of theatre and a spark of life. They will love your more outgoing side and will sweep you off your feet as they move the pace up a notch. And, if you are smart, you will let them think they are leading.
- Never embarrass them publicly – even slightly. If you have something to say to them, pull them over to a quiet corner and whisper your advice. They will appreciate this a great deal.
- In argument, be ready to joust, but don't play too hard. While tough and energetic, their sensitive feelings are easily hurt. Getting the balance right can be trial and error, so give it time.
- If you are feeling neglected, avoid the head-on approach. Appeal to their chivalry and inspire your rescue rather than tell them they are not doing their job.
- In day-to-day matters be ready for anything, and spice up the affair with lots of surprises, little gifts and caring gestures. Don't be put off if this seems expected – it probably is, but not necessarily in the egoistic way it appears. And you reap what you sow with an Aries Moon, so your generosity will be returned.
- Be patient with their impatience. Celebrate their energy and try to be uplifted by it yourself. Whatever you do, don't try to hold them back. They will lose interest quite easily and move on to the next fun adventure.

Aries Troubleshooting

☾ *How can you get them to take you and your feelings seriously?*
In some cases, this can be a challenge. The first step is to make sure that they are aware of how you feel, as there is a good chance that they are making their merry way unaware that anything is wrong. When you voice your needs, leave out any 'threatening' emotions or subtle suggestions that you are judging them. Appeal to their gentle side and ask for help in dealing with your problems rather than demand it. If they are ignoring your emotional needs, find a way to discreetly involve them. Appealing to the chivalrous side of their character will help – letting them 'come to the rescue'. Once you get their attention, to keep them involved give them a gentle reminder now and then.

☾ *How can you get them to be more supportive or responsive?*
Let's be real – the best way is for you to get their support is to show support, so make the effort to show that you are interested in their needs. At the same time send the subtle message that reciprocation is fun. Don't express your needs in a dreary or sombre way. Keep it upbeat and invite their participation rather than expect it. You don't want to appear too needy. Be ready to be independent and carry your own emotional weight, enjoy what reciprocation comes and always look ahead. This may not guarantee success, but it gives you the best chance to draw them into your life and your issues. Aries Moons are often supportive partners, but validating their affections and care will encourage them to give more of themselves, as they respond very well to positive reinforcement.

☾ *How can you re-establish communication?*
Aries Moons are often fiercely independent, freedom-loving and can be difficult to pin down. Don't be shy about initiating the contact yourself, but if there have been any problems keeping you apart, don't mention them, as this will make both of

you tense and derail the reconnection before it takes off. Take them by surprise, take the high road and suggest something fun, unusual or adventurous. Keep it light, informal and free and easy. Appeal to their active nature and love of anything new. If it's practical, make them the centre of the discussion, share your thoughts about them and don't be shy about being a little forward – they are likely to take it as a compliment as long as you don't seem to be pushy or trying to set the agenda.

☾ *What is the best way to apologize?*
Sincerity will make it easy. Do it when they are calm and appeal to the gentle side of their character. Admitting that they are right helps a lot. They tend not to hold a grudge once a problem is solved. Don't make the mistake of mixing your apology with a lesson in what is wrong with them. If you have issues to solve, apologize and get things back to normal and then pick a good time to deal with problems. Little gifts are always appreciated as peace offerings, but doing something active together – dinner, theatre, dancing – is more helpful.

☾ *How can you rekindle the flame?*
Expect to be challenged if they have lost interest due to hurt feelings. In any case the operative word here is 'spirited'. Capture their interest with spontaneity and stimulation. Break with tradition and explore new ways to entice them. Aries Moons love anything new and a change of pace should spark their interest again. Keep it real, though, as you will have to sustain it. But if you make them the centre of your genuine affections, you can't fail. When in doubt, to really get their attention, display your seductive side.

☾ *If the worst comes to the worst, how do you say goodbye without hurting their feelings?*
Avoid any suggestion that they are the cause of your leaving. If you are angry and want to get it off your chest, OK, but be ready for a strong emotional reaction. This is good advice for

almost anyone, but to lay blame at the Aries Moon's door will trigger their emotional defences and unless you want an argument it will likely get you nowhere. On the other hand, Aries Moons have a strong, natural 'self-healing' emotional quality and they are usually able to bounce back from life's challenges as long as their sense of self-worth has not been too seriously damaged. So, if you can keep things simple, lay the blame elsewhere and move on.

The Moon in Taurus ♉

Taurus makes a happy residence for the Moon and is considered 'exalted', or the best sign for the Moon, in both Western and Eastern astrology. Taurus Moons are big-hearted, pleasure-seeking and full of life. The combination of the Moon (emotions, mother, well-being, safety) and Taurus (felicity, nurturing, expansion, progress) hint at the fortune, goal and ambition of those whose Moon is in Taurus.

As the first zodiac Earth sign, Taurus is sensual and sensory. It is tactile and physical and, like the other Earth signs, Virgo and Capricorn, down-to-earth, practical and concerned with the tangible empirical world. Taurus is associated with finance, banking, farming, fruit, sweets and gemstones, all of which have connotations of prosperity and well-being. The Taurus Moon, therefore, tends to be fun-loving, spirited and socially active and enjoys life's myriad of pleasures.

In the cosmic zodiac court, the Taurus Moon is the chancellor of the exchequer – the minister in charge of ensuring the well-being of the court through prudent planning, fiscal discernment and well-guarded assets. The Taurus Moon chancellor provides the luxuries of the court and the good fortune of the citizens, and sets aside ample reserves against the event of calamity.

The Big-Hearted Pleasure-Seeker

A Taurus Moon epitomizes 'being well' and the striving for a prosperity that satisfies all aspects of material and spiritual being. In other words, if they can, these people will have it all – and why not? Quite often they do. As mentioned earlier, an astrological chart has thousands of factors and some of these may modify the Moon's expression, but in essence a Taurus Moon is considered an auspicious placement that strengthens and supports the character and life experience. Even where other factors in the chart lessen the strength of this symbolism, the individual will, in relative terms, be successful in fulfilling their cherished desires.

Taurus is ruled by Venus, which lends a sensual, artistic nature to the Taurus Moon, giving them an appreciation for the best they can afford. They take pride in their 'good taste' and aspire to the good life, whether in material possessions, friendships or love.

Among other things, the Moon represents the hearth and home, and it is quite normal to find Taurus Moons making their castles as cosy as they can. They enjoy quality decoration and often collect fine objects. They feel at home in fine surroundings and like a bit of plush. To make them happy, simply sit them down in a lush setting and offer them warm hospitality. They are attracted to art, music, good food and sweets, and may develop a measure of expertise in one or more of these areas if the rest of their chart supports it. Material assets comfort them and give them a feeling of security and well-being. While not necessarily only interested in material things, this is an intrinsic part of their nature and contributes a good deal to their values, attitudes and outlook.

A Taurus Moon strives for well-being, not necessarily in the healthy new-age sense (especially as they can indulge in rich diets and drink), but as an overall measure of material and emotional success. In fact, they are connected for Taurus Moon; material or financial challenges can be experienced by them as particularly difficult. If it were possible to say what all Taurus Moons would like, it would be a happy, well off, sensual life with just the right amount of spiritual spark. They aspire to do good, and if life gives them the means, they can be kind and generous and may be involved in charitable, social or community work.

Taurus Moons are happy-go-lucky in a sober kind of way and tend to be quite charming and likeable. It can be difficult to call them shy, but they do have a reserved side to their character and can be quite content to sit at the sidelines, watching rather than participating. There is a measure of self-contentment about them. Nevertheless, they also have a natural, easy-going warmth that puts others quickly at ease. Their friendly nature attracts others to them and they usually enjoy a busy social circle. This suits them well because a Taurus Moon does need others to feel truly complete. They can be true and lasting friends, and tend to be thoughtful in their dealings with others, making people feel welcome, cared for and the centre of attention.

Their keen social skills can, however, create problems for them now and then. They are so good at making you feel special that you can easily feel lost or abandoned when their affections are given to others. Remember, they are popular for being interesting, stimulating and able to make others feel the centre of attention. They put people at ease and whether at home, the office or at a party, a Taurus Moon will bring a gentle touch to the surroundings, especially if they make the effort to show you special favour.

The Stubborn Seeker

Taurus Moons are generally tolerant and accepting, but don't be surprised if they are not easily swayed to your way of thinking. Taureans like to build a sense of personal security through a well-developed set of principles that are not easily changed – or questioned. They can seem stubborn, and in fact are genuinely stubborn when they feel it's called for. Depending on other factors in their chart, this tendency can be reduced or magnified. In some cases, the strong will of a Taurus Moon can be expressed as dogmatic and overbearing, especially if they have expectations that are not being met. Don't be surprised by a slight tendency to use 'facts' to support their preconceptions.

Their strong will can surface especially in business and financial matters, which is why Taurean Moons can make good bankers, accountants and financial managers, with John Maynard Keynes the best example. They notice all the little details and can make 'practical' decisions if the facts don't add up, however disappointing it may be to others.

They tend to be ambitious people, at least within the circumference of their natural abilities, which often have an artistic or creative flair about them, and strive for a stable life. Their material side can make them feel inadequate or incomplete in spiritual or esoteric matters, however. They will try to fill this void with friends who offer them the chance to discuss existential and philosophical subjects. In fact, just having the friends will give them a sense of deeper well-being, a connection with something fulfilling and important beyond the mundane limits of tactile reality.

Another channel for their inner development comes from communing with nature. This will bring out the artistic inclinations of a Taurus Moon, but more importantly put them in touch with their emotional and intuitive side.

The most compelling side to their yearning for a spiritual completeness is their search for meaning in relationships. Even more than in friendships, they feel that a romantic partner should somehow be a companion in the journey to a deeper meaning of life, even if that journey is, in the end, limited to understanding the nature of their specific relationship. The best travel companion, one that will take a Taurus Moon well beyond their known limits is the quintessential, archetypal Taurus partner, the Scorpio Moon – deep, mysterious, inexplicable, seductive and transcendental. The Scorpio Moon can supply in full the magic the Taurus Moon needs to be whole.

Herein lies the chief paradox of a Taurus Moon – practical, sensible and focused on general well-being, yet attracted (sometimes secretly) to something that defies the logic that guides and stabilizes the rest of their life. Whether a Taurean is lucky enough to find the right Scorpio Moon partner, or another Moon sign such as Pisces or Aquarius, who brings this out in them, whether they dive deeply into mysteries or remain yearning for them, they know that their emotional maturity requires the addition of something divine. This has a mesmerising hold on them, and affects them throughout their life, if only perhaps from the periphery of their day-to-day being.

At the end of their journey they should come to realize that the material is but one part of the spiritual and that in a higher sense, the two are not incompatible. One does not invalidate the other, except when conspicuously absent from life. Finding a healthy balance between spiritual interests and material needs is an achievement that brings out the best of the Taurus Moon's talents.

Investing in a Relationship

Being in a relationship with a Taurus Moon offers many benefits, not least of which is a partner who is focused on creating well-being for the partnership. They are sensitive, caring, tender, sensual and can be natural romantics, although their practical side can dampen this at times, especially once the relationship is established.

They admire dependability and faithfulness, which they also aspire to – as long as their sensual nature does not get the better of them. Taurus Moons can be strong both emotionally and physically and have a stamina that helps them to be patient and tolerant. Their steadiness in relationships is a great asset, and when they give their hearts they are solid in their commitment. They naturally understand the power of commitment and the growth it brings. To them it's an investment in people, and worthwhile. Once they are ready, they are happy to settle down and are family-oriented.

Despite their practical side, Taurus Moons have delicate feelings, although they like to present a somewhat stoic face if they are hurt. Their trusting nature can be abused, however, and so they need to select a partner who will acknowledge their interest in a steady practical life, as well as lead them now and then on spiritual adventures.

When attracting a Taurus Moon you will need to appeal to both their fun-loving side and their dignified sense of privilege. Fine foods, pleasant surroundings and artistic ambience put them at ease and bring out the best of them. The seduction of a Taurus Moon is multifaceted, as they enjoy the chase but equally enjoy being pursued, and this can apply to both sexes. It is important that their partner has a relaxed attitude to intimacy and tenderness, as they usually expect lots of fondness and caressing, and enjoy cuddling and quiet evenings just tending to each other's needs.

The rigid side of the Taurus Moon's personality can, however, be expressed in their relationships. For instance, if they feel that they are right, they can be quite tenacious in holding their ground. One potentially irritating side of this is when they do it silently, trying to win an argument by stealth. When pushed, of course, they meet any challenge and are ready to argue the point convincingly. Emotionally, this has both a good and a bad side. On the good side, you have the reliability of a steady partner and know where you stand; on the challenging side, getting them to change their view, or to look at yours in a different way, can be difficult.

If you encounter this, the path of gentle persuasion is probably going to be more productive than a head-on argument. Appeal to their sweet side, not their strong side. And if you are trying to win an argument without having the facts, pertinent or not, you can forget it. There is a little Taurus in us all, but this particular trait is condensed with a Moon in Taurus and needs a bit of patience and strategy to deal with. Nevertheless, the Taurean nature is always ready to come to terms, if you can hold out whatever sweet incentive they find appealing.

In emotional matters, the Taurus Moon needs stimulation, and often relies on their partner to get things going. It is easy for them to get stuck in a rut and become complacent, especially when things are going really well. Their partner will need the right amount of push, pull and cajole to get them moving on to new things. This is great if your Moon is in Scorpio, Aquarius or Pisces, but probably challenging if your Moon is in an Earth sign like Virgo or Capricorn. While it may take some effort to get them moving – Taurus is symbolized by the strong-willed bull – they do appreciate it once they are in motion.

Taurus Moons also expect a good deal of discretion from their partners and are very pleased when they know how to keep a good secret, especially when it comes to financial, business or practical matters. But what they expect from others they can usually give in turn.

The Taurus Moon brings a lot to its valued relationships, not least an emotional ground that gives you a solid foundation to build on.

They are fun-loving, sensitive, sensible partners who have a good sense of humour, a love of refinement and a mind that is open to new ideas. Keep the relationship vital by challenging their views, opening up new vistas and weaving a bit of magic into their lives.

Taurus Top Tips

- Seducing a Taurus Moon requires grace, skill, tact and good taste. You will also need a good sense of timing. They respond to refined settings and cosy creature comforts. Think of Venus and you have the key to attracting them.
- They like to have a sense that they are in charge, so some finesse is required. Appeal to their sensual and fun-loving nature and offer easy-going exchanges. Don't rush matters. Gently ease into a deeper relationship and avoid giving a sense of being too dependent. They respond better when they are the one who notices your vulnerability.
- Friendship is an important part of any relationship for them. Balance and variety are also desirable – they like someone who enjoys the good life and is ready to play along in an easy-going manner. They have a timid side and don't respond too well to overly gregarious types.
- Genuine affection is the key to their heart, so if your feelings are real, don't be shy about sharing them.
- Endear yourself to them with care and attention if they are feeling melancholy. They expect a partner to be stable and there for them, and they enjoy private tranquil moments. They love gifts and you will score big time when you do the cooking.
- Show an interest in truth and beauty. Gallery visits, walks in the park or just sitting in gentle surroundings brings out their best nature and makes them feel comfortable opening up to you.
- Don't be fooled by their grounded, practical side. They are easily offended, which can be difficult because they won't easily let you know something's gone wrong. A touch of deference will go a long way.

- In an argument, be dignified, share your feelings and be ready to challenge and be challenged. If they are stubborn, give it time. You have a better chance of building a consensus by gentle persuasion than by intense argument.
- In day-to-day matters be constant, reliable and focused. Security is a big issue with the Taurus Moon, although not openly admitted. If they are in a rut, prod them into action. The unexpected and unusual will keep the relationship fresh.

Taurus Troubleshooting

- *How can you get them to take you and your feelings seriously?* This can be easy or difficult, depending on your own nature. Generally, Taurus Moons do in fact care even when they appear not to. If they have an emotional investment in the relationship, they will tend to want things to go well, but are often practical and a bit shy when it comes to emotional issues where they feel out of their depth. While they are attracted to deep emotions, they themselves can be reluctant when entering new emotional territory. So if they are holding back, take a little time to understand why. They tend to be responsive to others' needs, though, and don't like failing in emotional matters, so offering a little guidance, reassurance and validation will encourage their deeper involvement in your issues.

- *How can you get them to be more supportive or responsive?* Taurus Moons can have a strong sense of duty, purpose and responsibility. If the relationship means something to them it is unlikely that you will feel too neglected. If they understand that you are feeling neglected, it is likely that they will respond with whatever they have at their disposal. So make the time and effort to inspire them to action and appeal to their protective nature. They will need to feel that they can make a difference when it comes to giving you what you want. When they do respond to your needs, go out of your way to show them how well they have done. A Taurus Moon especially likes to be appreciated.

☾ *How can you re-establish communication?*

Appeal to their Venusian nature and soften them up by sending flowers, sweets or fragrant gifts. Cards are OK, whereas e-mails may not work, so if you use them be brief and cheery. Be gentle and ease into any communication with a light mood and a soft voice. Chance meetings don't work so well, so avoid being clever and contriving. If there has been something keeping you apart, avoid any mention of it, unless it is a must. If it is, be real, honest and quick about it. Meet in a pleasurable environment, somewhere romantic but not obviously so. Avoid triggering any need on their part to show the stubborn side of their character and where possible let them set the agenda for starting over again, however tense this may make you feel. Remember a Taurus Moon requires some patience. Appeal to their love of a laugh and good company.

☾ *What is the best way to apologize?*

Taurus Moons tend to be quite forgiving and remembering this should make your apology easier. Own up to your failure, but don't dwell on it. Acknowledge where you may have hurt their feelings and set reasonable expectations for the future. In other words, avoid promising what you can't deliver, because they have a good memory for such things. Best to under-promise and over-deliver. At the same time remember that the security-conscious side of their nature does need reassurance. Getting the balance right is important. Make the time and space for a proper apology rather than trying to slip it in, as their pride may say that they deserve more than a glossing over of the problem. As always, a show of genuine affection is sure to win them over. When in doubt, think flowers.

☾ *How can you rekindle the flame?*

This may not always be easy with a Taurus Moon. The key is to stimulate their sensual and romantic nature. Such a seduction will take some planning, because while the Taurus Moon is flirtatious early in a relationship, they can take time to commit, especially if they have lost interest. If the relationship is not working they may feel it's better to move on rather than look at the past. Concentrate on what elements did work in the past and use them in your exchanges. Create pleasant, seductive environments and show a good deal of physical affection. Lavish them with kindness and little courtesies. Certainly, gifts will help. If it's just a matter of breathing new life into a generally solid relationship, these suggestions will work well. If the problem is more 'structural' and affects their sense of values and security, the challenge may be bigger – and this means time and effort. In any case, getting them into the party spirit will always help.

☾ *If the worst comes to the worst, how do you say goodbye without hurting their feelings?*

Show concern for their feelings and go out of your way to give them the chance to talk if they want to. Taurus Moons tend to take life changes quite seriously and it will not be uncommon for them to feel that a break up will affect all the other areas of their life. They can have an inordinately strong response to rejection, even though they tend to have a grounded emotional nature – a combination that in itself can create conflict. Avoid trying to teach them a lesson by leaving them. In their own time they may understand what's happened, but not always in your time. If material assets are involved, be proactive in trying to create an equitable arrangement (if possible), as it is easy for emotional issues to get mixed into material issues for them. If handled well, a Taurus Moon can remain a loyal friend, even if the romantic side of things doesn't work out.

The Moon in Gemini ♊

A riddle wrapped in mystery inside an enigma, that's a Gemini Moon – but only if you expect conformity, predictability and a journey that is well signposted. Gemini Moons are often difficult to understand just because the rest of us have such a hard time keeping up with them. Like the shifting sands in a desert or the fleeting images in a smoky house of mirrors, the Gemini Moon has numerous qualities that are at once contradictory and yet, certainly to them, make perfect sense in the hermetic vessel of their fascinating personalities.

Angels and Fairies

The first rule when relating with a Gemini Moon is to be at ease with change and comfortable with the unexpected. If you enjoy a challenge, thrill, humour, practical jokes and quick wit, then the Gemini Moon is for you – which suggests that your Moon could be in Sagittarius, Pisces or even Aries.

Many of us approach the problem-solving of life by carefully filling in the first box, moving on to the second and eventually, if we are lucky, completing the form. This sequential and logical approach has little currency with a Gemini Moon because, unlike us, they can multitask and make relevant connections between unlike objects and concepts that we couldn't conceive of in our wildest imagination. This is one reason why Gemini Moons are sometimes categorized as mad – or genius depending on who is marking the exam. One doesn't really understand a Gemini Moon as much as marvel at their nature. In fact, many genuine and artistic geniuses have had their Moon in Gemini including Sati, Stravinsky, Debussy, Henri Breton, Henri Rousseau, Roman Polanski and John Cage – all of whom are enigmatic in character and work.

Gemini Moon is at once the jester, messenger, illusionist and inventor of the cosmic zodiac court, with the essential role of inspiration, insight and the proffering of Socratic questions and

Sphinx-like riddles that challenge and surprise in fits of fun and wonder. It is appropriate then that the ruler of Gemini is Mercury, the messenger of the gods and the fickle quick-footed embodiment of the cosmic mind and intellect. Mercury symbolizes thought, inspiration, eloquence, repartee, insight, originality and sudden flashes of imagination and so creativity is the hallmark of Gemini. Even if your partner's Moon in Gemini lacks the support in the rest of their chart to make them an Oscar-winning actor, without doubt their character and disposition will be scented by the tendency to create according to their abilities.

Gemini Moons are independent thinkers and are often quite original. They are able to weave a tapestry of attitudes and opinions that span a range of disciplines. If well-educated, they have the intrinsic nature of the polymath, and if not the least you can expect is a spectrum of trivia, word games and sophisms that tend to the polyglot. And yet, despite this jumble of mental puzzle pieces that form their strongly non-conformist picture, they reserve the right to change their views – immediately, even whimsically – and usually have a reputation for defending them strongly. Want a good and varied debate? Find a Gemini Moon, as this is what matters to them.

The adaptability of the Gemini Moon is their singular survival technique and their real strength, both intellectually and in relationships. Their ability to grasp the essence of an idea gives them an advantage and can put them in the lead in their chosen field of work. If they can quiet their busy mind, and sometimes busy speech, they can be very good at listening to their intuition, especially when it comes to other people. The danger they face with this is in listening to their mind and not their heart, which can lead them to jump to the wrong conclusions and can be a sore spot in their relationships. They tend to have good common sense but often ignore their own or others' practical counsel.

One teacher of mine used to call Gemini Moons 'angels and fairies', which probably doesn't fit well if you are an 18-stone decathlete or night-club bouncer, but it does illustrate an important point about the Gemini Moon, which is that regardless of the external package, they have a sweet, tender and caring heart and love a feather-light touch. They have an otherworldly, will-o'-the-wisp quality to their emotional nature and it is important to recognize this if you are to have the kind of satisfying, delicate emotional relationship that they can offer. This is especially notable with women who have their Moons in Gemini, giving an attractive subtle shimmer to their appearance and their interactions, particularly in the privacy of intimate relationships. If you are lucky to be in relationship with such a Gemini Moon, don't grasp too hard. Treat them with the delicacy that they expect, otherwise they will slip your hold and flutter away all too easily.

Embracing Quicksilver

Gemini Moons have a strong sensual nature, which can make them good lovers and partners. Sensuality, curiosity and a quick temperament can, however, cause problems if they draw the Gemini Moon into the wrong relationship. In this regard, it's important for them to curb their impetuousness and try to keep one foot on the ground – even while the rest of them is lifted by the wings of passion. If you are contemplating a relationship with a Gemini Moon and are more practically inclined, you may want to watch that your new partner doesn't get too carried away – or even carry you away by their infectious sense of wonder, discovery and light-heartedness.

The gossamer quality to their emotional fabric is a symptom of another side of their paradoxical nature and that is that they love to be emotionally in control. Although possibly not always in control themselves, they expect to be able to call the shots emotionally without too much objection from their partner. This means that when it comes to taking decisions and making commitments in relationships, the Gemini Moon likes to, shall we say, keep their options open. They love the thrill of the pursuit and of courtship, but will feel uncomfortable if things turn 'sticky' – meaning anything from predictable to claustrophobic. This is an aspect of their quicksilver quality and desire to escape the confines of the boring, dull, mundane, petty details of life. At one end of the spectrum, this trait will manifest as a near disregard for appearances and even a complete disregard for social convention bordering on the eccentric. How far each individual will go depends on many factors, but in relationships the Gemini Moon will certainly love to be in the driver's seat and will loathe backseat drivers.

How to deal with this? Delicately, patiently and ironically, with a certain amount of detachment. This may sound challenging, but for the right partner it can be stimulating, exciting and seductive. And in the game of seduction, there are a few tips worth noting when in relationship with a Gemini Moon. The first is to remain flexible. Think of the wind and emulate it, or at least agree to be swayed by it sometimes, refreshed at other times and once in a while blown over. Next is to find a balance between making the Gemini Moon feel desired and wanted, unfettered and independent. Don't be surprised if this takes some time and effort, or even if the balance is never really achieved but simply part of a long courtship game of adjustment and accommodation. Remember that the two faces of Gemini symbolize the ebb and flow of ideas, creativity and, of course, changeability.

The next tip is to give them plenty of room to lead with their spontaneity – even if at times it seems impetuous. In showing an enthusiasm to participate, you will be able to take part in setting the agenda and the direction of your journey together.

And the final tip is to make them feel special. Well, OK, I know we have to do this in any relationship, but some Moon signs need more of this than others. And remember to be genuine in this, or don't do it at all. Gemini Moons are quick to pick up on anything false and the last thing they need is to feel that you are making them feel special because *they need* to feel special and not because they really are!

If you are the jealous type, you could have a hard time with a Gemini Moon, if only because they are so naturally sociable. They thrive on stimulation, and thus tend to be outgoing and adaptable. They love being socially challenged and can't help rising to any occasion, even when it stretches them, bringing them to the edge of their talents and abilities. They see this as a chance to express the thespian in them and play centre stage. Of course, if you are a more staid type of person, you may well be embarrassed at the 'excesses' of your Gemini partner, so it's best if you have a fun-loving, adaptable side to your personality as well – or are at least a voyeur who enjoys seeing other people indulge in flights of fancy. Gemini Moons can be very comical, wacky and frivolous, so sit back and enjoy the ride.

Relating to a Moon in Gemini demands an understanding and acceptance of its mercurial nature. Just as quicksilver is fluid and flows around obstacles, so the Gemini nature will rebel against the imposition of rules and limits. In simple terms, it wants to be free and will do whatever is needed to grasp and protect that freedom. If met with strong limits, a Gemini Moon will respond strongly and has been known even to embrace danger or self-destruction rather than conform to the control of others. Of course, this is a somewhat rare occurrence; the most usual expression of this will be a quiet, quicksilver solution – to act the way they want and let you try to keep up.

It does little good to remonstrate with a Gemini Moon, unless of course you want to have an argument, but that doesn't work either because Gemini is an Air sign, which symbolizes a gaseous, insubstantial quality that is difficult to pin down. Want to debate? Be ready for a tour of subjects and ideas that don't fit the sequential patterns of good argument. 'Why are you changing the subject?' you will ask, and their response is, 'That *is* the subject!' Even when you think you have won, if you ask them, it's you who is the loser – 'You didn't get that?' Remember, they have the cosmic prerogative in originality and this imbues most of their approach to life, even something as tedious and mundane as a good argument about who said what when.

Keeping up with the Emotional 'Genius'

In fact, the Gemini quality of changeability expressed through the Moon, in the field of emotions where rules are at best fluid, results in someone who can be very difficult to pin down. The big question is, do they change as they appear to and the answer is paradoxically both yes and no. Gemini Moons even marvel at their own ability to discover emotional conditions and feelings they did not even know existed themselves. And this can happen quicker than you can say Hermes Trismegistus or the name of any other hermetic philosopher.

Gemini Moons will of course see this as part of their emotional 'genius' and are quite able to relish the experience of their new-found feelings – in many cases even dramatize them (which appeals to the artist in them). If you are not so quick off the mark, you will ask, 'Where did that come from?' The answer to this can be quite complicated, because it will not be the logical part of the Gemini Moon that answers but the emotional part, and you can bet they will be quite indignant that you have called into question the validity of their feelings. Of course, you are not questioning the sovereignty of their emotional territory, just their right to change the borders when it's convenient to them. Don't be surprised if they win the argument by working their way from polarities, inch by inch drawing to the centre – something like a three-dimensional chess game but maybe with fewer rules.

A good partner for a Gemini Moon therefore must have patience, a willingness to engage in regular effort, flexibility and a good measure of stability. Gemini Moons like all this because they are attracted to what they sometimes feel they don't have themselves – direction, a goal and a constant reference point. You will need to be simultaneously a straight shooter, a philosopher and a diplomat, which is why one of the best partners for them is the Sagittarius Moon. It's not that they will always like straight shooting – in fact they will probably complain about you being too direct – but emotionally this approach gives them a pivot, a central reference point from which they can irregularly orbit in their inquisitive pursuit of the new and unknown.

Insatiable curiosity is another trait that drives them on and helps them remain the perpetual emotional youth. The urge to know, to discover and to understand how things work is emblematic of the Gemini Moon, especially when it comes to emotional matters. They love to explore not only their feelings, but yours as well, although they are certain to expect your feelings to be more transparent than theirs.

Talk, talk, talk ... Expect a flood of conversation when they feel comfortable with you. Until then, they may keep up their guard, with the occasional quip as a deflective defensive mechanism. Once they are at ease with you, anything goes in conversation, which they love, but you may struggle to get a word in edgewise. (Don't let them drink too much coffee.) They also have a fairly developed ability to entertain themselves, so if you catch them talking to themselves, don't worry. The absent-minded side of their personality is only them engaging in satisfying private conversation with themselves.

One way of determining how well you are doing with a Gemini Moon is whether you have been able to keep their attention. A Gemini is prone to boredom, so their degree of interest in a subject (or the person they are speaking to), governs the degree of their presence in a conversation. This is one way that the Gemini naturally weeds out company that displeases or fails to challenge.

Once the relationship has been established, it is certain that you will play referee to Gemini's juggling-many-balls-at-once game. Their ability to multitask is a strength and a weakness. While they can dive into detail and resurface to a view of the bigger picture, their tendency is to spread themselves too thinly and even drive themselves to the point of exhaustion. Remind them to take some time to relax and recharge their batteries. This is especially important when they have got to the point where they mindlessly continue on their treadmill.

Another way in which you can help them is to keep them focused on their important goals. Their changeable and multifaceted nature can sometimes distract them. They need time to develop their strengths and their impatience can create problems such as failing to complete a job well and cutting corners unnecessarily in order to move on to the next object of interest. The goal is to settle down, at least to the extent that allows them to realize their potential.

When it comes to honesty in relationships, you may find them hard to pin down. Not necessarily because they are not honest, but more likely because they feel acutely uncomfortable when cornered or challenged directly. They are often direct and upfront with others, but if pressured, may fail to be transparent. In relationships with a Gemini Moon it's probably best to remember to give them the air, oxygen and space they need to feel safe – and then ask them about things rather than asking them to explain themselves.

Being in a relationship with a Gemini Moon will stimulate, inspire, entertain, sweeten, reveal, inform. It is never boring, predictable or ordinary. If you are artistic or need a partner who can act as a muse you could do very well with a Gemini Moon. All relationships take investment, each one a different type. A Gemini Moon gives a good return, especially if you like to play by similar romantic rules of the game.

Gemini Top Tips

- In seduction, be ready to be a conjuror and an escape artist, as the Gemini Moon can be easily attracted to anything new, but is also easily bored and distracted. With intimacy, they expect to be in the driver's seat, but at the same time they also enjoy the seduction of courtship. The big challenge is to read their mood, which can change in a moment, especially if you say the wrong thing or look the wrong way. You need to be firm but flexible and highly perceptive. A direct approach will rarely give you the result you want – but it is Gemini, so you never know. Conjure attractive romantic apparitions while escaping to a different, but equally attractive, fantasy if the amorous winds blow in a different direction.

- Be lively, fun-loving, light-hearted and inspired. Stay one step ahead by thinking of new and curious distractions, but let them take the reins, especially in moments of frivolity, amusement and courting.
- When they do show their inconstant nature, celebrate rather than berate it. Tell them how refreshing it is to have someone who is so diverse, so multifaceted. This will certainly endear you to them.
- Be flexible and ready for a change of plans. Fly with them and you have a fun-loving partner. Try to block them and it will be like trying to stop the wind – which carries on without even noticing your efforts.
- In arguments, they are highly sensitive and almost never forget a slight. In fact, they usually remember every detail. If you screw up, don't dwell on it as that won't get you anywhere. Instead, tactfully try to move the attention to more pleasant topics, without appearing patronizing or dismissive. Not easy, but it will improve your diplomatic skills.
- Need to say something touchy publicly? No problem – a wink, a nod or a subtle inference does wonders. They love word games, so play away embarrassing or difficult moments with clever comments or stimulating diversions.
- If, however, they do insist on talking something through, be ready to do meet them head on.
- In day-to-day matters variety is the spice of life. Gemini Moons are poetic by nature and love a romantic note, a flower or loving gesture. Keeping active and fresh is also the secret to keeping their attention and affections.
- Expect the unexpected and you are safe. They are romantic, lovers of fantasy and gentle and delicate in nature. Their emotions are very real to them and suffuse their being with energy. Show your love by speaking between the lines and you will have their interest. Spell it out for them and you may lose their attention. But if you love them for what they are, they will love you in return.

Gemini Troubleshooting

- *How can you get them to take you and your feelings seriously?* Gemini Moons are often misunderstood as uninterested or distracted. An important part of their nature is to set the agenda, if only because everyone else is too slow and they like to keep things lively. If you want to make your point, give it the time it needs and be ready to explore a few issues that may seem unrelated to you but that are important to them. Make your point as you go from one part of the conversation to the other and give them the benefit of the doubt. They may be listening to you and understanding what you are saying, even though it may appear to you that they are not. Getting them to acknowledge your needs will probably take more than one conversation – it is a process and a way of relating, not something that is finalized in one sitting. And don't forget to be patient with them if the conversation about your needs turns into one about theirs. The trick for you will be to show them how that is only one side of a two-sided coin.

- *How can you get them to be more supportive or responsive?* 'Stimulation', 'involvement' and 'exchange' are the key words for creating a more responsive relationship with a Gemini Moon. A demanding tone will not work at all. You stand a better chance of creating support through sympathy rather than through heavy-handed emotional demands. They tend to respond easily, though, as it is part of their nature. Appeal to this and invite, seduce or cajole them into being more supportive through discussion. It may work if you deal with the issue in the third person and look at the problem 'objectively' rather than making it too personal, because there will always be a part of the Gemini Moon personality that will feel that they are involved and responsive – just maybe not to your full satisfaction.

☾ *How can you re-establish communication?*

The challenge is more how to get the communication right than to re-establish it. Gemini Moons are naturally talkative and easily strike up conversation in a spontaneous way that can give you the impression you are getting somewhere, but in reality you may not be talking about the right things, or even the same things. So it's usually no problem to just give them a call and start talking, but to get it right remember the subject that is important to you, as it is likely that you will need to direct the conversation back there from time to time. The trick with a Gemini Moon is to catch their attention, so anything that stimulates, excites or creates fun is a good hook. Even when things have gone wrong, a Gemini Moon is able to remember the things that have gone right, and this is what you should focus on. They are not so indecisive as changeable, so be ready to go with the flow.

☾ *What is the best way to apologize?*

Simply sit together and say you are sorry. Then be ready to deal with their response and give them a little time to vent their feelings if they want to. It is good for the relationship if they want to express themselves, as they will feel listened to and you will get a chance to understand what is really going on inside them. Things are good when they are talking to you; when they don't, it's a sign that something is really wrong. Once they open up, if you want to make a good impression be ready to engage and move on, as while they are sensitive, they can quickly put hurts behind them. Gemini Moons usually have a good sense of humour, so once you get the more serious part of the discussion over, bring in a bit of levity.

☾ *How can you rekindle the flame?*

In simple terms, you either can or you can't with a Gemini Moon. If you can, being active, involved, talkative and romantic will help. To create romance where the passion has died down you will need to create a setting that inspires them as much as it does you. Gemini Moons can be fickle all at once and without cause, so creating a seductive setting also means being responsive and fluid. Travel is probably the best panacea for the Gemini Moon romantic doldrums. Pick a good day to leave (by reading *Panchang Moon Astrology* or going to www.panchang.com) and go anywhere that allows the two of you to take on new roles in the partnership. Failing that, a romantic holiday, a weekend in the mountains, a dinner at a special restaurant – anything fresh and out of the ordinary will bring in the spark you are looking for. When in doubt, for the best results express your love in a letter or poem.

☾ *If the worst comes to the worst, how do you say goodbye without hurting their feelings?*

Gemini Moons can have a nervous, changeable nature that affects how they deal with emotional conflict. Saying goodbye to them can be challenging, as it can result in a wide range of responses, from indifference to a need to cling to the relationship. It therefore needs arguably more care than with other Moon signs. It is best to be gentle, keep things clear and simple and, if at all possible, keep the exchange positive and hopeful. Expect that you may not be fully understood and give them the space to have their emotional reaction. There is a very tender part of the Gemini Moon that heals through communication, so if the situation is right, offer them the chance to talk about it. And if you come to the point of saying goodbye, it may be best to voice it once you are certain, rather than changing back and forth.

The Moon in Cancer ♋

Cancer is the queen of Moon signs. Both the Moon and the sign of Cancer symbolize the mother, mundane and divine, and the Moon's placement here suggests the role of the mother will be centrally important. Astrologically, the Moon is strong in Cancer, which emphasizes, even exaggerates, all things lunar – for better or worse. Cancer Moon is the queen of the cosmic zodiac court, symbolizing the principles of nurturing, protection, mental and emotional well-being, general good fortune, feelings, intuition, psychic abilities, digestion, house and home, land and place of birth, and relation to the feminine archetype, to name but a few.

The Sensitive Crab

One of the most important, but not immediately obvious, qualities of a Moon in Cancer is the need to protect name, reputation, appearance and personal dignity. Some may say that is important to everyone, but it is not quite as important to some as to others. The Cancer Moon is quintessentially sensitive, possibly one of the most sensitive Moon signs, and very private. Their inner world is sacred to them and they don't easily share it with others. They tend to be guarded and even defensive when it comes to revealing their vulnerabilities, hopes and desires.

It is not by accident that the ancients attributed the symbol of the crab to this part of the zodiac. In fact, there are many good reasons, especially when the Moon is in Cancer. A crab, with its soft interior, is quite vulnerable. Its shell, sometimes natural and sometimes borrowed, protects it from its harsh environment. It is its primary defence and its source of safety. A Cancer Moon also has a delicate inner emotional world. Cancer is the first Water sign in the zodiac and a Cancer Moon can experience waves of emotion that defy description but which are expressed most easily as tears or as silence. The shell for a Cancer Moon is their well-developed and cultivated reputation and appearance.

In simple terms, the defence mechanism of Cancer is the presentation of an image that keeps you from getting inside too easily. This is especially pronounced with a Cancer Moon. It's almost as though their external personality will keep you busy while they gradually begin feeling comfortable with you and learn to trust you. It is doubtful that you will ever find a Cancer Moon giving things away too easily when you first meet them. It takes time to develop a relationship with them and don't be surprised if you have to continually prove yourself along the way – and even much later in the relationship. Reaffirmation is a valued safety mechanism for them and in close personal relationships they will frequently like to know if everything is OK. The paradox of a Cancer Moon is that the emotional ego is strong, or let's say influential, much more so than the external ego, but it's the external ego that you need to get past in order to understand how they work and where their real strengths lie.

The Intuitive Home-Maker

Cancer Moons are often good providers, good business people and can be socially active, especially when an issue hits close to home. They are strong and determined – even dogged. Setting their mind to a task means it will get done and they won't stop until it is. They are durable, ever more so when the odds are stacked against them, as long as they don't give in to their periodic melancholies or emotional insecurities. Their strong spirit makes them tremendous allies. If they are on your side, you can rely on them, as long as circumstances do not conspire to threaten their safety, hearth and home. They are mortified when compromised by adversity or fate and tend to carry such wounds with them for a long time. In general, their loyalty, especially in love, earns them a good reputation.

The Cancer Moon is nostalgia personified. Early life experiences create their emotional fabric and where this has been traumatic, they will take a good deal of time to work through their issues – well into their middle age or beyond. The best medicine for any hurting Cancer Moon is lots of love and affection, a loyal partner who can mother them a little, putting a salve of reassurance on their hurts.

Like other Water signs, Cancer Moons are sometimes known for their pronounced psychic abilities. They rely more on gut instincts than they are comfortable admitting. This is because they are usually quite well-informed, down-to-earth people and like to make 'practical decisions' based on realism. Yet the more a Cancer Moon relies on their intuition, the more reliable it becomes. The well-known American psychic Lucille Van Tassel is a good example of Cancer Moon intuition, as she demonstrated her abilities from an early age and ranked in the top three gifted psychics tested in over 400 tests. While her case is exceptional and well supported by the other factors of her chart, most Cancer Moons have premonitions and deeper insights than many of us. This is especially helpful to them when they lack the 'hard evidence' they need. It's certain that they will tell you about the times they ignored their intuition only to regret it later. For this and other reasons the Cancer Moon can appear eccentric or unusual and not be easily understood at first. On first meeting them it quickly becomes obvious that they march to their own drum, even if the beat is irregular.

Because the Moon symbolizes the mind and mental processes, Cancer Moons also tend to rely on their mental powers. The idea of mind over matter is natural for them, because they have often experienced it. This, too, can contribute to their 'peculiar' side, especially when it comes to explaining how it is they have formulated their thoughts and conclusions. It is this trait that lends originality to their ideas.

Cancer Moons make good providers and can sacrifice a lot for the greater good of their loved ones. They know where their priorities lie and are industrious in going about ensuring the safety and protection of those in their care. If this appeals to you, then a Cancer Moon will make a perfect partner. This is especially true for a Capricorn Moon, who is also industrious and is willing to shoulder more than their fair share of the burden to keep things on an even keel.

Expect that a Cancer Moon will put lots of energy and attention into the home. A Taurus Moon thinks of home as a castle, whereas the Cancer Moon sees it as sanctuary – the secret hiding place away from prying eyes and busybodies, the place to cuddle and be secure. Assuming that other factors in the chart are supportive, they will love to decorate their home, making it very cosy, especially their bathroom and kitchen – food is our primary nurturing agent, so expect that a Cancer Moon loves to cook, or at least has a specialized palette. Home for a Cancer Moon is an important place of solitude and regeneration, symbolizing a reclusive part of their character that needs regular private time to remain physically and mentally healthy.

One of their quirky motivations is their silent competitiveness or sense of social striving that urges them to keep up with the standards that others are setting. This can make them victims of fashion, desirous of the latest gadgets or keen to improve the garden or add an extension to the house to create prestige and monetary value. They like to keep up with the Joneses.

Their ideal home has an ocean or water view, which mirrors their nature and is an impetus to their spirit and the uninhibited flow of their thoughts and emotions. Water is the perfect stimulus for Cancer Moon's creativity, even if all they have is the bath. They appreciate natural materials: wood, plants, fountains and the like, and also fine furnishings that are well designed, good quality and made from natural materials. Cancer Moons are born naturalists and enjoy being close to nature. Do you like pets? Animals are often Cancer favourites, helping them connect with their own deeply buried *primitif* within.

In cases where they don't get the home in good order (a rare occurrence), they feel out of place, unsettled and disconnected. This can be very unsettling to them and emotionally things will not be calm and peaceful in a Cancer Moon home that lacks the basic comforts (and then some). Don't forget that the home is analogous to their crab shell.

Entering the Shell

However, the Cancer Moon makes a great partner – warm, loving, affectionate, caring and protective. They can be very nurturing in their approach to relationships, as one would expect from a Moon in the sign that symbolizes mother and home. This caring extends to close friends, family members, lovers – anyone who has been patient enough to be accepted into the inner sanctum of their emotional being. Cancer Moons make affectionate partners and, like other Water signs, are hopeless romantics. They love to be courted, or to do the courting, and can be quite lavish and demonstrative when it comes to creating a good impression. If you have caught the eye of a Cancer Moon, expect flowers and lots of little whatnots that say 'I love you'. If you do get something, don't forget to show lots of appreciation, especially for the thoughtfulness and originality of their choice.

If you do forget, it is easy and natural for a Cancer to bear a grudge for a long time – especially when they feel neglected or that their reputation has been injured. If this happens they will make strong efforts to publicize their version of the story, well before you have even thought of acting. They won't forget it, either. Cancer Moons have an amazing memory, especially when it comes to affairs of the heart. In a moment, they can recall the slightest detail about an exchange you had with them when you first met 15 years ago (try your best to remember please), or even the way they felt when you forgot something important to them, which was relatively trivial to others. In more difficult cases, the memory of a relationship gone wrong can bind them to repeat negative behaviour patterns by unconsciously seeking similar situations. To avoid this, the Cancer Moon needs to consciously confront their hurt and let go of it to avoid becoming bitter and limiting the scope for future emotional contentment.

Their long memory can skew their perceptions not because they are emotionally rooted, but because they tend to look forward by looking at the past. This is part of their protective mechanism – they don't want to go to unsafe places and they tend to judge the new by reaching for what they know. They love to take stock of a situation by comparing it to past experiences, and often wistfully enjoy reminiscing about major events and milestones in their lives. If they are consciously aware of this tendency, they can use it to further their life aims by visualizing positive experiences and validations, projecting them forward in time away from the current situation. This is especially helpful when they are facing challenging and threatening circumstances.

The downside of Cancer Moons' great memories can affect their relationships when, for instance, a new friend or lover is unintentionally made to feel that they either have to live up to the past or to do better – which, as we all know, is a real pain. The best way to deal with this is to be sweetly direct and point it out to them. In doing so, remember that they are sensitive and even if they don't immediately acknowledge that they heard you, they probably did.

Side-Stepping Together

This leads us to another sticky defence mechanism of Cancer Moons – the tendency to side-step important issues. This is hard-wired into a Cancer Moon, and is symbolized by the crab's sideways walking. So Cancer Moons tend to manoeuvre around delicate issues instead of hitting them head on. This can be quite misleading because their erstwhile polished approach, aided by some level of diplomacy, can give you the appearance that they *are* dealing with the issues. Add into this some measure of that nurturing feel-good factor of Cancer and it is easy to walk away thinking that everything is resolved, when in fact they have done a good deflecting job, keeping you and the difficulty at bay.

It is not helped by the fact that emotional reactions are often suppressed with Cancer Moons until the point where they just have to vent their feelings – which can then seem distorted in relation to the issue, or inappropriate in terms of timing. Good timing is not always a Cancer Moon's strong point, as they tend to second-guess themselves, seeking to ensure that every step forward is a sure one.

How to deal with all this side-stepping? Mentally picture yourself sitting near them. If you can, and they are comfortable, move over and actually sit next to them. Take a piece of paper and outline the problem. Look at it together. Give them a sense that you are with them in dealing with the problem, not trying to get inside their hard shell to the soft, tender bits. Also, be ready to read between the lines. If Gemini Moon is a riddle wrapped in mystery inside an enigma, the Cancer Moon is just a mystery and likes to keep it that way. With a little practice, though, you will get to know their individual way of communicating.

When you are communicating back, directness hardly ever works, unless you have earned their undying, implicit and abundant trust – which usually takes a good deal of time. Just as a crab scurries quickly into its hole in the sand or shoots into a crevice as the surf breaks, so a Cancer Moon will head for the nearest exit when a direct aim is taken. Whether the exit is physical or effected by dispersing a distracting chaff of small talk, you can be sure that the straight approach almost never works.

In fact, Cancer Moons can do with a few tips on self-expression and how to create clear understandings in their relationships. Part of the challenge comes from those moments when the emotional sea swells with too many issues at once. This creates confusion and a jumble of feelings that they find difficult to sort out for themselves, not to mention expressing them clearly to others. Once they create an emotional order they are better equipped to talk about them sensibly. But don't expect a quick result with this. In the meantime, if confused, a Cancer Moon can communicate in a peculiar way and it can be frustrating for them when they fail to get the agreement of those around them. This is because they will often draw conclusions for you, without explaining the logic that brought them there. Trying to get this out of them can be tricky, so it's probably best to coax it out bit by bit. Cancer Moons dislike the unexpected, especially if it highlights their weaknesses, but when they do open up (thanks to your coaxing), they are usually pleasantly surprised at the positive reception. This can help them build confidence and assure them that taking risks has its good side.

Sailing the Seas of Love

The Cancer Moon is logically then a sometimes moody sign, prone to melancholy and expressing their emotions almost in synch with the rising tides and waning and waxing Moons. They are very lunar and very sensitive to nature and their surroundings. In a relationship with a Cancer Moon, you can help them avoid succumbing to negative moods, self-pity and melancholic indulgences. At the same time, it's important to know that they need them now and then. It's akin to emotional housekeeping – clearing away rubble by digging their hands in it. The best way to get them out of it is to remind them that they will miss out on opportunities if they get stuck in the wallow of 'poor me'. Another way to help them is to get them to open up about what ails them. Of course, this is not easy, but you can try and in the trying they will feel your support and may decide to share their problems with you.

If you are the problem and are guilty of creating the hurt, then it can be a challenge finding a way out and, depending on the level of their passions, you can expect them to need a chance to work through it with you on their terms. The trick for you will be knowing when this happens because it is a Cancer Moon's nature to keep things to themselves and store those hurts well away from prying eyes and busybodies. Then one of these hurts can unexpectedly bubble to the surface and catch you unaware. When this happens, acknowledge it and rather than challenge them with 'Why haven't you mentioned this before?', compliment them and express amazement at how long-suffering they have been. If you find this too much to handle, then it's going to be a challenge dealing with a Cancer Moon.

If a Cancer Moon is hurt they can express it by 'pinching' you – much as you would expect from a crab. The idea is to give you just enough hurt to let you know they are hurting. It may sound funny, but Cancer Moons may even like to pinch their lovers affectionately (maybe it will be love bites). If you are not within arm's reach, then a good substitute is a well-placed remark launched with just the right amount of stealth – not too obvious and giving *them enough time to retreat.*

If you are the one needing emotional succour, however, and are lucky enough to make your way into the heart of a Cancer Moon, you will find a soft, cosy, emotional resting place that offers a chance for healing and long-lasting growth. Once they let you inside, the Cancer Moon offers an experience like no other – a fluid, sweet, dreamy, undulating sea of nurturing emotions. Imagine the emotional equivalent of a Pre-Raphaelite painting and you have a clue to the romantic tempo of their feelings.

Cancer Moons love to encircle their loved one in a protective cocoon. Depending on who you are, this can be either good or bad. If you need security and thrive on help and protection, it's great. If you want a lot of freedom, and have a 'let's take it easy' approach, then you could find the warm embrace of a Cancer Moon too constrictive. In any case, at times you will have to put your foot down and stand up for your individuality, your own space and your own ideas. When a Cancer Moon indulges their bossy side, you could feel that it's their world and you just happen to be in it. Or maybe it's their movie and you are an extra – an important one, but an extra nevertheless. If the Cancer Moon knew you felt this way they would be horrified. That's the last thing they want for you – 'Just trying to help.' So, if you end up feeling hemmed in, to avoid rows, just be honest and spread your wings. Breaking free of the confines of the Cancer shell now and then doesn't have to mean demolishing it, just building an extension, for you. But ask them if they also want to break out and fly in the stars of the night sky. Otherwise they may feel left out.

In mature adult relationships this should not be a problem, just another move you make in the Cancer Moon cosmic dance. If, however, you are young and have a Cancer Moon parent there will be times when you will feel limited by the social expectations put on you – especially if you are coming to that age where you need to fly the nest. Remember, keeping up appearances is very important to Cancer Moons, so if you want to let your hair down, do it in a way that takes this into account.

A Cancer Moon makes a wonderful, caring and giving partner. If you can learn to play by the rules of their secret game of life, you will have a strong, loyal and sweet-natured ally. A relationship with a Cancer Moon, whether a romance or friendship, offers a lot and expects a lot. It's for people who love security, closeness and romance, and who are able to give it all back to their Cancer Moon partner in regular and equal measure.

Cancer Top Tips

- To succeed in seduction you will need to be perceptive, thoughtful and romantic. When in doubt, overdo the romance. Tasteful displays of affection, gift giving, romantic dinners and thoughtful gestures help a great deal.
- Be ready to reveal your feelings first – this is important for establishing trust. It can take time to hear their feelings in return. Still waters run deep, though, so you can bet a lot is going on inside. Let them express themselves in their own good time and be ready to read between the lines. There is often more in what they don't say than in what they do say.
- The best way to earn their trust is to be gentle with their feelings and allow them to come to you in their own good time. They do respond to demonstrative gestures, but this can also trigger a defensive mechanism of 'Let's wait and see'. If you are eager, this could dampen your enthusiasm. Some patience is needed, but it will pay off.
- Cancer Moons love a good time, but especially enjoy quiet, secluded, romantic settings full of creature comforts, nice fabric, flowers, pleasant scents, candles and soft warm rugs. If you want to make an impression, arrange for a cosy weekend away at a remote hideaway – as expensive as you can afford.
- Cancer Moons can be quite tactile, but again it works very well when they initiate the touching, especially in the early phases of a relationship. Once they are comfortable, they will expect and enjoy a lot of physical touching and intimacy. But before that don't be surprised if your advances are rebuffed, as they

need to keep a sense of personal space that they control. If you go rushing in it can create insecurity for them.

- Putting emphasis on togetherness, hearth and home, relating and personal intimacy fosters a Cancer Moon relationship. Expect to hear about it, verbally or otherwise, if they don't feel that you are giving enough attention to the partnership.
- They covet their privacy and will not tolerate it if you reveal their secrets. Once you have a relationship with them they will expect you not to allow anyone in to the envelope of your love.
- Arguments can be challenging – on one hand emotional and on the other silently emotional. There is little direct confrontation with a Cancer Moon, unless they are backed into a corner. Otherwise, expect them to deal with difficult issues tangentially – sideways. Arguments are rarely won with logic, as they are emotional personalities and tend to store their hurts deep inside, well beyond the reaches of any mental or intellectual probing.
- Giving free rein to the romantic in you gives you the best chance with a Cancer Moon. Poetry, flowers, scented oils, anything that pampers will help you win the heart of this nurturing and sensitive Moon sign.

Cancer Troubleshooting

- *How can you get them to take you and your feelings seriously?* It is very common for someone in a relationship with a Cancer Moon to feel misunderstood. This is not always fair, as a Cancer Moon is usually very caring and involved, but their nature can hide this even from those they are in a close relationship with. They may be thinking that in fact they are being quite caring, while you are feeling neglected. So the first thing to do, if you can, is to get them to look at your needs by hinting that they look outside their own emotional space. Create an empathy with them, and try to help them understand what it is like to be you in the relationship. Talk about your feelings so that they can listen and learn from you. Once they do, there is a chance they will respond, but the challenge is in getting them to that point.

☾ *How can you get them to be more supportive or responsive?*
If you are in a relationship with a Cancer Moon who is not supportive, think again and look closely at what is going on in the relationship or in you to give you that feeling. A Cancer Moon can be an extra specially supportive partner and if there is any real love in the relationship this has to show. An important question may be whether you are seeing their support. It is rare for a Cancer Moon to be truly indifferent, but if for some reason you happen to have a Cancer Moon partner who is breaking the zodiac mould, the best way to draw their attention to your needs is to get them to understand that their needs are served well when your needs are also met. And if and when they do meet them, make sure you make a big, happy fuss over it.

☾ *How can you re-establish communication?*
Regardless of the details of the relationship, there are a few points that will always help. The first is to both read and speak between the lines. The emotionally aware Cancer Moon is sure to pick up what is going on beneath the surface. Don't barge in, but gently approach them in an indirect way. This gives them the chance to feel comfortable with your effort. Create a soft mood in the conversation – inviting, cosy and secure. If you can, let them suggest a meeting before you do. Cancers are very romantic and respond well to gifts of any kind. This can be very helpful in touching their hearts and getting them to open up. Be ready to talk about your feelings first, read their subtle responses and express your interest when you feel that they are open and positive to your advances.

☾ *What is the best way to apologize?*
To be really smart you should avoid having to apologize in the first place, as the keen memory of the Cancer Moon will create a record of the transgression that you may have to live down

once or twice in the future. But if you have to apologize, do so sweetly, romantically, with flowers, gifts, generosity – in short, demonstratively. It will be important to acknowledge their hurt feelings – don't skimp on this. To apologize successfully, you will need to stroke the Cancer Moon, give to them and reassure them that everything is in order. This should give you splendid romantic and affectionate results.

☾ *How can you rekindle the flame?*
Think romance and double it. Assuming that you don't have to make up for transgressions (read above) and simply need to breathe new life into the partnership, anything romantic will do the trick. In this regard it is probably impossible to overdo it (as long as it's done in good taste) and any effort should have immediate and positive results (assuming that there is at least a small flame to kindle). Weekends away, surprise romantic dinners, gifts, poems, love letters, a fresh lick of paint on their favourite room (remember the house is important) – all these and more will give you the desired result. If you really want to score, recreate a wonderful experience that you shared together in the past, though take care to get the details just right.

☾ *If the worst comes to worst, how do you say goodbye without hurting their feelings?*
A part of the Cancer Moon will like to deal with any emotional upheaval by looking the other way, so don't be surprised if it takes extra effort to get them to recognize that you want to leave. Once the shock is over, their natural reaction will be to think in terms of self-protection, which could mean a break in communication or at least behaviour which underscores that you are out of the picture. This is a survival trait and should not be taken too seriously, especially as no matter what happens their future has your imprint on it, as they tend to think emotionally in terms of what's happened already in their life. As always, be gentle, kind and honest. Avoid strong emotions if you can and wherever possible let the relationship end on a positive note.

The Moon in Leo ♌

One word sums up the Moon in Leo – the Sun. (OK, that's two words.) Condensed into one symbol are all the qualities associated with this sign – pride, eagerness, energy, dignity and royalty. If Cancer is the queen of the zodiac, Leo is its king in every respect. Knowing this is the key to unlocking Leo Moon's inner secrets and realizing the many benefits they offer, as well as their particularly unique relationship challenges. Like all the zodiac signs that illustrate the duality of the material world, Leo colours our life experience simultaneously as joy and lessons, freedom and obligation, privilege and responsibility – and does so with all the pomp and emotional generosity of Midas himself.

The Golden King

Leo Moons have a golden quality that shines through all their dealings. They have a larger than life nature that seems to announce itself as they enter any room. Regardless of physical appearance, they exude a sense of self-importance, purpose and influence even in the most trivial of their exchanges. They are known for their pride and often have a sense of emotional confidence that sets them apart from the crowd. This is usually a positive, constructive type of pride that is based on a genuine care for others. Leo Moons possess a generosity of spirit and are sorely pained when, by reason of circumstances, they cannot help others in need. This is because Leo is the zodiac monarch, the sign that is the source of light and responsible for the well-being of all others. While this sounds grand and exaggerated, especially in humble human endeavours, in practice there is something of the benevolent monarch in all Leo Moons.

Leo Moons are naturally sociable and agreeable people. They can often bring new life to a gathering, and have a creative zeal that inspires and enthuses. They love to be at the heart of things and if you are looking for them at a party you can probably find them where the action is. People enjoy their company because everyone feels important in the company of someone important. They can bring purpose to even frivolous pursuits, which sometimes earns them a reputation for being too serious. In most cases, though, a Leo Moon possesses an idealism that attracts the attention and respect of others. You can therefore expect to find Leo Moons involved in social issues, charities, politics or other social groups of purpose.

One of the best qualities of a Leo Moon is their sense of generosity. This has a practical side in the form of giving, but also has an emotional component. Leo Moons have a naturally self-expressive quality about their feelings and if they are not feeling happy it is quite certain you will know about it one way or the other, either through outspoken emotional bursts or the pensive irritability that says simultaneously 'Go away' and 'Look what you've done'. The symbol of Leo is the lion and this Leo Moon trait is reminiscent of the guarding, protective side of the lioness, along with her tetchy side that says, 'Give me some peace to lie in the sun.' With a Leo Moon it is rare that you don't know where you stand. For the most part they are direct – for some, too direct – about their feelings, except when you have wounded their pride and invalidated their all-important sense of dignity.

Sometimes this pride can be their own worst enemy, painting them in to a corner where they have to keep up appearances and can't relax and really be themselves. This can usually be remedied by a word of encouragement, a change of scenery (Leo Moons love action) or a good joke, which can bring out their spontaneous and jovial nature. All these can also help to balance a more serious, ponderous side of their character that can depress their spirits. Their fiery and passionate nature ensures that they feel things very profoundly. They are also quite philosophical about their experiences and rely on this to give meaning where it seems wanting.

Leo Moons are in fact hopelessly attracted to the mysterious and esoteric sides of life, which is another aspect of their feline curiosity. They are seekers of wisdom and whether they gain this through the mundane school of hard knocks or a more structured study of philosophy, their ultimate aim is to 'influence through understanding'. Their search for understanding gives them an interest in a wide range of subjects that may include art, education and social welfare.

Leo Moons appear to have an innate wisdom that guides them and inspires them on their life journey. This forms part of their life strategy, which is to try and see the big picture. They tend to see things in a grand way and are not always concerned with the little details of life. What's important to them is to have a sense of direction and to put theory to good use in a practical way. Leo Moons tend to be 'doers' and loathe those who sit in their ivory towers ruminating about problems and solutions. They like action and like to see things getting done in a real way that doesn't waste time or resources.

The Inspirational Leader

Leo Moons are known for being born leaders. Examples of this are Benjamin Disraeli, Winston Churchill and John F. Kennedy. Another good example, but possibly less well known, is the medieval Indian religious reformer and avatar Sri Chaitanya Mahaprabhu. His concern for the spiritual welfare of all classes of people inspired what may be the world's first civil disobedience movement. He is known for his compassionate dealings and was also the first person to preach a supra-class doctrine that validated all people, regardless of their class or caste of birth – an especially revolutionary concept given the norms of his time and culture.

Whatever their circumstances, a Leo Moon's sense of destiny and concern for the welfare of others is a driving force that advances their ability to influence the destiny of others. Their sense of self-importance is not only a source of strength for them but also helps convey that they are someone who deserves a following. Regardless of whether it's global politics, the boardroom or the family circle, the leader in the Leo Moon must find expression if they are to have a sense of purpose and life fulfilment.

The leader in Leo Moons inclines them to executive or managerial positions. 'Being the boss' is something that comes easily to them. They like to be organized and like to organize others. In some cases they can set high standards for themselves and expect others to emulate them.

Expect a busy life around a Leo Moon. Although they love to take time out to relax, they also know the value of hard work and won't mind sharing that experience with you. Leo Moons love to create excitement in their lives and also like you to participate. It will take a very strong will not to play along with the desires of a Leo Moon and don't be surprised if, after putting your foot down, you find yourself going along for the ride. This will probably be due to their infectious enthusiasm and innate diplomacy. They can get people to do things they wouldn't normally do – willingly.

Leo Moons are good leaders, good listeners and good doers, but their Fire sign nature makes them first and foremost doers. At times they may give the impression of disregarding the opinion of others because they feel a sense of urgency that something has to be done. When their strategic thinking helps them draw conclusions in advance of others and prompts them to act, it can appear that they are too 'controlling' and 'bossy' and are therefore disempowering the people around them. While in the end they can be correct in their assessment, the impression that they are superseding the interests of others can work counter to their best interests. They then appear dogmatic or authoritarian – qualities most often attributed to Leo Moons and ones which can create resentment and a lack of co-operation. If this happens, then it's a cycle of disempowerment, because the Leo Moon will feel misunderstood and their pride will be hurt. So when they can, it's best to put more effort – and yes, in spite of their impatience, more valuable time – into validating others. If they can give them a piece of the action, their own prestige and influence will grow, making them more happy and secure. After all, no kingdom, no king.

Leo is the fifth house of the zodiac, which signifies artistic and creative expression. The soul and originality of the artist is symbolized by the Sun and pronounced Leo qualities in a chart point to the potential for artistic achievement. Julia Roberts, Robert Redford, John Travolta, Shirley Maclaine, Madonna, k. d. lang and Benjamin Britten are all Leo Moons. The attractive effulgence of these popular personalities is in large measure derived from their prominent Moons in Leo. While this standard of creative expression and success is rare, the qualities of originality, expression and creative confidence can be seen to some degree in all those with their Moon in Leo.

An artist without a gallery is of course as incomplete as a king without a throne, and to shine Leo Moon will need the chance for self-expression and creativity. Relationships offer them the chance for this type of expression and a friend or lover of a Leo Moon will be called on to participate, support and celebrate it. It is also important to encourage their creativity. You may not think your role in this is too important, but for the Leo Moon it is more valuable than you can imagine.

One trait that stands out with Leo Moons is their sense of a purposeful life. Destiny has ordained that they are who they are and it's only a matter of time before they realize their ultimate potential. Depending on the person, this can be endearing or off-putting, but for the Leo Moon it is a source of power and durability. This sense of purpose enables them to tolerate many inconveniences, as long as they feel that it is part of a grand plan. As soon as the magic has worn off and they feel their role is a bit part, they lose interest and become easily bored, not unlike their Fire-sign counterpart, the Aries Moon. Leo Moons therefore always need a sense of direction, a goal, a reason for being. If they don't have one, they will find one. There is nothing sadder than a monarch without a throne. The perpetual striving for a *raison d'être* is an important impetus in the success of Leo Moons and has expression in most areas of their life, but particularly so in their dealings with friends and lovers.

Loving the Benevolent Despot

In close relationships, a Leo Moon is affectionate, protective, thoughtful, calm, magnanimous, valorous and persevering. In love, they are idealistic and romantic in a 'principled' kind of way.

They always remember your kindnesses and are immensely loyal once they have given their heart to you. There is something naturally paternalistic about a Leo Moon and this comes across in relationships. They are there for you, to help and guide you, even if you don't know you need their good counsel. They are proactive in their friendships and have often thought through the cause and solution of your problem even before you have had time to acknowledge that you have one. Depending on the other aspects of their character, this trait will be expressed in a wonderfully supportive or insufferably overbearing way. In most cases, it's something in between and tends to be both supportive and well received, although the delivery can be at times strong, emotional, forceful or opinionated, especially when they are somehow involved emotionally as one of the ultimate beneficiaries of the advice. The trick with a Leo Moon, as with most of the signs, is to take the good with the bad and tolerate their exuberance if not be uplifted and supported by it.

In many ways, Leo Moons are a soft touch, because they are always ready to lend a helping hand or word of advice. You can expect a good number of people to flock to them for counsel, especially because of their sense of authority and their willingness to help. Hopefully, you will like people, or not feel inconvenienced by your Leo Moon partner taking centre stage.

In essence, a Leo Moon needs to be appreciated, and despite all the posturing, emotional insecurity or self-doubt lingers behind the regal façade. Maybe the crown is heavy and they need encouragement to keep things in order. They have a strong sense of duty and are generally responsible. Any encouragement, then, is guaranteed to please, even if they are not quick to show it, as it gives them a sense that their efforts are not in vain. Again, this stems from their sense of mission and purpose. The odd kind word will keep them from abdicating.

Negotiating Emotional Treaties

There will be times, however, when you will have to define your emotional territory with a Leo Moon, almost as though you are a neighbouring monarch who wants to conclude a treaty that establishes firm borders. When this happens, make sure that you conduct yourself 'monarch to monarch', with all the deference normally afforded to powerful sovereigns. Otherwise there is a decent chance that your border dispute will escalate into a full-blown conflict or result in a severing of diplomatic ties. There is one guiding rule when this happens and happily it's not that difficult to apply: to somehow remember that a Leo Moon is well intentioned – at least consciously – and that all they want to do is be your benefactor. Of course, this can only work when you are in close relationship with someone, otherwise such an attitude would be summarily guillotined in a revolution. But if you can meet the generosity of the Leo Moon with your own good nature and give them the benefit of the doubt, then the Leo Moon will be your valued ally. At court, the custom is to offer words of praise and then to get down to business and with a Leo Moon this is not a bad approach. If you tell them that you appreciate their concern and their good intentions, but can manage your life on your own, then you will go a long way to establishing the equal partnership in which both of you can thrive. Because, in truth, a Leo Moon needs a strong counterpart.

When confronting problems, Leo Moons can be quite determined, as long as they have a sense of direction and a plan of action. Making progress is important to them and they like to feel that they are advancing towards their goals, even if it's slow going. When they put their mind to it, they can be very determined, have a strong will and pride themselves on completing tasks and achieving goals. The biggest challenge to a Leo Moon is the constraints that limit their options and their ability to act. The frustrations that come from this can spark their more passionate and excitable side and land them in trouble. The main solution in dealing with limits for a Leo Moon is to 'work at it' and measure steady progress. Identify where they can make a difference and put their energies there. They also need to check their sometimes hot temper, otherwise it can have destructive results, especially in relationships. When it comes to dealing with others' shortcomings, Leo Moons should consciously extend their generosity to them rather than become impatient.

The chivalry of the Aries Moon finds a more mature astrological expression in Leo. If Aries is the young knight, Leo is the reigning sovereign. Leo represents the next octave of astrological Fire-sign qualities and symbolically the next platform of karmic/spiritual development in the journey of the soul to ultimate perfection. Thus, while the Leo Moon has a sense of self-importance similar to the Aries Moon, in contrast it may be more 'conscious' of subtle relationship dynamics. In some ways, it tends to be more encompassing of the needs and issues of others, by consciously embracing what Aries may otherwise be content to let pass by.

At the same time, this cycle of symbolic development is not complete and hints at a part of the Leo Moon that can be uncertain in relationships, where they need reassurance. Even in long-standing relationships the Leo Moon can appear to be cautious in its dealings with its partner – even to the point where they feel a distrust or doubt about them. Even at the worst of times this is infrequent, but it can cause friction, especially as the Leo Moon is not always aware of the level of demands they place on their partner. To keep this in check the Leo Moon needs to consciously work on this, and if these feelings arise, give their partner the benefit of the doubt. Life is a circle, and what you give out you tend to get back. If they can muster their natural leonine courage to validate and value their partner, then in most cases they can expect a proportionate reciprocation.

To be close to the Leo Moon is a privilege. They are strong, wilful, passionate and, at times, demanding partners. The spirited nature of the Leo Moon will give you energy, yet at times tax you. Their involvement in your life can create new opportunities and freedoms. In return they expect loyalty, honesty and energy. Like any relationship of value, there will be a sense of responsibility towards the Leo Moon, but without doubt you will also have a sense of privilege in being with a caring, romantic and affable partner. It's a court appointment that stimulates, philosophizes and shines brightly – so remember to bring your sunglasses.

Leo Top Tips

- To seduce a Leo Moon, tactfully appeal to their sense of importance and purpose. Their sense of mission and destiny applies as much to romance as it does to the rest of their life. Be kind and gently honour them, as much as you would stroke a cat. And, like a cat, give them the space and respect to respond to your overtures on their own good terms. Otherwise it is certain you will scare them away. In the case of the Leo Moon, seduction is, as the definition says, 'to entice or beguile into a desired state' – and to be effective, such enticement should not be too obvious.
- To attract a Leo Moon you should appeal to their sense of curiosity. Remembering to maintain your own sense of mystery will help enormously with this. The trick is to get them to come to you, or at least let them think they are making the moves.
- Appeal to their sense of the theatre of life and play up the special roles you both play on its stage. Beguile them by agreeing to play a supportive role and you will soon earn their allegiance, especially if you give them good reason to display their more regal, charitable nature.
- Adventure, excitement and being at the heart of things are important in a Leo Moon relationship. Be creative when it comes to thinking of new ideas and new entertainment. Don't let the relationship become predictable if you want to keep their interest.
- Arguments can be interesting and not a little heated, as Leo Moons are passionate by nature. It can take a good deal of effort to disengage, so if you must argue, make sure it's worth your while or a matter of important principle – a reason they respect easily.

- They can tolerate a challenge, even enjoy it, but they never suffer an insult easily, or forgive it quickly. The only way to kiss and make up with a Leo Moon is to admit your failings and appeal to their innate sense of justice. They almost always respond to honesty in another person.
- Coming to their rescue earns you an indelible place in their heart. Loyalty breeds loyalty with the Leo Moon. Think twice before you compromise their trust.
- In day-to-day matters, weave a bit of magic into the relationship with gestures that appeal to their pride of place in your heart. They are naturally generous and easily reciprocate with kindness. Gifts, even small ones, that celebrate their importance have great value to them.
- Vitality, enthusiasm, purpose and passion appeal to the Leo Moon. If you can reflect these qualities back to them, you are sure to capture their heart.

Leo Troubleshooting

- *How can you get them to take you and your feelings seriously?* Appeal to their sense of justice and righteousness as well as their natural inclination to respond to a call of distress. If life were a movie, they would love to play the hero or the heroine, so give them a chance to help, save, protect and respond. Definitely avoid unnecessary criticism. If you must highlight their faults, mollify them with assurances that you know that nothing was intentional. And if it was, well then it's a moment of rare weakness. In the first instance it is best to avoid taking the view that Leo Moons don't really care. Giving them the benefit of the doubt tends to bring the best out of them.

- *How can you get them to be more supportive or responsive?* At times, Leo Moons are prone to a mildly fickle emotional mood that can make them appear uninterested. As always, the best way to draw attention to your needs is to appeal to their high-minded nature and let them know you have wants. Of course, if you too are proud, you may feel that they should know this already. It's best not to act on this, though, as it won't get you far. When the Leo Moon does get it right, let them know, especially as the remembrance of their past successes are a key to their future ones.

☾ *How can you re-establish communication?*

Leo Moons have an adventurous, regal spirit which gives them an open nature that is often ready to respond to positive overtures. So, appeal to their sense of importance, valour and generosity. Be light-hearted, humorous and even ready to offer them a little challenge – in the right measure, and tactfully presented. Appeal to their chivalrous nature and of course in all cases treat them with the subtle undercurrent of deference due to someone of zodiac royalty. Compliments, therefore, usually work, as long as they are sincere. They may find it difficult to turn down an opportunity for a bit of fun, so appeal to their playful nature. And if you are clever you can always tease their curiosity, or their fantasy, to get a response from them.

☾ *What is the best way to apologize?*

Picture anything regal – king, queen, prince or lion. Appeal to their sense of dignity and reassure them that the problem was either not intentional or that it will not happen again. Give them the space to forgive you, but don't be put off if they have a mildly paternalistic tint to their response. Let it pass and get on with moving the conversation to hopeful, positive and future things. Leos like to think ahead. If possible, offer kind gestures, affection or gifts which demonstrate your sincerity (remember you are at court), and make sure you enquire whether your apology has made matters better and removed any hard feelings. And if it hasn't, set about stroking their hurt feelings with yet more kind words and gentle affections.

☾ *How can you rekindle the flame?*

Go back to your regal mental picture (see above) and let the spirit of that colour all your romantic efforts. Initially you can lead the way, but when your Leo Moon partner takes the bait, let them direct the proceedings. Leo Moons are highly romantic, passionate and vital by nature, so any chance to express that will lift their spirits and lift the relationship. Leo Moons revel in their destiny and purpose, so inspire their passion for the relationship by giving them an important centre-stage role to play in a way that stimulates their fantasy.

☾ *If the worst comes to the worst, how do you say goodbye without hurting their feelings?*

It is easy to offend a Leo Moon and special care needs to be taken to avoid hurt feelings and wounded egos. There may be no easy way to say goodbye (is there ever?), but the most important tip here is to take an open, honest approach in expressing why. While this may touch on delicate areas, the Leo Moon will appreciate the straightforward approach. They see it as a form of respect, and of course honour is very important to them.

The Moon in Virgo ♍

In the cosmic court, the sign of Virgo plays a number of roles, the most prominent of which is court advisor. This is because Virgo embodies the principles of discretion, analysis, probity and critical circumspection. Virgo is not easily bamboozled by flowery words or grand gestures. This is the zodiac's sign of the ultimate strategist, the chess player, the reserved observer who prefers to watch from the sidelines and act with caution, precision and good timing.

The Emotional Pedant

The planet Mercury rules Virgo and its well-known emblem is the virgin. Both symbolize Virgo Moon qualities. This is a different manifestation of the Gemini Mercury – less frivolous, more grounded and tending to the analytical and the pedantic, even in emotional matters. Virgo Moons do share certain qualities with Gemini – wit, humour, intellect, quick minds – but there is a gulf of difference, especially when it comes to more serious matters. And what could be more serious than matters of the heart?

Virgo is the sixth house of the zodiac, representing the ideal of service, of selflessness, giving, healing and care. Its role as counsellor derives from the Virgo willingness to stay on the fringes of the action and to not seek the centre of attention. Virgo Moons are often content putting others' needs and interests first, and thus it is not uncommon to find them working in consulting, the health service or government. Good examples of this include the diplomat Henry Kissinger and the doctor and author Deepak Chopra.

Virgo Moons have a nurturing quality that is mixed with an element of discipline. Unlike the Cancer Moon, whose nurturing is fluid, the Virgo Moon seeks to cultivate growth in a more 'structured' way and thus there is more of an element of discipline to the Virgo Moon nurturing. The emphasis is on conscious care and thus you will find that the Virgo Moon is very aware of the little details that would pass lesser mortals by. This often earns them the reputation for being too concerned about detail, a trait we will discuss (in more detail) later on.

The principle of purity plays a large role in the character of Virgo Moons. At the root of this trait is the striving for perfection, the attainment of the ideal – even to the point of the transcendent, a state unsullied by the mundane 'dirtiness' of this world. The Virgo Moon will often hanker for a state of purity, regardless of how inaccessible it may be. In fact, the further away, the more difficult to achieve, the purer it seems and the more desirable it is for them.

In practical terms, it is not very easy to live up to such a standard and if speaking candidly the Virgo Moon will tell you that it's a burden having such high ideals, but it seems there is nothing they can do about it. The struggle between the mundane and the ideal also earns Virgo Moons a reputation for being neurotic, too concerned about cleanliness, correctness, exactness, punctuality. It is easy for the Virgo Moon to lose sight of the wood for the trees, putting emphasis on details that seem almost irrelevant to a more strategic thinker. The trick for the Virgo Moon is to give this concern a strategic context – the detail has importance only within the bigger picture. The better they are able to learn this, the more relevant and effective their keen eye for what's right. In fact, the occasional view from the top of the mountain will give them some relief from the self-imposed pressure of having to look after every little detail all the time.

If you are in relationship with a Virgo Moon you can help them by giving them some objective input about keeping things in perspective. It is easy for them to become overanalytical and too wrapped up in their striving for perfection and struggle for order. Remind them that in an imperfect world, perfection is at best a state of mind rather than an embodied ideal. This can be very helpful to them when their own sense of human frailty makes them feel inadequate or incomplete. Remind them that the aspiration for perfection is a kind of perfection in itself and not always the end game. Of course, this can be difficult, especially when they are working in an environment which expects high standards or where there is a strong competitive element. Then you really have a job on your hands, but an important one, because they will need your support all the more.

Astrology concerns itself in large measure with symbolizing the dual material world, thus everything has both a good and bad expression. The good side to the Virgo pedantry for precision is their ability to work in demanding, detail-oriented fields of work such as healthcare, engineering, accounting, design and other endeavours that need attention to detail. On the other hand, there is nothing more painful for a Virgo Moon than for them to point the sharp end of their own critical nature at themselves. When they do, it can be difficult for them to break free and a bit of leverage from a friend or lover can help a lot. Otherwise, they can get in a rut of self-deprecation, self-doubt and melancholy.

On a more day-to-day basis you will often find a Virgo Moon being fastidious about their environment. Everything has a place and 'belongs there', so if you use it, please put it back where it belongs. How this is expressed varies from person to person. In some cases, the Virgo Moon will select just one or two areas which deserve this sort of attention, leaving other parts of their lives to an ordered chaos that only they know and understand. In most cases, however, this is expressed as a cyclical 'tidying up' and so while everything has a place, sometimes it's OK for things not to be there. Whether ordered or not, don't expect to be able to order things for the Virgo Moon, because they like to be in control. You can help, but ask before you move anything.

The Cosmic 'Fixer'

The sense of order so innate in a Virgo Moon is what makes them very good counsellors. Even if they somehow can't get their own life together, they will usually have an abundance of good advice on how you can sort out your chronic problems. On the one hand, this can make them seem a busybody, poking their noses into others' business, but on the other hand it can make them good and loyal friends. It is important to understand their deeper motivation if you are to develop a good sense of who they are and work out a viable partnership with them. The root cause is their desire to heal, to help and to please. In a sense, they are cosmic 'fixers' who have been sent here to help us sort out our lives. And if it seems that they don't have their own act together, this is not a problem for them and belies your immature understanding of who and what they are – for them, their ability to be concerned about you first is a form of sacrifice, a high-minded submission of their own interests to yours and to the greater good.

The Virgo Moon's striving for order derives from their sense of natural equilibrium and they are uncomfortable, even hindered, when an accustomed order is lacking. Taken to the extreme, this trait is part of what makes them dyed-in-the-wool creatures of habit. They do what works because they know it works. This is great when it comes to keeping systems alive, but not when change is needed, or when flux threatens the status quo. The Virgo reflex is to recoil from sudden change. They can deal with it when it's well thought-out, planned down to the detail and properly timed, but not otherwise. Virgo habit becomes a weakness when they forget to poke their head above the parapet to get a view of the bigger picture. In short, if left to their own devices, Virgo is the rut of the zodiac. To avoid this, now and then the Virgo Moon needs to take stock, use that analytical mind and revise their views. This helps to keep them fresh and lets their other strong qualities find expression, one of which is discrimination.

'*To discriminate*: To make a clear distinction; distinguish: discriminate among the options available. To make sensible decisions; judge wisely.' The discriminating quality of the Virgo Moon gives them a sense of refinement, polish and dignity. They have good powers of speech and a talent for conversation that sets people at ease. They can win over the minds and hearts of others with their well-chosen words and have a love for both truth and correctness, especially if they can express it diplomatically.

However, their speaking skill, combined with a sharp perception, can make them not only witty but also at times sarcastic.

This is not always intentional on their part, as they find themselves speaking ahead of their own sense of discretion. Best to treat these awkward moments with a sense of humour and move the conversation along. You can be sure the Virgo Moon will appreciate this once they have a moment to reflect on their *faux pas*.

Virgo Moons are usually quite perceptive when it comes to dealing with others, although they can make judgements too quickly. Like the mercurial Gemini Moon, they have a strong curiosity, but while the Gemini Moon expresses this as a desire to explore and experience, the Virgo Moon is much more concerned about scrutiny and understanding. Nothing superficial for the Virgo Moon – even if they draw the same conclusions as a Gemini Moon, or others in general, their methods of getting there tell them that they have a more reliable understanding.

This approach is fortified by their strong sense of purpose and direction. The very qualities that can put them into a rut also give them the ability to stay the course, to persevere beyond others' expectations or abilities. 'Steady wins the race' with a Virgo Moon. They normally accomplish what they put their mind to and have good levels of concentration, focus and stamina. They tend to become immersed in their work – in fact, can be workaholics with no other interests to get them away from their desks. Of course, this tends to make them very good at what they do and in time they usually succeed in creating a secure position for themselves based on their steadiness and reliability.

In general, they love to explore any new idea and put it to the critical Virgo test. The search for meaning gives the Virgo Moon an unusual way of linking ideas together, even if they don't seem to be related. This gives the appearance of originality but also in some cases, of eccentricity – in any case, both are related. This gives the Virgo Moon the capacity for self-satisfaction and a preoccupation with the pleasure of pure thought. They are thus often voracious readers, love magazines, word games and crossword puzzles and tend to be generally well informed. They tend to enjoy not only the stimulation of books, but also movies and multimedia. They are often attracted to philosophy, the study of sacred texts, wisdom traditions and matters related to the human condition such as psychology, sociology and anthropology. If other areas of the chart are supportive of these interests, a Virgo Moon offers a good basis to excel in these fields.

Virgo Moons have a yearning for faraway lands and are keen to explore other cultures. They tend to be fascinated by foreign traditions and are fond of travel. In fact, they often do very well living away from their place of birth. At the very least this gives them a chance to discover and cultivate broader aspects of their own personality. In foreign countries, their fortune tends to improve and travelling expands their horizons and gives them new perspectives on the human experience.

They tend to like the finer things of life and often have an artistic quality that can be expressed as an interest in music, writing or draughtsmanship. Their love of fashion gives them a medium for personal expression in their daily lives and they are often known for their originality and fine apparel, although for some tastes it may be too conservative.

Seducing the Vestal Virgin

If you are in a relationship with a Virgo Moon it is helpful if you also aspire, to some degree, to a similar excellence in your life and love. At least the appeal of the ideal and the pure should be something that you are comfortable with, although it may be helpful if you lighten up your Virgo partner a bit now and then, especially as they tend at times to be serious and a touch critical.

In this regard you should also be able to tolerate, accept, understand or welcome the kind of critical emotional faculty that comes with a Virgo Moon. This is not always easy and can come with mixed messages that are quite confusing. To understand this, we should begin at the beginning of a relationship with a Virgo Moon.

The first thing you will need is a desire for the hunt and the stamina to pursue what is not easily attained. A Virgo Moon's discriminating taste and critical eye can make you feel evaluated and sometimes found wanting. The Virgo Moon doesn't easily give their heart to anyone; the suitor has to prove their worth, pass the test and live up to the ideal love that lives in the heart of the Virgo Moon. It's therefore important to enjoy the chase and the challenge. You will need persistence, cunning, tact, discretion, humour, good taste and the ability to appeal to their sensual nature without giving a hint, especially to others, that that is what you are doing. Seduction takes place under the sacred veil, in the mystery garden, simultaneously expressive yet clandestine. Above all, you will need patience and you will need to be clever, because it can at times feel as though the Virgo Moon is as inaccessible as the vestal virgin ensconced in the temple of Diana.

Once you have set your mind to the task, nothing gross or boisterous, pompous or ostentatious will do. Wit and charm and, most importantly, devotion will win their hearts. You will get there by degrees. Expect to pass a few tests and remain patient when you feel that you deserve the reward: if it is withheld, it's because it is not in their nature to give themselves too easily. If they do, they will be prone to self-doubt and an inner ridicule that you will need to tend to, so, if you can, cultivate the relationship carefully over time – you will both be happier in the end.

And when you have won their hearts, expect to live up to the promised standards, because a Virgo Moon remembers all the little details of what bought their heart. A shallow or temporary interest is bound to fail with a Virgo Moon, so think in terms long and true. It's a relationship that demands that you walk your talk, otherwise you should expect the wrath of rapier emotions.

Perfect Just the Way They Are

In a relationship with a Virgo Moon, remember that they are always trying to live up to their sense of personal perfection. It is painful to them to be found wanting and anything that shows that is even more painful. So, although they are able to dissect themselves to a more precise and cruel standard than anything you are capable of, they are desperately pained if you are the person giving notice of any shortcoming. The first emotion they feel in this case is 'Don't you know I know that already!' Remember that playing along with Virgo means being honest in a discreet way – and this discretion applies equally to both genders.

Self-criticism helps create another Virgo trait, which has two main manifestations – competition and jealousy. In reaching for their goals, Virgo Moons can be quite competitive, especially when they feel that the competition is initiated from another party. While their first trait is to offer service and support, this can quickly change when their own service is challenged in the form of a critical view of their efforts, or worse. If the challenge comes from someone perceived to be encroaching on their emotional or relationship territory, this crystallizes into jealousy.

There is no gain to be realized in trying to *make* a Virgo Moon jealous, however. Not only can they be good competitors, but the wound they feel from such a slight is not easily forgotten. Sometimes, depending on the rest of the astrological chart, they may be prone to unwarranted fits of jealousy. To the observer, this may seem illogical, but comes from the Virgo Moon's own sense of inadequacy or striving for the acceptance of their partner. It is therefore important that their partner regularly offers sweet words and other comforts that tell them they are loved – and perfect just the way they are. And it is equally important that once their partner has proven their loyalty, they make the effort to check this tendency and give them the benefit of the doubt. This, together with a bit of give from both parties, will ensure a positive, reciprocal and contented relationship.

When the critical Virgo sword tip is pointed at you, it is best to deflect it, unless you enjoy a good debate. Try and help them shift this towards a more productive expression and encourage them to give up rigid attitudes that can create difficult or unmanageable conditions in your relationship. Maybe the best way to do this is to point out to them that they too are uncomfortable with it. Get on their side of the table and have what I call 'a 360° conversation', not one in opposition. With a little effort they will appreciate that you have helped to relieve the tension and opened up the chance for a bit of laughter and an 'easy does it' approach to life.

Whether it's in a relationship with a single person or with a team of people, the important challenge for a Moon in Virgo is to encourage others to buy into a mutual set of standards. Experience will always tell the Virgo Moon that it pays to create consensus. They will need to make their inclination to high ideals secondary to the process of creating consensus, but with practice they will come to know that this is a more effective way to build agreement, either at work or at home.

Despite the more challenging aspects of a Virgo Moon, they strive for self-satisfaction and contentment and a balanced relationship offers them the chance to bring out the best of their personality. To do this they need to ensure that they maintain a sense of individuality in their relationships. They should consciously try to be their own person and avoid relying too much on their partner for their sense of self-worth and life purpose. Getting the right balance with this is important in any relationship, but with the Virgo Moon it is essential to avoid a dependency that can severely limit their expression, creativity and inner value. It is also important for maintaining the spontaneity that is helpful and nurturing in a relationship. It will keep the partnership out of the rut and keep repetitive behaviour patterns from creating boredom and inertia.

Virgo Moons are practical, sensual and alluring if you are able to decipher the special codes that give you entrance to their hearts. They are immensely gratifying partners for the right person and offer a great deal of support for their chosen partner. Astrologically speaking, they are especially good for Aquarius, Libra and Cancer Moons, but are beneficial in many ways for anyone who resonates with their unique nature.

Virgo Top Tips

- Seducing a Virgo Moon requires some talent, a bit of patience and not a little artistry. You will do especially well and find the job easy if you are clever, witty, suitably self-effacing, sober, yet also mysterious, enigmatic and discreetly sensual. You will need to balance all this and be alluring but aloof, interested but not too taken. It really is a matter of drawing them to you in their own good time and keeping to their own sense of style and values – and boy, do they have them.
- In sensual matters, give them the space to open up and respond. If possible, let them initiate the proceedings and if it's going too slowly for your taste then gently, oh so gently, step by step, send out the right signals and respond accordingly.
- Not only patience but persistence is needed in the courtship process with a Virgo Moon, especially as it is counter to their nature to agree too easily. What you think is too easily is probably very different from what they think is too easily, and this will no doubt be part of your initiation into the Virgo Moon relationship.
- Having a good sense of humour is important. Even when you think it's not working or making a good impression, it probably is, so keep trying. A Virgo Moon will like you if you can laugh at yourself, as it tells them you don't take yourself too seriously, which in a roundabout way takes the pressure off them needing to take themselves too seriously.
- At first, when giving gifts, less is more. Take the time to get to know them a little before you spend lots of money only to be disappointed by their well-developed and critical sense of taste. They know what they like, your job is to find out what it is, and this can take a bit of trial and error.
- It can take time to understand that their critical comments can be their way of showing you their affection. While you may think this is backhanded, try to remember that it is their nature to better things and serve people. They may just be trying to help bring out the best in you. The best thing is to go with the

flow, take it in your stride and, if you can, thank them for it. Big points for you if you can.

- When it comes to feelings, they can appear reserved, even cold. Get around this by not reacting and relating instead to the more sensitive person inside them. This encourages them to reveal their feelings and if they do you can be sure you have their hearts, because they are quite careful when it comes to letting others in too easily.
- Virgo Moons like anything artistic, refined, polished and classy. They tend to enjoy classical styles, so nothing gaudy or flashy please. If anything, understate it on this one and you will be safe. If you are clever, you will sidestep their prudish or austere side by giving gifts that offer creature comforts that have discreet written all over them.
- Give them the space they need when they need it, otherwise you may see an abrupt, dismissive side to them. And when it comes to living in their space, remember that everything has a purpose and a place.
- In arguments, expect their logical side to sally forth into the fray. Emotion driven by logic is an awesome combination that needs wit, strategy and a cool head on your part. While they are shy by nature, if pricked they don't back down easily and certainly don't forget a slight. If you do err, then appeal to their sense of forgiveness, but don't expect them to forget too quickly.
- Keep the romance fresh by taking the lead. Suggest new interests, new places and new adventures. Overcome their reticence and push out from the familiar. You will need to work against the regularity of their nature and break the barriers and the boundaries (tactfully) now and then to keep the romance burning bright.

Virgo Troubleshooting

- *How can you get them to take you and your feelings seriously?* Virgo Moons take many things seriously, so it shouldn't be too difficult to pique their interest in any of your problems, as long as you are prepared for their critical analysis to shine some light on the cause. When it comes to feelings, the Virgo Moon can appear a bit cool at times, which needs to be understood as just part of their emotional language. Be ready to argue your case with at least a bit of logic or reason. This appeals to a Virgo Moon; to some extent they understand emotional issues by bringing their head into the service of their heart. If you can communicate your needs, pass the gauntlet of their scrutiny and appeal to their innate fondness for the underdog, you should have no problem attracting their serious attention.

☾ *How can you get them to be more supportive or responsive?*
This can be tricky, as Virgo Moons are discerning and sometimes cool in their approach and like to respond to what they think is a legitimate need. This, of course, means that you have to demonstrate legitimately that somehow they are not being as supportive as they should be. If you want to make headway with this, leave blame at the door, because they will tend to feel bad about not meeting your needs as it is. So, don't create unnecessary self-criticism in them, but gently and kindly show them that you need more and ask them to think about it. Bring their head into the service of your heart.

☾ *How to re-establish communication?*
A touch of diplomacy will always come in handy when appealing to a Virgo Moon. Express your interest with feeling but in a mildly detached way and make sure they know the doors of communication are open if, and when, that's what they want. Emphasizing that it's their choice won't hurt. You will not do well trying to coerce a Virgo Moon. The dance of relating with them takes some finesse and finding the balance between an open expression of interest and yet being OK without it can be part of that dance. Be prepared for them to show their discriminating, careful nature in agreeing to reconnect. Talking is very important, although it may make sense to exercise the

raconteur in you before suggesting something more intimate. Key words to remember include 'flexibility', 'acute perception', 'measured advance' and, above all, 'enticement'.

☾ *What is the best way to apologize?*
Humbly, patiently and honestly. If you can master this extra-ordinary task then you will be able to kiss and make up, but it may not be a one-two-three process. Virgo Moons are critical by nature and you will have to swallow at least something of your pride, as they are easily offended and tend to hold on to those hurt feelings maybe longer than some. Virgos give them-selves in a relationship and expect that you will live up to their ideals. If you don't, it is difficult for them to live down, as they feel that in part they may share in at least a little of the respon-sibility. You hurt them because they let you hurt them is an example of the logic. So make sure that when you apologize you do so for both of you and remember to mean it. Sincerity works wonders in a Virgo relationship, so dig deep and be real.

☾ *How can you rekindle the flame?*
Reconfirmation and recommitment are classic and cyclical parts of any Virgo Moon relationship. This is due to their need to examine, understand, re-examine and get it right. And keep it right. So if you are ready for the perpetual quest of romance then you will be able to keep the relationship fresh and alive. If, however, you are more human than that and let things slip, the key elements to rekindle the flame include reaffirming your love and offering demonstrations of love not just with gifts but more importantly with thoughtful action that includes the little details. For example, noticing their chair needed upholstering and making the arrangements, or realizing that they have run out of their favourite wine glasses and bringing some home along with a bottle of their favourite wine. This is worth a lot in a Virgo relationship. And of course, when in doubt, remember they love little gifts, especially anything that celebrates one of your most memorable experiences together.

☾ *If the worst comes to the worst, how do you say goodbye without hurting their feelings?*

Virgo Moons are very self-critical. They usually save the best of their scrutiny for themselves, which can make saying goodbye difficult, as they will take things to heart regardless of what you say. If you want to make it really easy for them then you could indulge in loads of self-criticism and help them to see you as undesirable. But, realistically, the best means at your disposal is making the point that it's best for you to move on and probably best for them as well. With any luck, the Virgo Moon may be able to bring their head to the service of their heart by thinking things through rationally. More than relieving the disappointment, it gives them a way to move on with their life.

The Moon in Libra ♎

A natural ability to understand and interact with people makes the Libran Moon the zodiac's court ambassador and emissary. Libra is the seventh house in the zodiac and is ruled by the good-natured planet Venus, both of which symbolize relationships, partnerships and social dealings. Libran Moons have a sweet, affable nature that makes them immediately likeable and attractive to others. They are known for their intuitive ability to help bring balance and harmony and often display a calming, steadying influence, even in difficult circumstances. Libra is, in a sense, the fulcrum of the zodiac, the middle point that symbolizes a stage of development in consciousness away from the individual self towards an outward-looking world view that recognizes the essential need to create harmonious relationships. Libra symbolizes our ability to transcend personal needs and interests for a higher cause, the greater good, the sublime. Libra Moons have an innate sense of this. They know somehow that life means growth through commitment and discipline.

The People Pleaser

Libra is the second Air sign of the zodiac, Gemini being the first. This imbues the Libra spirit with a light, changeable, open and involved nature. The essential being of a Libra Moon is focused on people. They tend to think of themselves with reference to how others view them. This is important to remember when you are in relationship with them, as they seek their own validation by what you say, or don't say. They are very aware of others' opinions, and this is a strength and a weakness – a weakness when others' opinions limit their own progress and cause them to doubt themselves. Whether positive or negative, their growth and development occur through their relationships with people.

Libra Moons are ruled by Venus, which gives them a love of fine objects and life's little pleasures. They often have good taste and a touch of extravagance. They are creative and often artistic, good examples being Marcel Duchamp and Edouard Manet. Because Venus is the planet of sensuality and creativity, the Libra Moon can also be imaginative. This is especially prominent in their childhood and helps them develop a rich inner world of fantasy and creativity. Sometimes, it makes the Libra Moon a good storyteller.

In any case, Libra Moons tend to be very sociable and involved with those around them. They are good at creating a pleasant atmosphere in which people can congregate. They like to be happy and cheerful, and are optimistic, encouraging and upbeat when it comes to dealing with others, even when their own moods are less than positive. In general, they can be quite spontaneous, especially with their sense of humour. In this they can be a bit theatrical and spice up any gathering. When you are down in the dumps, the Libra Moon will be ready and waiting with a kind word and plenty of good advice.

They also have a canny way of reading people, and are often quite accurate with first impressions, although it is true that this can colour the way they relate to someone from then on. It's a good idea if they can learn to give people the time and space to confirm what they have intuitively gleaned about them – just for that rare case when they are wrong.

The people-centric nature of Libra means that, like it or not, they are often surrounded by people. For the most part they do like it, and have a way of putting people at ease. The more expressive Libra Moons are known for being the glue at parties. They can be great networkers, linking the right people with the right opportunities and causes. It's not uncommon to find Libra Moons involved in politics or social activism, for example US Presidents Jimmy Carter and Dwight Eisenhower, South Africa's Nelson Mandela and France's François Mitterrand.

The tendency to political involvement comes from the inbuilt social radar of the Libra Moon and their ability to read the mood of the larger public, often in advance. They can excel at marketing and PR due to their knack of presenting an issue so as to get the most attention. They are also good at journalism, due to their ability to understand opposing views.

The more skilled of the Libra Moons demonstrate a further ability to reconcile opposing views by bringing people together and facilitating discussion. Libras can often broker constructive negotiation and are known for their mediation skills. The best of these will, at the same time, know when and how to conclude an agreement or precipitate settlements with the right touch of force. This is not very easy for most Libra Moons, as it runs counter to their nature. Those who can do it have probably learned the hard way that the Latin root of decision is dêcìdere, meaning 'to cut or sever'. Making choices means letting options go, and the constitution of the Libra Moon is not to let go, but to incorporate. The Libra Moon's nature is about facilitating the involvement and participation of others, of not denying anything. In a sense the Libra Moon is the place where yin meets yang, mingling them together in happy coexistence – or at least as happy as they can get.

The Reluctant Judge

The symbol of Libra is the scales but the Moon in Libra does not automatically imply that the person has achieved balance. On the contrary, it is more certain that they will struggle with or be striving for it in everything they do. Getting the perfect balance in anything is challenging, maybe impossible. It's rare when the greengrocer weighs your vegetables that the scales stop at an inert equilibrium. It is more likely that they continue to bob slightly up and down and the grocer is content to give a little or get a little more. Libra Moons can learn a lot from this simple analogy by agreeing to lose or gain, now and then, in order to keep the wheels of life turning.

Libra Moons and their partners will recognize the inability to make choices, the fretting to and fro as they move in their mind's eye from one perfect view to another and back again; seeing the equal validity of both options and therefore being unable to say to one, 'Sorry, you are not good enough.'

At one end of the Libran spectrum this can create inertia, which is all the more troublesome and frustrating for an Air sign that likes to have a sense of movement and progress. When the Libra Moon gets stuck, their inner turmoil is clear to see. And walking them through an analysis of the problem doesn't always work, as you simply end up retracing the steps they have already taken – frustrating in itself. The best way to help them is to emphasize the need for decision and reassure them that most of the time we can recover, even from bad decisions. Nothing is permanent. A Libra Moon has a way of seeing a decision as though it's a solidification of their thoughts, a congealing of ideas into an irreversible condition that is as weighty as stone. Their inner fear is then that they will have to live with their mistake forever. If Gemini Moon wants to do two things at once, Libra Moon has a hard time deciding which to do first – or at all. With practice, however, and age, they can reduce their indecision and thus also improve their sense of timing, which can be affected by their vacillation.

Surprisingly, this applies not just to the big things of life, but also to the little ones, whether it's choosing where to go on holiday or what to have for lunch. When you encounter this Libra trait – and you will – be patient if you can, encourage a decision and be ready to make one yourself without pulling the rug out from under them. Remember that the Libra Moon is about partnerships and they feel quite bad if they are holding up the show or if you decide to move on without their input – or without them.

The issue of choice is an extension of something more grave, and that is judgement. It's not by chance that the figure of blind justice has scales in one hand and a sword in the other. Libra Moons often have a love–hate relationship with making judgements. On the one hand, they hate them because they seem final, cutting, harsh and impersonal. They love to keep their options open, are ruled by sweet Venus and like things to be nice, and are very personal in their orientation. Everything about judgement runs counter to a large and important part of their character. On the other hand, the sign of Libra is about judgement. It's the fulcrum of the zodiac because it represents the growth that comes from dealing with life's limits and restraints.

Saturn, the planet of karma and discipline, is 'exalted', or in the strongest place he can be, in Libra. Yet there is something in the back of the Libra Moon mind that says that judgement implies obligation and karmic involvement – and that itself is a somewhat frightening concept to them. 'What if the sword is pointed at me?' is a fear lurking in the deeper recesses of their mind.

Nevertheless, Libra Moons often find themselves in the role of judge and they can be very good at it, once they embrace the cold facts. Their ability to see two sides of the picture and desire to find a balance can make them benevolent and understanding. Depending on the rest of the chart and their life experience, they can also be stern in their assessment of others. To some, they can appear somewhat unforgiving. Libra Moons have a sense of natural justice, an inner knowing that 'what comes around goes around'. To them, it's just a matter of time before someone gets their just deserts, even if it's another time, place or lifetime. This is a display of the deeper esoteric inclinations of Libra, which can take some getting used to if you haven't learned life's harsher lessons.

On a less serious note, this also gives them well-formed, strong opinions that they are ready to share. It will be sometimes easier for the Libra Moon to express opinions about ideas and events than about individuals. They love a good debate and like to become better informed about an idea by arguing their point of view. While it may seem that they are stuck in their way of thinking, in fact they are gathering new information as they go and you won't be surprised to find later that your discussion did indeed have an effect.

The Easy-Going Idler

Libra Moons are mostly considerate and benevolent, but don't be surprised if they don't know how popular they really are. The periodic self-doubt mentioned above can sometimes limit their sense of importance in the greater scheme of things. In fact, they often play a pivotal role – if you doubt it, just ask those around them – and enjoy extending a helping hand to others, even those who have not been kind or respectful to them in the past. While this is a laudable trait, they need to strike a balance, however, as they are often taken for granted. Their ability to empathize gives them a soft heart, but in tending to others' interests, they can forget their own basic needs. The Libra Moon has a tendency to live through those around them, including their close relationships, where their own sense of value comes from the feedback and validation they get from their partners. The Libra Moon has to be conscious of this and work wilfully to avoid it happening.

It's not uncommon, however, to see the Libra Moon's indecision, subordination of self-interest or generally easy-going nature result in a lack of motivation and ambition. All the pondering over which goal to go for may just result in the decision that it's easier to remain idle, just where they are now, going with the flow and drifting to that sometime day when a decision will be made, probably for them. This is a real pity and represents a great limit to the Libra Moon. It is a trait they will need to consciously work against. Their lethargy also leaves them open to be influenced by the needs and interests of other people, especially given their tendency to put others first.

To counter this, it is a good idea if Libra Moons spend some time planning their life direction. Of course, their reluctance to commit to the wrong path may keep them from chalking out a plan, but once they have a clear sense of direction they can bring out the best in themselves. The trick will be to have one, even if it's temporary or short term. The effort of making a plan will give them greater focus, even though they will want to review things from time to time as circumstances change.

Reassuring the Shy Romantic

When it comes to relationships, the Libra Moon is a natural. In friendship, they are loyal and helpful and you can count yourself fortunate to have them as a friend. In relationships, they are romantic, sensitive and generous and can often surprise their partner with thoughtful gestures, gifts and acts of love. They live for love, and expect or hope to be with their partner much of the time. They value togetherness in purpose, spirit and body. They have a poetic sense of love and often keep some kind of journal which chronicles their secret feelings. In all their relationships they are inspired by a sense of balance and like to give as good as they get. When the limits of life fail to match their romantic ideals, they are prone to melancholy.

In intimate dealings you will need to be proactive with a Libra Moon, maybe more than usual. They are quite good at reading the tenor of a relationship, although their self-doubt can cause them to fear for its safety. This can make them not jealous, but suspicious, something which they do not usually express directly. It will be important for you to read between the lines and reassure them as best you can.

The best way to capture the heart of a Libra Moon is to offer like-for-like in affections and generosity. Making them your focus and reaffirming their better qualities wins them over, as long as it's done genuinely, with a bit of humour and the right amount of charm. They are sensual by nature, quite tactile and like the warmth of a close embrace. Romantic settings are more thrilling for them than they will easily admit and if you want to make a good impression, then flowers and small gestures will be invaluable.

The inhibited, reluctant side to the Libra personality is reassured by open expressions of love and affection. They may tend to discount the importance of expressing their own feelings, ironically out of a misplaced deference for your feelings and maybe also out of concern that their tender advances will not be well received. They do tend to be shy when it comes to romance, but when they have established a close bond they are more confident and demonstrative.

These qualities, then, beg an open, demonstrative lover, someone who is willing to take the risk of expressing their love. A good example of this is the active, vigorous, adventurous, expressive and passionate Aries Moon. The Libra Moon finds an Aries Moon a good partner and is able to give Aries the kind of acceptance it desires, while being fed by Aries' love of fun and upbeat nature. Other suitable signs for the Libra Moon include Capricorn and Sagittarius.

Libra Moons make loyal, long-lasting partners. They don't give up easily and are not usually the one to break off a relationship. Getting the balance right with a Libra Moon means a loving exchange with a gentle partner.

Libra Top Tips

- The seduction of a Libra Moon is an artful dance of give and take, leading and being led, expressing your passion but being ready to respond to a slight change of mood or feeling. Libra Moons are very sensitive and sensual partners who are responsive to their lover's needs, but who also expect a high degree of perceptive awareness of their needs.
- The archetype of romance finds its full expression in a Libra Moon, so pull out all the stops with wining, dining, dancing and the final retreat to an atmosphere conducive to love. It should be a place of comfort and sweet refinement accompanied by music, flowers and delicate fragrances. This may work for most people, but for the Libra Moon it's *de rigueur*.
- Be expressive when wooing a Libra Moon. They have a poetic nature and appreciate creativity. They naturally respond to the stimulation of social settings, which helps lift their spirits and can create a sense of ease and relaxation for them.
- Be proactive in sharing your own feelings with them and don't be shy about showing them how you feel. If you lead the way in this, they will respond in kind, giving you the chance to establish a meaningful rapport.
- They tend to examine themselves by looking at their relationships, so if it's a new affair, take the time to reassure them and confirm your appreciation of who they are. Even if you are still uncertain, putting them at ease gives you the chance to get to really know them well.

- If you want to do something special for them, invite their best friends around for a dinner party where they are the centre of attention. Birthdays, anniversaries or any other good excuse will do nicely.
- They tend to enjoy togetherness. Even when they need private time, if the relationship is well established they will want to have you around. Doing things together, even the smallest of chores, gives them pleasure. And if you have to be away for a while, think about their feelings – call, write, send flowers or e-mails, anything to let them know how much you care gives them a boost and keeps them happy.
- Arguments are dreaded and wherever possible the Libra Moon will avoid confrontation. While this can be a good thing, it can also block the natural flow of a relationship. Some tension and a bit of friction can help you work through problems and understand each other. Libra Moons need to know that this can be done without jeopardizing the relationship.
- When giving gifts, think of natural, organic and refreshing items – perfume, bath salts and so on. Artistic or decorative items, especially jewellery, are winners and gifts that inspire their creativity are also a sure bet.

Libra Troubleshooting

- *How can you get them to take you and your feelings seriously?* It would be unusual for a Libra Moon not to take your feelings seriously, if only because relationships are so important to them. They may not take all your issues seriously, but if the relationship is at all genuine, they will likely indulge you in even your more petty concerns. To get them to take you seriously may also require you to express your seriousness towards their feelings. Libra Moons tend to be very reciprocal so being nice to them should earn you the same in kind. And you may find that any misunderstanding was more a matter of style and perception than substance.

- *How can you get them to be more supportive or responsive?*
  Partnerships are singularly important to them, so if they are not being responsive it probably means that you are part of the problem. Once you figure that out, approach them with your ideas about what you can do to be more supportive – and at the same time suggest where they can do the same for you.

- *How can you re-establish communication?*
  If communication needs to be re-established it is probably you who should lead the way, especially as the Libra Moon will likely ponder the pros and cons of calling, only to postpone it indefinitely. So, first make the effort and then remember that they are usually gentle, sociable people who have a soft heart and are open to relating. Even when things have been difficult, if you approach them with a little care, they will tend to be open-minded and easy-going. If you are going to suggest a meeting, lead the way again. Don't ask them if they want to meet, but rather suggest that you meet at a certain place – and probably at a certain day and time also. This may seem pushy, but if handled in the right way creates more of a chance to come together than keeping things open-ended. Suggest a festive, easy-going venue. Don't make them work too hard to get there and if the atmosphere is pleasant, things will have a chance of taking off again.

- *What is the best way to apologize?*
  First express how important the relationship is to you. Without this, you won't get on to other points in a meaningful way. After that, saying sorry for hurt feelings and explaining your foibles as a human being will help a lot. The good thing about a Libra Moon is that they will often meet you halfway, if you are honest in your expression. Venus rules Libra, so sweet gifts, flowers and other offerings will always help smooth over the rough issues. And when they have accepted your apology, a little reciprocation will affirm that it's not been forgiveness in vain.

☾ *How can you rekindle the flame?*
Romance is a natural interest for a Libra Moon and they tend to respond well to the right messages. Breaking away from the routine will always help and if you can frequently bring diversity into the relationship it will keep it fresh and your Libra partner happy. Pre-Raphaelite pictures, flowers, scents, candles, sweets, soft lighting and music, and quiet moments dedicated to each other is all that it takes to bring some joy and new life to a relationship with a Libra Moon.

☾ *If the worst comes to the worst, how do you say goodbye without hurting their feelings?*
Breaking off a relationship for someone whose Moon is in the archetypal sign of relationships is not going to be easy. Go gently and make the point, in your own way, that the balance between the two of you is not right and that to continue limits both of you. The real point is to make the cut as quick and painless as you can, once you have decided to make it.

The Moon in Scorpio ♏

Mysterious, alluring and magical – just a few of the qualities of a Scorpio Moon. Scorpio is elusive and secretive – hence potentially the most misunderstood sign of the zodiac. The Scorpio Moon is deeply, intensely romantic, very sensitive and highly intuitive, exuding an air of adventure, challenge and ultimate discovery.

The Clandestine Paramour

In the zodiac court, the sign is symbolized by a variety of roles that include the magi, secret agent, cryptographer and clandestine paramour. By nature, Scorpio Moons defy description and love to avoid detection. It can be quite difficult to categorize them and even when you get close, they love to slip your grasp to steal away undiscovered. One thing is for certain – they do not like being labelled, summed up or limited by the perception or assessment of others. They are a mystery because of their love of mystery and their desire to understand life's secrets.

Scorpio is the eighth house of the zodiac and, like Aries, is ruled by the planet Mars. The essence of this house and sign is transformation and regeneration. It symbolizes our individual or collective desire to achieve a state of being beyond our current limits, and in the highest sense, the attainment of some level of transcendence. Scorpio is about moving closer to our soul, our real selves, and finding freedom from the ordinary and the mundane. It acts as a doorway or portal through which we begin the long and often tedious process of personal transformation.

In medieval times, alchemical treatises emphasized the qualities of Scorpio because they represent the ability to transmute base metal into gold. The Scorpio journey begins with the mundane and traverses by degrees to the sublime. It is no surprise, therefore, that Scorpio embodies magical qualities and symbolizes the enchantment of becoming more than we are, or something else altogether. Who better embodies this aspect of the Scorpio Moon than Kahlil Gibran?

In general, Scorpio Moons exhibit these qualities in a number of ways. They have a probing, inquisitive nature that helps them plumb the depths of any chosen subject, especially those related to the esoteric and spiritual. They tend to be quite philosophical, but are at the same time non-conformist and love to challenge accepted wisdom in their pursuit for a genuine and personal realization of the truth. Their quest for knowledge will take them far and wide. The Scorpio Moon is likely to have at least an interest, if not an active involvement, in astrology, meditation and ancient cultures. To pursue the secret, to unravel the universe and its workings, to discover meaning and revel in understanding, these are the driving forces of a Scorpio Moon. When this striving is less esoteric, it can take on a decidedly scientific nature, which makes the Scorpio Moon's insatiable thirst for wisdom a real asset, not least because it will give them a compulsion for their work.

The best example of this is Albert Einstein, who took an interest in astrology and commented that it is 'a science in itself and contains an illuminating body of knowledge. It [has] taught me many things, and I am greatly indebted to it ... astrology is like a life-giving elixir to mankind.'[1] The author Umberto Eco is a good example of the depth of a Scorpio Moon, with his eminent scholarship, original ideas about semiotics and his breadth of esoteric knowledge.

The Scorpio Moon is often a quiet person, tending to a kind of introversion which is not so much a shyness as a reserve, a cautious withholding of themselves, at least until they get to know you and feel comfortable with you. It will be clear to you that while they are not saying much, they are conscious of everything going on around them. It is rare that the Scorpio Moon will miss anything.

Sometimes they can have a bit of voyeur in them, because they like to watch life from a private vantage point. They can therefore be good observers of people and will enjoy movies,

[1] Albert Einstein, *Cosmic Religion, with Other Opinions and Aphorisms*, Covici Friede, New York, 1931

theatre, the news, people watching, tarot cards, anything that lets them see the big picture while not getting too closely or immediately involved. Francis Ford Coppola's Moon is in Scorpio, which arguably is part of the reason for his keen cinematic eye, if not for his choice of genre. Other Hollywood Scorpio Moons include Dustin Hoffman, Warren Beatty and Gerard Depardieu.

In fact, Scorpio Moons are rebellious, avant-garde, artistic and original. Their penetrating natures help them break new ground, especially in artistic pursuits, the best example of this being Pablo Picasso. Much of the wild, unfettered, creative, intense nature of Picasso had its roots in his Scorpio Moon. His well-known penchant for passionate relationships and his desire to find the perfect love can also be astrologically attributed to Scorpio.

The Subtle Sensualist

Scorpio Moons are sensual people who have a magnetic, attractive quality that can be captivating, especially if your Moon sign is Taurus, Pisces or Cancer. If so, then you will no doubt be drawn to the magic of the Scorpio sexuality, which is a mixture of subtle intensity, expectation, uncertainty and a hint of excitement – a potent allure. This will be stronger or weaker depending on the house placement of the Moons in the respective charts. In any case, though, the feelings will be palpable – assuming, of course, that there is a physical attraction, which is the essential in any match.

There is a lot more to the Scorpio Moon than just sensuality, however. They can be truly dedicated and fiercely loyal partners. When a Scorpio Moon gives their heart, there is probably nothing more binding. While it may take time to win them over and to create an intimate bond, once you have a mutual trust they are special partners indeed.

There is also a yearning in the Scorpio heart, often felt very intensely, for a level of personal achievement and inner fulfilment. The subtle quality of this yearning may be best expressed by a sense of urgency to discover what will complete them, make them whole and lift them up higher. It is a feeling that is difficult to express in words and finds a better expression in dreams. Although subtle, its effect is powerful, compelling the Scorpio Moon to be ever conscious of the need for that inner perfection.

It is no wonder, then, that their nature is strong, intense and moving. The Scorpio Moon can perceive meaning even in the most ordinary of experiences. Nature speaks directly to them, again in a way that is not easy to convey unless your Moon is in Pisces, or maybe Cancer. For this reason, verbal communication with a Scorpio Moon can leave you feeling that much is left unsaid, and if you are in a relationship with one, you will certainly need to develop your intuitive and non-verbal skills to fully understand what's going on. If you are the kind of person who likes to keep things simple, uncomplicated, maybe more on the surface, then the Scorpio Moon may be too deep and subtle for your liking.

Their love of freedom, originality and their rich inner world can also make them eccentric. The Scorpio Moon does not like taking the beaten path; even when they tend to conservatism, it is their own personally embellished brand. They are not easy followers, so expect them to express a need to change things slightly if you are working together on a project. Maybe more than many of the Moon signs, they contain a knot of contradictions not easily unravelled.

Beguiling the Secret Lover

It takes time to get to know a Scorpio Moon, so be patient, especially if they are quiet or withdrawn. At first they are likely to interact with you with small, often imperceptible and seemingly inconsequential comments, gestures and sideways glances. These actions are a kind of radar that helps the Scorpio Moon assess your reaction, nature and character, while you remain unaware of it. Needless to say, the Scorpio Moon is very aware and you may notice that behind the reserved façade, there is a lot going on, which earns the Scorpio Moon the reputation for being intense and mysterious.

In time, they will open up and you can get to know them better. If you express your appreciation of secrets and good discretion, it is likely that they will feel more comfortable with you, but they will certainly ask you to talk about yourself first. When they do voice their opinions, you can expect them to be frank and a touch diplomatic. You may have to read between the lines, as they can be subtle in their expression, at times appearing to talk in riddles and double meanings. If you are shy or insecure, this can leave you feeling uncertain about where you stand.

In simple terms, the Scorpio Moon likes privacy and secrets. They are not boisterous and are unlikely to be demonstrative. They are more demure and refined in their dealings. A paradox of the Scorpio nature is their ability to swing to extremes, sometimes showing intense interest in someone or something, and then in the next moment nonchalantly walking away, detached as always. The intrinsic quality of reformation and regeneration expressed in their character means that you will see some degree of the anarchy that often precedes creativity.

In fact, they are accustomed to holding their views and feelings close to their chest and tend to scrutinize new ideas carefully before accepting them as their own. Their thirst for knowledge doesn't mean they are easy to convince or persuade. Bringing a Scorpio Moon round to your way of thinking takes time and patience. Don't expect quick results. It's best if you are just as happy if they don't ultimately agree with you, because otherwise you could be disappointed. The Scorpio Moon certainly doesn't like to be pressured, and the best way to gain their agreement is to tenderly cajole them and give them lots of space and respect.

When confronted or dominated, there is a contrariness to the Scorpio Moon which should not be underestimated. There is no force on Earth that will easily get a Scorpio Moon to your side of the fence and if coerced, the fundamental Scorpio urge for freedom will take control. If anyone is going to be in control, it's the Scorpio Moon. This often creates misunderstanding and distrust in their relationships. Taken at face value some people think that the Scorpio Moon simply wants to override others. For the most part, this is not the case. The Moon is highly sensitive in the sign of Scorpio, giving feelings of vulnerability, heightened awareness, preoccupations and fears, both real and imagined. Scorpio Moons thus desire respect in all their dealings, and ideally preferential treatment – which helps assure them that the relationship is a safe and stable one for them. While this principle can vary widely according to other factors in a person's chart, it will certainly constitute a large and important part of their character.

The symbol of the secret lover is appropriate here, because the Scorpio Moon will, like a secret lover, expect attention, care and understanding, all in a way that is not so obvious as to draw others' attention. Scorpio Moons tend to be painfully self-conscious and while they are good at hiding it, it can nevertheless affect their confidence. The last thing they want is to draw attention to their delicate feelings, or any special treatment that you offer, and you will earn their respect and gratitude if you are able to handle emotional or romantic matters with care and discretion.

Do not make the mistake of airing private matters publicly, because this can hurt them beyond words, or forgiveness. They tend to feel things deeply and can carry hurts with them for a very long time. They will let you know it by hurting you back, letting fly with a cutting remark that really stings – another reason why the ancients chose the symbol of a scorpion for this part of the zodiac. The suddenness of their expression is most likely due to their failure to express themselves and their tendency to keep things in long after you have forgotten them. There is also a compulsive side to their nature, which means that their salvos are not always intentional, but are instinctual, especially when they are hurt in some way. If this catches you by surprise, rather than respond straightaway, give a moment's thought to what you have done, consciously or unconsciously, to cause pain, then do your best to heal the wound with a little attention and the salve of affection.

The range of emotional expression is very broad with a Scorpio Moon; even after you have known them for some time you can expect surprises now and then. While anger is not uncommon at difficult moments, the most likely Scorpio expression is a silent, painful brooding which can be very difficult to tolerate, especially if you are also very sensitive. They are usually aware that this and their sharp tongues can land them into hot water, and so they have to work consciously to avoid taking things to the extreme. Getting the right balance of self-expression and restraint is important for the Scorpio Moon and something that they usually perfect as they get older.

Transforming Love

Transformation is an important part of the Scorpio life mission, which manifests as a tendency to tear down, in order to build up again. This phoenix-like urge applies pre-eminently to emotional matters where periodically the Scorpio man will want to redefine the relationship, discover new meanings and challenge existing emotional patterns. A typical expression of this will be the need for the two of you to redefine your love and attachment for each other, sometimes by playing one of those bittersweet dramas where you separate only to reunite in greater mutual intensity. Depending on your own nature, this can be something of an emotional roller-coaster ride, but if it's excitement, striving for freshness and relevance, and emotional adventure that you crave, then the Moon in Scorpio is for you.

Scorpio Moon is strongly intuitive and often psychic, which like all qualities has its good and bad side. On the good side you can expect them to pick up on how you are feeling and what may be bothering you. They can be proactive and helpful with this, especially when it comes to getting you to talk about repressed feelings or thoughts that need expressing. It's also not uncommon for them to have premonitions, insights and dreams of the future. This is very handy, but some people are not comfortable with knowing things in advance – unless they are stockbrokers. You'll be fine if you are comfortable with a partner who can read at least your feelings and maybe something of your mind, and has a pretty good idea of what's going on. The downside of this trait is sometimes a tendency to be suspicious and to think that what they feel is what is really happening. If they become sceptical or even jealous, the Scorpio Moon can take some convincing that all is well.

For a loved one, however, the Scorpio Moon can be long-suffering and in some cases this helps to fulfil a kind of yearning for the experience of profound romantic self-sacrifice. The Scorpio Moon is capable of a deep and intense quality of love. When they love you, they throw their whole being into relating with you. Their amorous embrace has a binding, seductive nature that envelops your being. You too will be expected to give of yourself, to offer maybe more than you might with a less demanding love. For some, this is highly captivating and for others, slightly unnerving.

Scorpio Moons also have their own subtle and sometimes difficult to understand emotional language: deep, intense, yearning, but changeable and sensitive. In a moment it is possible for you to unconsciously say or do something that rubs them the wrong way, and it may take some time and effort before you understand the cause of their mood change. In truth, it is not possible to change this tendency in a Scorpio Moon and the best way to deal with it is to accept it, enjoy it and sometimes just watch it in wonder. The Scorpio Moon deserves the stability and earthiness of a Moon sign like Taurus, who can act as a steadying influence and may not be reactive to the ebb and flow of the Scorpio Water sign.

The heart language of Scorpio first and foremost wants to be understood, but not revealed. They want their feelings to be perceived, but not exposed. They want to be respected, and yet not be taken too seriously. They want to be serious and deep, but don't want to dwell on feelings or have you look too closely at what goes on inside them. In a sense, they want you to see them deeply but not directly. To do this you will have to look at them, emotionally speaking, with a sidelong glance that tells them you understand them, without revealing how much you understand. When you can do this, you will have their heart and their abiding affection, because you have pierced the mystery of their being and understood the sensitivity and simplicity of their love – however complicated it seems on the surface.

Being a partner to a Scorpio Moon means travelling with them on their journey of personal evolution – a journey of their soul. The karmic theme of this journey is the transformation of latent potential into higher-minded achievement. It is certain that this is an exciting, unpredictable, demanding, but rewarding journey – and if you choose to take it with them you can expect an uncommon depth of love and life experience.

Scorpio Top Tips

- When seducing a Scorpio Moon, the real question may be 'Who is doing the seducing?' One thing that is certain is that the Scorpio Moon will play an equal part in the seduction, if – and only if – it's a game they want to play. If you have been able to spark their interest then they are willing partners. But they are particular and can be very discerning in matters of romance.
- Their deep and secret moods are instantly changeable, so be ready to respond to a shifting emotional landscape. This requires a measure of awareness, adaptability and love of mystery. In loving the Scorpio Moon you will have to love the enigma in them and enjoy the surprises as they come, one of which is their intensely sensual, feeling mood which can make them captivating lovers.
- They are profoundly romantic and often have a knack for the art of love. They are exotic by nature and are stimulated by unusual, original settings. Creating the right ambience is important when courting a Scorpio Moon, so give free rein to your fantasy.
- Don't expect that you will change them to suit you. The trick is to get to know their nature and work with it, not against it. If anything, expect that relating with them will change your life in many ways, thanks to their transformative personality.
- The range of personal expression is quite broad with Scorpio Moons, with some enjoying seclusion and intimacy and others ready for a busy night life. It's likely to be a bit of both for most,

but feel your way in the relationship to find out your Scorpio Moon's inclinations. Taking note of the subtle hints earns you their respect and affection. Reading between the lines is a basic skill for being in a relationship with them.

- You may want to share your feelings with them, but don't have too many expectations when it comes to getting them to open up too quickly. This can take time and a bit of effort. Nonetheless, taking the lead with emotional honesty will make them more comfortable with you, which can help as long as you don't mind the tension of uncertainty if they don't respond in kind.
- While they may not easily admit it, or openly accept it, they do enjoy your praise and words of affection and encouragement. Even if they are not the communicative type, you can score points with compliments, provided they are genuine and not overstated.
- They tend to take their relationships seriously but in a way not always obvious to others. With an argument you may have your hands full, as they can plumb depths of emotional expression which can surprise you. They can also retreat to their inner world, pouting and sulking, so when it comes time to make up you will need to make an extra effort to soothe their wounded feelings. Spending too much time explaining how hurt you are can complicate things, making them feel bad and aggravating their own wounded feelings. Best to give energy to new romantic exchanges rather than rehash the past. This will keep the relationship, light, upbeat and rewarding for both of you.
- Simple gifts given with feeling have real meaning to a Scorpio Moon. To impress them, give them something related to one of their more discreet passions or interests. This will tell them that, like them, you are someone who sees beyond appearances.

Scorpio Troubleshooting

☾ *How can you get them to take you and your feelings seriously?*
Seriousness is a by-word for the Scorpio Moon. Getting them to take your feelings seriously may be another matter, as they tend to have an inward-looking, rich and self-contained emotional world, one that has its own inner tumults and issues to be resolved. If you can let them know that you understand their feelings, though, you have a very good chance of them responding to yours. It is always better to appeal to their deeply sensitive nature and their ability to feel the needs of others than to confront them with criticism. That will result in certain failure. Once they take an interest, you should be prepared to go deeply into the issue, as they will want to get to the root of the problem. But ask for help, don't demand it.

☾ *How can you get them to be more supportive or responsive?*
The emotional lens of a Scorpio Moon magnifies feelings more than anyone other than another Scorpio Moon can understand. Thus, what you consider a slight concern may be felt by them as something deep and real. The trick is to get the communication and understanding right. If you want their support you may have to accept a level of involvement from them that is more than you expect. They bring an intensity to matters they care about, which in some cases can make you feel that they are taking over, rather than just giving you good advice or support. This needs a bit of emotional translation, where you filter out the intensity or emotional control to see the care and concern they are giving. Getting more response from them is more tricky, as they tend to be deep and often preoccupied with their own issues. Be ready to offer practical suggestions that you think they can agree to, and don't present these as something they 'must' do.

☾ *How can you re-establish communication?*

Delicately, with a bit of detachment, and hopefully with a certain amount of allure and mystery. Appeal to their curious nature and their compulsion to need to know what is going on. If you want to get really dramatic, send them flowers, cards or gifts – anonymously, maybe with a hint about the identity of their secret admirer. When you do talk to them, don't spill all the beans, as at least a little secrecy is an important ingredient to keeping their attention. On the other hand, don't play too hard to get – that's their job and they don't take to competition, or at least not from their lover. If you have hurt their feelings, read the section below, but if you have just lost contact, you will lure them with expressions of love and affection – but don't expect an immediate response. If at first they appear distant, paradoxically you are probably doing OK.

☾ *What is the best way to apologize?*

Sit and meditate for a few minutes, as you will need to be composed and focused. Assume the most deferential of moods. Be caring, sensitive, giving, thoughtful and, hand on heart, say you are sorry – once, twice, thrice ... as many times as it takes without overdoing it. But if you are not sincere, forget it. They will know. Small gestures, gifts and little services are essential and make the process easier. Whatever you do, don't backtrack and suggest that they are partially to blame. And don't expect immediate results. Give it time. Stay positive.

☾ *How can you rekindle the flame?*

If there is any real attraction in the relationship you should have no problem increasing the passion with a Scorpio Moon. Of course, it requires a deft hand, and maybe a little planning, but if you give free rein to your romantic inclinations even the smallest spark can ignite quickly. Remember to bring in a touch of magic and a flavour of the discreetly theatrical. Suitable settings are important. Throw in a well-meant compliment. Learn to speak and read between the lines, but be ready for intensity and passion when the opportunity arises. Poems and cryptic messages of love are almost sure to inspire them.

☾ *If the worst comes to the worst, how do you say goodbye without hurting their feelings?*
In situations like this it is almost impossible for them not to feel hurt or slighted. Knowing this will help you have the right expectations when saying goodbye. Don't think that they are going to take it in a happy-go-lucky mood. The best that can happen is that they somehow lose interest in you at the same time – which will make things easier for both of you. Be sensible and avoid saying anything that will pinch their sensitive nature.

The Moon in Sagittarius ♐

Sagittarius is the cosmic force that stands against the sell-off of the soul. It is the esoteric role of Sagittarius to guard truth, justice, honesty and wisdom. Sagittarius is a protector of the cosmic court and embodies the role of general, judge, legislator and sage. It is not surprising, therefore, to find that a Sagittarius Moon is a champion for a just cause and strives to hold as closely as possible to life's deeper values, whether spiritual, moral or ethical.

Sagittarius is the third and final Fire sign in the zodiac and in a manner of speaking represents the mature development of this astrological element. It has the passion, vigour and martial sense of Aries and the royal, dignified nature of Leo. But maybe more than these two, it is characterized by the near mythical figure of the Vedic warrior-saint, the *Rajarishi*, who blends into one person the wisdom of the sages with the power and majesty of the monarch. This romantic character embodies a godly sentiment that strives to satisfy the spiritual and corporeal needs of the citizens. Many cultures also have their Sagittarius Moon sage-monarchs, including Solomon, King Arthur, Bhisma, the regent and a protagonist in India's epic *Mahabharata*, and Emperor Yao, the mythical Chinese Emperor who created the game of Go.

The Practical Philosopher

This archetype colours the Sagittarius Moon to give an inner passion, vigour and striving for justice. They are chivalrous and love to offer help and support to others. They tend to feel that this is part of their purpose in life. In general, they are sensible counsellors, because they have a knack of putting themselves in others' shoes. Although they are philosophical, their advice is usually practical and down to earth and their caring nature makes them both good friends and good lovers. They also love to champion the underdog, and are quick to defend those less advantaged. Even when their external personality is introvert, they will have a powerful inner world that yearns for truth, purpose and justice.

You can expect to find them involved in some form of practical philosophical activities, whether it's politics, humanitarianism, ecology or religion. Where introversion limits association with such causes, the Sagittarius Moon will nonetheless tenaciously hold on to their sense of justice, even in the face of strong opposition.

This means that it can be difficult for the Sagittarius Moon to tolerate wrong-doing, either their own or that of others, and thus they tend to aspire to high ideals that can be difficult to live up to. When they fail to live up to them, they can suffer melancholy and self-doubt, castigating themselves for not being as perfect as they know they should be. This is not limited to high-minded philosophical ideals and can express itself in a number of ways, such as the desire to excel at work, home, play, relationships or even the smaller things of life. There is something of the perfectionist in the Sagittarius Moon, although this tends to be more sweeping or big picture than the finer, detailed perfectionism of the Virgo Moon.

When the Sagittarius Moon doesn't make the grade, they can be defensive about their faults and are good at debating their foibles into a context that makes the faults seem almost desirable. Don't forget they represent the cosmic advocate. If you are in a relationship with a Sagittarius Moon and have to point out their shortcomings, you need to use a little diplomacy. The best way to get their attention and agreement is to present a context, a strategic viewpoint that identifies the fault but simultaneously highlights their strengths.

Sagittarius Moons can react strongly if they feel they are being unjustly accused or criticized. Don't bother if you don't have a good case to back you up because their sense of justice is so strongly ingrained.

If they feel that their dignity has been offended, they will fight long and hard, but privately can become preoccupied with self-examination and doubt. This can be distracting and painful for them, as their own sense of justice causes them to truly examine whether they are at fault. Sometimes, this can result in them fingering the wound, making themselves feel worse and taking their eye off what really matters. When this happens, they can lose their vital drive, so important to a warrior-sage, becoming despondent or succumbing to inertia. They should at all costs try to avoid this and when it happens, acknowledge the wound but move on as quickly as they can towards a more positive goal. And of course they like nothing better when the tides have turned, and fate lets them show you how wrong you have been.

The Purposeful Visionary

The astrological symbol of Sagittarius is the centaur with bow and arrow in hand. This combines the intellect and will of the human spirit with an equine passion focused into the aim and precision of the archer. The Sagittarius Moon thus has a strong will, inner passion and sense of purpose. They strive for purpose and work to find it. Their life energy is the meaning that comes from the lofty aspects of the sign. This applies to most things, but especially so to their emotional being and sense of values. The Sagittarius Moon needs a goal and a vision, and don't be surprised if it's a grand one at that.

There is nothing more challenging to them than to lack a target or to remain undecided. Experience tells them that he who hesitates is lost. Progress inspires them, and even helps redirect them towards the right goal should they start off in the wrong direction. It is almost better for them to do something, anything, rather than nothing at all, because in the action there is the momentum. It takes less energy to redirect a moving object than an inert one, especially if the inertia is weighted down by confusion or doubt. A word of caution, though: there is another side to the coin and there is always the chance with a Fire sign that they might act impetuously without seeing the consequences. The Sagittarius Moon really needs the 'ready, aim' before they fire.

In emotional matters, therefore, Sagittarius Moons seek a relevance, certainty and purpose in their relationships. They need a sense of progress, direction, improvement, not only in how they are relating to the other person, but also in how the relationship itself is developing. If you are a more passive or introverted Moon sign, such as Virgo or Taurus, you may feel that the Sagittarius Moon is too concerned with the need for 'reason'. It can be annoying when they want to take stock of where the relationship is headed rather than just sitting back and enjoying the ride.

This trait is, however, the catalyst for the Sagittarius Moon's well-known leadership qualities. Astronaut John Glenn, General George Patton and US founding father George Washington are good examples of the Sagittarius Moon's strong sense of purpose and determination, so important to good leaders. This also puts them at the forefront of change, as they like to be at the front leading the charge into unknown territory, which excites them and lifts their spirits. Degas, Matisse and Rauschenberg did this for the art world and are good examples of Sagittarius' natural dexterity and fondness for working with their hands.

This pioneering quality often inspires Sagittarius Moons to seek their fortunes in foreign lands, and almost always they enjoy the allure of other cultures and exotic places, and the chance to learn and grow that comes from travel. The Sagittarius Moon tends to do well in foreign countries or when they leave their place of birth some distance behind. They are natural globe-trotters, which gives them plenty of good stories to spice up the conversations of which they are so fond.

The full, unadulterated expression of the Sagittarius Moon makes them adventurous and audacious to the point of appearing reckless. Yet even in their most unbridled moments they have a sense of direction – not always evident to others – which helps them to their goal. They are enterprising and like to rise to any challenge as best they can, and they do aspire to the inner discipline needed to realize their ambitions.

They also passionately love their freedom and will do anything to avoid feeling constrained. They often fear confinement of any type and will go to great lengths to avoid being checked in their progress. This is perhaps one of the few influences that may cause them to bend their strong principles, supported, of course, by good and philosophical argument.

Offering the Freedom to Fall in Love

To attract a Sagittarius Moon you will need to give them the space they need to be themselves if you don't want them to bolt. You will know when you have earned their trust when they feel comfortable opening up and expressing their faults to you. This is something that doesn't come too easily – well, to anyone really, but especially to a Sagittarius Moon. The irony for them is that such an openness endears them even to their opponents, not to speak of a close partner.

Once they commit, they are dedicated and loyal and make great partners. They are protective of their partner and friends and you will be able to count on them when you are in a bind. When you have a problem, their optimism alone can help you find a way through to a solution. Their positive outlook and enthusiasm can lift you up, especially when combined with their usually good sense of humour. They can be fun to be with. They are very romantic, as one would expect, and love to wow their lovers with gifts, surprises and unusual demonstrations of love.

Sagittarius Moon partners are trustworthy. They pride themselves on sticking to their commitments and are saddened when life demands a compromise that impinges on their values. This can be their great strength or their weakness, as they may not be as flexible as they need to be in a complicated shades-of-grey world. Their pressure valve for this is their philosophical attitude, which can help them reconcile themselves to the oddities and imperfections of life, as long as they don't allow their passionate emotional nature to get the better of them. This also gives them a great deal of comfort and underscores a nature that seeks meaning even in the small things. It further helps them to reconcile themselves to their own problems and gives them the chance to take something good out of even the most difficult of situations.

Drawing the Arrows of Love

When their 'principle-first' view of life becomes too strident, however, the Sagittarius Moon can become difficult or overbearing. They can think, rightly or wrongly, that the force of their emotions can help them push through any obstacle, sometimes earning them a reputation for being pushy. The choice for them is which battles are worth fighting and which are better ignored.

Sometimes they are so focused on what they think is important that everything else seems irrelevant or a distraction. There is the story in the *Mahabharata* of the five youthful Pandava princes who were studying archery with Dronacharya Guru. Arjuna, the best of the students, faithfully hit even the most difficult targets. His guru asked him what he saw as he took aim. Did he see the tree? 'No,' came the answer. 'The bird?' 'No' yet again. 'The neck of the bird?' 'Yes, the neck.' 'Only the neck?' 'Only the neck.' To which his guru exclaimed that this kind of focus is what makes a brilliant archer. To some extent this idea finds expression in Sagittarians, as their focus gives them the goal, but sometimes to the detriment or neglect of other things. They are therefore known for being intense, driven and able to deliver, but are often catching up with things left undone.

A good marksman hits the target with the bow fully drawn. Regardless of whether it's openly expressed or emotionally felt, the Sagittarius Moon almost always has a fully drawn bow at the ready. You may find this challenging if you are the kind of person who accepts life's paradoxes more easily; not needing answers to all the questions.

In some cases the Sagittarius Moon can see meaning in almost anything, and will express this with a display of absolute conviction – and there is nothing more forceful than a Sagittarius Moon being 'right' about what is right. While they sometimes are right, the extreme expression of this attitude can limit their ability to discern what is really happening around them. Not too infrequently they are surprised by life's sudden turns of Fate and complex entanglements. It can take courage to stand up to them and meet them head on. But if you have the guts to do it, in most cases you will find that they are not as rigid in outlook as it first appeared.

In fact, the Sagittarius Moon has a gentle simplicity of spirit that is not always evident at first hand. They love nature for its harmony and splendour, and have a passionate poetic quality to their hearts that expresses itself in grand gestures. Anaïs Nin, a Sagittarius Moon, is depicted by one biographer thus:

> 'Indeed she can be described as a witch of words. Very early she sensed the magical power of words to produce states of being, such as ecstasy, languor or dread. Her ambition was to transform the ugly realities of life into beauty, as the beast in fairy tales becomes the handsome prince after achieving a certain wisdom. She desired to distil the pure from the dross.'[2]

This touches on the magical side of the Sagittarius Moon and its focus on purity, transcendence and heightened experience.

On the more mundane side, they do not easily tolerate the slights of others and are often quite sensitive, more than would be expected from a warrior-sage. So don't be surprised by their occasionally strong emotions. Those around them often learn – sometimes the hard way – that they are only influenced by sweet words, never by force, despite being sometimes forceful in their own expression – another aspect of their 'royal' nature.

In fact, despite a generally compassionate nature, they don't always suffer fools gladly and can be quite direct. So, if you are in a relationship with them, it would be useful to be comfortable with their candour.

Also, their thirst for newness and excitement can make them restless or pensive. If you see this in them, act as a sounding-board to get them talking. Getting them to share their ideas is the first step to inspiring action in them.

[2] Valerie Harms, 'Stars in my sky', *www.anaisnin.com*

The Sagittarius Moon lives for authenticity, aspires to genuine relationships and in the purest sense isn't shy about challenging or being challenged. To bring out the best in them, you should give them the chance to express their principled, chivalrous and romantic nature. You will need to have a sense of magic about life, love a good debate now and then, and be willing to give as good as you get. Sagittarius Moons make good partners for Gemini Moons, but also do well with Pisces and Leo Moons. Having a Sagittarius Moon partner means that you have a soulmate who will help safeguard the value of your own deeper self and be ready to defend your right to express it.

Sagittarius Top Tips

- To seduce a Sagittarius Moon you will need the same passion, fiery nature and sensuality as they have, combined with discretion and good timing. Appeal to their chivalrous, romantic imagination, their free spirit and their sense of adventure. Add in a bit of pomp, a subtle touch of amorous quarrel and a gentle hand to capture their spirit.
- They love a challenge and don't give in easily, so don't be too easy yourself or you will lose your appeal. And yet avoid being too cool, as this dampens their interest and can hurt their feelings. If slighted, they quickly feel that they can't be bothered and beat a hasty retreat.
- Sagittarius Moons can be open and direct, and you will know they feel comfortable with you when they share their deeper feelings. If they do, they often expect that you will do the same, so if you are shy you will need to find a way to pacify them. But don't let them think you are hiding something, as they can get on their high horse and expect you to open up and tell all – nothing they wouldn't do themselves in your situation!
- They are passionate and sensual, and tend to respond to the needs of their lover if they are aware of them, which is one good reason to open up to them.

- They are adventurous and usually willing to explore new territory. They like a partner who appreciates their strong points and helps them with their weak areas – confidence, ironically, being an issue. The right partner will be able to give them a pep talk without making them feel judged or weak.
- They are caring partners if you have proved your loyalty. They like to lead and direct, and have a sense of purpose to everything they do, even small matters. If you are clever you will play along and if you want something else, then appeal to their strong sense of partnership to get your way.
- They like a good argument – well, debate may be a better word. The worst thing for them is to have a partner who doesn't engage, so make yourself available if you want a happy Sagittarius Moon. If you do want an argument, avoid getting personal. Keep the discussion at the level of ideas and it will be OK. Playing dirty rankles them and brings out their pure passion.
- As they are romantic and have a good sense of fantasy, give them gifts that are original and unusual. You can take more risks with this than you would normally, as they enjoy the thought of the deed more than the object, so you can't go far wrong.

Sagittarius Troubleshooting

- *How can you get them to take you and your feelings seriously?* Appeal to their sense of justice and their inclination to help others. Be open about how you feel – if anything, they respond better to honesty than diplomacy. Suggest practical ways in which they can help you with your problems. Like Leo Moons they have a touch of royalty about them, so tell them what good they are doing, while suggesting areas they can work on. If the issue is feelings, then tell them your feelings. Don't assume that they already know. Lastly, speak to their sense of partnership and suggest they empathize with your situation, which is something they can usually do quite well.

☾ *How can you get them to be more supportive or responsive?*
Express your needs clearly. Give them a target to focus on. Try not to confuse them with mixed messages or sketchy communication. If you can identify the problem, they are sure to try and help you if they care about you. They don't lack interest, but they can be driven and focused, so with their sights set on one goal, they may neglect others. Making them aware that there are other important issues that need attention will usually do the trick.

☾ *How can you re-establish communication?*
Sagittarius Moons are mostly open, direct, honest and straightforward – well, at least they try to be, or think they are. So surprise them and make the call. Chances are they will be open to your communication. Be upbeat, positive and suggest a meeting, but prepare the way with a hint or two about how you feel and what you think the agenda will be. In any case they usually love a good conversation. Appeal to their sense of humour and their love of action and adventure. Avoid being dour, self-obsessed or pessimistic. (If you feel like that, try to hide it.) They usually have a broad area of concern and small talk can be a good way to break the ice.

☾ *What is the best way to apologize?*
If an apology is needed, don't postpone it. Get the essence of what you want to say in your mind and share it with them. Sagittarius Moons can move on quickly and sever emotional ties if they feel that they have been 'unjustly' treated. So simply say you are sorry. It is rare for them to hold a grudge or want to punish you for your faults. Apologizing to a Sagittarius Moon is a lot easier than it can appear on the outside.

☾ *How can you rekindle the flame?*
Think of what has previously excited their passion and go with that. Give them more of the same, but maybe in a new or original way. The regal side of Sagittarius is easily pleased when they see that you have been thoughtful about what

pleases them and this more than anything can win their hearts. They are passionate and responsive by nature, so if there is a spark to fan you shouldn't have too hard a time. The main thing is to show strong interest and be demonstrably excited to be in their company. When in doubt, be a little theatrical, but always genuine.

☾ *If the worst comes to the worst, how do you say goodbye without hurting their feelings?*
A strong sense of duty colours their character and they may not want to give up easily. So it's important to give them the chance to warm up to the idea, otherwise they may still try and make a go of it. They are sensitive and tend to be proud. Remember this when giving the bad news. Then it's best to let them get on with their new life and do the same yourself, rather than trying to find a compromise that soothes hurt feelings. It's difficult to have it both ways when saying goodbye to a Sagittarius Moon.

The Moon in Capricorn ♑

Capricorn is the mountain citadel of the cosmic court. It symbolizes the rock-solid foundation of prosperity – stability, austerity, reliability and permanence. It is the last of the evolving Earth signs and is, in a manner of speaking, the backbone of the zodiac upon which all things practical are built. The keeper of this citadel is the clever, meticulous merchant prince whose industry sustains and nurtures the court in residence. He is methodical, diligent and ambitious.

From the vantage point of their mountain view, the Capricorn Moon sees things strategically and objectively. They tend to be quite structured in their approach to life and are usually comfortable solving problems in a methodical, even plodding, way that often guarantees them the right results. They like the 'tried and true', and often stick with their way of doing things.

The Cool Lover

Capricorn Moons tend to have a serious, reserved nature and generally like to think of themselves as 'detached', cool, unaffected and sagacious. Even when their external ego is more outgoing or demonstrative, the Capricorn Moon will maintain their reserve, hiding sensitive feelings behind the walls of their emotional stronghold. First impressions may suggest that they are the least emotional of the Moon signs. This comes from the 'grounded' quality of their emotional being, which is not easily ignited into expressing itself in a passionate or exaggerated fashion. Like all inhabited fortresses, there is a lot going on inside the walls, however, and a closer inspection reveals that Capricorn Moons are sensitive and have the same emotional intensity as the next person. While they don't often express it, they can be moved to emotional extremes that, once underway, are sometimes difficult to subdue. This slow to start, hard to stop quality is symbolized by the well-known emblem of the Capricorn mountain goat and is characteristic of other sides of their nature.

Once they have spied where they are going, the Capricorn Moon can be doggedly determined and single-minded. They like to use their analytical skills to compartmentalize the different aspects of a challenge and to then address one part at a time. This applies also to their feelings, which they tend to try and analyse – a difficult task, as emotions tend to be self-validating and beyond the rules of intellect. Nevertheless, the effort is made because the Capricorn Moon likes to know where they stand and likes the certainty of being able to control matters. This is their sensible side – wanting to be practical with feelings – which can now and then make them appear manipulative or controlling. They grow in wisdom and confidence with age, though, and eventually learn to tread softly in these areas and to be a little more laid back.

The well-known determination of Capricorn is a primary strength that helps them succeed in their undertakings and tends to make them industrious, hardworking and long-suffering, especially if they are motivated by gain or practical pursuits. The tenacity of Capricorn Moons is found in the charts of Alfred Nobel, Henry Ford, John D. Rockefeller and Andrew Carnegie, all of whom represent the quintessence of the industrial merchant prince. Capricorn Moons often have skills in business, industry and commerce, especially as Capricorn is the zodiac sign of business. It's therefore no surprise to find that the chart of the USA has a Capricorn Moon (countries and companies also have charts, based on their time of incorporations). While a Leo Moon will make one lion-hearted and determined, a Capricorn Moon gives one the durability, drive and fortitude to overcome obstacles on the path to success. 'I persevere' is the motto that helps them realize their hopes and dreams.

They can be immensely patient, especially when they have a clear sense of where they are going. When dealing with obstacles, their patience is a great strength as long as they feel they are making progress, however meagre that progress may seem to others. 'An obstacle is an opportunity' for those whose charts express the purest expression of Capricorn. There is no backing down for them: rather they muster whatever it takes to meet and outdo their adversaries. By nature they tend to be competitive and this is demonstrated in the charts of many athletes, including André Agassi, David Beckham, Carl Lewis, Tom Watson, Jana Novotna, Monica Seles and Maria Butyrskaya. Probably the most notable of the indomitable Capricorn Moons is Muhammad Ali, who personified the determination, discipline and finesse associated with Saturn, the proprietor of Capricorn.

The reason Capricorn Moons are rugged is that life has often taught them hard lessons early in life, urging them to adopt a 'can do' approach. Experience tells them that there are no easy answers in life, and that to make it, they must work hard and keep their nose to the grindstone. They bring this to their relationships, with a mood to 'make it work', and once they commit they are very reliable partners. However, Capricorn Moons also know that luck plays a big part in success and they never give up on the idea that a bit of good luck will come to help them at the right time. In a manner of speaking, they are 'children of providence' and know that for all their feet-on-the-ground outlook, fortune has a strong influence in the affairs of life.

The deeper qualities of the Capricorn Moon can be found in this idea, as they synthesize the idea of free will and the hand of Fate to celebrate their individual power as the architects of their own fortune. Capricorn symbolizes karma, or life-work and the fruits of one's efforts. This gives them the ability to reconcile a philosophical respect for forces greater than themselves with their own sense of will-power and desire for success. Theirs is thus a quiet, personal philosophy that harmonizes their being with life's limits, while seeking to expand their reach and their personal gain.

The Sober Pragmatist

They are not usually given to feeling sorry for themselves, at least not in a self-indulgent way where they become too self-absorbed and inactive. They can, however, become quite moody, sombre and deep, which could be a cause of worry for a partner who doesn't realize that they need time, like their zodiac opposite of Cancer, to dwell and reflect on important, private matters. This introspection also serves to help them plan their actions. When you see them like this, it's best to let them retreat to their mountain cave and in time they will come out ready for action.

In taking action they like to look before they leap. They know that sure-footedness takes precision and care and it often takes time for them to ponder their options. In truth, they have a proclivity for getting stuck in the proverbial rut: planning and pondering their way to inaction. A good partner for the Capricorn Moon will act as a catalyst here and a sounding-board to help them weigh up the facts. Just be ready to lock horns with them to get them moving.

Capricorn's tendency to prepare comes from their sense of strategy and forward thinking. If they are ponderous, it's because the last thing they want is to wind their way up the mountain and find themselves at an impasse. Capricorn Moons are known for their ability to shoulder more than their fair share of the load. They can even feel that unless there is an element of struggle or work involved in something, somehow it's not real or valuable. To them, life takes effort. While this gives them purpose, it can not only limit their options, but can manifest a pessimism that limits their happiness.

The practicality of their nature makes them realistic and strong in their feelings. They usually know where they stand, but are also prone to quiet moments of self-doubt or uncertainty. To counter this they may express themselves strongly or voice opinions that seem inflexible. This doesn't always work in their favour, for shy or delicate people tend to think they are boastful or self-obsessed, and stronger people will, like them, want to rise to challenge them. One of their challenges is to find an effective way to communicate, and usually for them this is best done with simple, direct and clear expression.

The Capricorn Moon also has to learn how to step out of its mountain fortress and let people get to know them more intimately. This is especially important in intimate relationships when genuine feelings are hard to hide. Although it will take time, and will likely happen in gradual steps, allowing themselves this kind of openness in relationships will create trust and understanding, which the Capricorn Moon needs and deserves.

Valuing a Relationship

At first glance, the combination of the emotional Moon and the sober, rational Capricorn may seem incompatible, but the combination is reconciled in the tendency to channel emotional energy into work and to seek emotional gratification through activity. In simple terms, this can make them career-centred or even workaholics. They need to put their heart (Moon) into their work, and they can become quite despondent when stuck in a dead-end job. While they will often continue to work at it, they find no satisfaction from it and when they realize this, it's time for them to move on to new things if they want to be happy.

This can also create for them a personal value system that applies the standards of one life area to the other. So, emotional matters are appreciated for their 'value'. Despite this mixing of work, heart, life and love metaphors, though, relationships are much more important than work. This is the paradox of the Capricorn Moon – their strong desire to be in a feeling relationship and their struggle to express the depth and seriousness of their feelings in a heart language that another heart will easily understand. Imagine an inner force that wants to expand, countered by a limit that keeps it hidden. This is a hint of how some Capricorn Moons can labour to open up and be at ease in their relationships.

So don't be surprised if the Capricorn Moon appears dismissive when they are dealing with 'troublesome' or irrational emotions. This can seem rough or inconsiderate, but is in fact more a by-product of their own discomfort in dealing with feelings they don't have or don't understand. They will also take the same approach to work that fails to gratify them. The right partner for a Capricorn Moon will reassure them and encourage them to be themselves and be at ease with their feelings. This is an important area of growth for the Capricorn Moon and their partner can play a big role in helping them develop an acceptance of emotional issues, an openness of feeling, and a greater sense of freedom in dealing with them.

With intimate relationships, they like to be careful and considered before making a move. This can result in a less spontaneous approach to love, making them seem cool or uninterested. But the slow to act, hard to stop quality comes into full effect in matters of the heart with a Capricorn Moon. Once they have finished assessing, they are as passionate and driven – maybe more so – than the next person, and passion coolly expressed is an intriguing and captivating combination of qualities.

What a Capricorn Moon needs from a relationship is a good dose of optimism, frivolity and reassurance. This will help them loosen up and give them a more well-rounded and satisfying emotional life. They need a partner who is balanced and gives as much as they take. Their cautious approach means they don't easily understand the more impetuous of the Moon signs, although they may secretly admire them while openly commenting that maybe they are a bit foolhardy. For a Gemini or Aries Moon who likes a breezier, more light-footed way of living, Capricorns can seem too pedantic and unadventurous. In truth, they do have an adventurous side, it's just that they depart fully prepared and ready to go the duration. They do well with Libra Moons, who round them out and bring the right amount of levity and sociability. A Cancer Moon is considered the perfect partner for them – caring, home-loving, emotive, giving and nurturing.

In turn, they will be responsible partners who will shoulder more than their fair share of the emotional load, even to their own detriment. This applies not only to love relationships, but also to friendships. If they come to feel that they have given too much of themselves, though, they can feel disadvantaged or taken for granted. It is easy for them to get carried away by such feelings and become sceptical or suspicious, which can further hurt their relationships. This only makes matters worse, as they tend to feel bad about feeling bad and yet don't know how to get out of such a rut. At such times, getting them out into nature helps them to relax and brings out the best of them – especially if you can get them to a windy mountaintop. The natural vista frees and nourishes their spirit.

Making It Work

In emotional matters, their determination gives them real staying power and the ability to press on with difficult emotional or relationship issues. When discussing a problem, be ready for a careful, deliberate look at all the options and don't be surprised if they point out things you have overlooked. Their cool scrutiny will help both of you find an answer. If, though, after a long effort, they fail to move forward, their goat-like nature comes into play and they can put their head down to hit problems head on, often with a stubbornness that is hard to beat.

Working out a problem with the stubborn side of the Capricorn Moon can be daunting, especially if you hope to get them to entirely change their point of view. There is little to be gained from a frontal assault, as it will only trigger their natural defences, causing them to want to hold their ground. In old Indian poetry, arguments are referred to as 'the thunder and lightning of love', and only the largest bolts, those of mythical proportions, are a match for the immovable mountain. In everyday life, strategy, diplomacy and a bit of compromise are much more effective. Of course, the Capricorn Moon is good at this as well. The best thing is to adopt a playful attitude and get them to the chessboard to see who will win, lose or draw. In any case, be ready to be flexible and give them the sense that you have heard them and that they have not had to let go of everything. If you are clever in relating with a Capricorn Moon you will 'give a little to get a little', letting the thunder of conflict intensify your passions.

If it's a reliable, stable partner you are looking for, then Capricorn Moons are as good as they come. They have strong characters, and their friends and lovers usually come to rely on and admire them for this. They tend to lean toward the hard-working, trustworthy and predictable end of the social spectrum and therefore make good parents, loyal friends and sound business partners. They also exhibit these qualities in regard to social and charitable interests. They have open minds, although they love a good debate, and they strive to understand life and love with both their minds and their hearts. Understanding which they are using at any one time can be challenging, but with time and practice you will be able to see how for them the two are closely connected. They can appear quite strong and confident, but also need as much nurturing as the next person. The challenge for you will be to gain entrance to their mountain fort, which you can do by taking the risk of showing your own vulnerable side before they do – which brings out their own noble qualities. It can take some time to unravel the special language of their heart, but having done so, you can talk your way into the fortress of their heart to find a safe, secure place that has lots of room for you and for others.

Capricorn Top Tips

☾ Seducing a Capricorn Moon requires patience, a bit of strategy and the will to let spontaneity prevail. Appeal to their earthy sensuality and stimulate their interest with tactile, gentle, physical affection. But don't rush things, as the Capricorn Moon has its own sense of timing in romance. Endear yourself with soft-spoken expressions of affection and don't worry if their reaction is not immediate or what you expect. There is a part of their emotional personality that is surprised when someone makes amorous overtures and as they are not known for quick or spontaneous emotions it can take time before they show their appreciation. Of course, once they are romantically inspired, expect to see their determination and single-mindedness.

☾ The steady drip of water wears away the hardest of stone. Patience and persistent affection will eventually help them feel at ease with you. Whatever you do, don't try to force your way into their hearts. This may work with other signs, but not with

Capricorn. And if they feel you are insincere they can be particularly resistant and stubborn.

- Sincerity characterizes their approach to relationships and you can expect an earnestness about romance which helps them overcome any feeling of insecurity they have in this area of their life. You can get closer to them by sharing their practical down-to-earth values.
- Like their Earth-sign cousin Virgo, they can appear cool and aloof. If you choose to share your feelings with them you have a better chance of getting them to open up. If they appear distant, make the effort to get close. For the most part they will appreciate the effort.
- Don't waver in the relationship if you want to keep them as partners, as loyalty is a cornerstone of their character. If they do stray, they will still retain a sense of loyalty to an important partner, which, while contradictory, is reconciled by their earnest nature.
- Bring some levity to their lives and keep things fresh with plenty of entertainment and fun. They can become quite serious and overly responsible and need someone to remind them that relaxation helps rather than hinders them in doing their duty.
- Express your feelings to them, as they are good listeners and will benefit from hearing your views on life. Don't expect too much gushing emotionalism from them in return, however, as they are more measured than that.
- When it comes to arguments you will have your hands full, as any disagreement can trigger their sceptical and stubborn nature. It is not easy to win an argument with them as they tend to not so much ignore it as rise above it. They can have very fixed views and it can be difficult to convince them otherwise. Facts, figures, logic and practical reference will help a great deal, even when it comes to dealing with 'irrational' emotions. You don't so much win an argument with them as coax them to your way of thinking in gradual increments. And sometimes it is just better to let them win.

- In all cases, a good sense of humour help you to keep the relationship light and fresh. Capricorn Moons have an element of self-effacement to their character and appreciate it when you are not too taken with yourself either. This may be due to their own insecurity, but certainly if you bring yourself down rather than raise yourself up, you will find a ready and easy-going partner in them. Your good sense of humour will also help when they show their more critical, melancholic or serious side. It's best not to overreact at such times. If you let it all pass it will be a relief to you and to your Capricorn Moon.
- You may need to lead when it comes to breaking new ground and to stay the course if they show their stubborn side. Soften them up with thoughtful gifts which have a practical side to them – something they can use, as opposed to space-taking decoration for instance. And lighten their spirits by taking them out to leave the work behind and ... just have fun.

Capricorn Troubleshooting

- *How can you get them to take you and your feelings seriously?* The sober, aloof Capricorn can be difficult to understand. But if you dig beneath the cool surface you may find that they are more concerned than you first thought. Don't expect them to always know just what you are feeling, though. This can help you avoid disappointment. But if they are aware that you are having a problem, it is almost certain that they will take it seriously. This doesn't mean that they will know exactly what to do. You can help here by giving them a few tips on what you are expecting or how they can help in very practical terms. Tell them what is going on with you and suggest how they can help while giving them the space to respond in their own way.

- *How can you get them to be more supportive or responsive?* Supportive may be more easy than responsive. If the relationship is well established, the Capricorn Moon is usually quite protective and caring. If relatively new, the Capricorn Moon is usually looking to ensure that the relationship is worthy of care, and this can take some time. While maybe less expressive than others, they are, though, earnest in their intent to support their partner. In fact, they usually shoulder more than their fair share of the burden in a relationship. So, if you are feeling neglected it will be helpful to tell them. They may be surprised or pained and the problem may be more about communication than a lack of real interest on their part. Taking the time to read between the lines of subtle Capricorn emotions and being alert to their tendency to understatement will help build better communication and understanding.

☾ *How can you re-establish communication?*

Don't be put off by their cool nature. Ignore, if you can, any aloofness and try to touch their deeper, often hidden need for emotional connection and nurturing. Play it cool yourself, don't expect too much and take a gradual approach. If you can, tempt them with a bit of fun and excitement, but don't go overboard. Be sensible, as they like that, but also add in a bit of humour. As they are able advisors, you may even want to ask their help with something small that doesn't take too much commitment on their part. Lastly, if you show some determination, maybe persistence, it can help, assuming there is the potential for genuine interest on their part.

☾ *What is the best way to apologize?*

Say you are sorry, acknowledge your offence, put the time into communicating that you are sensitive to their feelings (even if they don't respond too readily) and avoid letting the conversation degrade into ponderous moods that take you nowhere. Once hurt, a Capricorn Moon tends to hold on to those feelings. This may be countered by bringing a light-hearted touch to the conversation, perhaps a modest amount of humorous self-mockery. What you want to do is draw them out emotionally, get them to talk about their feelings and to engage with you outside the confines of their self-protective barriers. Once you have appeased them with a little gentleness, their sensible side will let them get on with life and love.

☾ *How can you rekindle the flame?*

Take them by surprise, be spontaneous, affectionate, creative and out of the ordinary. Ignore or make light of any reluctance on their part and do your best to place them at the core of a new celebration of romance. Jump up from the rut and if possible go somewhere new and exciting. Whether a weekend at a nice hotel, a trip to sunny climes, or hillwalking and rambling, taking a break in the natural world will lift their spirits and stimulate discussion. To fan the flames of passion, indulge your intimate fantasies. If appropriate, an openly seductive approach will work wonders with a sometimes timid Capricorn Moon.

☾ *If the worst comes to the worst, how do you say goodbye without hurting their feelings?*

Don't gloss over important issues, be sensible and a touch serious. If the relationship is well established, expect them to try and make it work, and to assume more of the burden. Letting go does not come easily to a Capricorn Moon. Avoid making it their problem and focus on the 'realism' of separation as a positive step for the both of you. Although pained by your departure, they may not openly express their real feelings. Don't try to force this, as it's their way of managing disappointment. Wherever possible, emphasize the 'progressive' and once you have talked it through, don't linger. In the best case you may find that they take a refreshingly pragmatic approach, which will give you the chance to remain friends and support each other.

The Moon in Aquarius ♒

Aquarius is the entire court in the zodiac cosmos. It represents all the people, from courtesans to subjects of every grade and quality. It is everyone and everything – the body politic. The educational leaning of zodiac Air signs is fully expressed by Aquarius as the mature stage of learning – the mingling of spirit and matter, and the practical application of higher knowledge for the benefit of the citizens. It symbolizes nourishment of the body and enlightenment of the soul and is found in the Aquarius emblem of a man pouring water into a pitcher, the water being spirit and wisdom, the pot being the body and matter, and the figure variously representing man, the sage and God.

The sign of Aquarius paradoxically celebrates the humble individual as the cynosure of the cosmic court. It suggests that governments are good to the degree that their citizens prosper – spiritually and materially. Systems, structures, rules and regulations have value when they nourish the individual and help them succeed in their personal growth, wisdom and happiness.

These lofty ideals find expression in the Aquarius Moon, giving them first and foremost a sense of the big picture and what really matters. Aquarius Moons are socially conscious, active and energetic – and whatever cause they adopt, they put their heart and soul into it. They get involved in issues big or small, and play an important role of building awareness of issues that affect us all.

The Idealistic Revolutionary

The Aquarian principle is a kind of social conscience that moves the focus from individual selfishness to important matters that concern us all. This often places Aquarius Moons at the cutting edge of new ideas, where they act as a catalyst for awareness, consciousness raising and sometimes a bit of radical rabble-rousing. They are the revolutionaries of their times and tend to be forward-thinking. They are known for their visionary qualities and a mystic aura that can make them larger than life characters.

They have an intuitive understanding of what makes us all tick, and their emotional nature, tinged with its futurist qualities, makes them born leaders within the sphere of their social status and influence.

The heart is the inner force that drives us toward our destinies. With Aquarians, the power of their convictions and their concerns is heart driven, which gives them a potency to achieve big things. In fact, there are many examples of great figures whose Aquarius Moon illustrates this idea, including Dr Martin Luther King and his wife, Coretta Scott King, and the pacifist–activist, Cesar Chavez. The revolutionary qualities of Aquarius Moons manifested in the lives of Che Guevara and Huey Newton, whereas the mystical, trend-setting side of this sign and all its eccentricity is probably best illustrated in the Aquarius Moon of Dr Timothy Leary.

Aquarius represents the mass of people: what concerns us, what worries us and what inspires us. Even when they are not the person creating the trend, Aquarius Moons have a knack for knowing about trends well before they appear. It is not uncommon to find them working in marketing, communications or the media. They also tend to display an artistic bent and are sometimes setting their own trends with their writing or painting. Jean-Paul Sartre's writing stimulated a generational debate about existentialism, and the works of Goethe, Camus and Ginsberg forged new territories and gave voice to the concerns of their respective generations. Sometimes, an Aquarius Moon will embody the spirit of a generation in this way, or capture the essence of a mood or feeling that grips everyone at the time. There may be no better examples of this than Princess Diana and Marilyn Monroe, both Aquarius Moons who, in dying tragically, created an iconic impression of themselves in the hearts of the generation who mourned them.

While famous examples like the above are rare, the same principles and ideals manifest in the hearts of Aquarius Moons who like to be where it's happening, whether it's politics, fashion, art or social activism. This gives them the ability to relate to people. They are usually warm-hearted, friendly and able to put people at ease. They tend to make friends easily and are conduits for networks of people, so hopefully if you have an Aquarius partner, you enjoy having a busy social life. They are good people brokers and like to bring people together for good causes, good parties or good conversation.

The Spiritual Adventurer

They have a strong curiosity and are motivated by a desire for wisdom and understanding. They tend to be open-minded, non-judgemental and like to be well informed. If they are passionate about a subject, expect that they will have facts and figures to back up their point of view, but don't worry, as they are quite good at giving others the space they need to express themselves. While they can be politically adept, they are often at the cutting edge of new ideas, which can put them outside the mainstream or at the fringes of real influence. They are better at drawing up strategy than glad-handing, but sometimes their natural human warmth and likeability does put them at the forefront.

Aquarius Moons are very sensitive to their environment and like to create atmospheres of comfort and congeniality. They have a natural understanding of the harmonies of nature and are able to go to the depths of the ecological argument to see that the problem lies first of all in the way people think. They are attracted to ideas like *feng shui* and other systems which seek to harmonize people with their environment. They have a strong sense of our interdependence on nature and our environment, which is an extension of their philosophical and spiritual interests. They also have a keen interest in self-development subjects, which may include poetry, art and meditation.

The mystical side of their nature gives them an intuitive grasp of how spiritual energy threads its way through the fabric of life. They find a great deal of solace in these ideas and not only actively seek to understand them, but also try as best they can to experience them in a genuine way. They are thus spiritual or humanist adventurers, ever on a quest for wisdom and understanding. This journey takes them naturally into the exploration of new subjects. Due to their questioning nature, they tend not to adhere to run-of-the-mill attitudes and while they tend to appreciate spiritual ideas, they are not always religious in the strict or dogmatic sense of the term. This is because, in their view, religion is the outer form of an ideal that is universally true and applicable. This lets them sit at the table of any culture, feel comfortable and find the common ground that brings people together.

We find another expression of their quest in anthropology; they enjoy meeting foreigners and travelling to foreign places. In fact, the more they travel, the broader their horizons, and they learn a lot from their adventures which they are then inspired to share with others.

This touches on the teacher in them, which is quite pronounced and which they like to demonstrate in a practical and informal manner. As an Air sign, they like a sense of freedom and shy away from limits and constraints. Their broadmindedness tends to emphasize the need for a new, exploratory approach to learning and old school discipline seems to them a form of punishment and certainly not an incentive to develop and grow. They are so conscious of this that they will give others a wide berth when it comes to imposing their own standards or ideals on them, although they will vigorously argue their point of view. They are educational reformers, even if their job has nothing to do with teaching.

The never-ending quest of the Aquarius Moon keeps them moving, exploring, evaluating, collecting and accepting the diversity that is the fabric of life, so if you are looking for someone with more solid or fixed views then you should probably look elsewhere. To pin them down to one way of thinking or being is paramount to killing them by limiting their ability to experience the diversity of life. However, if you have an open mind, or want your mind opened, then an Aquarius Moon is just for you.

A driving force behind the Aquarian nature is the urge for transformation and regeneration through ideas. Their wide range of interests gives them an understanding of many subjects, which may include psychology, understanding people, the healing arts, creative interests; anything where the mind can find stimulation and expansion. No matter how good life is, it can never be as good as it could be, and in any case the world is so full of faults that it gives them more to do than they have time for. The essence of their karmic purpose is service through knowledge and understanding. They try to do this gradually and gently and usually have the Saturnian patience to nurture progress along. If, however, they feel that a just cause demands it and that no progress is being made, they launch their revolutionary passion to try and create change the radical way. Stubborn and unreasonable behaviour is sure to trigger this kind of reaction with an Aquarius Moon.

If you need a champion, then think about an Aquarius Moon. There is nothing that galvanises them into action more than the underdog or the disadvantaged. As a result, they also tend to make very good counsellors and social workers, as they can give tirelessly of themselves for others' benefit.

Dreams and hopes inspire and guide them on their life journey and it's important for them to remain true to their vision. 'Never lose sight of the goal' should be their catchphrase. In any case it is rare for them to lose heart and if you do, you can count on them to help you find it.

If they lose their way, however, the Aquarius Moon can become listless and morose. In dealing with life's challenges, it is important that they take a passive attitude to obstacles – they do better to go around them rather than to hit them head-on like their neighbouring Capricorn. A certain amount of detachment is a good tool for Aquarius and will help them manage life's ups and downs more effectively, helping them to step over problems as they make steady progress.

Supporting the Cause

A positive mental attitude is the core strength of the Aquarius Moon, and their vision and practical optimism will help them deal with challenges that come their way. This is part of their sense of purpose, of life mission, and it is important that their close relationships validate this for them – it is doubtful that a critical or pessimistic partner will last long with them. Preferably, their partner will understand their idealism and see it as a source of strength and inspiration for both of them. At best, their partner will validate their highest ideals and support them in their struggle to realize them.

To attract an Aquarius Moon you will need to be flexible, perceptive, a little challenging, a touch mysterious and also playful. You will have to appeal to their desire to know. Try to attract them with subtlety and finesse. They are often uncomfortable with a too-direct approach and prefer a gentle seduction in which they are equal partners – dancing to a natural rhythm.

You will be particularly successful in a relationship with them when you can demonstrate that you understand what they are thinking or feeling before they express it. To do this you will need to be observant and be able to read between the lines, where a lot goes on for the Aquarius Moon. They like perceptive people, as they themselves tend to observe more than the next person, and this will tell them that you are similar spirits.

Aquarius Moons are usually quite romantic and expressive when it comes to sharing their feelings – not always verbally, but in gentle, subtle gestures that tell you how they feel. Indeed, they are very sensitive and value their emotions, often saying that their feelings are as important as their mental judgement. This is a good example of the evolution of Aquarius, as it shows how the sign combines emotions and intellect into one complementary whole. An intimate relationship with an Aquarius Moon can be ethereal and almost otherworldly, as though the two of you are on a magical adventure of feeling, insight and the sharing of unspoken understandings.

The Aquarius Moon makes a good partner when exploring ecstatic moods and exotic atmospheres. They have an artistic way of creating a setting that inspires sensuality and their mystical leanings may spark an interest in subjects like Tantra and the *Kamasutra*. Romance is thus a deep experience that brings out a devoted quality in them. They will express their love poetically, tenderly and sometimes with a touch of genuine humour. They like the playful side of love and, thanks to the Air-sign quality of Aquarius, can easily change their moods to enhance the romantic setting.

As their partner, they expect that you will want to take part in their journey and not be a passive bystander. This comes from their commitment to realize their destiny and from a romantic nature that seeks a union that is as transcendental as it is sensual. Jumping into a close relationship with an Aquarius Moon means being willing to explore life's mysteries with them. While common interest is important in any relationship, with Aquarius it is essential. Lacking at least a mild interest in big issues, social concerns, philosophy or the mystical side of life will disadvantage you in a relationship with them, as they will tend to lose interest in a partner who is not 'deep' enough.

Learning the Personal Touch

For an Aquarius Moon, part of the reason why their lover should be ready to share an interest in the abstract is because their pronounced social abilities actually belie a mild handicap when it comes to making deep emotional and personal connections. Depending on the chart, they can struggle to descend from their lofty place of ideas to the tangible nitty-gritty of relationships. This is not usually chronic, but more periodic, and it will depend on the individual involved. If you are a sensitive person and want to have lots of reassurance and affirmation, though, you may feel out of place with an Aquarius Moon, thinking them distant, uninterested or lacking passion. If you learn the Aquarius language of the heart, you will, in time, come to find that this is not as 'personal' as it seems, but more a character trait that needs to be understood and managed rather than changed. Of course, you can make efforts to bring them down from their Valhalla, and you will succeed, but their natures urge them to soar, so once you get them down, be ready to take off with them again and enjoy the journey.

Another trait that can be misleading is the Aquarian Moon's intolerance for the petty things of life. Again, this comes from their preoccupation with the big picture and their tendency to dismiss what they consider inconsequential or irrelevant. This trait can be expressed in emotional matters and is easily misunderstood as lack of interest or care. If you have an important issue to discuss and want their participation, the best way to get their attention is to explain how important it is to you. This will ensure that you have a better chance of getting their ear and once you do they are usually sympathetic. They can be good listeners, although they will try to *understand* your feelings rather than *feel* your feelings, meaning that there is a gap to bridge when bringing them into your more sensitive emotional space.

The reverse is true when they have emotional needs, and their quick nature is likely to expect you to be ready for anything, so don't get too upset if there seems to be a double standard here. Remember that Aquarius is a higher octave than Libra and Gemini and, to some extent, shares in a few of their Air-sign qualities.

A relationship with an Aquarius Moon can be stimulating, uplifting, challenging, enigmatic, otherworldly, inspired and involved. It can take you to places you might not normally go and as long as you are open-minded, you will learn and grow along the way. Aquarius Moons have a knack of bringing the creative out in others, so with them you may also discover new sides to your personality. If you are ready to explore new territory, then the Aquarius Moon may well be the partner for you.

Aquarius Top Tips

- Seducing an Aquarius Moon can be a stimulating adventure and a unique emotional experience that initiates you into a subtle sensuality that is tinged by the realm of thought. Desires and principles, passions and concepts blend together in the Aquarius heart and create the chance for an emotional experience that is creative, transformative and inspirational.

Don't be surprised if the Aquarius Moon is a past master in the realm of sensuality and weaves a bit of magic into the seductive exchange. Even if inexperienced, they will have a natural sense of the sensual world.

- If you want to be romantically successful with an Aquarius Moon you will need more than just an attractive physique, as they like to bring their soul into the romantic experience. In sensual matters, they are reaching for more, and expect more, than the ordinary. To seduce them you should appeal to their creative and inspired nature, keep a little mystery about yourself and hint that there is more to discover together than separately.
- The setting for any romance should be suitably exotic, mystical or fantastic. Candles, scents, flowers, breezes and the right music will all help. Most importantly, remember to address yourself to the whole person, the whole being in the exchange, or you could lose their interest quickly.
- Appeal to their love of ideas. Express your interest in the big picture and issues that affect all of us – anything that stimulates discussion and their passion for understanding. If you are clever, you will entice them with the promise of gaining a greater understanding of life by relating with you.
- As they are communicative they will tend to share their feelings, but not if it seems self-indulgent or petty. Keep this in mind when you have tender feelings and are needy. Making the right approach is important in getting the attention and sympathy of an Aquarius Moon. On the other hand, they have a soft spot for the underdog and are usually ready to lend a helping hand, so appeal to that part of their nature if you have a problem.
- They generally love going out, social events and anything new, unusual or exciting. They especially enjoy meeting people, so be ready to share them with others, especially at parties. Arrange dinner parties, clubbing and other active pastimes to keep the relationship lively and progressive.

- Avoid hemming them in with emotional demands. They can get claustrophobic and need their space, so don't be too needy too regularly. The other side of this coin is that they can be difficult to pin down, so you should be confident when dealing with them.
- Arguments can be interesting, polemic and spirited. Aquarius Moons can be elusive and will often side-step issues. If you feel they are doing that, be ready to argue your case convincingly – with good examples, of course. Making up is generally not that hard to do, as they tend not to get bogged down in boring details or hold grudges.
- When it comes to gifts, offer items that are sensual, imaginative, thought-provoking or poetic. Decorative or artistic gifts are good, as are personal gifts that satisfy their love of comfort.

Aquarius Troubleshooting

- *How can you get them to take you and your feelings seriously?* Discreetly link your concerns to their ideals. Express your problems within the context of their own important values, but be subtle in doing so. Force or insistence rarely works with Air signs, so avoid trying to rope them into dealing with your emotional needs. They have a subtle way of thinking of relationship issues in abstract or intellectual terms, which can be a clue to how to stimulate their concern for your feelings, depending on the person. To get them to look at your needs more closely, emphasize that a closer connection will bring out the better qualities of both of you and give you the chance to explore a deeper, more meaningful love. But don't get clingy, as that will certainly send them in the other direction.

- *How can you get them to be more supportive or responsive?* Communication is the key ingredient here. Take the time to be together, create meaningful dialogue and take the lead in showing an interest in their needs and issues while expressing your own. When talking about your issues, give the impression that you are looking at the problem 'objectively' and not that they are the cause. Dealing with matters side by side will create togetherness and mutual understanding. It will also be easier for them to deal with a problem as an idea, rather than as a failure on their part. Remember that while they can be distracted, even eccentric at times, they are also responsive by nature, especially to anything which helps bring them closer to their ideal of a perfect union. In contrast, when they get it right, let them know and make it their personal success.

☾ *How can you re-establish communication?*

Aquarius Moons are insatiably curious and have a wide range of interests. They are open, communicative and non-conformist, so the best approach is one that is bold, open, stimulating, inventive and original. They usually like engaging conversation, so start a discussion and gradually bring it round to an invitation to a party or social event. Emphasize your shared interests, but be ready to bring in new ideas that broaden the discussion, if only to challenge their minds and pique their interest. Suggest a meeting that is easy, such as a quick coffee which lets the both of you feel free and not obligated. Keeping expectations to a minimum will help them feel a get-together is natural, not contrived. If things have gone wrong in the past, avoid them in discussion and emphasize the positive, the hopeful and the ideal. Be laid back, not too eager, and create the experience of enjoying each other's company and conversation again.

☾ *What is the best way to apologize?*

To err is human, to forgive divine. If you play the human role, they will most likely be happy to play the divine role. Be sincere, admit your failings and appeal to their higher nature. They can easily forgive and even forget, so a genuine apology should stand you in good stead. Be generous and offer a gift or other gesture of reconciliation that will touch their naturally romantic heart.

☾ *How can you rekindle the flame?*

A combination of the exotic, erotic and sensual will be the perfect potion to heighten feelings of love and desire. Poems, flowers and a well-planned romantic setting will help. Activity and diversity are important to keeping the relationship fresh and vital, and this includes socializing, dancing and other forms of entertainment. Create the sense that the relationship is going somewhere and that together you are taking it to a new level. Don't revisit the past, but forge ahead to a new future.

☾ *If the worst comes to the worst, how do you say goodbye without hurting their feelings?*

If you are saying goodbye, there is a good chance they will know it before you get a chance to say it. If you can, deal with things 'conceptually' and not as an emotional failing on their part. They tend to be adaptable and can recover from rejection quickly, though they are likely to ponder the deeper, more philosophical side of the experience for some time. Emphasize that you are both moving on to new experiences, where you will find enrichment and make progress in life. In short, be philosophical about it without ignoring their delicate feelings or being insensitive.

The Moon in Pisces ♓

Pisces is the last of the Water signs and the final sign of the zodiac. It is mysterious, sensitive, deep and profoundly intuitive by nature. It is magical and enigmatic, difficult to understand but very pleasant to be with.

The Pisces Moon plays the role of wizard, sage or hermit in the cosmic court because it embodies knowledge and the highest secret truths offered in the service of others. Almost every culture has its mystical wizard or high priest who symbolizes wisdom incarnate, and invariably their role is to protect truth and propagate knowledge. Merlin is a good example of a sage who is compassionate but also detached from the world he tries to help – so characteristic of the wise man's ability to be in the world, but not of it. Here but not here, involved but detached, feeling but aloof – the Pisces Moon in a paradoxical nutshell.

The Sensitive Mystic

It takes some time to understand the Pisces Moon. They tend to resist easy labelling, although a little experience will quite easily help you pick one out from the crowd. They are a wonder all of their own and have a special allure that seems to invite your investigation into who they are – a journey that is almost as endless as they are deep.

Layer by successive layer you will find that the Pisces Moon holds many secrets and possesses many subtle qualities. They are one of the most sensitive of the zodiac signs, and are often known for their strong intuition and psychic talents. Pisces is ruled by Jupiter, known in Sanskrit as *Guru*, and thus Pisces Moons are philosophical and appreciate life's deeper mysteries. They are given to deep thought and are usually content contemplating in their own quiet privacy. They can reflect on a subject for a long time, and sometimes need prodding with external stimuli to come back to normal consciousness. They have an insatiable curiosity, which frequently lands them into trouble, and are always seeking new levels of meaning and understanding, even in the most simple events of the day. It is difficult for a non-Piscean Moon to comprehend, but they are naturals at meditation and easily slip into daydreaming, reveries and fantasies. This gives them a strong creative quotient and a vivid imagination that can captivate you if you are able to get the shy Piscean to open up and reveal their inner secrets.

Pisces Moons are generous and thoughtful, non-judgemental and usually like to reflect on all sides of an issue before they draw a conclusion. When they do, they like to think that it is a wise judgement, but they are not usually too worried about being wrong or admitting a fault. They can be quite philosophical about life.

Pisces Moons are attractive personalities that are likeable for their easy-going nature. People gravitate to them, especially when they feel a need for comfort or understanding, which come naturally from a Pisces Moon. They often have a healing spirit about them and are able to intuit the needs, wants and hurts of others. This is not always apparent to the casual observer, but that is because the Pisces Moon has its own heart language, a special vocabulary of emotion that tends to work beneath the surface, quietly and gently.

In a sense, Pisces symbolizes the final stage of evolutionary soul development. This can make Pisces Moons uninterested in mundane subjects and material possessions, and keen adherents of esoteric knowledge or spiritual values. They are strongly intuitive, which often gives them psychic abilities and premonitions. This may be most easily noticed in their childhood, when their capacity for fantasy has not been dulled by the imposition of social norms. In this freer state, they are more open to receive the subtle influences which give psychic impressions and they are more likely to reveal them if they find a person genuinely willing to listen to them. In their early stage of life, their rich inner world is a source of wonder and inspiration and its influence tends to last long into adulthood, inspiring the more creative and original side to their nature.

The Creative Romantic

The creative element to their character is strong and in some cases will actually manifest as artistic ability. Painters whose Moon was in Pisces include Braque, Dali, Warhol and Renoir, each of whom demonstrated, in their own way, the romantic and fantastical elements of Pisces. The Piscean romantic shades, poetic depth and philosophical insight into human nature are found in the charts of Chekhov, Pasternak, Tagore and Twain. If your Pisces partner is not endowed with such august talent, you will nevertheless still find an original, expressive and eccentric creative spirit that loves to indulge in decorative, playful and inspired living spaces. Pisces Moons love social gatherings and if there is anywhere they can let their hair down, it's at a party or dancing in a club. They tend to have a unique sense of style, enjoying fine clothes and ornaments. Even when they dress simply, they do so with a panache that sets them apart from the crowd – which is one of the more extrovert tendencies of the Pisces Moon.

The love of home and a penchant for displaying fine objects are strong elements in the Pisces Moon, although it may take some time before you get used to the love of clutter, which they prefer to describe as 'ordered chaos'. An interesting side of their personality is their lack of interest in objects which don't live up to their standards – they have the ability to do without rather than lower their standards. In terms of daily living, it is important for them to retreat to their 'hermitage', to pull away from the hustle and bustle of life, in order to stay in touch with the inner world that strengthens and supports them.

They are more fond of ideas than details, which they tend to discount as troublesome and irrelevant. It's as though the minutiae of life will ground them down and keep them from the pleasure of their inner creative world. In short, the nitty-gritty is boring to them and without sufficient reason to be 'in the world' they can easily float off to a dreamy contentment all their own. They therefore do well with an Earth sign, such as the perfectionist Virgo Moon or the practical Taurus Moon, who can draw them back down to earth while celebrating and enjoying the Piscean other-worldliness.

The Pisces Moon is more emotional than logical; in fact they have their own 'feeling-logic', which, at least to them, explains the dynamics of emotions and is self-justifying in its own right. It is a rare soul who can get them to express the rules of this logic. The Pisces Moon does not express itself easily in words. They are usually taciturn, shy and retiring. It is very unusual to find an extrovert Pisces Moon and even when you do, they almost certainly will not reveal their inner secrets. If for some reason they do let you into their emotional world, it will be a treat and a privilege, and this in itself suggests that they hold you in high esteem.

If this doesn't happen, then be patient, because the challenge with the Pisces Moon is to get them to understand what is happening outside them. Their tendency to introversion can make them more inward-looking than most, and this can make them appear eccentric and absent-minded. There is every chance that they are distracted or disconnected from what is happening around them. Where this would worry another person, a Pisces Moon will be quite content at letting 'the little boring details' pass them by.

To communicate with them, you will probably be more successful by sitting down and meditating, visualizing them and sending them a psychic message, than trying to get them to understand something by talking. This may seem like an exaggeration, but for many Pisces Moons it is not far from the truth, as they tend to be sensitive, keenly aware and often in tune with the subtlety of nature and their surroundings. They are accommodating and can be quite fluid in their approach to life, with a flexibility that lets them bend with the wind like no other Moon sign. They can find it difficult when it comes to taking charge and having it their way. They have to make an extra effort to exert their will, otherwise it is much too easy for them to go with the flow and end up in a place or relationship where they don't want to be.

The sign of Pisces is the essence of giving and self-sacrifice, and the Pisces Moon is one of the most naturally compassionate signs. It is not just a matter of a mental or intellectual view of suffering, but rather something they feel as personal, almost physical in themselves; they have the ability to actually feel the pain and discomfort of others. This is another side to their mystical nature and allows them to truly place themselves in another's shoes. This can apply not only to people but almost any living thing, and thus the Pisces Moon represents not only self-sacrifice but a tendency to non-violence. It is rare to find that a Pisces Moon will actually be aggressive or hurtful, except in cases where the rest of the chart strongly counters their exceptional compassion.

Romancing the Selfless Soul

In relationships, Pisces Moons are therefore able to empathize and share their feelings and affections delicately and thoughtfully. In fact, they are the ultimate romantics. In some cases this is so strong that their capacity for fantasy, deep feelings and dreamy desires cloaks them and their partners in an intoxicating romantic opiate. This can create a private insular world, where both partners feel safe and secure, shielded from life's petty realities. When they love, they love intensely, and they are able to give themselves to their partner in a way that defies easy description. They are creative in their expression of love and while generous with little gifts, they love to receive them even more. Flowers, perfume, fragrant oils, anything exotic touches their heart and sets their romantic imagination in motion. They are sensitive lovers who are quite giving and thoughtful when it comes to satisfying the needs of their partner. They are able to create wonderfully conducive atmospheres for amorous exchanges. When they give their heart, it is accompanied by all the lofty feelings and ideals associated with selfless and divine love – a good example of this being Joan of Arc's Pisces Moon. Their love can be very deep, so deep that even their partner may fail to understand its depths. 'Still waters run deep' never had a truer subject than the Pisces Moon.

Ideally, their partner should share an interest in their desire for adventure, personal growth, spiritual or mystical interests and, on a more mundane level, good causes such as charities. Their nature is to make a contribution – to their own inner life and to the lives of those around them. In a real sense, self-improvement is a cornerstone of their being, and the theme of enlightenment and growth through contribution, sacrifice and sharing is an idea that will ring true to most Pisces Moons. Their key word is 'belief', based not on dogmatic statements, but on real, inner-life experiences. They are often content with the reward of virtue itself and tend not to strive for recognition or kudos from those they help. Their partner will certainly benefit personally from such a giving nature, but will also have to share in something of the same interest to ensure harmony of purpose in the relationship.

Pisces Moons may be even more giving than they should be, as they tend to feel the needs of their partner even when they haven't expressed them. This is a special trait that makes Pisces Moons desirable partners, but if their partner is selfish, it is possible that the Piscean will find themselves giving to someone who takes but who doesn't give back. This can be especially challenging to them, as they are usually tolerant and can continue to give well past the point where they should say something to bring some balance to the relationship. This also comes from an insecure part of their character that values the other person more than themselves. In time, they often learn that this is not a good way to manage their relationships, but it takes regular effort on their part to stand up for themselves and not be taken advantage of. Their soft heart can bind them to relationships that don't work for them, because they can't bear to break away. Being cruel to be kind is just not in their vocabulary and it can take some hard lessons before they learn that the right relationship is one where they are getting as much as they are giving.

There are other cases, however, where Pisces Moons are so much in their own world that they make a special type of radical reformer – one who thinks the world should live up to their romantic and high ideals and who quite easily disregards the usual rules of life by being 'above it all'. Basically, they simply disagree with the way things are done, and they just do what is so easy for them, which is to ignore it.

Living Up to the Ideal

If life is kind to them, the Pisces Moon will not have too many disappointments in love. Yet it is difficult for the mundane world to live up to their romantic visions. They can be very forgiving, but tend to hold on to hurt feelings for a long time, not unlike their Water-sign relatives Cancer and Scorpio Moons. Almost any emotional experience leaves a lasting impression on them, which gives them a kind of register they refer to when any experience comes their way. If they have been hurt, it can take some time before they give themselves easily again, but give they must – it's their nature – and it's sure that they will find someone to bestow their affections and healing love on. Indeed, their affections do have a healing quality and astrologically this is symbolized by Pisces being the sign of healing retreats, places of rest and hospitals. Ideally, the healing in such places will have an element of the caring and giving that a Pisces Moon is capable of.

Their shy natures can make them too sensitive, however, and if you have to confront them about a troublesome issue, they do tend to withdraw. This can be frustrating if you are the more straightforward type and you may think that they are avoiding the issue – which to some degree is likely to be the case, but not in the 'sneaky' sense, more in the sense of 'Is this really necessary?' or 'I am not equipped for this.' Of course, their nature won't let them say that to you, but it's what they are thinking. If you are smart, you'll avoid taking a direct, boisterous or confrontational approach with them as they will tend to pull back and clam up. Gently ease them out and try and get them to deal with the issue in partnership. Maybe the best way is to share your concerns in an oblique way that gives them the space to come to your rescue, which they love to do.

If you are a down-to-earth person who likes things to move to a regular and reliable beat, it is sure that a Pisces Moon will test your patience. It is often seen that they can have, almost stubbornly, their own clock and own sense of personal time – which for the most part is rarely in synch with that of others. If this is the case with your Pisces Moon partner – and there are exceptions – then it's best to adjust your expectations and go with the flow. This will keep everything smooth and easy, and in any case your exhortations probably won't do much good anyway.

When it comes to problem-solving, again Pisces Moons take an unorthodox approach, this time surprising others with their ability to deliver solutions from unexpected places. This is the magician in them, which they subtly demonstrate by dealing with obstacles by using mind over matter. They tend to understand the natural order of things and are able to influence or connect with that order through their will-power or their strong talent for visualization. While they can't always explain how this works to others, it is a skill they put to good use in supporting their partners.

On balance, the Pisces Moon is a wonderful partner who gives more than they get. If you are not too picky, can be flexible and enjoy going with the flow – not to mention the eccentricities and otherworldly absent-mindedness – then a Pisces Moon is a good partner for you. The Virgo Moon offers a perfect counterbalance to the Pisces Moon – although they are not known for their easy-going, flexible nature, their pedantry and structure offer a lot to Pisces and Pisces in turn gives them a high-minded and flexible way to bring out their best. Other suitable signs include Taurus, Sagittarius and Capricorn. With a Pisces Moon it's a magical mystery tour, so, for the like-minded, all aboard!

Pisces Top Tips

☾ Seduction of a Pisces Moon has a dream-like quality that unfolds in subtle stages to reveal a passionate, sensual lover. It is not always easy to see this in them thanks to their quiet nature. Appearances can be deceiving, so give the gentle Pisces time to respond to your advances and show their lively fantasy. You can judge how well you are doing more through their body language than anything they say. This is a good hint as to the best way into their heart – softly, sweetly, patiently. Between the lines a lot can be said.

- A special setting is not always required for the seduction of a Pisces, thanks to their ability to create their own romantic ambience within themselves. If you are lucky, that is the place you will be led to in your romance. But if you want to make special preparations, create a secluded, well-appointed 'cave' where you can both hide from the busy world. Think sensual and be sensual in setting your romantic stage and you won't go wrong.
- It can be difficult to understand the deep feelings of a Pisces Moon and it is probably easier to get them to open up by revealing your own feelings. It can be difficult to get verbal validation from them – and that will certainly not happen quickly. It takes time to coax them out of their inner seclusion, so open up first and get the ball rolling. They are not intentionally secretive – they have a rich inner world which is as real as anything outside, and they may reveal it to you.
- They love a good time and can be real party animals, so if you want to see the wild side of your erstwhile retiring partner, get them out clubbing, partying and socializing. You may be surprised how popular they are with others. If you lose them at a party, look for where the most fun is happening – they are probably the cause of it.
- It can be frustrating when it comes to arguments, especially if you want someone who will engage with your own passionate nature. Pisces Moons don't win arguments verbally, but by quietly retiring to their corner and waiting it out. The more you try to force them out into the open, the more they will retreat. So, if you have important issues to resolve and are passionate by nature, make sure you help them feel secure and appeal to their peace-loving nature, otherwise they won't engage.
- Pisces Moons have a sense of inner confidence, although they are not really known for being extrovert. But if you need help with something, appeal to this solid inner core and you will benefit from sage advice.
- They are easy to please when giving gifts, but the more thought that goes into the gift, the more it will be appreciated,

even if it's something simple or inexpensive. Maybe the best gift to give is anything that pampers them and appeals to their sensual nature.

Pisces Troubleshooting

☾ *How can you get them to take you and your feelings seriously?*
Pisces Moons are naturally, deeply empathetic. As long as they are not absorbed in their own dilemmas, they will be there to help you with yours. If you feel they are not taking you seriously, it may be because they are genuinely not aware of what is going on with you. Make the extra effort to spell it out for them in the nicest possible way, ask for their advice and appeal to their compassionate nature. Also, give them some time to respond. They tend to work to their own life rhythms, which are not always in synch with those around them.

☾ *How can you get them to be more supportive or responsive?*
Getting a Pisces Moon to be outgoing or externally supportive can be a challenge, although not impossible, as they are very caring by nature. Getting them to be responsive may be too much to ask, at least if you are expecting them to do what non-Pisces people do. One thing that is certain – if they care about you, they are often thinking about you or feeling how you are, even at a distance, and even when they may not be aware of it. In this sense they are quite supportive. If you want a more open expression of this, let them know what it is you are looking for in detail. Be patient, hope for the best and expect that it may take some time and more than one conversation.

☾ *How can you re-establish communication?*
Pisces Moons are gentle and receptive and therefore usually make reconnecting easy. Re-establishing 'communication' in the strictest sense of the term may be another thing, as the Pisces idea of communicating is quite unique. This means that if you want to link up again, it is likely that you will need

to make the first move. When you do, take the softly, softly approach. No great expectations or big pressures. Draw them back into the relationship with sweet enticements. While they may not be talkative, they are very good listeners, which can help when you have something thought-provoking or romantic to say.

☾ *What is the best way to apologize?*
Make amends with deeds more than words. Pisces Moons can almost feel when you are genuinely contrite. Small gestures and a soft, unassuming apology should be more than enough to bring about their easy forgiveness. Make the point that you know how deeply they feel any slight and that you appreciate their patience. Any attempt to show that you understand their deeper feelings will be appreciated, especially if you say it without saying it.

☾ *How can you rekindle the flame?*
Think creatively, act seductively and touch tenderly. Be romantic, poetic and considerate at every turn. Be demonstrative with your love – create secret love trysts, leave one rose, send a card for no good reason, focus on gentle gestures that remind them of you, tell them you love them more deeply than words can describe. With this as the strategy, the rest is detail and will fall into place naturally.

☾ *If the worst comes to the worst, how do you say goodbye without hurting their feelings?*
Pisces Moons are very emotional and tender, so tread carefully. Expect that there will be hurt feelings of some kind. Be open and honest, but don't go into too much detail, as they will likely feel what is going on without you having to spell it out. Express your appreciation for what did work, thank them for the good times you shared and wish them well on their journey. Do your best to leave them feeling good about themselves – not always an easy task, but a worthwhile and rewarding one.

Chapter 4

The Spice of Life ... and Love

We are all different. That's what makes life interesting. In love, it's the difference that creates attraction. But it really works when it's balanced, or grounded by similarity. Vedic and Panchang Moon astrology looks at relationships as a dance of energies, an interplay of natural, even cosmic qualities that play out in different ways according to who is our dancing partner.

To be powerfully involved in a relationship, you have to be aware – conscious of these energies and how they create the dynamic moves of your own dance. If your partner moves one way, if it's contrast you want, you move in another. If you or your partner seeks harmony, you agree to move the same way, while always remaining the individuals you are. People whose relationship has lasted for 30 or 50 years will undoubtedly say that their dance combines the differences as much, if not more, as the similarities.

This is a magical way of looking at relationships. A relationship seen from this perspective becomes a celebration of qualities and influences that are larger than life. It's this kind of magic that we all look for and hope for early in a relationship, but which usually gets lost in the humdrum of living our lives. We usually call this familiarity, but in fact it is really unfamiliarity, in that we have forgotten how those plays of energy attracted us in the first place.

Reconnecting with the dance of our partner is the magic we all long for and need in our relationships.

Whatever kind of dance you are in – passionate, wild, fluid, sensuous, thoughtful, reflective, internal – the essence is in knowing how your partner moves. This lets you dance *with* differences, rather than clashing with each other. It's about working with the things that 'don't work'.

The comparisons below highlight a few major themes in the interaction of two Moon signs. The idea is to give a hint of the emotional dynamic between the two signs, the subtle dialogue between two hearts, the scent of roses ...

Each sign's astrological element of Earth, Water, Fire or Air gives a quick reference to the type of each Moon sign. Classical astrological texts consider some of these 'naturally compatible' and these are highlighted with a star (★). These do not, of course, guarantee relationship bliss, but rather illustrate how the dynamic between the two Moon signs enhance and complement each other. This hints at the emotional dialogue that the Moon sign in question is ideally looking for.

To avoid repetition, comparisons between any two Moon signs are made only once. So, for instance, 'Aries and Taurus' covers 'Taurus and Aries'. For ease of reference, you can consult the index to find the page for any two sign comparisons. Lastly, each of the comparisons that follow reveal even more of the character and subtle nuances of each moon sign.

Aries and...

Aries (Fire and Fire)

A potent, energetic combination with lots of fire, passion, wilful expression, vying for prominence, action and fun. This will be inspiring, challenging, encouraging and enthusing. Two Fire signs create drive, momentum and purpose. They are sensual and sexual, with strong urges. Both are impetuous, restless and inquisitive and in continual pursuit of independence and new ground, seeking to overcome barriers and set new standards. This is a partnership that can express a potent rebellious and revolutionary spirit, striving for change and high ideals. A positive focus is a must – career, family, children or good causes. Love of influence and a thirst for importance energizes the relationship to achieve and succeed, but there is the chance of conflict, argument, competition and strong emotions.

Make some space for personal needs and development and take turns playing centre stage. It's important to remember to air sensitive feelings well before either needs to exert their will or control the relationship. There is a need to let off steam and vent tensions.

This strong combination demands respect and care but keeps both youthful, active and fresh. It will never be dull. The monthly Moon phases are felt particularly strongly, creating regular cycles of helpful/challenging influences. Agree to direct energy to the outer world and have fun doing it.

Aries and Taurus (Fire and Earth)

A potent, emotive and expressive partnership. A will to lead is symptomatic of Aries' approach and can invigorate the relationship if they remember to allow the gentle, nurturing, easy-going Taurus to tone them down and settle their restless spirit. A more mellow pace gives Aries a chance to direct their lust for life into fruitful, practical efforts which build security and stability for the relationship – something Taurus needs and likes to engineer.

Intimately, it can be an interesting mix of strong passions, tactile sensuality and heady sexuality. Both have feelings that are sensitive, but expressed differently, with Aries more open and Taurus more reserved. Aries should try to read between the lines and, to stimulate passion, offer something that pleases Taurus' love of beauty and fine things.

Aries likes attention and expects total support, and should be patient when Taurus seems a little restrained. The sober, practical Taurus is not trying to hold them back, but is just being cautious, sensible and thinking of all the possibilities. Aries should not let their stubbornness frustrate them or be too affected by their periodic moodiness. And it's better for Taurus to let the primal Aries energy enliven them and get them out of any rut they may be stuck in.

Aries/Taurus is an interesting mix of energies with a bit of push/pull that keeps feelings vigorous and alive. But be ready for a touch of ram meets bull along the way.

Aries and Gemini (Fire and Air)

High energy, exhilarating, manic, inspired, creative, original and motivational – Fire and Air combine to fuel a passionate, sometimes frenetic relationship. Regular verbal communication is essential and keeps things on track. Aries needs to use tact and flexibility, not force or will, when dealing with Gemini's sensitivities and changeability. Both partners are capable of impulsive, impetuous action, which is good for creativity and expression, but also potentially disruptive, chaotic or destabilizing. There is a slight tendency to wild, adventurous and thrill-seeking expressions in various areas of life. This is an intense relationship that can be positive and productive if both partners work at being cool and a bit detached, and look for solid ground. Be mindful to curb restless tendencies with regular goal-setting.

Intimately, this is a whirlwind of hit or miss sensuality, depending on the mood. When it's right, it's perfect; when wrong, it's frustrating with pent-up nervous energies seeking release. Both are sensual, but delicate Gemini can be as fickle as they are flirty, which, combined with Aries' intensity, can result in exhilaration or tempest. Both need and deserve each other's more delicate approach – which can take time and practice.

However, this is a lively, vivacious partnership that is uplifting, changeable and never boring, especially if both partners take the time to talk, listen and synchronize their speed and approach. Aries needs to know when to relax, pull back and let Gemini 'fly'. This is best done by remembering their own love of freedom. The trick for Aries is to develop the emotional lightness of touch that a Gemini Moon expects and to be ready for unexpected course changes. Also, Aries should remember that although Gemini loves people and new experiences, this does not necessarily invalidate Aries' centre-stage role.

Aries and Cancer (Fire and Water)

A partnership that lets Aries play a chivalrous, supportive and dynamic leadership role, as long as they remember that the grounded, deep and strongly emotive nature of Cancer sets the agenda for mutual well-being and emotional security. Getting this right can take some effort, but be immensely rewarding. Aries should express their more regal nature in a thoughtful, considerate and respectful manner that doesn't make the Cancer Moon feel as though a charging knight has breached their sanctuary. A little effort here, and a little time, will earn the Cancer Moon's trust and give Aries the chance to bask in the limelight at centre stage. Cancer can then let their natural affection, nurturing and support flow unrestricted to Aries, which in turn will give them a real boost in confidence and purpose.

Aries needs to remember that Cancer has a long emotional memory – a generally foreign concept to the Aries Moon – and should avoid intense emotional confrontations that appear threatening. While this may be just the Aries vigour, and in time Cancer will forgive, they won't easily forget, which can make the Aries Moon self-conscious and, in some cases, unnecessarily rebellious or negative.

At best, this can be a good partnership that is spirited and full of variety. The intuitive, protective side of Cancer brings out the best in Aries, but can also stifle their more primitive side, and this will need some effort to resolve now and then. Aries' energy is positive for Cancer, giving just the right jolt to shock them out of their sometimes moody self-absorption. Both signs are strong and can grow with the right amount of respect, space and acceptance of each other's different qualities.

Aries and Leo (Fire and Fire)

Proud, energetic, strong, emotional and passionate – there is a natural connection between these Moon signs, as long as they both want a relationship that is emotionally intense, grand and regal. Inspiring, creative, supportive and respectfully challenging – the two bring out the best in each other. It is a generally easy exchange, with an emotional fluidity that recognizes the best and the worst in each other. Dignity is the byword here, with both needing the right amount of respect – deference, if you will – although Aries will at times have to give way to their Leo Fire sign. This can create discord – two strong, emotional and proud characters vying for importance – so it's best to enjoy the joust and agree that both win in the end.

At times, Aries may be challenged and even feel upstaged by Leo's magnanimity and emotional grandeur. One thing is certain: both signs can degrade to sulking if feelings are hurt. The wise Leo will give way to the more impetuous Aries and exert a measure of confident warm-hearted influence by diplomatically guiding and encouraging. It's not that difficult to see the Leo in Aries.

Intimately, the combination is pleasant and passionate, and there is a natural sympathy between the two signs that can make romance grand, lofty and uplifting. A natural excitement, energy and drive will give the couple an attractive aura that sets them apart from the crowd. If the two can live with the cyclical need to jockey for position, which to them is a pleasant sport in itself, then they can have an active, sociable and mutually compatible affair.

Aries and Virgo (Fire and Earth)

Two different styles of emotional energy combine here to create a vivid contrast that, if managed well, can make an enlivening relationship. The outgoing, ebullient Aries may, however, find it hard to understand the restrictive tendency in prudent, reserved and emotionally cautious Virgo. This is just Virgo's careful nature not wanting to 'jump in' without looking. Simply said, Virgo puts the head before the heart, and Aries the heart before the head. Aries may feel that Virgo is too critical, inflexible or analytical, which can trigger Aries' fear of restriction or, worse, their regal ego, causing them to put their foot down – not a wise thing to do with a Virgo Moon, who will easily rise above an emotional rant and thus reinforce the struggle for dominance. Aries can never win by exerting their will over Virgo.

This may also express itself in intimate matters, with the Aries *primitif* being too gregarious for the more discriminating Virgo. If Aries chivalrously takes the lead and expresses their passions more discreetly, though, Virgo will gradually feel safe in the relationship and will respond. Aries should remember that Virgo places an importance on style and any rebuke is not as personal as it seems. The resolution of this kind of struggle can help both partners build an understanding of what works for them, so give it time.

Virgo seeks a personal standard of refinement, whereas Aries tends to be happy with the adventure of seeking. Shared interests will be important in this partnership and verbal communication will be necessary to create understanding and acceptance. Aries will need to invest time and patience to make it work. The challenge for Aries/Virgo is to balance contrasting styles of outgoing vs reserved, easy acceptance vs critical inspection, breaking barriers vs building them, lust for life vs prudish reserve. While this may be overstating the contrast, these themes will animate the relationship and give both parties a decent amount of stimulation and challenge. The key here is for both to recognize, accept and work with the strengths of their partner.

Aries and Libra (Fire and Air) ★

A perfect match. The two natures naturally complement each other, creating harmony, energy and agreeableness. Both partners appreciate the qualities of the other: Aries enjoys the sociable, flexible, accommodating, partner-centred style of Libra, who in turn is inspired, uplifted, motivated and reassured by Aries' sense of purpose and confidence. Libra doesn't mind Aries' strong emotional personality or desire for influence, and the active but flexible Libra Air sign fuels the restless, impulsive Aries while helping to channel their energies productively into efforts that support the partnership. The Libran humour loves the jocular, independent Aries, who in turn loves the chance to play to the Libran audience.

Romance and sex are bolstered by an emotional harmony that enhances loving exchange. It's passionate, feeling, tactile, sensual and lively, yet tender and sympathetic. Each offers the other the right amount of challenge without triggering defence mechanisms or insecurities.

Communication is generally fluid and the ease of emotional relating gives a solid base on which to build a relationship. Libra is a good buffer or absorber of the Aries intensity and can offer the respect Aries needs, while being free to question their direction and purpose. Aries' drive gives the Libra Moon a chance to rise above indecision and find direction. Both signs have a youthful, fun-loving spirit. The combination brings a natural empathy and a mutually intuitive sense of emotional needs and wants. Both partners will feel comfortable with fulfilling the other's needs.

Aries and Scorpio (Fire and Water)

Both signs are ruled by Mars, but have very different expressions. The vigorous Aries, outward-looking, adventurous and impulsive meets the more reserved, brooding and intense Scorpio. One can feed the other, but this requires awareness and some tact.

The Scorpio Moon may be uncomfortable with the gregarious, emotional Aries and may at first feel some measure of challenge, competition or uncertainty. Aries in turn may feel out their depth in understanding the delicate, mysterious emotions of Scorpio. Both need to play centre stage, but their styles are very different, with Aries needing open recognition and energy and Scorpio wanting the same attention, but in a more subtle, less obvious, even more silent fashion. Scorpio will revel in the nuances, whereas Aries will be bolder. This can work, but it can also trigger strong emotions and intense exchanges that take time and energy from each.

Of the two, Scorpio has the best chance of being patient and understanding, but Aries should never take this for granted, as it will pinch Scorpio's sensitive and sometimes vindictive nature. Both signs can be self-absorbed and need to be thoughtful about reassuring and giving to their partner. Scorpio's possessiveness can inspire Aries, but not if they feel it impinges on their freedom or free will. Both need space but also togetherness. There is also a martial wild side in both, which can trigger licentiousness, overindulgence or a tendency to go to extremes. All in all, it's a high-energy, transformative and deeply passionate relationship.

Aries and Sagittarius (Fire and Fire)

A good combination that gives both partners the chance to express their passions, energy, drive and commitment while developing a directed, focused and sensible emotional exchange. Sagittarius brings a maturity to the fiery Aries nature and lends a sense of vision and wisdom without jeopardizing the free-wheeling, ambitious side of Aries. There is a strong similarity between the two which encourages creativity, originality and a kind of philosophical understanding and acceptance of each other and of life.

There are also good chances for conflict and strong emotions, but a resolution is likely to be easily reached and each partner will have the chance to grow and learn from the challenge. Aries is quicker off the mark than the more prudent Fire sign Sagittarius, but both can stimulate, enliven and encourage each other, especially as both have an adventurous spirit and a lust for advancing in life.

Humour, joviality and practical jokes will all come easily. Open, frank Sagittarius is just what Aries needs and Aries is able to reply to any challenge in kind. Aries can benefit from Sagittarius' wisdom, while Sagittarius likes the Aries drive and youthful spirit.

Romantically, this is a good combination, with a generous amount of mutual passion, sensuality and tenderness. Sagittarius is more moody than Aries and may at times brood or need space, which Aries should not take as a rejection and in time may consider as an opportunity to learn something of the rich inner world of their partner.

Both are inspired by, and active in, good causes and together they are a potent mix of energy, vigour and strong principled feelings. All things being equal, they will bring out the best in each other.

Aries and Capricorn (Fire and Earth)

Two different natures combine to challenge and stimulate through opposition. The steady, cautious, practical Capricorn can be too sober for vivacious and emotional Aries, but understanding and a conscious agreement to direct mutual energies and emotions towards practical, tangible goals can counter this. This brings both styles of being into a complementary endgame, giving Aries a focus for their drive and desires and Capricorn reassurance that there is value for effort.

Conflicts can arise, however, especially when dominating Aries tries to lead and Capricorn stubbornly refuses to submit. One is the ram and the other the goat of the zodiac, so head-to-heads are inevitable. It can be easy for the more reserved Capricorn to dampen the Aries' *joie de vivre* with their characteristic emotional inhibition. Aries needs to coax Capricorn into action by offering support and a bit of positive thinking. A sense of working together, side by side, is an effective way for Aries to express their drive and the more timid Capricorn to put their strength behind the cause. In this, responsible Capricorn does need to avoid taking on too much in an effort to please and should remember that Aries is a loyal and dedicated partner.

Emotions here can blow hot and cold, and both partners can get carried away one moment and feel uncertain the next. Getting the timing right is important and the style of approach can help. In time, romance can be solid and steady and the pair can feed each other's respective needs. But this can only happen when they celebrate the differences between them as being more valuable than the similarities.

Aries and Aquarius (Fire and Air)

A workable, agreeable relationship that offers mutual stimulation, excitement and emotional opportunity. Aries can express their energy without too much concern, as Aquarius will be fed and enthused by their drive. Aquarius is likely to have all the right channels to direct the Aries energy – even the more revolutionary or anarchistic tendencies. Aquarius thinks big and is involved in causes and with an Aries has the right partner to work at important social issues.

There can be conflicts, though, especially when Aquarius is busy with friends, networks and causes and appears too aloof or preoccupied to acknowledge Aries' emotional needs. It is helpful that both tend towards optimism, live active social lives and love to explore new ideas. Both are adventurous, although Aries may not be as well prepared in setting off on their discoveries as their partner.

Intimacy is important to both, but Aries will need to explore the more subtle side of Aquarius to understand their undulating and enigmatic sensual moods. When romantically in synch, there will be passion, excitement and fun at intimate times. The Aries Moon may be rebuffed if they express themselves too forcefully, however – while Aquarius is an inspired sign, it is less impulsive or impetuous than Aries.

Aries enjoys Aquarius' need for company, but in order to feel unfettered should break away now and then to explore new territory alone. Aries tends to a more openly emotional nature, whereas Aquarius can be more of an ideas person, a little cool and at times distant. But the combination does work if there is a sharing of interests, moods and ambitions – as both signs are ambitious.

Aries and Pisces (Fire and Water)

Harmony through diversity here, with the passionate Aries mingling with the shy, retiring and deep Pisces. Pisces Moons are good partners for Aries due to their passive, sympathetic, agreeable nature, which gives Aries' will to dominate free rein. Pisces needs to remember to stand up and be counted now and then, though, otherwise potent Aries can be the only driver, while Pisces recedes into the background. Aries needs to celebrate their Pisces partner, get them centre stage now and then (difficult for a Pisces Moon) and let them know how important they are.

The primal Aries energy motivates and encourages, which is what Pisces needs to get them out of their dreamy, emotional passivity. In turn, Pisces should try to introduce Aries to their inner world, which will be a wonder for Aries and help them relax and find a measure of emotional serenity. Mysterious, spiritual or occult Pisces subjects will also inspire Aries.

Aries benefits from Pisces' intuition, wisdom and guidance, but needs to remember to not run roughshod in their desire to lead. It takes time to understand the deep Pisces Moon who will rebel in the face of any excessive show of force.

Both are actually rebels, but Pisces is more secretive and stealthy in their anarchy than Aries. Both love parties and enjoy being with people, although on the surface Aries will lead the way with this. Pisces is hardly impetuous and impulsive, which can sometimes restrict Aries' sense of drive and freedom.

In romantic affairs, the passion of Aries will suit Pisces, who will love the chance to introduce Aries to a deeper understanding of the meaning of love and love-making. If there is a suitable setting with music, soft lights, luxury and even a bit of poetry, both will be assured of tender passion.

Taurus and...

Taurus (Earth and Earth)

Venus meets Venus in this partnership, creating strong affections, pronounced sensuality and heightened sensitivity. This can be quite a compatible combination that is naturally romantic and erotic. A love of life's refinements makes the couple lovers of truth and beauty and lends a strong sense of enjoyment to the affair, while an acquisitive urge helps put the focus on practical, material possessions, creature comforts and general well-being.

Both are constant and loyal, and are emotionally deep – ironically, in contrast to their material inclinations. Both know the importance of nurturing a love and have a fundamental need to create a secure, tranquil home environment.

When there is agreement, the emotional relationship is easy, sweet and helpful. When conflict arises, both can show a stubbornness that is difficult to back down from – so someone, somehow, will have to learn to let go first. Take turns.

Extra effort needs to be made to explore the more subtle side of life, otherwise the partnership can become claustrophobic or limited by the couple's own sense of material well-being and this will cause both partners to seek something more exciting, even forbidden, in order to get close to life's mysteries. It's best if this is done in tandem.

Expect that lunar phases will have some effect on the harmony of the relationship. In particular, when one feels stress, it's quite likely the other does as well. This will require a conscious recognition and effort to exercise the more patient, stable and firm qualities of the Taurus Moon.

Taurus and Gemini (Earth and Air)

A stimulating combination that blends the constancy of Taurus with the variability of Gemini. This meeting of opposites – Taurus' steady, practical and grounded reliability and Gemini's capricious, flighty, nervous restlessness – can make a complementary partnership. The firmly-rooted Taurus gives Gemini a pivot, a resting-point and the necessary stability to seek out and explore the new and unusual. Conversely, the creative, inspired and complicated Gemini can spice up the sometimes drab dependability of the Taurus Moon.

Gemini keeps things fresh, humorous and prankish, which appeals to the Venusian Taurus who, like Gemini, is sociable, fun-loving and fond of luxury and privilege. Taurus may gripe now and then about Gemini's unpredictable side – and for good reason, as it knows that someone has to rein Gemini in – but secretly Taurus would greatly miss their partner's capricious and enlivening spirit.

Both are moody in their own unique way. Taurus can be brooding, stubborn and resistant, whereas Gemini's feelings are feather-light, quixotic and often inexplicable. When they are both irritable, they should retire to their separate corners. This will help keep things fresh, which is necessary because each has a very different emotional nature. It is likely that Taurus will be the partner who needs to exercise a more proactive understanding, which is not usually a problem because their petulant moments are less frequent, though often longer-lasting than those of the mercurial Gemini. With their tranquil, self-satisfied view of life, Taurus Moon will be a calming influence on the vacillating disquiet of Gemini. This helps Gemini sift through their multifaceted interests to focus on the issues that really matter, but it can also frustrate Gemini when Taurus is inflexible or 'too practical'.

Venus and Mercury are creative and artistic, and the Taurus/ Gemini combination gives both partners a good outlet for enjoying music, art and other mentally stimulating pursuits. It also suggests that in romantic matters there is a good level of understanding, so expect sensitivity, tenderness, thoughtfulness and lots of caring gestures. The ethereal quality to the Gemini sexuality can leave Taurus disoriented at times, but a lot of positive exchange is possible in this partnership.

Taurus and Cancer (Earth and Water)

There are common natures and interests with these two sensitive, practical, domestic signs. It will be rare to find anything out of place, ill planned or hastily conceived with this combination, especially as both are very security-conscious and plan ahead for all contingencies. Cancer feels cosy with stable Taurus and together they can create a pleasant, sensual and satisfying life. Once Taurus passes the test and is admitted into the Cancer shell, they can both decorate their chambers to their hearts' content and enjoy each other's private company and affections.

Together they make an indomitable pair, knowing just what they want and how to get it, and feeling certain about what's right. The downside may be smugness or overconfidence, but the insecure qualities of Cancer will help to balance this out.

In the best case, the sensitive, intuitive Cancer, who tends to hypersensitivity and even psychic inclinations, will satisfy Taurus' need for something other than the predictable day-to-day. Both are creative and have artistic tendencies, but are also moody, melancholic and inward-dwelling. Cancer benefits from Taurus' foresight, which helps wake them from their tendency to dreamy, unconscious reveries.

This is a highly emotional relationship, full of deep feelings, sensitivities and yearnings. There is a lot of mutual expectation here – each must live up to the high standards of the other. Failing to do so can cause frustration, though it is likely that discord will be triggered by practical issues (money, etc.), rather than by inconsiderate behaviour. This is also a deeply romantic combination that loves all things Valentine. Pronounced sensual and sexual expectations will keep both partners active and satisfied.

Taurus and Leo (Earth and Fire)

The proud, fiery, emotive and expressive Leo Moon contrasts with the slightly more retiring but no less proud Taurus. Two such strong emotional natures need mutual respect to bring out the best in each. A subtle underlying friction will have a productive effect by creating cycles of challenge and adjustment, difficulty and resolution that polish both partners and enhance their mutual strengths.

When things are working harmoniously, both are mutually strengthened especially with the confident, generous Leo Moon emboldening its more reserved Taurus partner. However, when Taurus has one of its moody moments, Leo's direct approach can seem intrusive or irritating. If Taurus says as much, Leo's sensitive feelings will be easily hurt. At times like these Leo needs to take a more diplomatic, laid back attitude which will help sooth the troubled Taurus heart, giving it the time it needs to mend on its own. This approach will help steer the relationship clear of unnecessary complications.

When it does work, though, it works well, with the practical view of Taurus and the valiant, passionate energy of Leo combining to good effect. Leo enjoys a bit of aggrandizement, ego-boosting and gentle stroking from their partner, whereas the Taurus Moon is more understated, tranquil, less demonstrative, but both enjoy the good life and may stimulate the hedonistic in each other. Taurus is more 'feminine' and Leo more 'masculine' in spirit, regardless of gender, and this clue can help any Taurus/Leo partnership.

In romantic affairs, both express their love of beauty, loyalty and respect. Taurus is sensual and Leo passionate. Leo enjoys feeling that their partner comes to them, and is both open and warm-hearted in receiving the affections of their lover.

Some trial and effort will be needed to fit all the pieces of the Taurus/Leo puzzle. But when they fit, they make good partners, stimulating just the right strengths in each other.

Taurus and Virgo (Earth and Earth)

Stable, reliable, solid and predictable – both share similar values and admire level-headed thinking and practicality. So they naturally understand each other, although there are some significant differences. Virgo tends to be led by the head and, although secretly quite emotional, likes to think that they are well in control of their emotions. Needless to say, this in itself can create inner conflict, but when it comes to relationships, Virgo may try and extend this control to their partner. So balance is needed here. Taurus, in contrast, is more easy-going, sensitive, almost fluid, which doesn't always fit well with the analytical, critical side of Virgo. In this regard, a bridge is needed, an agreement that Taurus' feelings are accepted at face value and not dissected. And maybe Taurus will indulge the Virgo need to know and understand.

Taurus likes the luxuries of life, whereas Virgo can prefer simplicity, sometimes to the point of austerity. When Virgo likes the finer things they really are finer, because they have an eye for detail that is the envy of any connoisseur.

Taurus is sensual and tactile and enjoys close, comfortable relationships. Virgo needs this kind of relationship to bring out their best qualities, but can at first appear almost cool when it comes to intimate relations. Happily, Taurus usually understands this and can patiently earn a place in the Virgo heart with refined manners, kind gestures and gentle overtures. Virgo is definitely a sign that needs courting, often in the 'old-fashioned' way. Once an intimate relationship is established and mutual trust exists, both partners can grow in affection and loyalty to each other and this gives Virgo the chance to offer a special quality of love that puts the needs of Taurus before their own. A nice touch, really.

Taurus and Libra (Earth and Air)

Both signs are ruled by Venus and thus they share a number of traits, including sociability, a friendly demeanour, a thoughtful and caring nature and a generally gentle approach to relationships. But their dissimilarities can either challenge or deepen their relationship.

Libra's indecisiveness and periodic lack of direction are just the opposite of Taurus' firm grip on reality. Libra needs clear goals and Taurus can provide them, or at least offer a well-defined pathway for finding them. Conversely, Libra offers Taurus the lightness of touch, flexibility and happy silliness to help free Taurus from being too rooted in boring predictability. Open communication is needed for this exchange to work, however, otherwise Libra can feel that the solid Taurus is judging them or, worse, causing self-doubt or insecurity – both of which come too easily to the Libra Moon. This is troublesome to Libra, who puts great value on their relationships, to the point where they can become overly dependent on their partner. Taurus can then feel that Libra lacks a fluid approach and seems competitive, resistant or standoffish. Talking helps here, as do reassuring gestures that put each other at ease.

When there is conflict, both can be sulky and brooding, and while Taurus is maybe the more grounded, flexible Libra, whose purpose is harmony in relationships, will probably make the first gesture for reconciliation. Taurus loves truth and beauty and Libra will have to work at sharing their real feelings honestly, not holding back or hoping that any problem will just disappear.

Libra is highly romantic, with strong desires and yearnings. If comfortable with their Taurus partner, they will demonstrate their deep longing with easy and open affection. Like Taurus, they are natural pleasure-seekers and intimacy between the two can bring passion, depth of feeling and real bonding.

Taurus and Scorpio (Earth and Water) ★

A mystical and harmonious combination that can blend material and spiritual ideals for mutual well-being. Taurus and Scorpio are ideally suited to each other and although very different, complement each other. Taurus is confident and grounded and able to remain fixed while Scorpio experiences a wide range of changing emotions that are at once sweet, affectionate, tempestuous, enigmatic and intense. The mystery of Scorpio captivates, almost mesmerizes Taurus, drawing them into the deeper, secret recesses of their emotional being. Taurus likes this because it is the ideal use of their practicality and sober disposition. It means that the material abilities of Taurus have a higher service to render via the Scorpio relationship.

This deep combination brings out the best in both partners. Taurus will not take it too seriously when Scorpio is moody or pinching – in fact it has an erotic aspect for them, almost like a love bite. Taurus can absorb the intensity of Scorpio and Scorpio can celebrate the gravity of Taurus – especially as Scorpio is not a frivolous spirit. Soberness aside, Scorpio appreciates Taurus because they share a sensual, pleasure-seeking nature. Taurus' moods seem trivial compared with the depth and range of emotions experienced by the Scorpio Moon. Taurus is in awe of this and captivated by it, and, while knowing it's inaccessible, would love to somehow understand it, if not experience it.

In short, they nurture each other through opposites, while enhancing the better parts of their natures. Emotions can run high and when it comes to conflict, both are capable of throwing their whole being into the exchange. But for a well-established Taurus/Scorpio relationship, this is usually just a prelude to more affectionate dealings.

Taurus and Sagittarius (Earth and Fire)

Strong emotional natures that combine both harmonious and challenging traits offer this partnership a chance for growth through acceptance, openness and understanding. Both signs are personable, friendly and generous. They have a good sense of humour and enjoy life's pleasures, especially good company and free expression. Sagittarius offers Taurus a philosophical partner who inclines to the pursuit of wisdom, which deepens and satisfies Taurus' need for growth. Both are creative, though Sagittarius thrives on bursts of inspiration and vision, driven by a rich inner being that, while attractive to Taurus, is difficult for them to fully comprehend.

Freedom is a must for Sagittarius, so much so that they can forfeit other gains and privileges if it is threatened. Tensions can arise when the more staid, cautious Taurus presents practical limits which to Sagittarius are mere troublesome details. When there is agreement, however, the chancellor Taurus can work well with the warrior-saint in Sagittarius – but they both must be conscious of the goal and take time to build that agreement.

There is an element of wisdom in both signs – in Taurus a wisdom of life in the 'real world' and in Sagittarius an 'other-worldly' wisdom. The trick is to be aware that in truth they are but two aspects of one wisdom. This will help both partners overcome any sense of challenge, worry or fear, for example when Sagittarius speaks their mind openly and forcefully, causing their opinions to appear as a threat when they're not, or when Taurus is intractable or withholds their affections or appreciation for the proud Sagittarius. Most importantly, both will need to find productive ways to channel any competitive moods that arise.

Both are passionate in romance. Fiery Sagittarius will make the attempt to lead the way (regardless of gender), seeking to set the standards, quicken the pace and establish the goals. Taurus can win them over with a touch of deference. Both are caring, sensitive and strong signs with big hearts and good intentions. Both can grow through the relationship and learn to appreciate very different points of view.

Taurus and Capricorn (Earth and Earth)

A natural combination that fosters material growth and prosperity due to mutual interests in material well-being, financial success and a desire to measure up to the highest standards. The sensible

Taurus inspires the hard-working, responsible Capricorn and validates their practical values. Capricorn is, however, more reserved, austere and withdrawn. Taurus will be the more sociable, with Capricorn querying the value of time spent 'unproductively' in 'idle socializing'. So, the easy-going Taurus could find the more sober Capricorn restrictive or deflating, but in truth Capricorn needs the emotional lift that Taurus can provide. This helps open up the fun sides of both characters and deepens the relationship.

Both are acquisitive and measure success, even emotional success, at least in part, with a material yardstick. Capricorn leads the way with this and is usually work- or career-fixated. Taurus will appreciate this up to a point and will then cry out for the more subtle side of life.

There can be some challenges with romance, but with a bit of time and effort a strong common bond can be established. Taurus needs patience with Capricorn's inhibited and introverted emotions. The feelings are there, you just have to dig to find the treasure. When you do and can get Capricorn to open up, there is a great heaving sigh of relief and strong gratitude that you have lifted a burden from them. The only problem is their tendency to bury again, so be ready for treasure-hunting from time to time.

In general, Taurus can help Capricorn build confidence and Capricorn can validate Taurus' sensitive, caring nature. The big challenge is to avoid getting into a rut, succumbing to pensive moods and stifling the relationship with too much predictability. From time to time each partner needs to break the mould and surprise the other. This will keep things fresh, fun and intimate.

Taurus and Aquarius (Earth and Air)

A good combination characterized by agreement, mutual understanding, common interests and an easy exchange of ideas and emotions. The broad concerns and interests of Aquarius help broaden Taurus' horizons, with both partners stimulated by an exchange of ideas. Taurus helps Aquarius realize their dreams, with practical ideas on how to bring visions into concrete reality.

Aquarius in turn gives Taurus a larger outlet for expressing their love of truth and principles. The caring and humanitarian concerns of both are accentuated in the partnership.

Taurus offers a good basis for the sociable Aquarius and knows how to help them build lasting foundations for the future. Both have high hopes, but Aquarius reaches for the stars. This appeals to Taurus, who may be too down-to-earth to reach that high, but who is inspired by the gesture itself. It's certain that Aquarius will want to pioneer new territory, which will keep the relationship fresh and dynamic. In return, Taurus can help keep Aquarius on the ground and balanced.

Romantically, both partners are able to express affection and deeper emotions, but they need to be careful not to drift apart in the convenience of a well-established relationship, with Aquarius pondering lofty ideals and Taurus busy with mundane concerns.

The tranquil, self-satisfied nature of Taurus complements the mystical Aquarius and stimulates a potent love that is as uplifting as it is sensual. Intimate connection is likely to open new levels of experience for both partners, rounding them and deepening their understanding of nature, life and themselves.

Taurus and Pisces (Earth and Water)

Sensual, stimulating, exploratory, revealing and pleasing – each of these Moon signs offers the other the chance to balance their nature. Pisces gives Taurus an introduction into the ethereal world of dreams, feelings, intuition and fantasy, whereas Taurus offers Pisces a chance to connect now and then with what is happening in so-called 'reality'.

The Pisces experience may appear to be too much for the Taurus Moon, but deep down is really just what they are yearning for. Flexible, yielding, agreeable Pisces flows with the tide and bends with the wind – something that is not so easy for the fixed, and sometimes stubborn, Taurus, who can be frustrated when they fail to understand just how ethereal Pisces can be. Soon enough Taurus will find that no amount of remonstration will change the Pisces Moon, it is really a matter of loving them for who they are and, if Taurus is smart, agreeing to take that magical mystery ride that's on offer.

Sexually, there is compatibility, with both partners having a pronounced sensuality. Both are sensitive, but Pisces introduces Taurus to a new level of tenderness and feeling. Indeed, both tend to be quite tactile. Both love music, poetry and art, and they stimulate each other's imagination. Taurus may be surprised by the Pisces openness and agreeableness, especially when it comes to sensual issues.

In many ways this is a good partnership, especially when there is a balanced exchange of natures and abilities, with Taurus helping to ground Pisces, who in turn helps Taurus discover new levels of inner experience and meaning in life and love.

Gemini and...

Gemini (Air and Air)

A busy, frenetic, hectic and sometimes complicated partnership. Gemini is symbolized by twins and the combination of two Gemini Moons may figuratively equate to four emotional people!

There are pluses and minuses in the partnership. On one hand it has a sociable, active, creative and inspired nature. When both are feeling good the energy runs high and the relationship overflows with good fun, wacky and original behaviour and a flood of conversation and good ideas. The attitude of both partners is similar but frequently changeable, and the proximity of another Gemini Moon can quicken the pace of inconstancy, instability and unpredictability. Gemini is a restless, adventurous sign that is compulsively driven by their curiosity. So while Gemini symbolizes communication, there is the risk that when lots of talking is going on, no one is really listening, especially as Geminis tend to think they know what the other person is going to say before they say it and try to lead the conversation to where they think it's going – or where they want it to go. It's a three-dimensional, verbal chessboard that can get quite confusing.

The frequency of change and susceptibility to concurrent lunar influences means there will be great highs and some troublesome lows. When things get tetchy and moods conflict, both should retire to their private space and let tensions pass.

Romantically, it can be very interesting, especially as both have similar natures, heightened sensitivities and a quick, reactive nature. When intimacy works, it is wonderfully uplifting and satisfying and can be very sensual and scintillating, but due to the potential for sudden shifts of mood, is often accompanied by surprises, distractions or strong emotional exchanges.

This can be an interesting, satisfying partnership if both feel they can do without a stabilizing influence and want to plumb the depths of the Gemini nature.

Gemini and Cancer (Air and Water)

Strong winds make turbulent seas and this combination brings adventure, excitement and a few challenges along the way. They are neighbouring signs and are sensitive to lunar phases that touch both Moons simultaneously, creating cycles of choppy waters and smooth sailing. On the whole, they complement each other well, but some adjustment will be needed as the relationship grows.

Cancer loves stability, constancy and reliability, so the Gemini changeability and flighty emotions can rub them up the wrong way. Cancer needs to open up to their Gemini partner and see the humour and entertainment they provide. In turn, Gemini needs to make a conscious effort to let their Cancer partner know how much they appreciate their devotion and nurturing. This comes quite naturally for them, but they do need to make the effort and not just 'think' they have told them – something easily done for Gemini.

However, Gemini is sure to keep Cancer fresh, young and active, which for the most part they appreciate. Common goals will help reassure Cancer, keep Gemini focused and solidify the relationship on a practical basis.

Romantically, Gemini's flirtatious, sensual nature helps draw the emotional Cancer out, and the intimate exchanges can be quite deep, easy and fun. Gemini needs to take care with Cancer's long emotional memory, though, and make sure that any slights or hurts are dealt with not just quickly but thoroughly, otherwise it can hamper the smooth growth of the partnership.

Cancer can help Gemini direct their multifaceted emotional and mental energies, and should not be too concerned if Gemini seems distracted or inattentive. If they repeat themselves a couple of times the message should get through. In turn, Gemini can ease Cancer's insecurity and periodic mood swings by reaching out and reassuring them that everything is OK. Gemini should also try to heed Cancer's premonitions and deep insight, especially as Gemini tends to gloss over things.

Ultimately, this is a good match of different natures that keeps both parties happy with regular communication and private time centred on the cosiness of the home and the mutual security of the relationship.

Gemini and Leo (Air and Fire)

A positive, constructive tension helps both partners direct their emotions productively, accompanied by energy, enthusiasm, a touch of friction and sparkly debates. They are mutually supportive, tend to relate easily and understand each other's emotional framework. They can also work effectively with the more challenging sides of their respective natures.

Leo enjoys mercurial Gemini, especially their jesting, lively spirit. Leo also likes the flirty, sensual and proactive side of Gemini, as it appeals to the Leo sense of playing centre stage. The multitude of thoughts, ideas, attitudes and feelings challenges Leo and gives fodder for debate and stimulation for conversation and romance.

Leo even likes the 'frailer' and slightly dependent moods of Gemini, and feels able to play an important role in protecting their valued partner (responsible Leo is the zodiac king). So Leo will offer counsel and direct the spontaneous energy and moods of Gemini, even though they will sometimes be rebuffed, as Gemini regularly needs space and Leo can be a bit emotionally overbearing at times.

Nevertheless, the exchange between these two zodiac signs creates strong desires and passions, mixing sensual, ethereally seductive Gemini with hot, emotive, gregarious Leo. Sparks do fly with intimate exchanges, which are generally satisfying.

Leo needs to curb any tendency to jealousy, especially regarding Gemini's wanderlust and sociability. Otherwise there is the risk of pushing Gemini away, which is very easy to do with restless Gemini. On balance, though, there is a good exchange of compatible emotional natures.

Gemini and Virgo (Air and Earth)

Here the jester meets the court mandarin in a combination that spans the range of mercurial symbolism. This is a celebration of wit, energy, intellect, creativity and verbal bantering, with a swirl of complementary and contradictory emotional characters. Expect amusement, pyrotechnics and mutual growth.

While very different in substance, these signs are two states of Mercury and secretly, hermetically, spy themselves in each other. So while Gemini jests, it does so with the hidden seriousness of Virgo, and while Virgo pedantically analyses, it does so with a good measure of mocking self-effacement. This is a circus of nuance and *double entendres*, able to keep both partners and bystanders entertained and enlivened.

Gemini's seductive caprice is just the medicine for Virgo's cool, decorous sense of romance, which in turn grounds Terpsichorean Gemini. Gemini is able to penetrate the prudery of Virgo, as though cleverly winking acknowledgement of Virgo's deeply amorous emotional nature that pines to break free – but of course only to the right lover. Few Moon signs can pull this off and even Gemini will sometimes ham it up too much for Virgo's comfort. But at least both will enjoy the act, laughing about it in their own way.

Virgo can stimulate Gemini but also frustrate them with a taciturn or controlling mood. While Virgo likes to keep things simple and in place, Gemini will splay their energies, creating an emotional clutter that urges Virgo to get out their duster to tidy up the mess. The ebb and flow of this drama is guaranteed to keep both partners on their feet, stimulated and happy to celebrate the paradox of their incompatibly compatible natures.

Gemini and Libra (Air and Air)

This is a creative combination that is a catalyst for mutual self-expression and personal progress. Like meets like with a difference here, and the improvisational Gemini is a perfect complement to the light-footed Libra, with both enjoying a high sociability quotient. Bells will ring at their first meeting and the similarity of emotional character will be immediately conveyed to each other. It can get the pulse running, especially as there are many common outward interests. Both signs represent duality – Gemini with their twins, Libra with the two sides of their scales. While Gemini tends to bounce back and forth from one to the other, at least Libra has a fulcrum – which in this partnership is the place to operate from. The test is to keep things in balance.

Communication flows smoothly and it is likely that there is a strong, subtle, almost psychic, link between the two. There are challenges, such as Libra's need for dependability contrasting with their tendency to indecisiveness and Gemini's changeability. It is easy for nothing to get done, or too much of the wrong thing to get done, which can frustrate and limit both partners. The challenge here is to get grounded, create goals and keep centred. Libra may be the better of the two at doing this, but will chaff at the thought of 'making all the decisions'.

Venus and Mercury are good friends, though, and, as the lords of Libra and Gemini respectively, create a smooth path to romance. The two signs share a love of refinement and a delicate approach to intimacy, although the distracted Gemini can cause Libra some unspoken worry. Nevertheless, the exchange is sensual, tactile, exciting and satisfying and feeds the emotional well-being of both. Together they can be flirty, silly, affectionate and amusing, but will need to find common ground to keep each other from drifting and losing interest. Their careers and work ethic are a good place to begin. Once settled, this is a flowing emotional exchange.

Gemini and Scorpio (Air and Water)

Very different natures can make for strange bedfellows or a highly original, almost eccentric partnership. At first glance the light, airy, jocularity of Gemini is hardly compatible with the deep, ultra-sensitive Scorpio Moon, challenging both to find common ground and mutual acceptance.

Both are unpredictable for different reasons. Gemini loves diversity, expressive, almost theatrical changes of personality and the freedom to be whatever the mood dictates. Curiosity is the Gemini trait, which to Scorpio seems superficial for their transient fancifulness. In contrast, Scorpio's changeable moods are deeply rooted and fulsomely experienced. Gemini flies high, Scorpio dives deep – both ironically searching for the same transformative experience.

Neither may feel at ease with explaining or justifying their emotional natures to the other, but for the partnership to work there has to be common ground, possibly in this case their fascination with mysteries. It is important that they work together, rather than withdrawing to their own spaces. They need to talk to each other to create common ground and demystify themselves to each other otherwise the tension between them could be symbolized by competition, suspicion or fear. Gemini is the jester that the court spy Scorpio fears may spill the beans and reveal the state secrets. This is a hint at the underlying dynamic which both partners will no doubt recognize, but which needs further exploration to deepen the relationship.

Romantically, things are intense and tempestuous, with deep Scorpio meeting, examining and exploring the more delicate Gemini emotions which would rather be accepted than understood. Intimate relationships, assuming they reach this far, are passionate and can be inspiring. The trick for both will be to recognize the deeper emotions, common to them both, which manifest in different ways.

Gemini and Sagittarius (Air and Fire) ★

The sage can disguise himself as a jester and the jester may mockingly dress like a sage, but beneath these impersonations lie natures that are complementary and celebrate the same wisdom. In this relationship, each has the chance to stimulate the best in the other. Sagittarius is inspired by Gemini's range of expression and being, seeing it as imaginative and creative. This resonates with Sagittarius, who also has a rich inner world. In turn, Sagittarius' direct, frank and powerful emotions stimulate and enliven Gemini, who recognizes a perfect partner – kind-hearted, flexible and generous, while at the same time being strong and offering the solid foundation Gemini needs.

Both are great lovers of freedom and are able to conceive of sailing off to explore distant shores. In each other's company they ignite a sense of adventure which fuels the passions that draw them together. Sagittarius brings drive and focus, while Gemini brings inspiration and levity, which appeals to the generally jovial nature of Sagittarius. Gemini often forgets the goal, but Sagittarius will remind them. Sagittarius' forward-looking goal-setting will also temper Gemini's inconstancy and help Gemini control their restless mind and sometimes turbulent emotions.

Both are moody in their own way, with Sagittarius tending to swings of inspiration and melancholy. Gemini helps here with tender concern that lifts Sagittarius' spirits, especially as Sagittarius, like the other Fire signs, needs recognition and reassurance now and then. When they have it, Sagittarius is ready for anything, which is what Gemini loves most about them. This combination is an emotional basis for a solid, prosperous partnership.

Gemini and Capricorn (Air and Earth)

The lively spirit of Gemini is a boost to the sober Capricorn, who benefits a great deal from the partnership. Gemini can be the antidote for Capricorn woes, if they are allowed into the mountain lair to spread some good humour. In turn, Capricorn can offer Gemini the stability and emotional grounding they often need and help them direct their abundant energies to a productive goal.

The challenges here come from the contrast of natures. The pensive, reticent and reserved Capricorn may seem too serious for Gemini, who loves the freedom to be unpredictable and contradictory. Capricorn may feel that Gemini is unreliable, or even too nervous for their emotional nature, which loves rock-solid predictability and evenness of spirit. Gemini can feel that serious, steadfast Capricorn appears domineering or overbearing. Of course, this can be countered if both agree to let Gemini be affable and Capricorn be gladdened by the experience. Gemini can help Capricorn open up, express themselves and find happiness, but should accept that there are limits to this expression and should not try to make Capricorn conform to their own free-wheeling nature – even if this is attempted with the most delicate of persuasions.

This can be a good combination if each is given plenty of space for self-expression and there is not a lot of expectation of changing basic characters. Then there is a good chance for a solid relationship and a satisfying emotional and intimate life together.

Gemini and Aquarius (Air and Air)

A happy combination that enlivens both partners and emphasizes the best of their natures, which are similar and compatible. This is a socially-centred type of relationship in which both partners work harmoniously together and interact with an ever-increasing group of acquaintances and friends. The vivacious Gemini satisfies the Aquarian need for stimulation, good company, quick wit and an exchange of ideas. Mercury and Saturn rule them respectively and this gives Aquarius the ability to support, nurture and, in the right measure, guide and discipline the Gemini nature. Gemini in turn takes Aquarius back to their roots, to their more primal Air-sign nature, helping them expand their ideas and interests. Together they can broaden each other's horizons metaphorically and practically, with a fondness for travel and foreign ideas and cultures.

The combination also helps to foster learning and mutual growth, stimulating – even challenging – each other to reach higher and further in their quest for wisdom and an understanding of life. This will no doubt express itself as an interest in art, music and the finer pursuits, according to their natural tastes. Both are open and love new ideas, feeding each other with news, trivia and contrasting views of important issues. This exchange enlivens and fosters personal and professional growth for both.

As always, there are challenges, here stemming from the pair both being Air signs, which tends to keep them aloft in the realm of ideas, some small, most big, and making it difficult to be practical at times. There is, though, a creative and a spiritual element to the partnership and a mutual desire to explore philosophy and self-development. It will not be surprising to find these two involved in some way with social, religious or spiritual groups.

There is a natural and easy exchange of feelings in this partnership, although at times Aquarius may tend towards superciliousness, which can hurt the delicate feelings of Gemini. Romantically, there is a strong compatibility – in fact, both are not only hopelessly romantic by nature but also have strong fantasies that energize their romance and intimate dealings. These two Moon signs offer each other a good basis for developing a deep and meaningful relationship.

Gemini and Pisces (Air and Water)

The court messenger meets the hermit in this combination, which gives some idea of who does most of the talking. Despite the obvious differences, though, this can be a very compatible combination. Both have a lightness of being that gives them a love of finer ideals. They can encourage each other in the pursuit of wistful, fanciful notions, dreamy states of mind and delicate emotional moods. While their individual experiences of this will be different, there is a common interest that binds them to explore the more subtle sides of life hand in hand.

Agreeable, flexible Pisces can easily play along with the changeable Gemini and even enjoy their moodiness and many contradictions. The wise Pisces is able to reconcile these and value all the aspects of Gemini, which will endear them to Gemini – just what Gemini needs, really!

However, there is a chance that the combination of easy-going Pisces and the scattered Gemini can flounder in vague, directionless busyness. This can have its emotional expression as well, which deserves attention and conscious effort with goal-setting and communication to clarify feelings and attitudes. In cases where Gemini tendencies are strongly pronounced, the Pisces Moon may be disadvantaged by the self-interest which will distract Gemini from keeping the relationship balanced. Pisces will then have a hard time not only communicating what is really happening but also getting Gemini to listen and respond.

When it goes well, this relationship can be very nice and the romantic nature of both can put them into an imaginative, sensual and emotive world of their own. Pisces will prefer to be there more often than Gemini, but in general the two are amorous, caring and tender with each other.

Cancer and...

Cancer (Water and Water)

Common emotional natures give this partnership an abundance of energy, and mutual attachment and the potential for a strong bond and immense sense of togetherness. Everything will centre on the partnership and there is a strong inward-looking tendency that puts security, nurturing and creature comforts top priority. The home will be very important and you can expect it to be nicely decorated and comfortable.

The risk here is that the couple may become too inward-looking and lose sight of the bigger picture. While the fluid, intuitive and deeply emotional nature of both contributes to a strong sense of well-being, it can also result in one or the other feeling confined or restricted at times. Cancer Moon is impressionable and easily influenced, and each partner should take time for personal interests outside the partnership.

Nevertheless, the fervent, devoted and nurturing qualities of Cancer make for a strong partnership in which there is an ease of understanding. The early phases of the relationship can get a bit humorous with each partner tentatively, carefully feeling the other out. But once they arrive at a comfortable understanding, both are intensely loyal and are not easily swayed from their commitment.

Both are also so emotional that when things go wrong they can become intensely brooding and moody. This is a partnership that is run by the lunar phases with both becoming hypersensitive, melancholy or despondent at the same time in the month – one triggering off the other. At times like these it may be good to take a break from each other, create some space and come back refreshed.

Overall, though, this can be a powerful combination if both partners make the effort to balance emotional experience and self-preservation through diversifying their interests and enriching each other by reaching out to others beyond the limits of their domestic kingdom.

Cancer and Leo (Water and Fire)

An interesting, stimulating and compatible partnership that combines the regal nature of the Leo zodiac king with that of the Cancer queen. Regardless of the gender of each, these natures are symbolized by the Sun and Moon respectively, magically interacting to create a rich and satisfying emotional tapestry. Both are intuitive, but Leo expresses this with focus, vigour and action to bring it out into the world, whereas Cancer tends toward introversion. When they are in synch, Leo helps Cancer make good use of their intuition, and stimulates them to be more and do more with their natural gifts. In turn, Cancer's nurturing and thoughtful nature feeds the proud Leo, helping them feel respected and loved – so important for the Leo Moon in any partnership.

Warm-hearted, responsible, diplomatic and magnanimous Leo will comfort sensitive Cancer, offering stability and direction. Because Leo loves to lead and Cancer is impressionable and easily led, Cancer will, however, need to put some energy into keeping a sense of separate self. Regardless of gender, Leo will be the one who wants to lead on the dance floor.

Both are highly sensitive in their own way and when it comes to romance there can be deep feelings, hyper-sensuality and an intense intimacy. The pair stimulate each other's creative, expressive and artistic natures, and can develop a deep attachment. Cancer can even tolerate Leo's sometimes overbearing self-importance once the relationship is solidly established, though until then Leo should restrain this trait and wait for Cancer to understand their more generous and sensitive qualities. In time, these will become especially endearing to Cancer.

The combination will tend to make a popular couple who display the right balance of verve and decorum, outspoken expressiveness and delicacy in relating – a good combination that is also very sensitive to the emotional ups and downs of lunar phases.

Cancer and Virgo (Water and Earth)

This relationship can really work if both partners make the effort to understand their unique natures and emotional language. The practical, prudent Virgo offers a sensible and supportive nature to the security-minded, domestic Cancer. Both tend to be quite grounded, thinking ahead about life's inevitabilities. Even Virgo's analytical, perceptive traits can complement the deeply emotional, subterranean quality of Cancer, giving Virgo the ability to understand Cancer without much explanation.

On the other hand, Virgo likes to put the thinking side of their emotional being (if that is not a contradiction in terms) before their more emotional side and this can create some discomfort for Cancer, who is 'all heart'. When the cool, calculating, anxious aspects of the Virgo nature come out, it can leave Cancer a bit despondent or with hurt feelings.

Cancer's giving, tender nature helps Virgo, though, and can be a moisturizing salve to Virgo's hurts. Cancer can help Virgo open up and express themselves. In turn, Virgo needs to realize that Cancer needs a comfortable, secure home if there is to be harmony. Both signs can be very introverted, especially when hurt, and it could be challenging to see who will reach out to help the other in times of conflict. Virgo will try to use their head, Cancer their heart, and they should agree to meet somewhere in the middle.

This can be a sensitive, intimate and revelatory romantic partnership with the caveat that reconciliation is needed to bring out their amorous best. Cancer needs to be conscious of Virgo's ultrasensitive, emotionally timid nature when it comes to intimacy. The more relaxed, sensual side of Cancer can help Virgo find a way to express their passions and feelings. Both place a great importance on privacy and discretion, so there is no need for concern for either in regards to feelings being revealed to others.

Cancer and Libra (Water and Air)

Self-awareness and the celebration of differences can make this a strong working partnership. The Libra Moon puts great value on the happiness and well-being of their partner, and their love of luxury, sociability and affectionate nature complement the sensitive, emotional Cancer.

A Cancer Moon can create a strong personality, someone who knows what they want, even if they don't express it so well. In contrast, a Libra Moon can be indecisive and unsure about their direction and thus Cancer can take a place of prominence and influence in the partnership. If this happens, Cancer will need to reassure the sometimes insecure Libra, making sure that they take time to understand their concerns.

Libra can be long-suffering for their partner, but can become bitter if the partner fails to meet them halfway and take their share of the load. Libra needs communication, especially verbal communication, and this is not something that always comes easily to Cancer. Also, Libra tends to be straightforward and Cancer will need to check their sideways approach to difficult issues if they want to keep Libra's respect. Cancer will tend to be more moody than Libra and this can be a concern for Libra, though they will respond easily to Cancer's needs, as long as Cancer doesn't use their melancholies to control the relationship.

There is the potential for balanced give and take here, with both partners able to show kindness and affection to each other. Cancer can give focus and direction to Libra and the partnership can be amicable, caring, fun-loving and amusing. Romantically, it can be strong, as both are sensual. Of the two, it can be more problematic for Libra, who may feel that Cancer is too complacent or self-satisfied to give them what they really want. It is important for Cancer to remember this if they want to retain harmony and solid mutual understanding.

Cancer and Scorpio (Water and Water)

Maternal symbolism is strong in both but for different reasons, which gives the relationship a central theme of simultaneous attraction and conflict – which, if managed well, can make this a strong, compatible, loving partnership.

Both signs are very deep and sensitive, and have to recognize their own emotional needs if any serious relationship is to take place. Cancer may be less intense than Scorpio but no less emotional, and it will be easy for the extreme aspects of Scorpio to hurt them. Of course whenever Scorpio is extreme, it is because they are driven by their own deep-rooted feelings. Neither partner will find it easy to express exactly what is going on and it will be important that they learn how to read between each other's lines to make it work. This should be quite easy for both, though, as long as the will is there.

So much of the Water element in a relationship makes for a very interesting emotional playing-field, one that can be caring, entertaining and certainly not dull. Cancer has a pronounced ability to provide nurturing and understanding, which is just what sensitive Scorpio needs but is not always open to accept. Cancer should recognize a bit of themselves in Scorpio and where possible try to be patient with their sometimes tempestuous partner.

Cancer tends to be more self-satisfied than Scorpio, quite possibly due to a positive and caring mother image. Scorpio Moons can have a more complicated relationship with the mother. Thus the two signs can be a good mix if both are willing to play their own role and let the other play theirs. Cancer can learn a lot from the varied interests of a Scorpio Moon, especially with regard to spirituality and magical ideas. Scorpio will definitely introduce Cancer to a deeper side of their emotional Water nature.

Expect a highly intuitive, psychic, emotional partnership that romantically can be as intense as it is satisfying. Both are deeply, helplessly romantic by nature and this more than anything is the area where the relationship can thrive.

Cancer and Sagittarius (Water and Fire)

The Sagittarius warrior-sage meets the zodiac Cancer queen to create a passionate, intense and sometimes complicated emotional experience that sparks each into action and keeps them growing, searching and questioning.

Cancer will attempt the seduction of Sagittarius with charm, tact and grace. Remember that Cancer rarely, if ever, makes a direct frontal assault, whether martially or amorously. This delicate sensitivity will appeal to Sagittarius, who will find it alluring, mysterious and sexual. They may try to conquer it with a direct, winning display of high energy, strong will and vivid emotions, which will also be attractive to Cancer. So there is almost a jockeying for position and influence between these two signs, which can keep things fresh and stimulating but also be challenging.

At times, the strong and focused nature of Sagittarius is too direct for Cancer, who may feel under siege from the Sagittarius potency. Sagittarius is intrepid, inconstant and manic and likes to direct their heart energy out into the world. Cancer is more inward-looking, secretive and recessive. Sagittarius may not understand Cancer's more complicated nature, but there is no point in expecting Cancer to change as it is one of the more resilient signs. This contrasts with Sagittarius, who often has personal experience of the need to change and adjust their approach to life in order to succeed. Both will have to learn to celebrate their different natures and give each other the space to be themselves.

Sagittarius can, however, give Cancer the direction and vision they need and sometimes lack. The fiery Sagittarian nature is a catalyst for action and is just what Cancer needs when they retire too long to their feeling recesses. Cancer is sometimes more like a lake than an ocean, and can be resistive to force, but if Sagittarius uses their more diplomatic side they can make good headway. They should remember that losing their patience does no good at all.

The partnership can work if there is a will to make it work, but expect a see-saw of emotions, issues and themes. This will appeal to both the adventurous Sagittarius and the emotional Cancer, as long as they keep the mystery in the relationship and avoid the rot of familiarity.

Cancer and Capricorn (Water and Earth) ★

Opposites not only attract but also reflect each other. At a deeper level there is something of one in the other, which creates understanding, acceptance and endearment. This is certainly the case with the Cancer/Capricorn partnership. These are opposites by zodiac position and quality and yet who complement each other perfectly.

The industrious, hard-working, responsible Capricorn appeals to the domestic, sensible and family-oriented Cancer, and they can create a working partnership in which each feeds the other with the appropriate emotional nurturing. Cancer's caring and affectionate qualities, their 'moist' tenderness, are just what the 'dry', sober, reticent Capricorn needs to feel wanted and respected. The responsible Capricorn can shoulder almost any burden and willingly does so for a partner. They are able to put the happiness of another before their own needs and this trait endears them to Cancer, who sees it not just as loyal, but also intensely romantic. The theme of sacrificial love colours this partnership and encourages each partner to extend themselves beyond their limits for the other's benefit.

Both are shy and reserved but for different reasons. Cancer is full of feelings and often turbulent emotional energies, but doesn't feel safe revealing them to others. Capricorn's feelings are repressed and restricted. They tend to put limits on their own emotional expression and, like Cancer, are waiting for the right partner who can see beneath appearances and celebrate who they really are. This is something Cancer does easily, thanks to their intuitive skills and deep perceptions. Cancer can actually feel another's feelings and this makes it easy for the taciturn and even sombre Capricorn.

Romantically, they are highly suited to each other and can connect amorously without the need of words or boisterous and embarrassing expressions. They are able to tell each other how they feel with their touch, and that is enough for this sensitive couple.

Cancer and Aquarius (Water and Air)

While not opposites, this combination has a number of contrary qualities which offer the chance of growth through resolution and the opportunity for each partner to deepen the other's view of life by seeing the world through very different emotional eyes.

Aquarius tends to be a big-picture person, driven by a yearning for feelings that rise above the singular needs of one person and tend to the needs of all. This is an emotionalism that is mystical and while almost intellectual, it is nonetheless a valid emotional viewpoint. In contrast, Cancer tends to think that charity begins at home and likes to ensure that the basics are taken care of before looking further afield. This is not to say that Cancer fails the social awareness test, but rather that the two natures tend to have a different focus, and this brings both challenges and opportunities for the relationship.

Cancer can feel that Aquarius' concerns are too ethereal to be practical and may worry that Aquarius may float away on a breeze of lofty ideas. Aquarius may feel that Cancer fails to understand their high-minded transpersonal values. This is the gap that needs to be bridged, either through acceptance or through participation in each other's interests, in order for the relationship to work.

On the plus side, there is a lot of common ground, as both are naturally sociable, although Cancer may be more selective than Aquarius, who finds people fascinating in general and is interested in exploring human nature and new ideas. While Cancer tends to be more circumspect in this regard, they are sociable and affable and can play along in the company of others as long as they get time alone with their Aquarius partner.

Cancer and Pisces (Water and Water)

These two are very compatible, as both are symbolic denizens of Poseidon's watery kingdom. This is a festival of feeling, impressions, dreams, intuitions, yearning and hypersensitivity. Each will understand the other to such an extent that they are the quintessential couple who can communicate across a room without words or gestures.

This can also be a moody swirl of sentiment and shadowlike impressions that can make both partners susceptible to the other's emotional states. While this can result in melancholy and sometimes feelings of inferiority and insecurity, for the most part both partners will feel comfortable even in the more challenging emotional depths and can adjust to the high tides and choppy seas of their combined feelings.

There is a conscious understanding of each other's sensitivity and this helps both overcome the uncertainties of their lives. Of the two, Pisces tends to be more introverted, but is able to offer a lot to Cancer in a spirit of service and deference that makes Cancer feel confident and secure.

The principal challenge in the partnership is that both are impressionable, inward-dwelling and ultra-sensitive. Without some effort this can result in a dreamy loneliness where both are preoccupied with the relationship and fail to reach out beyond their own watery domain. To avoid this they should get out and socialize, get involved in the community and explore the creative and artistic inclinations that they have in common.

Romantically, this is something potentially very special. Each will give the other the chance to explore the depths of their amorous and highly sensual natures. Despite Pisces' quite reserved nature when it comes to intimate dealings, they will feel at ease with expressing their sensuality and sexuality openly, and this can be a big attraction to the Cancer Moon.

Leo and...

Leo (Fire and Fire)

The combination of two Leos is certain to create a fun-loving, jovial, warm-hearted partnership. It can be a passionate affair that is fiery, intense, upbeat and exciting, while challenging by reflecting back each other's traits, both good and bad. Without doubt these two will understand each other, but will need to find a way in which they can take turns playing centre stage or ascending the throne of importance.

This larger-than-life, attention-getting couple will seek out an active social life and may at times compete for social influence. They will be generous and proactively involved in their community, family and work. They both love to lead, so it's best that they each have some area of their life they can call their own. Whether social, political or charity work, they need a field where they can do some good and be respected for it. They may also express their combined creative drive, which demonstrates their instinctive power and forward-looking qualities.

Romantically, the combination is potent, passionate and driven. Their leonine natures animate their intimate exchanges and lend an air of excitement and adventure to the relationship. While this can make the romance very special, it can also make it very sensitive and prone to moments of upheaval and discord, especially at delicate times in the monthly lunar phases. Expect lightning and thunder at such times, especially as neither partner shies away from a challenge. It's not in their nature to give up territory and, taken to extremes, their relationship can be like two monarchs divvying up the kingdom. If it gets like this, they should remember that the bed belongs to both of them and, as the old adage goes, they should never let the sun go down on their anger. Of course, storms are exciting to the Leo Moon, and there will be no problem as long as they are but the prelude to love.

Leo and Virgo (Fire and Earth)

The service-minded, discreet Virgo and the royal Leo make a natural combination whose respective qualities, although very different, complement and support each other. Passionate Leo brings excitement and stimulation to Virgo and keeps them from falling into a comfortable rut. Leo is challenging to Virgo, but can lead rather than bully thanks to their diplomatic nature, which appeals to the retiring, cool-headed Virgo Moon. Virgo is discretion personified and applies a rigid measure to all their relationships – happily for Leo, their strong, larger-than-life personality passes the Virgo muster.

Virgo also plays an important role for Leo by helping to keep things balanced, prudent and composed. Unlike Leo, it takes a while for Virgo to let themselves go emotionally and this emotional austerity of Virgo helps keep Leo dignified and focused. Golden-hearted Leo brings a shine to Virgo's emotional experience and illustrates how they can express their refined qualities in a way they can be proud of. So Leo helps to build the Virgo confidence, in part because Virgo's lord, Mercury, is adaptable and mutable, giving Virgo the profound ability to learn from their life experience.

There can be challenging moments. For instance, it can take a great deal of effort for Leo to recover if their sense of grandeur rubs critical Virgo up the wrong way. Humble pie is not the first option on the Leo menu, but it can be served cold if Virgo feels Leo is insufferable in their self-importance. On the other side of the coin, Leo's pride is easily wounded if the Virgo suspicion or jealousy is unfairly pointed in their direction. Virgo is expected to know that Leo is above such petty and common foibles – and even if they aren't, it's not Virgo's place to point it out. But in truth it is, because there is no one better equipped critically than Virgo.

Romantically, however, they are well suited and they make a good couple, whose complementary traits can bring out the natural humour and wit in both.

Leo and Libra (Fire and Air)

Fervent Leo's and the more modest Libra's compatible and contradictory qualities kindle an exuberant, sometimes feverish affair. The combination is full of promise but, like many of these Moon-sign pairs, needs a measure of conscious effort to make the most of what is on offer.

Each partner is a catalyst for the other, bringing out the best through some challenges which contrast with the mostly positive disposition of both signs. Leo is forthright, directed and has a sense of what they want out of life – just what is often missing from the more indefinite Libra. Libra's more flexible nature moderates the fiery-tempered Leo, while Leo's emotional confidence has a stabilizing influence on Libra, helping them off the fence of indecision while boosting their sometimes tenuous sense of self-worth. Libra gives Leo the respect they hanker for and a feeling of central importance – something that tends to bring out the best of Leo's leadership, generosity and responsibility. There is nothing more appealing to a Leo than a good cause, and what better cause than an admiring partner who needs their help?

The principal challenge comes when each seeks to dominate or express themselves excessively, Leo with their pride and strong emotional ego, Libra with the deference that puts them at the whim of Leo the lion-hearted. Libra may also restrict Leo's progress through their indecision, though this is rarer.

They are a good match socially, as the gregarious Leo, diplomatic, open and inventive, gets plenty of opportunity for fellowship via the people-loving nature of Libra. Both have a love of luxury and the privileges of life and if they don't get them can become despondent. Together, however, there should be enough emotional drive to move them to get what they want from life. When it comes to humour, they can set the house on fire. Amusements, jokes, silliness and demonstrative behaviour combine to make them the life and soul of the party, although it is likely that Libra will be the quieter of the two.

Romantically, the union combines passion and desire, urges and deep longings to create an active and sensual intimacy.

There is every chance that this combination will result in a happy and prosperous exchange.

Leo and Scorpio (Fire and Water)

An intense, transformative combination that is sensual, passionate and at times a tempest of emotion, but which suits both partners' distinctive natures. Both have strong desires, especially Scorpio, who is yearning personified, and who can stimulate the same in the naturally passionate Leo. Leo is less complicated, or complex, than Scorpio and may have a hard time understanding the sensitive, changeable and enigmatic quality of Scorpio. Leo is more direct – what you see is what you get – whereas with Scorpio what you see is only a secondary by-product of what is really going on deep down inside. This, however, does not hinder the adventurous Leo, whose feline curiosity will draw them to further investigate captivating Scorpio.

Both personalities are attractive in their unique ways and Scorpio will admire Leo for their energy and confidence, but will also feel that this contrasts with their own hidden insecurity or personal doubt. Leo needs to acknowledge this and potentially adjust their interaction with Scorpio now and then, using a little diplomacy to try to get Scorpio to express their feelings. Chances are, though, that Leo will still need to read between the lines and be happy to live with a lot of mystery.

The passions of both make for an interesting romance which can be deep for both. Problems will arise if Scorpio subtly influences the relationship in a way that makes Leo feel powerless or without any voice. It is doubtful whether Scorpio will do this openly, directly or even consciously, but it could tax Leo's none-too patient nature and result in emotional tensions between the two. Leo will need to learn that greater power in the relationship will come through acceptance and flexibility rather than through force or show of will.

Leo and Sagittarius (Fire and Fire)

An exciting, compatible and sometimes combustible combination. Both are knight-warriors and there is a similarity of nature and ease of exchange between the two. They complement and challenge each other and can bring out the best of each other's characters, especially imagination and creativity.

This is a potent mix that gives energy to the relationship and helps the pair express themselves both as individuals and as a couple. Sagittarius supports Leo with their philosophical moods, helping them deal with life's challenges and disappointments, which Leo feels strongly and can take quite personally. In turn, when Sagittarius suffers from depressive moments, Leo offers the right amount of emotional lift and encouragement, helping to revitalize Sagittarius and keep them on track. The similar natures and the angular relationships of their positions on the zodiac mean that they not only understand each other but can also support each other, as when one is weak the other may be strong.

The challenges will come from strong emotional egos expecting the limelight and not getting it. Arguments can be accompanied by a display of fireworks which can leave both feeling tender and misunderstood. Sagittarius may need to take the first step to soothe hurt feelings and keep things sweet.

They both have a zest for life and tend to throw themselves into whatever they are doing. In romance, this sparks strong passions and a sensual agreement that can be very pronounced, depending on the rest of their charts. They both love the finer things in life and as a couple will tend to be aspirational. Mutual motivation keeps them fresh and vigorous.

Leo and Capricorn (Fire and Earth)

Extroverted and introverted natures combine here to create the potential for tension which, if handled well, can give good results. Both will need to be flexible, as by nature they bring an element of challenge to each other and one may not wish to bend to the will of the other. Of course, this will depend in large measure on the rest of their charts, but from a Moon-sign perspective both will need to agree to some amount of accommodation.

At first, convivial Leo and reserved Capricorn may eye each other somewhat suspiciously, judging from a distance whether or not they are real characters. Ironically, both usually are, but existing at nearly opposite ends of the zodiac spectrum, they have their own style of expression. Capricorn is concerned with life's duties and obligations, and puts these before anything else. Leo is also very dutiful, but tends to be less sombre about managing this than Capricorn. Capricorn is more sceptical than Leo and in extreme cases can be cynical as a result of life's disappointments, which they suffer well, but not gladly.

Leo tends to deal with problems by seeing past them, while Capricorn lives in their immovable citadel, which symbolizes their approach to problems – 'I won't budge.' Their obstinacy and sheer will are their strength, but at times also their weakness. Where the relationship may not work is when they are too concerned with the style of approach, rather than its substance.

Romantically, Leo will need to show some patience with Capricorn, who is less emotionally demonstrative and expressive. Trust needs to be established, but once this is done the caring, generous Leo nature can reflect back to Capricorn their abundance of good qualities. With this, a satisfying intimate relationship is guaranteed.

Leo and Aquarius (Fire and Air) ★

Another 'perfect' Moon-sign match – the happy meeting of the zodiac king with his beloved and prosperous citizen. The compatibility of these two symbols is obvious and characterizes the generous, protective leadership of Leo and the broadminded, ideals-inspired Aquarius. This is a stimulating combination in which both partners have a natural affinity based on shared values. The regal Leo is naturally fed by the attentive, socially-minded and sympathetic Aquarius who adores the Leo mind and gives it that central place of importance that makes Leo feel so much better. Meanwhile, the fire of the Leo character inspires the lofty thoughts and mystical feelings of Aquarius. Both signs are dynamically political in nature and are catalysts for mutual action. Whether that is for the local school or something large scale, like the environment, the combination is virile.

The two share a love of wisdom and are attracted to the magical aspects of life. Both are equally instinctive and original, and reflect each other's qualities. Leo inspires Aquarius to action, and can give a sense of purpose and a channel for their wealth of ideas and ambitions.

Romance is potentially strong in this relationship, with each partner being lifted higher by the spirit of the other. While there are in fact many dissimilarities between them, this is a case of the attraction of opposites. For instance, Leo tends to be singular in nature, whereas Aquarius is plural. Leo can be quite satisfied on their own, but Aquarius needs the company of others to be complete. In so many ways it's a good match.

Leo helps ground Aquarius who in turn helps raise Leo to new heights through the discovery and introduction of new ideas, as well as vigorous debate and the exchange of views. Both are content to celebrate the differences while enjoying the similarities, and this, if nothing else, points to their natural compatibility.

Leo and Pisces (Fire and Water)

There may not be a combination that flexible, amenable Pisces cannot accommodate. Some, however, may present more of a challenge than others and Leo may be one such case. Leo the emotional extrovert meets Pisces the prototype introvert – the king on his tour of the land encounters the hermit sitting quietly in his retreat. They couldn't be more different, but that will not stop the inquisitive Leo from exploring the depths of mysterious Pisces, especially as both recognize that there is much they can learn from each other.

The yielding, agreeable Pisces appeals to centre-stage Leo, but offers an indirect challenge through their nearly amorphous and enigmatic quality. The Leo Moon loves to challenge and be challenged, and it is not uncommon for a Leo to be called argumentative when in fact they are only enjoying the polemical exchange of debate. The problem Pisces poses to Leo is that they rarely offer a tangible disagreement that would satisfy Leo's love of joust.

In contrast, the active, lively and outgoing Leo may be too strong for the sensitive Pisces, who likes to communicate subtly and mostly without words. Leo may be too external for Pisces, who leads a rich inner life. It would be Pisces' hope that Leo can enter their more ethereal inner world to explore their feelings, fantasies and dreams – something maybe akin to the hermit inviting the king (and his entourage) to stay a while at the hermitage. Pisces may also be easily led by Leo and succumb to their strong blandishments, but both will be only superficially satisfied. So the challenge is to stay awhile and explore each other more deeply.

Romantically, Pisces can open new doors for Leo, who in turn feels that Pisces gives them the chance to easily express their strong emotions. Leo is likely to be surprised by the confidence of Pisces in intimate affairs, which can enamour Leo further.

While there are big differences in style and approach, this combination can work if both partners seek to understand and relate to each other's unique emotional qualities.

Virgo and...

Virgo (Earth and Earth)

Discriminating, careful and observant Virgo has a mirror reflection with another Virgo partner, creating a combination that works either very well or not at all. In the latter case this would be due to the discomfort of being with someone too alike in emotional character and outlook. While such a combination is not impossible, it may be unlikely, as a consequence of Virgo's tendency to apply their talents for the benefit of dissimilar natures.

Where it would work, both partners would embody each other's vision of perfection – an unlikely attainment for a normal mortal. In truth, the Virgo Moon has immense emotional potential, but their expression remains under the lock and key of that rare person who has proven their worth with discretion and proper behaviour. It could be easy for one Virgo to display that to another and thus such trust can be established. But the task of living up to each other's ideals then gets underway and this can result in the mutual striving for refinement and a distilled prudence whose scent is pure and astringent.

Possibly the biggest challenge to such a couple is the tendency to become mutually dependent on a methodical, repetitive, analytical approach to life to such an extent that it limits their vision and growth and their inherent freedom to seek the new and unproven.

In emotional and intimate matters, a Virgo/Virgo combination could result in mutual respect for their emotional timidity and reserve – which can work but again doesn't expand their horizons. Both need a measure of warmth and demonstrative love, one that breaks the silent Virgo barrier to intimacy. If the other aspects of the astrological charts balance this out with a more gregarious tendency, though, both may have the perfect partner of their dreams.

Virgo and Libra (Earth and Air)

There are a number of compatible traits that can make this combination work well. Both have a reserved nature, even friendly Libra, and this creates an easy understanding. Libra can also be deferential and accommodating, which suits Virgo's somewhat inflexible nature.

Libra can create the chance for the reserved Virgo to manifest whatever adventurous spirit lies within and offers Virgo the compatible, refined affection it needs to grow in self-confidence and intimacy. Libra tends to be quietly pleasure-seeking, which opens the door for Virgo to relax their rigid standards while not feeling that they have compromised their principles. Virgo, on the other hand, gives a grounded, reference point to the sometimes aimless Libra. Virgo is immensely practical, which is a big help to Libra when they're trying to decide on a course of action. In particular, Virgo can lend their analytical skills and help bring the Libra mind from the polarities of an issue to the fulcrum.

At times, Libra may be pinched by the sharp, critical nature of Virgo, which can leave people feeling exposed and vulnerable – an interesting trait for a Moon sign who avoids the same for themselves externally but who internally can be overly self-critical. Virgo needs to make themselves available to the love and affection that Libra has to offer and stop second-guessing both themselves and their partner. This can then help Virgo open up to receive the softening love of sensual Libra.

Virgo and Scorpio (Earth and Water)

This will undoubtedly be a unique emotional exchange due to the two characters involved – deep, penetrating, hypersensitive and secretive Scorpio and the analytical, critical and perceptive Virgo, who can struggle to express their deep, highly-refined emotions. Nevertheless, after a time of trial and error, if there is ample physical attraction the partnership can work because of these very traits.

Scorpio enjoys Virgo's critical, discriminating nature as long as it is not directed Scorpio's way. If it is, it can result in hurt feelings that cause pain to both partners and disrupt the smooth flow of emotional exchange. A Scorpio Moon can be very sensual, at least in mind if not in body, and their passions require the right partner who is free for intimacy in the secret fashion of Scorpio. There is a good chance that Virgo will feel safe with this hidden approach, although they may chafe at the intense, subterranean nature of Scorpio passions. This is not something that Virgo can pass judgement on, but should try to understand and accept to make the partnership work. Scorpio in turn needs to understand the more reserved, timid nature of Virgo and adjust their approach where possible.

Virgo can apply their analytical, caring and service-minded nature to helping Scorpio in their yearning for self-knowledge and deep understanding. A little feedback from insightful Virgo can help Scorpio understand their deeper yearnings, and Virgo's healing care can help ease the pain of that yearning. Scorpio will also give Virgo a great deal, not least of which will be the chance to hear a similar analysis of themselves offered up unexpectedly in a way that rivals the best of what Virgo is capable of. This is revelatory and will teach Virgo a lot. In doing this, however, Scorpio needs to recognize that Virgo can be immensely self-critical and disparaging. Virgo needs a gentle hand to help keep them soft and virginal, just as Scorpio needs a tender hand to keep them from feeling the same pain of yearning for the best self they know they are capable of.

Virgo and Sagittarius (Earth and Fire)

A potentially challenging but rewarding relationship where two dissimilar natures offer just the right amount of friction to polish and refine, stimulate and inspire each other. The fiery, regal nature of Sagittarius appears strong, even dominant to the retiring, reserved Virgo Moon. There is a level of emotional confidence, at least a potent sense of self, that Virgo feels lacking in and this can deepen their self-criticism. It can be hard to warm to a strong character who brings this up, but if Virgo musters up the courage, they will find that Sagittarius is generous, thoughtful and pleasingly easy-going, which is just what Virgo needs but has a hard time finding in themselves.

There is a meeting of minds when it comes to thoughtful, philosophical discussions. Virgo loves to understand the working of life's secrets and Sagittarius is wise enough to stimulate fruitful exchanges.

Sagittarius is more extrovert than Virgo and if this doesn't intimidate Virgo it can encourage them to greater self-expression. Sagittarius will need to adjust to the picky and sometimes small-minded or pedantic nature of Virgo – something that is not easy for Sagittarius, as they are much more of a big-picture person than a detail-oriented person. Of course this can be complementary, with Virgo reminding Sagittarius about the tedium and Sagittarius helping Virgo out of the rut and into a more profound life strategy.

Virgo can offer Sagittarius the kind of recognition and support they hanker for, but Sagittarius also needs to make time to be free and unfettered if they are to enjoy the best of Virgo without tiring of their more prudent, restrictive nature.

Romantically, it can be a good match, as Sagittarius has the dignity of heart to respect the reserved Virgo nature, work with it and celebrate it. Virgo can be enthused by the chivalrous Sagittarius and feel understood and accepted, which is all-important for a Virgo Moon.

Virgo and Capricorn (Earth and Earth)

There is nothing more practical than this combination of Earth signs, which works fluidly and harmoniously with mutual understanding. Both are practical, methodical, analytical and ambitious. Virgo gives Capricorn support and insight and can inspire them to reach their full potential. With a Virgo partner, Capricorn feels that they can go far and bear even more burdens in their quest to build a solid foundation for their fortress.

Both are also retiring, shy and reserved, and the big challenge for them may actually be to meet and start talking. Once this is done, they will find they have a great deal in common, both being cool-headed, loyal, discerning and long-suffering.

On the challenging side they may be too alike in some respects, thereby reinforcing the more difficult or inhibiting sides of their natures. Their mutual caution may limit their choices and risk-taking and when Capricorn's emotional repression meets Virgo's critical nature it can deaden the exchange and sap it of the emotional moisture it needs to keep fresh and healthy. Both are also prone to being self-critical and dissatisfied. This can motivate them to succeed but also give them a dour, almost negative view that is unlikely to bring out the best of their respective emotional characters. Lastly, their sense of reserve may also hinder the much-needed emotional demonstrativeness needed to bring some cheer to the party ... To counter this, they should both go to the funfair now and then – if only to keep young in heart and spirit.

Romantically and sensually, there is a lot of common ground and mutual styles of expression. They will understand a lot of each other – maybe more by what is not said than by what is said – but it can be helpful if now and then they open up and share their feelings one way or the other. Once they are comfortable with each other, though, there is a good basis for satisfying intimacy.

Virgo and Aquarius (Earth and Air)

Understanding and compatibility blend with a modest element of tension here to create a stimulating, solid basis for a relationship. The expansive worldview of Aquarius helps open Virgo up to new vistas, while Virgo's down-to-earth nature helps Aquarius structure their thoughts and actions to create practical results.

Virgo also offers Aquarius a foil to test their unproven ideas with debate and a good argument now and then. Aquarius shouldn't think Virgo an easy pushover when it comes to fielding their radical notions. Virgo's austerity of mind and sometimes suspicious worldview make it the perfect balance for Aquarius, who can too easily discount other partners for lack of critical faculty. No dearth of that in the Virgo department.

On the other hand, Aquarius breathes fresh air into the often circumscribed life of Virgo, helping to break down some of their more inflexible barriers and bringing them out into a diverse emotional world. This is particularly the case if Aquarius offers access to their view of mystic reality and otherworldly ideas.

On the downside, Aquarius needs to give Virgo the space to ploddingly follow their lead and should be patient with Virgo's ultra-sensitive nature, which can be pricked when Aquarius puts on superior airs that rub Virgo up the wrong way.

On the whole it can be an interesting romantic relationship, one that helps Virgo explore their emotional nature and hidden sensuality in a safe, careful way. In turn, Aquarius can connect with and be inspired by the supra-mundane romantic ideals of the Virgo Moon.

In truth, this combination can result in a powerful healing partnership that feeds both, helps others and brings more light to the world. Virgo is hugely giving when it comes to the needy and the social mind of Aquarius can apply this to the big picture.

Virgo and Pisces (Earth and Water) ★

Yet another archetypal zodiac partnership that blends contrasting qualities to create a union whose whole is greater than the sum of its parts. The emotional fantasy of Pisces with their rich inner world is probably the closest that the Virgo sense of perfection will ever get – if only because the Pisces ideal is more transcendent than mundane. The sensitive, alluring and sensual Pisces is at once inviting and unthreatening to the careful, shy Virgo, who finds in Pisces someone that for once isn't offended, put off or disenchanted by their sharp, critical eye. The Pisces Moon acts like a gaseous fluffy-sweet cloud that absorbs whatever inconsistencies exist in the expression of Virgo, who finds this immensely gratifying, healing and liberating. Virgo is happy to be free of the critical tendency that they secretly desire to abandon and Pisces aids that abandonment, being detached from the sordid views of the right and wrong of this world. What a relief for Virgo.

Romantically, the exchange is even deeper, as the emotional depth of Pisces invites Virgo to discover a reality that defies logic, where only feelings, impressions and sensitivities are valid and everything else is unimportant. In the Pisces hermitage, Virgo can be their deeper feeling self that celebrates a perfection beyond rules. Here, Virgo discovers that the rules are but the poor stand-in that is needed when the pure entity is absent. Here, Virgo feels safe and free, away from the prying eyes of the world, able to enjoy embraces without the pain of self-consciousness.

In exchange, Virgo is able to bring balance to Pisces, who does need to operate in the 'real' world now and then. Virgo gives Pisces the necessary grounding – not too much, just enough, thank you – and the solidifying discretion to express emotions in a relevant and understandable way. Discriminating Virgo, however, knows better than to reveal everything – a trait that is reassuring to the secretive Pisces.

Libra and...

Libra (Air and Air)

Phone calls, visits, company, people – this combination creates a hub of social activity. If this partnership shares a household it will be a place where people come for comfort, pampering and listening. Both partners have people at the centre of their busy lives, willingly or not, as even when they tend toward introversion, life will conspire to put lots of people on their path, as it is through people that the Libra Moon grows.

Libra Moons love a good laugh and are sometimes downright silly. They will also be thoughtful and courteous and pleasure-seeking by nature. They make great company and are good medicine when you are feeling down in the dumps.

The main challenge here is if the two Libra Moons feed each other's ponderous plodding indecision they can end up in an endless cycle of reviewing all the options but never taking action. They could thus fall into a proverbial rut that in extreme cases becomes more like a maze. If this happens, they should sit down, pick a decision and take it – if only to get things moving.

Like other pairings of the same astrological Moon sign, expect that the cycles of lunar phases will bring highs and lows to the relationship, potentially making both partners sensitive at the same time. An awareness of this will help channel pent-up feelings productively.

This is a loving, sensitive partnership that is strongly sensual and is inclined to a refined life. According to their means the Libra Moons will aspire to comfortable surroundings and a measure of luxury. The emotional bond between the two can be quite strong, as the Libra tendency is to put great emphasis on their partner. There will be a lot of affection, sensitive feelings and tender exchanges. Both will enjoy the quiet of their private life and need to take the time and energy to nurture and protect it.

Libra and Scorpio (Air and Water)

There is a good level of compatibility with these two zodiac neighbours, especially when they are aware of each other's strengths, weaknesses and emotional language. If they are not, it could be challenging for both, as the contrast between them can make them seem at odds with each other.

Libra's sensitive, delicate nature puts great value on the happiness of their partner. In some cases, a Libra Moon will actually 'live through' the life of their spouse, which, depending on the people involved, can be a good or a bad thing. The Libra Moon likes to talk, relate and have a good sense of where they stand with their partner and the hypersensitive, moody and emotionally introverted Scorpio can present problems here. Scorpio can vacillate in emotional extremes, being withdrawn one moment and boldly and unexpectedly open another. Scorpio also likes their privacy, needs it in fact, and the socially-involved Libra may make this difficult, bringing stress to the relationship. But maybe the most challenging aspect will be the see-saw of emotional swings and adjustments, especially when Libra attempts to adjust willy-nilly to the mood swings of Scorpio. It is very difficult for Libra to sit quietly at the fulcrum and not respond to a changing emotional landscape, but this is precisely what must happen here, because not only does Scorpio usually not want so fine a response to their moods, but also it would be difficult to know exactly when they did. Libra needs to be content with having a deep-feeling partner and celebrate by observing rather than reacting to Scorpio's more unpredictable qualities. This will be helpful to both partners and keep the relationship fresh and easy.

Romantically, this can be a very passionate affair, with the mixing of Mars (Scorpio) and Venus (Libra), the two planets that symbolize the polarities of the two lovers and their passion. Both are sensual, especially Scorpio, and both are subtle in nature, which gives ample opportunity for romantic fun, games and surprises. This can be an exciting and satisfying combination for both partners with the caveat that both are highly sensitive and prone to react too strongly or quickly even to innocent remarks. Keeping this in mind will help make the most of this passionate combination.

Libra and Sagittarius (Air and Fire)

Fire and Air are compatible elements and combine to create strong passions, excitability, intense feelings and a wide emotional experience for both partners. Sagittarius' love of freedom and striving for a higher ideal will inspire and encourage principled Libra, who responds well to the frank expression of feelings voiced by Sagittarius, although there is a chance that the more delicate Libra may feel overwhelmed by the force of this expression. Sagittarius provides a strong emotional partner for Libra, who by inclination tends to depend on their partner and draw strength and stamina from them. In contrast, Libra may be less open about their deeper feelings and it will require subtleness and delicacy for Sagittarius to read between their emotional lines. Both tend to be diplomatic by nature, though, and the natural insight of Sagittarius will help in reading the refined but sometimes vague, even distant Libra.

Sagittarius offers Libra a partnership of direction and purpose, with the chance to jump into action and have some adventures. The trick for Libra will be to overcome their possible lack of vision and indecisiveness and play along with the more gregarious Sagittarius. A little practice should provide the confidence to feel safe in the process.

Both are giving, generous and thoughtful – of each other and others – and also share a kind of restless tension of expectation. There is a good basis for humour and fun-loving exchange. Romantically, it is a strong partnership, with both living according to a romantic, high-minded ideal. There is plenty of scope for affection, sensuality and happy intimacy, though the more passionate Sagittarius may sometimes find the inconstant, moodiness of Libra disconcerting or deflating. This is a periodic but likely occurrence.

While the two natures are different, there is enough common ground to create a content, yet striving partnership aspiring to larger-than-life goals and ambitions.

Libra and Capricorn (Air and Earth)

This can be a flowing, harmonious combination that presents the couple's differences in a positive, supportive light. The Libra 'lightness of being' offers Capricorn a lift and inspires them to set their ambitious goals even higher. Libra also helps them 'lighten up' and free themselves of their heavier moods, which are not their most becoming asset.

Libra's evocative romantic nature also encourages Capricorn to loosen their emotional restrictions. Libra will be able to do this in an alluring way that helps check Capricorn's sceptical attitudes and genuinely triggers a strong interest from the forthright Capricorn. The sociable, humorous, amusing qualities of Libra remedy what ails Capricorn, who is able to respond in kind, in their own style.

In turn, Capricorn helps ground and support the irresolute Libra, because, above all, Capricorn knows how to create supportive, reliable emotional structures – which, of course, endears them to the partner-first side of Libra. While Capricorn may be less capricious than Libra, they do offer a solid emotional backdrop for Libra to play their part with confidence – something that doesn't always come easily to Libra.

Emotionally and romantically the partnership can thrive, with Libra helping Capricorn discover or explore their sensual, tactile nature. Intimacy can be strong and abiding and the thoughtful Libra will be able to penetrate the impervious Capricorn to find a gentle nature hidden in their deeper recesses – a discovery that will gladden the erstwhile retiring Capricorn.

Libra and Aquarius (Air and Air)

An abundance of similarities makes the few differences here stand out as mere embellishments to naturally harmonious emotional natures. There is an easy exchange of emotion and outlook between these two signs, with the potential for a strong bond and long-lasting relationship.

Both are lovers of ideas, ideals and people. In a sense, it is the meeting of the zodiac diplomat with all the citizens – good symbolic harmony. The exchange can foster the creative abilities of both and will certainly stimulate them to express themselves to each other and to the world. The Aquarius need for connecting with people is easily met via Libra's sociability – in fact, they both help each other in this regard. Aquarius also helps deepen Libra's view of life by sharing their more rarefied ideals and large-scale concern for issues such as the environment, politics or social work. Where the focus is more on down-to-earth matters, both partners may be active politically or socially, and in other cases the more philosophical nature of Aquarius will take Libra on an adventure of the mystical heart.

Both have strong desires, ambitions and longings, and together these passions are fanned to more intense expressions. This may even result in the couple hoping for fame and recognition. They will be equally dependent on each other, but Aquarius can at times appear more aloof to the needs of the partnership than Libra, who needs patience when it comes to the more lofty Aquarian tendencies. In contrast, Aquarius needs to make the necessary time for their Libra partner and realize that the partnership is more important to Libra than anything more abstract.

Both are hopeless romantics and have a good chance of living up to each other's high expectations. Intimate dealings have an *élan* that, in the right moments, stimulates ecstasy and transpersonal feelings of love.

Libra and Pisces (Air and Water)

Here the differences outweigh whatever similarities may bring these two signs together. Knowing this may be the key to getting more from the relationship and ensuring that both partners feel satisfied and understood.

The deep, and often elusive, quality of introverted Pisces can challenge Libra, who always feels the need to connect and relate, even if only sitting quietly side by side reading a book – although a discussion would be better. Pisces needs to bring Libra more actively into their romantic heart centre, which satisfies and enlivens Libra and can deepen the relationship. Then Libra can use their more social nature to create the chance for Pisces to show their love of celebration, parties and fun – a quality that can seem paradoxical in the subterranean Pisces.

Like any relationship there will be moments of friction or misunderstanding, due in part to Pisces maybe not fully understanding Libra, who in turn may feel it a struggle to be heard and understood. The best way to deal with this is through discussion that highlights their different approaches to communication – Pisces being led by feelings, Libra needing more open and verbal communication.

In terms of sexuality, it can be a satisfying partnership, one that is capable of intense feeling and intimacy. Both Libra and Pisces are pleasure-seekers and will likely feel comfortable in the bedroom, and it is here that ties of affection and understanding will be easily formed.

Scorpio and...

Scorpio (Water and Water)

The emotional exchange of two Scorpio Moons can span the entire spectrum. The Scorpio emotional repertoire can give the relationship Gothic dimensions, transcendent aspirations, reclusive and ultra-sensitive fears and suspicions, intense compulsive yearning for love, an uninterested aloofness – and everything else above and beyond.

This combination can work if both parties are conscious of what lies within each other's hearts and agree to respect the mirror image of each other – which is quite possible, for if anyone can understand a Scorpio Moon it is another Scorpio.

The depths of emotional intensity in this partnership are profound. The two Scorpios can stimulate each other to dive ever further into uncharted emotional terrain, a mutual revelation that can electrify and invigorate. Romantically and sexually, both yearn for a partner who can journey with them in an intrepid adventure to the centre of their heart. By nature, they are passionate, sensual, affectionate, petulant and complicated. This can be an engrossing physical relationship and will certainly not be boring, repetitive or mundane.

There is an old astrological saying that Scorpio is represented by the scorpion – sensitive, reactive and irascible – but also the eagle – visionary, high-flying, discerning and expansive. In the mix of two Scorpio Moons the choice for both will be which of these traits to live out. The strong likelihood is that they will choose both, now and then, but always aspire to the best they can be.

The trick for both will be to fly high even when their delicate, reactive natures are hurt and to avoid hurting because they have been hurt. The way to do this is to remember how much of each lies in the other and give not just respect but also the tender touch each deserves.

Scorpio and Sagittarius (Water and Fire)

These two zodiac neighbours share common traits in uncommon ways. Both have an intensity of being. Sagittarius expresses their vivid inner experience, often with emotional eloquence, into the outer world. In contrast, Scorpio, who may have the biggest emotional lexicon of the zodiac and a greater intensity of inner experience, rarely projects everything out to the world – their expressions are indicative only, small but potent samples of what lies within. Sagittarius is outward-looking where Scorpio is inward-feeling.

In terms of communication, Sagittarius tends to a frank diplomacy, whereas Scorpio is inclined, when forced by circumstance, to say just what they feel with an apparent disregard to how it is received. Mixing the two does not always work, but does offer a lively exchange that challenges the best of both natures. Sagittarius may be too open, direct or 'intrusive' for the more reserved, easily-pained Scorpio, whereas their secretive tendency will prick the curiosity of Sagittarius but may also frustrate them, as their need to know and understand can remain largely unfulfilled by the Scorpio universe.

Both are freedom-loving and loathe the idea of any form of restriction, but each may ironically try to limit the other in their striving for certainty and security. To avoid this, each needs to give the other a wide berth to manoeuvre emotionally. This means respect, a touch of distance and agreeing to keep a measure of mystery alive in the relationship.

The pair can work intimately and romantically, but may find that the phases of the Moon blow hot and cold on their amorous affections. Knowing this can give the couple a better understanding of each other's sensitivities and desires, which are strong for both. An interesting, challenging and passionate relationship that has elements of tension and attraction.

Scorpio and Capricorn (Water and Earth)

Appearances can be deceiving, especially with this partnership, where a semblance of common traits are found on closer inspection to have very different causes. Both signs can appear melancholic, shy, retiring and emotionally aloof, but in the case of Capricorn this is an expression of their cool reserve, whereas with Scorpio Moon it's a veil that conceals their more turbulent feelings. Like the mountain citadel, Capricorn seems emotionally distant and this is a defence against strong emotions or the more irrational side of human nature. Keeping cool is their way of managing the unknown. The distance of Scorpio is misleading because, although hidden, their emotions lie just beneath the surface – conscious, observant and at the ready. The real nature of Scorpio, with its abundance of intense feeling, is mostly well beyond the rational grasp of Capricorn.

This will disadvantage Capricorn in the relationship if they try to understand Scorpio using their usual rational yardstick. Capricorn tends to control or manage their environment and Scorpio is well beyond this. It would be better for Capricorn to accept the enigma that Scorpio often is and give it space. That way the relationship could potentially open new emotional pathways for Capricorn to explore.

Scorpio in turn needs to manage their own expectations of Capricorn, who tends to withdraw from the kind of feelings Scorpio is capable of. If this happens, Scorpio should not feel neglected, but accept that Capricorn offers a practical, solid basis and is a reliable partner. The metaphor of the zodiac spy taking refuge in the citadel is not a bad one and with this Scorpio will realize that Capricorn offers a much-needed secure emotional foundation, however staid it may appear to Scorpio.

Romantically, the mix can work, but only if each allows the other to get closer to their distant emotional world. Risks need to be taken here, but they can pay off. When both Moons reach acceptance and understanding, the combination can be passionate and earth-shaking.

Scorpio and Aquarius (Water and Air)

The mystical inclinations of both signs create the potential for deep agreement, a meeting of minds and a melding of hearts. But like any mystical journey this will not be without its challenges, symbolized by the dissimilar natures of Saturn and Mars, the owners of Aquarius and Scorpio respectively.

Aquarius thinks expansively and includes a host of others in their big concerns, whereas Scorpio tends to a self-absorption. Aquarius seeks meaning in a broad universality, an open outward-looking inclusiveness that celebrates the importance of everyman as all men – typical of their Air-sign thinking nature. Scorpio in contrast seeks meaning through their inward-looking, soul-searching, ultra-personalism that puts self-importance first. In this they feel symbolically representative of every man, emphasizing a transcendence that can only be achieved first and foremost by the soul within. Their liberation is a victory for everyone and they know that without one being free, none can be free. So both approach the same subject by different means and as long as they stay true to their natures and avoid labelling their styles, they can celebrate their mutual aim and find common ground.

Romantically, Scorpio will inspire the sensual, pleasure-seeking side of Aquarius, who in turn will appreciate a partner who is very passionate and intensely sensual. Aquarius needs to remember that Scorpio is possessive and in certain circumstances also jealous, and should therefore balance their social life with reassurance and time spent alone with the Scorpio Moon, who will enjoy quiet, candlelit dinners and good music and the intimacy of just the two of them on their own.

Scorpio and Pisces (Water and Water)

The transcendent aspirations of Scorpio have their mature expression in the easy-going, gentle Pisces, giving this couple a lot of common ground. Pisces can both understand and accept the impenetrable Scorpio Moon and celebrate their intuitive, feeling nature, which is so like their own. While both have their high-minded qualities, they are also pleasure-seeking and can stimulate each other's passions, arousing primal urges for a magical intimacy rich in feeling and visionary quality. This passion has an intuitive quality that speaks in subtle tones from heart to heart, reaffirming the depths of their watery beings.

While both are seductive, Scorpio is more dominant and expressive, Pisces more passive and surrendering. Pisces symbolizes self-sacrifice and universal love, which can offer Scorpio a healing salve for their tender heart. Pisces will need to hold their own, though, as it is easy to succumb to the stronger Scorpio with an emotional deference that can sometimes leave Pisces vulnerable.

Both will be interested in exploring the mysteries of life and love, and may even express this by combining sexuality with spirituality in the form of Tantra and similar principles. Pisces also symbolizes moksha, or liberation from the bondage of mundane existence, thus the combination with Scorpio results in a freedom-seeking couple.

Emotional, fluid, flexible and impressionable natures can bring a high degree of fantasy and dreaminess to this pair. They need to help each other keep their feet on the ground, as they can lack discipline and structure. However, the exchange of moods fosters creativity, insight and an intuitive view of reality. It is possible that they will strengthen each other's psychic talents and bring out each other's originality.

Sagittarius and...

Sagittarius (Fire and Fire)

An easy but passionate understanding exists in this partnership due to the couple's common emotional natures that tend to celebrate their regal, driven, energetic passions. This is a philosophical combination that encourages interpersonal growth through the striving for wisdom, understanding and higher knowledge. It is rare for the Sagittarius Moon to bend to the yoke of prejudice, especially as they know that their all-or-nothing nature will take them as far as any small mind can go. They know that any man is capable of what all men can do and tend to rein in their lower nature by aspiring to high ideals which include an interest in justice and democratic freedom. The squaring of this potency with two Sagittarius Moons makes for a strong couple who seek truth and justice for all at every turn.

Both are passionate, moody and sometimes depressive and it will be easy for one to trigger this in the other, especially with the help of the lunar phases which will emphasize their joint emotional ups and downs. They will need to help each other with this. The easiest way will be talking things through, being honest and revealing their minds to each other. This will bring a relaxing of mental tensions as well as help them put small problems into context.

Both are sociable and tend to have large networks of friends and acquaintances with whom they generously share themselves. This is an energetic, caring partnership that is ready to champion the underdog and loves to be where the action is, particularly in opening up new territory.

Romantically, this is an impassioned combination that can result in tremendous highs and sulking, despondent lows. Each has a good understanding of the other's emotional needs, but at times there could be a mild competition for whose needs are met first. If a third party enters the scene, this competition can degrade into jealousy. Intimately, the couple are close, sensitive and engaging, sparking each other's amorous natures with jest, trickery and originality.

Sagittarius and Capricorn (Fire and Earth)

Both signs have a stoic, principled, strong-willed nature, which gives them plenty of opportunity to create mutual understanding and harmony. Their different approaches to life are also complementary, with each able to help with the other's weaknesses and shortcomings.

The freedom-loving, inspired and outgoing Sagittarius offers a boost to the emotional morale of reserved, serious Capricorn. Sagittarius brings a positive, can-do spirit which Capricorn is able to use to progress towards their important goals. Both signs tend to be ambitious and aspirational, but Capricorn has a sobering, practical influence on the sometimes overly optimistic Sagittarius. Capricorn offers practical support and grounding, which aids Sagittarius in their mission of personal growth and material well-being. In turn, Sagittarius' optimism can soften the hard edges of Capricorn's sceptical view of life, helping them make greater use of their talents. There is a good chance that both can harness the energies of the other for their mutual benefit.

The challenges will come when Sagittarius becomes depressive or listless and Capricorn is also depressive, or emotionally restricted, and unable to lend a hand. So the pair can get quite moody at times, especially as they are zodiac neighbours and are influenced by the lunar phases one after the other. This means that there are likely to be strong swings of mood, from perky positivism to peevish pensiveness. Knowing this will help them manage these temporary swings so that they can remain focused and keep on track.

Capricorn benefits from the philosophical view of Sagittarius, although at times probably finds it unsatisfying. Any other sign than Sagittarius and Capricorn could find their 'theorizing' simple-minded or self-serving, but Capricorn knows all too well that when push comes to shove Sagittarius is ready to argue their case.

Romantically, there is a good likelihood of compatibility, although it may require Sagittarius to make sacrifices for Capricorn. However, the Sagittarius romantic thunderbolt may be just what is required to set off a romantic avalanche in Capricorn's mountain retreat. If that happens, give them plenty of room.

Sagittarius and Aquarius (Fire and Air)

The high-minded, wisdom-seeking qualities of both give ample ground for a solid friendship and inspiring romance. Sagittarius can inspire Aquarius like, perhaps, no other sign in their striving for truth and universalism. Sagittarius naturally understands the esoteric, wistful and sometimes ethereal ponderings of Aquarius and unlike other signs will not feel left out or ignored when Aquarius takes time to contemplate. On the contrary, Sagittarius is a willing meditation partner.

Both are fed by the other's intrinsic emotional qualities, Aquarius by the inspiring, thought-provoking Sagittarius, Sagittarius by Aquarius' concern for people, social and global principles and big-picture view of life. They combine to produce a generous couple who can easily put the needs of others before their own, and who are often involved in charitable and social projects.

There is a scintillating intimacy between the two, as the vigorous and fiery nature of Sagittarius excites the receptive fantasies of Aquarius and Aquarius' lofty, almost otherworldly nature triggers the philosopher and warrior passions in Sagittarius. Sagittarius may prove to be more easily content alone, whereas the urge for company, stimulation and involvement will take Aquarius further afield to explore new relationships and experiences. While Sagittarius is also very sociable, they may not always accept this Aquarian interest in more and more social experience, and think it inane. To counter this, Sagittarius needs to remember, like Scorpio for that matter, that Aquarius grows with social interaction and to restrict this does little good. Of course, this may be just the Sagittarius concern for playing a central role in their partner's life, so Aquarius needs to put conscious effort into making their partner feel loved, appreciated and needed. Soldiers get into trouble when they feel unappreciated and as Sagittarius is the zodiac general it's a good idea to show regular appreciation.

This is a relationship that has a lot going for it, not least of which is good communication, the sharing of interests and ideas, and the right amount of difference to galvanize the mixture into a harmonious working whole.

Sagittarius and Pisces (Fire and Water)

Both signs are ruled by Jupiter, which gives them a natural affinity and mutual appreciation, although the differences between them are strongly pronounced. Both have a thirst for wisdom and knowledge, and in a sense represent the evolution of the warrior-sage to the final zodiac stage of renunciation symbolized by the hermit. This symbolism represents the wisdom-in-action of Sagittarius and the wisdom-of-being in Pisces. This is the symbolic key to understanding the relationship dynamic at work in this partnership.

Pisces has less outreach than Sagittarius and is happy with a quiet inner contentment – no need for grand emotional gestures, it's enough to feel it, or be it. Sagittarius usually appreciates this as 'action in inaction', the idea that a state of being in itself is strong enough to effect change or get results from the outer world. Still, despite this understanding, Sagittarius is an action-in-action sign and can get frustrated with the laid-back Pisces, especially when there is practical work to be done. Pisces will benefit from the Sagittarius prodding, if their sensitive feelings aren't hurt or their strong ego roused (yes, even Pisces has an ego). Assuming that Pisces stays flexible, they can make good use of the Sagittarius push to get into action and advance their own interests.

There is a mutual respect between the two signs and both have a strong creative quality and active imagination. They can share a very close intimacy and tend to know what each other is feeling and thinking. Both are sensual and passionate, although Pisces can probably surprise Sagittarius with their unexpected intensity and sensuous inclinations.

Capricorn and...

Capricorn (Earth and Earth)

It is certain that work and practical progress in life will be a central theme in this relationship. The challenge will be to ensure that the deeper, tender emotional needs of both are met by more than success at work or managing the details of day-to-day life. To do this, both partners will need to consciously enliven their relationship with outside stimuli such as travel, holidays and an active social life. The key here is to create diversity, because variety is the spice of life – and there is nothing worse for this couple than to fall into a rut of the routine and predictable.

Assuming that other qualities in their charts help them, however, they will be able to develop a solid relationship that can take them far in life. Regardless of their status in life, they will emphasize work and the responsibilities they have to each other and to others. Their extraordinary patience will help them tolerate many inconveniences as they fulfil these obligations. They are loyal, steadfast and trustworthy, and this can make up for any lack of frivolity in their partnership.

However, the tendency to emotional reserve in each other's company can put too much emphasis on what they don't have as opposed to what they do have. In some cases this can manifest as a sense that somehow they don't deserve better, which, if they are not careful, will become a self-fulfilling prophesy.

Maybe the easiest way for them to lighten up their relationship will be by combining career, financial and relationship interests. While this can be tricky, and not always viable, it may be more possible for the practical Capricorn Moon than for others and would bring in a mix of interests, thus allowing them to share in each other's achievements and successes. Whichever way they choose, the important (but maybe unspoken) goal should be to invite as much outside stimulation as possible to animate and invigorate their romantic exchange.

Capricorn and Aquarius (Earth and Air)

Both signs are ruled by the disciplinary, karmic planet Saturn, which gives them the chance for an emotional kinship that can bring out the best of both. The stimulating, questioning and sociable Aquarius offers the right pick-me-up to the more sedate Capricorn, bringing them out into their diverse world of ideas, causes, concerns, friends and acquaintances. This can do wonders for Capricorn, whose work or professional concerns can benefit through such networks, but of course the real benefit to Capricorn is the chance to feed their heart with agreeable social interaction.

Aquarius may be challenged to get Capricorn to budge from their cautious vantage point, but then again this is just the kind of challenge the humane, caring and generous Aquarius is built for. The connection offers them the chance to examine and re-examine their ideas and attitudes thanks to Capricorn's doubting and sometimes sceptical approach. The exchange softens both partners, opening up Capricorn's mind and helping Aquarius to make their ideas more practical.

The challenge here will come if either partner tries to force their views and moods on the other. This will result in hurt feelings, the entrenchment of attitudes and a withdrawal of emotional access. This can be difficult and as the two are zodiac neighbours, nerves can fray more easily during certain lunar phases. The trick here is for each to give the other the respect they deserve, otherwise it can be difficult to pull back and undo thoughtless hurts.

Intimate relations have a strong, binding, intricate quality to them, with an element of yearning and intensity. Very deep feelings can develop between the two and the softer side of Aquarius can bring Capricorn into a safe, secure emotional space in which to stretch and feel free. The astrological kinship can make this a lasting partnership, especially when the best of each is freely expressed.

Capricorn and Pisces (Earth and Water)

An agreeable combination that can satisfy the needs of both, especially when they are aware of their distinctive emotional natures. Pisces' sweet, gentle and giving nature helps soften and support Capricorn and, in turn, Capricorn offers Pisces solid ground, a loyal and dependable partner and help with channelling their talents productively into the outer world.

Capricorn can lovingly bolster Pisces' confidence, helping to remove their hidden feelings of inferiority or self-doubt. This is a great boost to Pisces, who needs a good sounding-board in a partner, a person who is in some measure similar – quiet, reserved and not too boisterous. Capricorn helps put Pisces at ease and gently coaxes them into expressing themselves – something which does not often come easily.

Both will feel emotionally comfortable in the other's company, but the reticent Capricorn may feel insecure or uncertain at times. This can arise when Pisces appears 'too far away', lost in their rich inner emotional world, leaving Capricorn lonely or isolated – something they feel naturally. If, somehow, the couple can overcome any barriers to expressing their own feelings and understanding each other's concealed feelings, though, the relationship should thrive. Pisces should be able to help with this by creating a soothing, sensual setting of creature comforts where both feel at ease, secure and stimulated to share their inner thoughts. Pisces may also decide to bring this out to the party arena, which will bring fun, excitement and energy to the relationship.

Lastly, it is certain that Pisces can play an important role in introducing their Capricorn partner to the subtle side of life, something Capricorn may at first resist, but will benefit from. This will help Capricorn explore their own feelings, which can be quite powerful when given expression.

Aquarius and...

Aquarius (Air and Air)

This couple will be at the centre of social events, stimulating discussion, causing debate and proposing new ways of thinking. They will inspire in each other inventive and original ideas which sometimes border on the eccentric and unusual. Their combined creative sense will make them fashionable, if not fashion victims. Their love of people, causes and movements will draw them to friends and acquaintances, *soirées* and parties, events and even demonstrations.

The big-picture view in each partner magnifies the importance of an issue and impassions their commitment to it. The energy of this partnership can breathe an urgency into even trivial things. Given the mystical side of the two Aquarius Moons, you can also expect them to read messages from events in nature or their surroundings from time to time. Certainly they will put value in 'reading' their environment or 'feeling' the situation before taking important action.

They are also catalysts for learning and demonstrate a thirst for knowledge and wisdom. This can take on a markedly artistic quality if other astrological factors are supportive. Regardless of the finer details of their external egos, it is certain that they inspire in each other a sense of mission and purpose that makes them quite passionate.

Romantically, this is a couple seeking to experience higher levels of intimacy and ecstasy. The mixing of two Air signs infuses the relationship with vigour and intensity but can make it unstable, changeable and fickle. The challenge is to stabilize their emotions and give them direction and focus. Like all partnerships between the same Moon sign, expect that the lunar phases and other astrological influences will create cycles of varied experience that both challenge and deepen the relationship.

Aquarius and Pisces (Air and Water)

The emblem of Aquarius is that of a man pouring water from one pot to another. This symbolizes a mixing of matter and spirit, ideas and action, theory and validation, renewal and establishment. Speaking esoterically, the spirit, ideas, theory and renewal have their deeper source in the neighbouring sign of Pisces. Aquarius, if you will, borrows the meditative potency and conceptual energy of Pisces and pours them into the tangible physical realm for everyone's benefit. This is symbolized by the constellation of Purva Bhadra (Alpha and Beta Pegasi), which straddles Aquarius and Pisces and to some extent suggests why Aquarius ideas can appear eccentric at times – they lose some of their archetypal potency in the translation from the unconsciousness of Pisces to the mass awareness of Aquarius.

If both partners in an Aquarius/Pisces relationship have a sense of the connection between the two zodiac signs, they have a key for understanding how to harmonize their relationship and make the most of it. Pisces is a master of dreams and fantasy – and just as dreams talk to us in apparently unintelligible ways, so the Pisces Moon can transfer imperceptible signals of inspiration to the mystical Aquarius. Whether these are transmitted through feelings, body language, spoken ideas or psychic impressions, they will stimulate Aquarius into action.

This principle has a romantic component as well – the subtle signals sent to the unconscious part of Aquarius by the sensual, intuitive Pisces can make them appear highly seductive. This can be a satisfying romantic partnership if Aquarius can learn to check their tendency to bring the mundane side of their awareness into the interaction with dreamy, romantic Pisces. Of course, the more practical side of Aquarius has a role to play, but not in the realm of intimacy.

Pisces and...

Pisces (Water and Water)

Too much easy-going agreeability may leave both partners floating in an emotional ocean of dreamy, feel-good sentimentality – not an entirely bad thing for two signs symbolized by fishes. Whatever the details of a double Pisces relationship, it is certain to be so subtle that much of what goes on between them will be imperceptible to the average bystander.

Still waters run deep and this applies doubly to this combination, which can make their union one that is deep, satisfying and mutually nurturing, or one that fails to really connect emotionally. This, of course, is due to the depth of the two Pisces' inner worlds, which they tend to experience happily alone – which to some extent precludes the need for the more overt kind of emotional connection. This relationship is like two hermits meeting! While such a meeting can result in lots of conversation, storytelling and note-taking, it can also end up with both looking impatiently at their sundials. The trick is to get this couple to share their rich inner worlds with each other, bringing each other into a heart world they create together. Of course, when this happens the next challenge may be to get them to surface from their diluvial depths to connect with the rest of us!

The challenge in this partnership is obvious. The two Pisces Moons will need to help each other navigate the day-to-day world, including tidying up, and will be especially prone to the concurrent vagaries of lunar phases and planetary influences.

Together, however, they can create a fantastic romantic world that defies both logic and description. If they are able to inspire in each other the necessary passion to connect, they can go on to experience a special intimacy and the wonderful, dreamy sensuality of two Pisces hearts mingling.

Epilogue

Early on in my career, my partner Pandita would join me in astrological group discussions to explore our charts. Afterwards she would sometimes remark that she shared some of the character traits of another group member. Sometimes more, other times less, but often there was some common ground, although both the charts and the external personalities were very different. Those of you who have read all, or most, of this book may feel that you too share in some of the other traits described. There is a good astrological reason for this, as all the 12 zodiac signs play a role in some area of our lives, even when the Moon, Sun or Rising sign is not in them. If a particular sign appears dormant in our personality, its symbolism nevertheless colours some part of our experience or personality.

This symbolism gives us a way to understand more of each other, as indeed there is a part of us all that is Aries, Taurus, Gemini, Cancer, Leo, Virgo, Libra, Scorpio, Sagittarius, Capricorn, Aquarius and Pisces – even if it is a small part. And there is a part of us all that is prince, chancellor, jester, queen, king, counsellor, diplomat, spy, warrior-sage, merchant prince, citizen and hermit – zodiac characters that embody one of the many sides of our personalities. This is just one reason why the magic of legend and the characters of fairy-tales continue to warn, teach, guide and inspire long after we have grown too old to 'believe' in them.

These are archetypes dancing in the mandala of life. If we can recognize how they are dancing in another person, then we can recognize something of ourselves at work in them – which, if nothing else, can help us be more open-minded and tolerant. Recognizing our common traits may also inspire greater compassion and give us all a chance to keep a more harmonious and prosperous court.

Michael is available for personal and business consultations, life coaching and workshops at www.moonastrology.com, by e-mail at mdg@panchang.com and at the following address and phone numbers:

Panchang Ltd
PO Box 2837
Bath
BA1 2FR
England

Tel: +44 1225 786500
Fax: +44 1225 339222

Appendix

Find your Moon Sign

Finding your Moon sign is easy using the tables below. To find your Moon sign you will need three things: your date of birth (year, month and day), the approximate time of your birth and the time zone of your birthplace.

The first thing to do to find your Moon sign is look up the year of your birth on the left-hand side of the page, then find the month of your birth on the left column. The days of every month are in the top row of each year, numbered from 1 to 31. Locate the date of your birth, run your eye down to the month of your birth and make a note of the number, if there is one, and the astrological glyph. If you don't know the glyphs, don't worry, a small table on page 235 tells you what they are.

The number next to the glyph (if there is one) tells you what hour of the day (using the 24-hour clock) the Moon entered that particular zodiac sign from the preceding Moon sign. If there is only a glyph there, then that is the sign your Moon is in.

Take the actress Meg Ryan, for example. She was born on 19 November 1961 in Connecticut, USA. Find 1961, then November and run your finger across the page to 19 to find that '♈18' appears there. This tells you that on that day, at 6 p.m. (GMT) the Moon entered Aries. All the times in the table are given as Greenwich Mean Time (GMT) – Greenwich, England. If you were not born in the UK and the GMT time zone, simply add or subtract the number of times zones for your place of birth (*see* the Time Zone table below).

Now, Ms Ryan was born in Connecticut, which is Eastern Standard Time (EST). A look at the Time Zone chart below tells you that EST is –5 hours behind GMT, that is, 5 hours earlier. Deduct 5 hours from 6 p.m. to find that the Moon entered Aries at 1 p.m. EST (18 – 5 = 13, or 1 p.m.). Anyone born on that day in that time zone after 1 p.m. has their Moon in Aries. Ms Ryan was born at 10 a.m. and therefore her Moon is in Pisces.

Some other examples:

- If you were born in Los Angeles (–8) on that day then you would *deduct* 8 hours from 6 p.m., which means the Moon entered Aries at 10 a.m. Pacific Standard Time (PST). (18 – 8 = 10, or 10 a.m.)
- If you were born in Hong Kong (+8) on that day then you would *add* 8 hours to 6 p.m., which means that the Moon entered Aries at 2 a.m. on the next calendar day, 20 November. (18 + 8 = 26, – a 24-hour day = 2, or 2 a.m.)

Calculating your Moon sign using these tables has a margin of error of approximately 2 per cent. If you want to be absolutely accurate about your Moon sign, please visit www.moonastrology.com or www.thorsons.com, where you can get your free Lunar report which tells you your Moon sign with negligible margin of error.

Time Zones

00 Greenwich Mean Time	+13 Nuku'alofa
-01 Azores	+12 Wellington
-02 Mid-Atlantic	+11 Solomon Islands
-03 Buenos Aires	+10 Canberra
-04 Atlantic	+09 Tokyo
-05 Eastern	+08 Singapore
-07 Mountain	+06 Dhaka
-08 Pacific	+05 Karachi
-09 Alaska	+04 Abu Dhabi
-10 Hawaii	+03 Moscow
-11 Samoa	+02 Cairo
-12 Date Line	+01 Berlin

Note: If daylight saving time is in effect at the time and place of your birth, subtract an extra hour.

Astrological Glyph Table

♈	Aries
♉	Taurus
♊	Gemini
♋	Cancer
♌	Leo
♍	Virgo
♎	Libra
♏	Scorpio
♐	Sagittarius
♑	Capricorn
♒	Aquarius
♓	Pisces

1930	1	2	3	4	5	6	7	8	9	10	11	12	13	14	15	16	17	18	19	20	21	22	23	24	25	26	27	28	29	30	31
Jan	♑4	♑	♒16	♒	♒	♓4	♓	♈14	♈	♉19	♉	♊21	♊	♋20	♋	♌19	♌	♍20	♍	♍	♎1	♎	♏9	♏	♐21	♐	♐	♑10	♑	♒22	♒
Feb	♒	♓10	♓	♈20	♈	♈	♉3	♉	♊7	♊	♋7	♋	♌6	♌	♍7	♍	♎10	♎	♏17	♏	♏	♐3	♐	♑16	♑	♑	♒4	♒			
Mar	♓16	♓	♓	♈1	♈	♉9	♉	♊14	♊	♋16	♋	♌17	♌	♍17	♍	♎20	♎	♎	♏2	♏	♐11	♐	♑23	♑	♑	♒12	♒	♓23	♓	♓	♈8
Apr	♈	♉14	♉	♊19	♊	♋23	♋	♋	♌1	♌	♍3	♍	♎6	♎	♏11	♏	♐20	♐	♐	♑7	♑	♒19	♒	♒	♓7	♓	♈16	♈	♉22	♉	
May	♉	♊1	♊	♋4	♋	♌7	♌	♍10	♍	♎14	♎	♏20	♏	♏	♐4	♐	♑15	♑	♑	♒4	♒	♓15	♓	♓	♈1	♈	♉6	♉	♊9	♊	♋11
Jun	♋	♌12	♌	♍15	♍	♎20	♎	♎	♏3	♏	♐12	♐	♑23	♑	♑	♒11	♒	♒	♓0	♓	♈10	♈	♉16	♉	♊19	♊	♋19	♋	♌19	♌	
Jul	♍21	♍	♍	♎2	♎	♏9	♏	♐18	♐	♐	♑6	♑	♒18	♒	♒	♓7	♓	♈18	♈	♈	♉1	♉	♊5	♊	♋6	♋	♌5	♌	♍5	♍	♎8
Aug	♎	♏14	♏	♏	♐0	♐	♑12	♑	♑	♒0	♒	♓13	♓	♓	♈0	♈	♉9	♉	♊14	♊	♋16	♋	♌16	♌	♍15	♍	♎16	♎	♏21	♏	♏
Sep	♐6	♐	♑18	♑	♑	♒6	♒	♓19	♓	♓	♈6	♈	♉15	♉	♊22	♊	♊	♋1	♋	♌2	♌	♍2	♍	♎3	♎	♏6	♏	♐14	♐	♐	
Oct	♑0	♑	♒13	♒	♒	♓1	♓	♈12	♈	♉21	♉	♉	♊3	♊	♋8	♋	♌10	♌	♍12	♍	♎13	♎	♏16	♏	♐23	♐	♐	♑8	♑	♒20	♒
Nov	♒	♓9	♓	♈20	♈	♈	♉4	♉	♊9	♊	♋13	♋	♌16	♌	♍19	♍	♎22	♎	♎	♏2	♏	♐8	♐	♑17	♑	♑	♒5	♒	♓17	♓	
Dec	♓	♈4	♈	♉12	♉	♊17	♊	♋19	♋	♌22	♌	♌	♍0	♍	♎4	♎	♏10	♏	♐16	♐	♐	♑1	♑	♒13	♒	♒	♓2	♓	♈14	♈	♉22

1931	1	2	3	4	5	6	7	8	9	10	11	12	13	14	15	16	17	18	19	20	21	22	23	24	25	26	27	28	29	30	31
Jan	♉	♉	♊3	♊	♋5	♋	♌5	♌	♍6	♍	♎10	♎	♏15	♏	♐23	♐	♐	♑9	♑	♒20	♒	♒	♓9	♓	♈22	♈	♈	♉8	♉	♊13	♊
Feb	♋15	♋	♌15	♌	♍15	♍	♎16	♎	♏21	♏	♏	♐5	♐	♑15	♑	♑	♒3	♒	♓15	♓	♓	♈4	♈	♉15	♉	♊23	♊	♊			
Mar	♋2	♋	♌3	♌	♍2	♍	♎2	♎	♏4	♏	♐11	♐	♑20	♑	♑	♒9	♒	♓21	♓	♓	♈10	♈	♉21	♉	♉	♊6	♊	♋11	♋	♌13	♌
Apr	♍13	♍	♎13	♎	♏14	♏	♐19	♐	♐	♑3	♑	♒15	♒	♒	♓4	♓	♈16	♈	♈	♉3	♉	♊11	♊	♋17	♋	♌21	♌	♍22	♍	♎23	
May	♎	♎	♏1	♏	♐4	♐	♑12	♑	♒22	♒	♒	♓11	♓	♈23	♈	♈	♉10	♉	♊17	♊	♋23	♋	♋	♌3	♌	♍5	♍	♎8	♎	♏10	♏
Jun	♐14	♐	♑20	♑	♑	♒6	♒	♓19	♓	♓	♈7	♈	♉18	♉	♉	♊1	♊	♋5	♋	♌8	♌	♍11	♍	♎14	♎	♏18	♏	♐22	♐	♐	
Jul	♑5	♑	♒15	♒	♒	♓3	♓	♈16	♈	♈	♉2	♉	♊9	♊	♋13	♋	♌15	♌	♍17	♍	♎19	♎	♏23	♏	♏	♐5	♐	♑12	♑	♒22	♒
Aug	♒	♓10	♓	♈23	♈	♈	♉11	♉	♊19	♊	♋23	♋	♋	♌1	♌	♍1	♍	♎2	♎	♏5	♏	♐10	♐	♑18	♑	♑	♒5	♒	♓17	♓	♓
Sep	♈6	♈	♉18	♉	♉	♊4	♊	♋9	♋	♌11	♌	♍11	♍	♎11	♎	♏12	♏	♐16	♐	♐	♑0	♑	♒11	♒	♓23	♓	♓	♈12	♈	♈	
Oct	♉1	♉	♊11	♊	♋18	♋	♌21	♌	♍22	♍	♎22	♎	♏22	♏	♏	♐0	♐	♑7	♑	♒17	♒	♒	♓5	♓	♈18	♈	♈	♉6	♉	♊16	♊
Nov	♊	♋0	♋	♌6	♌	♍8	♍	♎8	♎	♏9	♏	♐10	♐	♑15	♑	♑	♒0	♒	♓12	♓	♓	♈1	♈	♉13	♉	♊22	♊	♊	♋6	♋	
Dec	♌11	♌	♍15	♍	♎18	♎	♏19	♏	♐21	♐	♐	♑1	♑	♒9	♒	♓20	♓	♓	♈9	♈	♉21	♉	♉	♊6	♊	♋12	♋	♌17	♌	♍21	♍

1932	1	2	3	4	5	6	7	8	9	10	11	12	13	14	15	16	17	18	19	20	21	22	23	24	25	26	27	28	29	30	31
Jan	♍	♎0	♎	♏3	♏	♐6	♐	♑10	♑	♒18	♒	♒	♓4	♓	♈17	♈	♈	♉5	♉	♊15	♊	♋21	♋	♋	♌0	♌	♍3	♍	♎5	♎	♏8
Feb	♏	♐13	♐	♑18	♑	♑	♒2	♒	♓13	♓	♓	♈1	♈	♉14	♉	♉	♊0	♊	♋7	♋	♌10	♌	♍11	♍	♎12	♎	♏14	♏	♐18		
Mar	♐	♐	♑0	♑	♒9	♒	♓20	♓	♓	♈8	♈	♉21	♉	♉	♊9	♊	♋17	♋	♌21	♌	♍22	♍	♎22	♎	♏22	♏	♏	♐0	♐	♑6	♑
Apr	♒15	♒	♒	♓2	♓	♈15	♈	♈	♉4	♉	♊15	♊	♊	♋1	♋	♌7	♌	♍9	♍	♎9	♎	♏8	♏	♐9	♐	♑13	♑	♒21	♒	♒	
May	♓8	♓	♈21	♈	♈	♉10	♉	♊21	♊	♊	♋7	♋	♌14	♌	♍18	♍	♎19	♎	♏19	♏	♐19	♐	♑22	♑	♑	♒4	♒	♓14	♓	♓	♈3
Jun	♈	♉16	♉	♉	♊3	♊	♋12	♋	♌20	♌	♌	♍1	♍	♎4	♎	♏5	♏	♐5	♐	♑7	♑	♒13	♒	♓22	♓	♓	♈10	♈	♉23	♉	
Jul	♉	♊10	♊	♋19	♋	♋	♌1	♌	♍6	♍	♎10	♎	♏12	♏	♐14	♐	♑17	♑	♒22	♒	♒	♓7	♓	♈18	♈	♈	♉7	♉	♊18	♊	♊
Aug	♋3	♋	♌8	♌	♍12	♍	♎15	♎	♏18	♏	♐21	♐	♐	♑1	♑	♒7	♒	♓15	♓	♓	♈2	♈	♉15	♉	♉	♊2	♊	♋12	♋	♌17	♌
Sep	♍20	♍	♎22	♎	♏23	♏	♏	♐2	♐	♑7	♑	♒14	♒	♓23	♓	♓	♈10	♈	♉22	♉	♉	♊11	♊	♋21	♋	♋	♌3	♌	♍6	♍	
Oct	♎7	♎	♏7	♏	♐8	♐	♑12	♑	♒19	♒	♒	♓5	♓	♈17	♈	♈	♉5	♉	♊18	♊	♊	♋5	♋	♌13	♌	♍17	♍	♎18	♎	♏17	♏
Nov	♐17	♐	♑19	♑	♑	♒1	♒	♓11	♓	♈23	♈	♈	♉11	♉	♉	♊0	♊	♋11	♋	♌21	♌	♌	♍2	♍	♎5	♎	♏4	♏	♐4	♐	
Dec	♑4	♑	♒9	♒	♓17	♓	♓	♈5	♈	♉18	♉	♉	♊6	♊	♋17	♋	♋	♌2	♌	♍9	♍	♎13	♎	♏15	♏	♐15	♐	♑15	♑	♒18	♒

1933	1	2	3	4	5	6	7	8	9	10	11	12	13	14	15	16	17	18	19	20	21	22	23	24	25	26	27	28	29	30	31
Jan	♒	♓1	♓	♈12	♈	♈	♉1	♉	♊13	♊	♋23	♋	♋	♌8	♌	♍15	♍	♎20	♎	♏23	♏	♏	♐0	♐	♑2	♑	♒5	♒	♓11	♓	♈20
Feb	♈	♈	♉8	♉	♊21	♊	♊	♋7	♋	♌15	♌	♍21	♍	♍	♎1	♎	♏4	♏	♐7	♐	♑10	♑	♒14	♒	♓20	♓	♓	♈5			
Mar	♈	♉17	♉	♉	♊5	♊	♋16	♋	♋	♌0	♌	♍5	♍	♎8	♎	♏10	♏	♐12	♐	♑16	♑	♒21	♒	♒	♓4	♓	♈13	♈	♈	♉1	♉
Apr	♊13	♊	♊	♋1	♋	♌10	♌	♍15	♍	♎17	♎	♏18	♏	♐19	♐	♑21	♑	♑	♒3	♒	♓10	♓	♈20	♈	♈	♉8	♉	♊20	♊	♊	
May	♋9	♋	♌19	♌	♌	♍1	♍	♎4	♎	♏4	♏	♐4	♐	♑4	♑	♒8	♒	♓16	♓	♓	♈2	♈	♉14	♉	♉	♊2	♊	♋15	♋	♋	♌2
Jun	♌	♍10	♍	♎14	♎	♏15	♏	♐14	♐	♑14	♑	♒16	♒	♓22	♓	♓	♈8	♈	♉20	♉	♉	♊8	♊	♋21	♋	♋	♌8	♌	♍17	♍	
Jul	♎22	♎	♎	♏0	♏	♐1	♐	♑0	♑	♒2	♒	♓6	♓	♈15	♈	♈	♉2	♉	♊15	♊	♊	♋3	♋	♌14	♌	♍22	♍	♍	♎4	♎	♏8
Aug	♏	♐10	♐	♑10	♑	♒12	♒	♓15	♓	♈23	♈	♈	♉9	♉	♊22	♊	♊	♋10	♋	♌20	♌	♌	♍4	♍	♎10	♎	♏14	♏	♐17	♐	♑19
Sep	♑	♒21	♒	♒	♓1	♓	♈8	♈	♉18	♉	♉	♊6	♊	♋18	♋	♋	♌4	♌	♍12	♍	♎16	♎	♏19	♏	♐22	♐	♐	♑1	♑	♒5	
Oct	♒	♓10	♓	♈16	♈	♈	♉2	♉	♊14	♊	♊	♋2	♋	♌13	♌	♍21	♍	♍	♎1	♎	♏3	♏	♐4	♐	♑6	♑	♒10	♒	♓16	♓	♓
Nov	♈0	♈	♉10	♉	♊21	♊	♊	♋10	♋	♌22	♌	♌	♍7	♍	♎11	♎	♏13	♏	♐13	♐	♑13	♑	♒16	♒	♓22	♓	♓	♈6	♈	♉16	
Dec	♉	♉	♊4	♊	♋17	♋	♋	♌6	♌	♍16	♍	♎22	♎	♎	♏0	♏	♐0	♑23	♑	♑	♒0	♒	♓4	♓	♈12	♈	♉22	♉	♉	♊10	♊

1934	1	2	3	4	5	6	7	8	9	10	11	12	13	14	15	16	17	18	19	20	21	22	23	24	25	26	27	28	29	30	31
Jan	♋23	♋	♋	♌12	♌	♍22	♍	♍	♎6	♎	♏10	♏	♐11	♐	♑10	♑	♒10	♒	♓13	♓	♈19	♈	♈	♉4	♉	♊17	♊	♊	♋5	♋	♌17
Feb	♌	♌	♍4	♍	♎12	♎	♏18	♏	♐20	♐	♑21	♑	♒21	♒	♓23	♓	♓	♈4	♈	♉12	♉	♊23	♊	♊	♋12	♋	♋	♌0			
Mar	♌	♍10	♍	♎18	♎	♏23	♏	♏	♐3	♐	♑5	♑	♒7	♒	♓9	♓	♈14	♈	♉21	♉	♉	♊7	♊	♋20	♋	♋	♌8	♌	♍18	♍	♍
Apr	♎1	♎	♏5	♏	♐8	♐	♑11	♑	♒14	♒	♓18	♓	♈23	♈	♈	♉6	♉	♊16	♊	♊	♋4	♋	♌17	♌	♌	♍3	♍	♎9	♎	♏13	
May	♏	♐15	♐	♑17	♑	♒20	♒	♒	♓0	♓	♈6	♈	♉14	♉	♉	♊0	♊	♋12	♋	♋	♌1	♌	♍12	♍	♎19	♎	♏22	♏	♐23	♐	♐
Jun	♑0	♑	♒2	♒	♓5	♓	♈12	♈	♉20	♉	♉	♊7	♊	♋19	♋	♋	♌8	♌	♍20	♍	♍	♎4	♎	♏8	♏	♐10	♐	♑9	♑	♒10	
Jul	♒	♓12	♓	♈17	♈	♈	♉2	♉	♊13	♊	♊	♋1	♋	♌14	♌	♌	♍2	♍	♎12	♎	♏18	♏	♐20	♐	♑20	♑	♒20	♒	♓20	♓	♓
Aug	♈0	♈	♉8	♉	♊18	♊	♊	♋7	♋	♌20	♌	♌	♍8	♍	♎18	♎	♎	♏1	♏	♐5	♐	♑6	♑	♒6	♒	♓7	♓	♈9	♈	♉15	♉
Sep	♉	♊1	♊	♋14	♋	♋	♌3	♌	♍14	♍	♍	♎0	♎	♏7	♏	♐12	♐	♑15	♑	♒16	♒	♓17	♓	♈19	♈	♈	♉0	♉	♊9	♊	
Oct	♋21	♋	♋	♌10	♌	♍21	♍	♍	♎6	♎	♏12	♏	♐17	♐	♑21	♑	♑	♒0	♒	♓2	♓	♈5	♈	♉10	♉	♊18	♊	♊	♋5	♋	♌18
Nov	♌	♌	♍6	♍	♎14	♎	♏20	♏	♐23	♐	♐	♑2	♑	♒5	♒	♓9	♓	♈13	♈	♉18	♉	♉	♊2	♊	♋13	♋	♋	♌2	♌	♍14	
Dec	♍	♍	♎0	♎	♏5	♏	♐8	♐	♑9	♑	♒11	♒	♓14	♓	♈19	♈	♈	♉1	♉	♊10	♊	♋21	♋	♋	♌10	♌	♍23	♍	♍	♎9	♎

1935	1	2	3	4	5	6	7	8	9	10	11	12	13	14	15	16	17	18	19	20	21	22	23	24	25	26	27	28	29	30	31
Jan	♏16	♏	♐19	♐	♑19	♑	♒19	♒	♓21	♓	♓	♈0	♈	♉7	♉	♊16	♊	♊	♋4	♋	♌16	♌	♌	♍5	♍	♎17	♎	♎	♏1	♏	♐5
Feb	♐	♑7	♑	♒6	♒	♓6	♓	♈8	♈	♉13	♉	♊22	♊	♊	♋10	♋	♌23	♌	♌	♍11	♍	♎23	♎	♎	♏8	♏	♐14	♐			
Mar	♑17	♑	♒17	♒	♓17	♓	♈17	♈	♉21	♉	♉	♊5	♊	♋16	♋	♋	♌5	♌	♍18	♍	♍	♎5	♎	♏14	♏	♐21	♐	♐	♑1	♑	♒3
Apr	♒	♓4	♓	♈4	♈	♉7	♉	♊13	♊	♋23	♋	♋	♌12	♌	♌	♍1	♍	♎11	♎	♏20	♏	♏	♐2	♐	♑7	♑	♒10	♒	♓12	♓	
May	♈14	♈	♉17	♉	♊22	♊	♊	♋8	♋	♌20	♌	♌	♍8	♍	♎19	♎	♎	♏3	♏	♐9	♐	♑13	♑	♒16	♒	♓19	♓	♈21	♈	♈	♉1
Jun	♉	♊7	♊	♋16	♋	♋	♌4	♌	♍16	♍	♍	♎4	♎	♏12	♏	♐17	♐	♑20	♑	♒22	♒	♒	♓0	♓	♈3	♈	♉8	♉	♊15	♊	
Jul	♊	♋0	♋	♌12	♌	♌	♍0	♍	♎12	♎	♏21	♏	♏	♐3	♐	♑5	♑	♒6	♒	♓6	♓	♈9	♈	♉13	♉	♊21	♊	♊	♋7	♋	♌18
Aug	♌	♌	♍7	♍	♎19	♎	♎	♏6	♏	♐12	♐	♑15	♑	♒16	♒	♓15	♓	♈16	♈	♉19	♉	♉	♊2	♊	♋13	♋	♋	♌1	♌	♍13	♍
Sep	♍	♎2	♎	♏13	♏	♐21	♐	♐	♑1	♑	♒2	♒	♓2	♓	♈1	♈	♉3	♉	♊9	♊	♋18	♋	♋	♌7	♌	♍19	♍	♍	♎7	♎	
Oct	♏19	♏	♏	♐4	♐	♑10	♑	♒12	♒	♓13	♓	♈12	♈	♉13	♉	♊17	♊	♊	♋1	♋	♌13	♌	♌	♍2	♍	♎14	♎	♎	♏0	♏	♐9
Nov	♐	♑16	♑	♒20	♒	♓22	♓	♈23	♈	♈	♉0	♉	♊3	♊	♋10	♋	♌21	♌	♌	♍9	♍	♎21	♎	♎	♏7	♏	♐15	♐	♑21	♑	
Dec	♑	♒1	♒	♓4	♓	♈7	♈	♉9	♉	♊13	♊	♋19	♋	♋	♌5	♌	♍17	♍	♍	♎5	♎	♏16	♏	♐23	♐	♐	♑4	♑	♒7	♒	♓10

1936	1	2	3	4	5	6	7	8	9	10	11	12	13	14	15	16	17	18	19	20	21	22	23	24	25	26	27	28	29	30	31
Jan	♓	♈13	♈	♉16	♉	♊21	♊	♊	♋4	♋	♌14	♌	♌	♍2	♍	♎14	♎	♎	♏1	♏	♐9	♐	♑14	♑	♒15	♒	♓16	♓	♈18	♈	♉22
Feb	♉	♉	♊4	♊	♋12	♋	♌22	♌	♌	♍9	♍	♎22	♎	♎	♏10	♏	♐19	♐	♐	♑0	♑	♒2	♒	♓2	♓	♈2	♈	♉4	♉		
Mar	♊9	♊	♋17	♋	♋	♌4	♌	♍16	♍	♍	♎4	♎	♏17	♏	♏	♐3	♐	♑10	♑	♒13	♒	♓13	♓	♈12	♈	♉12	♉	♊16	♊	♋23	♋
Apr	♋	♌10	♌	♍22	♍	♍	♎10	♎	♏22	♏	♏	♐9	♐	♑18	♑	♒22	♒	♒	♓0	♈23	♈	♉23	♉	♉	♊1	♊	♋6	♋	♌16	♌	
May	♌	♍4	♍	♎17	♎	♎	♏4	♏	♐15	♐	♑23	♑	♑	♒5	♒	♓8	♓	♈9	♈	♉9	♉	♊11	♊	♋15	♋	♋	♌0	♌	♍11	♍	♎23
Jun	♎	♎	♏11	♏	♐21	♐	♐	♑5	♑	♒11	♒	♓14	♓	♈17	♈	♉18	♉	♊21	♊	♊	♋1	♋	♌8	♌	♍19	♍	♍	♎7	♎	♏19	
Jul	♏	♏	♐5	♐	♑12	♑	♒17	♒	♓20	♓	♈22	♈	♈	♉1	♉	♊5	♊	♋10	♋	♌17	♌	♌	♍3	♍	♎15	♎	♎	♏3	♏	♐14	♐
Aug	♑21	♑	♑	♒0	♒	♓2	♓	♈4	♈	♉7	♉	♊11	♊	♋17	♋	♋	♌1	♌	♍11	♍	♎23	♎	♎	♏11	♏	♐23	♐	♐	♑6	♑	♒10
Sep	♒	♓11	♓	♈11	♈	♉13	♉	♊16	♊	♋23	♋	♋	♌7	♌	♍18	♍	♍	♎6	♎	♏19	♏	♏	♐7	♐	♑16	♑	♒20	♒	♓22	♓	
Oct	♈21	♈	♉21	♉	♊23	♊	♊	♋4	♋	♌13	♌	♌	♍0	♍	♎12	♎	♎	♏1	♏	♐13	♐	♑23	♑	♑	♒6	♒	♓8	♓	♈8	♈	♉7
Nov	♉	♊8	♊	♋11	♋	♌19	♌	♌	♍6	♍	♎18	♎	♎	♏7	♏	♐19	♐	♐	♑5	♑	♒13	♒	♓17	♓	♈19	♈	♉19	♉	♊19	♊	
Dec	♋21	♋	♋	♌3	♌	♍12	♍	♍	♎1	♎	♏13	♏	♏	♐1	♐	♑11	♑	♒19	♒	♒	♓0	♓	♈3	♈	♉5	♉	♊6	♊	♋8	♋	♌12

1937	1	2	3	4	5	6	7	8	9	10	11	12	13	14	15	16	17	18	19	20	21	22	23	24	25	26	27	28	29	30	31
Jan	♌	♍21	♍	♍	♎8	♎	♏21	♏	♏	♐9	♐	♑18	♑	♑	♒0	♒	♓5	♓	♈9	♈	♉12	♉	♊14	♊	♋17	♋	♌22	♌	♌	♍6	♍
Feb	♎16	♎	♎	♏5	♏	♐17	♐	♐	♑3	♑	♒8	♒	♓12	♓	♈14	♈	♉17	♉	♊20	♊	♊	♋1	♋	♌7	♌	♍14	♍	♍			
Mar	♎1	♎	♏13	♏	♏	♐2	♐	♑12	♑	♒18	♒	♓21	♓	♈22	♈	♉23	♉	♉	♊2	♊	♋6	♋	♌13	♌	♍22	♍	♍	♎8	♎	♏21	♏
Apr	♏	♐10	♐	♑21	♑	♑	♒4	♒	♓7	♓	♈8	♈	♉8	♉	♊9	♊	♋12	♋	♌19	♌	♌	♍4	♍	♎15	♎	♎	♏3	♏	♐16	♐	
May	♐	♑4	♑	♒13	♒	♓17	♓	♈19	♈	♉18	♉	♊18	♊	♋20	♋	♋	♌1	♌	♍9	♍	♎21	♎	♎	♏9	♏	♐22	♐	♐	♑10	♑	♒20
Jun	♒	♒	♓2	♓	♈5	♈	♉5	♉	♊5	♊	♋6	♋	♌9	♌	♍16	♍	♍	♎3	♎	♏16	♏	♏	♐4	♐	♑16	♑	♑	♒1	♒	♓8	
Jul	♓	♈12	♈	♉14	♉	♊15	♊	♋16	♋	♌18	♌	♌	♍0	♍	♎10	♎	♏22	♏	♏	♐11	♐	♑22	♑	♑	♒7	♒	♓13	♓	♈18	♈	♉21
Aug	♉	♊23	♊	♊	♋1	♋	♌4	♌	♍9	♍	♎18	♎	♎	♏6	♏	♐19	♐	♐	♑6	♑	♒14	♒	♓20	♓	♈23	♈	♈	♉3	♉	♊6	♊
Sep	♋9	♋	♌13	♌	♍18	♍	♍	♎3	♎	♏14	♏	♏	♐3	♐	♑15	♑	♒23	♒	♒	♓4	♓	♈7	♈	♉9	♉	♊11	♊	♋14	♋	♌19	
Oct	♌	♌	♍2	♍	♎11	♎	♏22	♏	♏	♐11	♐	♑23	♑	♑	♒9	♒	♓14	♓	♈16	♈	♉17	♉	♊18	♊	♋20	♋	♋	♌1	♌	♍8	♍
Nov	♎18	♎	♎	♏5	♏	♐18	♐	♐	♑7	♑	♒18	♒	♒	♓0	♓	♈3	♈	♉4	♉	♊3	♊	♋4	♋	♌7	♌	♍13	♍	♎23	♎	♎	
Dec	♏11	♏	♏	♐0	♐	♑13	♑	♑	♒0	♒	♓9	♓	♈14	♈	♉15	♉	♊15	♊	♋14	♋	♌15	♌	♍20	♍	♍	♎5	♎	♏17	♏	♏	♐7

1938	1	2	3	4	5	6	7	8	9	10	11	12	13	14	15	16	17	18	19	20	21	22	23	24	25	26	27	28	29	30	31
Jan	♐	♑19	♑	♑	♒6	♒	♓15	♓	♈21	♈	♈	♉1	♉	♊2	♊	♋1	♋	♌2	♌	♍5	♍	♎13	♎	♎	♏0	♏	♐13	♐	♐	♑2	♑
Feb	♒12	♒	♓20	♓	♓	♈3	♈	♉8	♉	♊10	♊	♋12	♋	♌13	♌	♍16	♍	♎22	♎	♎	♏8	♏	♐21	♐	♐	♑9	♑	♒20			
Mar	♒	♒	♓3	♓	♈9	♈	♉13	♉	♊16	♊	♋19	♋	♌22	♌	♌	♍1	♍	♎7	♎	♏17	♏	♏	♐5	♐	♑17	♑	♑	♒4	♒	♓12	♓
Apr	♈16	♈	♉19	♉	♊22	♊	♊	♋1	♋	♌4	♌	♍9	♍	♎16	♎	♎	♏1	♏	♐13	♐	♐	♑2	♑	♒13	♒	♓21	♓	♓	♈2	♈	
May	♉4	♉	♊5	♊	♋6	♋	♌10	♌	♍15	♍	♎22	♎	♎	♏8	♏	♐20	♐	♐	♑9	♑	♒21	♒	♒	♓6	♓	♈12	♈	♉14	♉	♊14	♊
Jun	♋14	♋	♌16	♌	♍20	♍	♍	♎4	♎	♏15	♏	♏	♐3	♐	♑15	♑	♑	♒4	♒	♓14	♓	♈21	♈	♈	♉0	♉	♊1	♊	♋0	♋	
Jul	♌0	♌	♍3	♍	♎10	♎	♏20	♏	♏	♐9	♐	♑22	♑	♑	♒10	♒	♓20	♓	♓	♈4	♈	♉9	♉	♊11	♊	♋11	♋	♌11	♌	♍12	♍
Aug	♎17	♎	♎	♏3	♏	♐15	♐	♐	♑4	♑	♒15	♒	♒	♓2	♓	♈10	♈	♉16	♉	♊19	♊	♋21	♋	♌21	♌	♍22	♍	♍	♎2	♎	♏10
Sep	♏	♐22	♐	♐	♑11	♑	♒22	♒	♒	♓8	♓	♈16	♈	♉21	♉	♉	♊2	♊	♋4	♋	♌6	♌	♍8	♍	♎12	♎	♏19	♏	♏	♐6	
Oct	♐	♑18	♑	♑	♒6	♒	♓16	♓	♈23	♈	♈	♉4	♉	♊7	♊	♋10	♋	♌13	♌	♍16	♍	♎21	♎	♎	♏4	♏	♐14	♐	♐	♑3	♑
Nov	♒15	♒	♒	♓1	♓	♈8	♈	♉12	♉	♊14	♊	♋16	♋	♌18	♌	♍22	♍	♍	♎4	♎	♏12	♏	♐22	♐	♐	♑10	♑	♒23	♒	♒	
Dec	♓10	♓	♈18	♈	♉22	♉	♊23	♊	♋23	♋	♋	♌0	♌	♍4	♍	♎10	♎	♏18	♏	♏	♐5	♐	♑17	♑	♑	♒6	♒	♓18	♓	♓	♈4

1939	1	2	3	4	5	6	7	8	9	10	11	12	13	14	15	16	17	18	19	20	21	22	23	24	25	26	27	28	29	30	31
Jan	♈	♉9	♉	♊11	♊	♋10	♋	♌9	♌	♍11	♍	♎15	♎	♎	♏0	♏	♐11	♐	♐	♑0	♑	♒12	♒	♒	♓0	♓	♈11	♈	♉18	♉	♊21
Feb	♊	♋21	♋	♌21	♌	♍20	♍	♎23	♎	♎	♏6	♏	♐17	♐	♐	♑6	♑	♒18	♒	♒	♓6	♓	♈17	♈	♈	♉1	♉	♊6			
Mar	♊	♋8	♋	♌8	♌	♍8	♍	♎9	♎	♏15	♏	♏	♐0	♐	♑12	♑	♑	♒1	♒	♓12	♓	♈22	♈	♈	♉6	♉	♊12	♊	♋15	♋	♌17
Apr	♌	♍18	♍	♎20	♎	♎	♏0	♏	♐9	♐	♑20	♑	♑	♒8	♒	♓20	♓	♓	♈6	♈	♉12	♉	♊17	♊	♋20	♋	♌23	♌	♌	♍2	
May	♍	♎5	♎	♏10	♏	♐18	♐	♐	♑4	♑	♒16	♒	♒	♓4	♓	♈14	♈	♉20	♉	♉	♊0	♊	♋2	♋	♌5	♌	♍8	♍	♎12	♎	♏18
Jun	♏	♏	♐2	♐	♑12	♑	♑	♒0	♒	♓13	♓	♈23	♈	♈	♉6	♉	♊9	♊	♋10	♋	♌11	♌	♍13	♍	♎17	♎	♎	♏0	♏	♐9	
Jul	♐	♑20	♑	♑	♒8	♒	♓20	♓	♓	♈8	♈	♉15	♉	♊19	♊	♋20	♋	♌20	♌	♍20	♍	♎23	♎	♎	♏6	♏	♐15	♐	♐	♑2	♑
Aug	♒14	♒	♒	♓3	♓	♈15	♈	♈	♉0	♉	♊5	♊	♋6	♋	♌6	♌	♍5	♍	♎7	♎	♏12	♏	♐20	♐	♐	♑8	♑	♒20	♒	♒	♓9
Sep	♓	♈21	♈	♈	♉7	♉	♊13	♊	♋16	♋	♌17	♌	♍16	♍	♎17	♎	♏20	♏	♏	♐3	♐	♑14	♑	♑	♒2	♒	♓15	♓	♓	♈2	
Oct	♈	♉12	♉	♊19	♊	♊	♋0	♋	♌2	♌	♍3	♍	♎3	♎	♏6	♏	♐12	♐	♑21	♑	♑	♒9	♒	♓22	♓	♓	♈9	♈	♉18	♉	♉
Nov	♊1	♊	♋5	♋	♌9	♌	♍11	♍	♎13	♎	♏16	♏	♐21	♐	♐	♑6	♑	♒17	♒	♒	♓6	♓	♈17	♈	♈	♉2	♉	♊8	♊	♋11	
Dec	♋	♌14	♌	♍17	♍	♎20	♎	♎	♏1	♏	♐7	♐	♑15	♑	♑	♒2	♒	♓14	♓	♓	♈2	♈	♉11	♉	♊17	♊	♋19	♋	♌20	♌	♍22

1940	1	2	3	4	5	6	7	8	9	10	11	12	13	14	15	16	17	18	19	20	21	22	23	24	25	26	27	28	29	30	31
Jan	♍	♍	♎2	♎	♏7	♏	♐14	♐	♑23	♑	♑	♒10	♒	♓22	♓	♓	♈11	♈	♉21	♉	♉	♊3	♊	♋5	♋	♌6	♌	♍6	♍	♎8	♎
Feb	♏12	♏	♐20	♐	♐	♑5	♑	♒16	♒	♒	♓5	♓	♈18	♈	♈	♉5	♉	♊13	♊	♋16	♋	♌17	♌	♍16	♍	♎16	♎	♏19	♏		
Mar	♏	♐1	♐	♑11	♑	♒23	♒	♒	♓11	♓	♓	♈0	♈	♉12	♉	♊21	♊	♊	♋2	♋	♌4	♌	♍3	♍	♎3	♎	♏4	♏	♐9	♐	♑17
Apr	♑	♑	♒5	♒	♓17	♓	♓	♈6	♈	♉18	♉	♉	♊3	♊	♋9	♋	♌13	♌	♍14	♍	♎14	♎	♏15	♏	♐18	♐	♐	♑1	♑	♒11	
May	♒	♒	♓0	♓	♈13	♈	♈	♉0	♉	♊8	♊	♋15	♋	♌19	♌	♍22	♍	♎23	♎	♎	♏1	♏	♐4	♐	♑10	♑	♒19	♒	♒	♓8	♓
Jun	♈20	♈	♈	♉7	♉	♊15	♊	♋20	♋	♋	♌0	♌	♍3	♍	♎6	♎	♏9	♏	♐13	♐	♑19	♑	♑	♒4	♒	♓16	♓	♓	♈4	♈	
Jul	♉15	♉	♊23	♊	♊	♋4	♋	♌7	♌	♍9	♍	♎12	♎	♏15	♏	♐20	♐	♐	♑3	♑	♒12	♒	♓23	♓	♓	♈12	♈	♈	♉0	♉	♊8
Aug	♊	♋13	♋	♌15	♌	♍16	♍	♎17	♎	♏21	♏	♏	♐2	♐	♑9	♑	♒19	♒	♒	♓7	♓	♈20	♈	♈	♉8	♉	♊18	♊	♋23	♋	♋
Sep	♌1	♌	♍1	♍	♎1	♎	♏3	♏	♐8	♐	♑15	♑	♑	♒1	♒	♓13	♓	♓	♈2	♈	♉15	♉	♉	♊1	♊	♋8	♋	♌12	♌	♍12	
Oct	♍	♎12	♎	♏12	♏	♐15	♐	♑21	♑	♑	♒7	♒	♓19	♓	♓	♈8	♈	♉21	♉	♉	♊7	♊	♋16	♋	♌21	♌	♍23	♍	♎23	♎	♏23
Nov	♏	♏	♐0	♐	♑5	♑	♒13	♒	♒	♓2	♓	♈15	♈	♈	♉3	♉	♊13	♊	♋21	♋	♋	♌3	♌	♍7	♍	♎9	♎	♏10	♏	♐11	
Dec	♐	♑14	♑	♒22	♒	♒	♓9	♓	♈22	♈	♈	♉10	♉	♊20	♊	♊	♋3	♋	♌9	♌	♍13	♍	♎16	♎	♏19	♏	♐21	♐	♐	♑0	♑

1941	1	2	3	4	5	6	7	8	9	10	11	12	13	14	15	16	17	18	19	20	21	22	23	24	25	26	27	28	29	30	31
Jan	♒7	♒	♓17	♓	♓	♈6	♈	♉18	♉	♉	♊4	♊	♋11	♋	♌15	♌	♍19	♍	♎22	♎	♎	♏1	♏	♐4	♐	♑9	♑	♒16	♒	♒	♓2
Feb	♓	♈14	♈	♈	♉3	♉	♊13	♊	♋20	♋	♋	♌0	♌	♍2	♍	♎4	♎	♏6	♏	♐10	♐	♑16	♑	♑	♒0	♒	♓10	♓			
Mar	♈22	♈	♈	♉11	♉	♊22	♊	♊	♋6	♋	♌11	♌	♍12	♍	♎12	♎	♏13	♏	♐16	♐	♑21	♑	♑	♒6	♒	♓16	♓	♓	♈5	♈	♉18
Apr	♉	♉	♊6	♊	♋15	♋	♌21	♌	♍23	♍	♎23	♎	♏22	♏	♐23	♐	♐	♑3	♑	♒11	♒	♓22	♓	♓	♈11	♈	♈	♉0	♉	♊12	
May	♊	♋22	♋	♋	♌5	♌	♍9	♍	♎10	♎	♏9	♏	♐9	♐	♑12	♑	♒18	♒	♒	♓4	♓	♈17	♈	♈	♉6	♉	♊17	♊	♊	♋4	♋
Jun	♌12	♌	♍17	♍	♎19	♎	♏20	♏	♐20	♐	♑21	♑	♑	♒2	♒	♓11	♓	♈23	♈	♈	♉12	♉	♉	♊0	♊	♋9	♋	♌17	♌	♍23	
Jul	♍	♍	♎2	♎	♏4	♏	♐5	♐	♑7	♑	♒12	♒	♓20	♓	♓	♈7	♈	♉20	♉	♉	♊7	♊	♋16	♋	♌23	♌	♌	♍4	♍	♎8	♎
Aug	♏11	♏	♐13	♐	♑16	♑	♒21	♒	♒	♓4	♓	♈15	♈	♈	♉4	♉	♊15	♊	♊	♋1	♋	♌7	♌	♍11	♍	♎13	♎	♏16	♏	♐19	♐
Sep	♑23	♑	♑	♒5	♒	♓13	♓	♈23	♈	♈	♉12	♉	♉	♊0	♊	♋10	♋	♌17	♌	♍20	♍	♎22	♎	♏22	♏	♏	♐0	♐	♑4	♑	
Oct	♒11	♒	♓20	♓	♓	♈7	♈	♉19	♉	♉	♊7	♊	♋19	♋	♋	♌3	♌	♍7	♍	♎8	♎	♏7	♏	♐8	♐	♑10	♑	♒16	♒	♒	♓2
Nov	♓	♈13	♈	♈	♉1	♉	♊14	♊	♊	♋2	♋	♌11	♌	♍17	♍	♎19	♎	♏19	♏	♐18	♐	♑19	♑	♒23	♒	♒	♓7	♓	♈19	♈	
Dec	♈	♉8	♉	♊20	♊	♊	♋7	♋	♌18	♌	♌	♍1	♍	♎5	♎	♏6	♏	♐5	♐	♑5	♑	♒8	♒	♓15	♓	♓	♈1	♈	♉14	♉	♉

1942	1	2	3	4	5	6	7	8	9	10	11	12	13	14	15	16	17	18	19	20	21	22	23	24	25	26	27	28	29	30	31
Jan	♊2	♊	♋13	♋	♌23	♌	♌	♍7	♍	♎12	♎	♏15	♏	♐15	♐	♑16	♑	♒18	♒	♒	♓0	♓	♈9	♈	♉21	♉	♉	♊10	♊	♋21	♋
Feb	♋	♌6	♌	♍12	♍	♎17	♎	♏21	♏	♐23	♐	♐	♑1	♑	♒4	♒	♓9	♓	♈18	♈	♈	♉5	♉	♊18	♊	♊	♋5	♋			
Mar	♌14	♌	♍20	♍	♎23	♎	♎	♏2	♏	♐5	♐	♑8	♑	♒12	♒	♓18	♓	♓	♈3	♈	♉14	♉	♉	♊2	♊	♋14	♋	♌23	♌	♌	♍5
Apr	♍	♎8	♎	♏9	♏	♐11	♐	♑14	♑	♒18	♒	♒	♓1	♓	♈10	♈	♉21	♉	♉	♊10	♊	♋22	♋	♋	♌8	♌	♍15	♍	♎18	♎	
May	♏18	♏	♐18	♐	♑20	♑	♑	♒0	♒	♓7	♓	♈17	♈	♈	♉4	♉	♊16	♊	♊	♋5	♋	♌16	♌	♌	♍0	♍	♎4	♎	♏5	♏	♐4
Jun	♐	♑4	♑	♒7	♒	♓13	♓	♈22	♈	♈	♉10	♉	♊22	♊	♊	♋11	♋	♌23	♌	♌	♍8	♍	♎13	♎	♏15	♏	♐15	♐	♑14	♑	
Jul	♒16	♒	♓20	♓	♓	♈4	♈	♉16	♉	♉	♊4	♊	♋17	♋	♋	♌4	♌	♍14	♍	♎20	♎	♎	♏0	♏	♐1	♐	♑1	♑	♒2	♒	♓5
Aug	♓	♈12	♈	♉23	♉	♉	♊11	♊	♋23	♋	♋	♌10	♌	♍19	♍	♍	♎2	♎	♏6	♏	♐9	♐	♑10	♑	♒12	♒	♓15	♓	♈21	♈	♈
Sep	♉7	♉	♊18	♊	♊	♋7	♋	♌18	♌	♌	♍2	♍	♎8	♎	♏11	♏	♐15	♐	♑17	♑	♒20	♒	♒	♓0	♓	♈6	♈	♉15	♉	♉	
Oct	♊3	♊	♋15	♋	♋	♌2	♌	♍11	♍	♎15	♎	♏18	♏	♐20	♐	♑23	♑	♑	♒2	♒	♓8	♓	♈14	♈	♉23	♉	♉	♊10	♊	♋23	♋
Nov	♋	♌11	♌	♍20	♍	♍	♎1	♎	♏3	♏	♐4	♐	♑5	♑	♒8	♒	♓13	♓	♈21	♈	♈	♉7	♉	♊18	♊	♊	♋6	♋	♌19	♌	
Dec	♌	♍6	♍	♎12	♎	♏14	♏	♐14	♐	♑13	♑	♒15	♒	♓19	♓	♓	♈2	♈	♉13	♉	♉	♊0	♊	♋13	♋	♋	♌2	♌	♍13	♍	♎21

1943	1	2	3	4	5	6	7	8	9	10	11	12	13	14	15	16	17	18	19	20	21	22	23	24	25	26	27	28	29	30	31
Jan	♎	♎	♏1	♏	♐1	♐	♑0	♑	♒0	♒	♓3	♓	♈9	♈	♉18	♉	♉	♊6	♊	♋19	♋	♋	♌8	♌	♍19	♍	♍	♎4	♎	♏9	♏
Feb	♐12	♐	♑12	♑	♒11	♒	♓13	♓	♈17	♈	♈	♉1	♉	♊13	♊	♊	♋2	♋	♌14	♌	♌	♍1	♍	♎9	♎	♏15	♏	♐19			
Mar	♐	♑21	♑	♒22	♒	♓23	♓	♓	♈3	♈	♉10	♉	♊20	♊	♊	♋9	♋	♌21	♌	♌	♍8	♍	♎15	♎	♏21	♏	♏	♐1	♐	♑4	♑
Apr	♒6	♒	♓9	♓	♈13	♈	♉19	♉	♉	♊5	♊	♋17	♋	♋	♌6	♌	♍16	♍	♎23	♎	♎	♏4	♏	♐6	♐	♑9	♑	♒12	♒	♓16	
May	♓	♈21	♈	♈	♉4	♉	♊13	♊	♊	♋1	♋	♌14	♌	♌	♍1	♍	♎9	♎	♏12	♏	♐14	♐	♑15	♑	♒18	♒	♓22	♓	♓	♈3	♈
Jun	♉11	♉	♊21	♊	♊	♋8	♋	♌22	♌	♌	♍9	♍	♎18	♎	♏22	♏	♏	♐0	♐	♑0	♑	♒1	♒	♓3	♓	♈9	♈	♉17	♉	♉	
Jul	♊3	♊	♋15	♋	♋	♌4	♌	♍17	♍	♍	♎2	♎	♏8	♏	♐10	♐	♑10	♑	♒10	♒	♓11	♓	♈15	♈	♉22	♉	♉	♊9	♊	♋21	♋
Aug	♋	♌10	♌	♍23	♍	♍	♎9	♎	♏16	♏	♐20	♐	♑21	♑	♒21	♒	♓21	♓	♈23	♈	♈	♉5	♉	♊15	♊	♊	♋3	♋	♌16	♌	♌
Sep	♍4	♍	♎15	♎	♏23	♏	♏	♐4	♐	♑6	♑	♒7	♒	♓7	♓	♈9	♈	♉13	♉	♊22	♊	♊	♋10	♋	♌23	♌	♌	♍11	♍	♎21	
Oct	♎	♎	♏4	♏	♐10	♐	♑13	♑	♒16	♒	♓17	♓	♈19	♈	♉23	♉	♉	♊7	♊	♋18	♋	♋	♌7	♌	♍19	♍	♍	♎4	♎	♏10	♏
Nov	♐15	♐	♑19	♑	♒22	♒	♒	♓1	♓	♈4	♈	♉9	♉	♊16	♊	♊	♋2	♋	♌15	♌	♌	♍3	♍	♎13	♎	♏19	♏	♐23	♐	♐	
Dec	♑1	♑	♒3	♒	♓6	♓	♈11	♈	♉16	♉	♉	♊0	♊	♋10	♋	♌23	♌	♌	♍12	♍	♎22	♎	♎	♏5	♏	♐8	♐	♑10	♑	♒10	♒

1944	1	2	3	4	5	6	7	8	9	10	11	12	13	14	15	16	17	18	19	20	21	22	23	24	25	26	27	28	29	30	31
Jan	♓12	♓	♈16	♈	♉22	♉	♉	♊7	♊	♋18	♋	♋	♌6	♌	♍19	♍	♍	♎7	♎	♏15	♏	♐19	♐	♑21	♑	♒20	♒	♓20	♓	♈23	♈
Feb	♈	♉4	♉	♊13	♊	♊	♋0	♋	♌13	♌	♌	♍1	♍	♎13	♎	♏23	♏	♏	♐5	♐	♑8	♑	♒8	♒	♓7	♓	♈8	♈	♉11		
Mar	♉	♊19	♊	♊	♋6	♋	♌19	♌	♌	♍8	♍	♎19	♎	♎	♏5	♏	♐13	♐	♑17	♑	♒18	♒	♓18	♓	♈18	♈	♉20	♉	♉	♊2	♊
Apr	♋12	♋	♋	♌1	♌	♍14	♍	♍	♎1	♎	♏11	♏	♐18	♐	♑23	♑	♑	♒2	♒	♓4	♓	♈5	♈	♉7	♉	♊12	♊	♋20	♋	♋	
May	♌9	♌	♍21	♍	♍	♎9	♎	♏17	♏	♏	♐0	♐	♑5	♑	♒8	♒	♓11	♓	♈13	♈	♉16	♉	♊21	♊	♊	♋5	♋	♌17	♌	♌	♍5
Jun	♍	♎17	♎	♎	♏1	♏	♐7	♐	♑11	♑	♒14	♒	♓16	♓	♈20	♈	♉23	♉	♉	♊5	♊	♋13	♋	♋	♌1	♌	♍13	♍	♍	♎1	
Jul	♎	♏10	♏	♐16	♐	♑19	♑	♒21	♒	♓22	♓	♓	♈1	♈	♉5	♉	♊12	♊	♋21	♋	♋	♌8	♌	♍21	♍	♍	♎9	♎	♏19	♏	♏
Aug	♐2	♐	♑5	♑	♒6	♒	♓6	♓	♈7	♈	♉11	♉	♊17	♊	♊	♋3	♋	♌15	♌	♌	♍3	♍	♎16	♎	♎	♏3	♏	♐11	♐	♑16	♑
Sep	♒17	♒	♓16	♓	♈16	♈	♉18	♉	♊23	♊	♊	♋9	♋	♌21	♌	♌	♍9	♍	♎22	♎	♎	♏9	♏	♐19	♐	♐	♑1	♑	♒3	♒	
Oct	♓3	♓	♈2	♈	♉3	♉	♊7	♊	♋15	♋	♋	♌3	♌	♍16	♍	♍	♎4	♎	♏15	♏	♏	♐0	♐	♑7	♑	♒12	♒	♓13	♓	♈13	♈
Nov	♉14	♉	♊16	♊	♋23	♋	♋	♌10	♌	♍22	♍	♍	♎11	♎	♏21	♏	♏	♐6	♐	♑13	♑	♒18	♒	♓21	♓	♈23	♈	♈	♉0	♉	
Dec	♊3	♊	♋8	♋	♌18	♌	♌	♍6	♍	♎18	♎	♎	♏5	♏	♐13	♐	♑19	♑	♒23	♒	♒	♓2	♓	♈5	♈	♉8	♉	♊12	♊	♋18	♋

1945	1	2	3	4	5	6	7	8	9	10	11	12	13	14	15	16	17	18	19	20	21	22	23	24	25	26	27	28	29	30	31
Jan	♋	♌3	♌	♍14	♍	♍	♎3	♎	♏14	♏	♐22	♐	♐	♑4	♑	♒6	♒	♓8	♓	♈11	♈	♉14	♉	♊19	♊	♊	♋2	♋	♌11	♌	♍22
Feb	♍	♍	♎11	♎	♏23	♏	♏	♐8	♐	♑14	♑	♒16	♒	♓16	♓	♈17	♈	♉20	♉	♉	♊1	♊	♋8	♋	♌18	♌	♌	♍6			
Mar	♍	♎18	♎	♎	♏6	♏	♐17	♐	♐	♑0	♑	♒3	♒	♓3	♓	♈2	♈	♉3	♉	♊7	♊	♋14	♋	♋	♌0	♌	♍12	♍	♍	♎0	♎
Apr	♏13	♏	♏	♐0	♐	♑9	♑	♒13	♒	♓14	♓	♈13	♈	♉13	♉	♊15	♊	♋20	♋	♋	♌6	♌	♍18	♍	♍	♎6	♎	♏19	♏	♏	
May	♐6	♐	♑15	♑	♒21	♒	♒	♓0	♓	♈0	♈	♉0	♉	♊1	♊	♋5	♋	♌13	♌	♌	♍0	♍	♎13	♎	♎	♏1	♏	♐12	♐	♑20	♑
Jun	♑	♒3	♒	♓7	♓	♈9	♈	♉10	♉	♊11	♊	♋14	♋	♌22	♌	♌	♍8	♍	♎20	♎	♎	♏8	♏	♐19	♐	♐	♑3	♑	♒8	♒	
Jul	♓12	♓	♈15	♈	♉17	♉	♊20	♊	♊	♋0	♋	♌6	♌	♍16	♍	♍	♎4	♎	♏16	♏	♏	♐3	♐	♑11	♑	♒15	♒	♓18	♓	♈20	♈
Aug	♉23	♉	♉	♊3	♊	♋8	♋	♌15	♌	♌	♍0	♍	♎12	♎	♎	♏0	♏	♐12	♐	♑20	♑	♑	♒0	♒	♓2	♓	♈3	♈	♉5	♉	♊8
Sep	♊	♋14	♋	♌22	♌	♌	♍8	♍	♎19	♎	♎	♏8	♏	♐20	♐	♐	♑5	♑	♒10	♒	♓12	♓	♈12	♈	♉12	♉	♊14	♊	♋19	♋	
Oct	♋	♌4	♌	♍14	♍	♍	♎2	♎	♏15	♏	♏	♐3	♐	♑14	♑	♒20	♒	♓23	♓	♈22	♈	♉22	♉	♊22	♊	♊	♋2	♋	♌9	♌	♍20
Nov	♍	♍	♎8	♎	♏21	♏	♏	♐9	♐	♑20	♑	♑	♒4	♒	♓8	♓	♈9	♈	♉9	♉	♊9	♊	♋11	♋	♌16	♌	♌	♍2	♍	♎14	
Dec	♎	♎	♏3	♏	♐15	♐	♐	♑2	♑	♒10	♒	♓16	♓	♈19	♈	♉20	♉	♊20	♊	♋21	♋	♋	♌2	♌	♍10	♍	♎21	♎	♎	♏10	♏

1946	1	2	3	4	5	6	7	8	9	10	11	12	13	14	15	16	17	18	19	20	21	22	23	24	25	26	27	28	29	30	31
Jan	♐22	♐	♐	♑8	♑	♒16	♒	♓21	♓	♓	♈1	♈	♉4	♉	♊6	♊	♋8	♋	♌12	♌	♍19	♍	♍	♎5	♎	♏18	♏	♏	♐6	♐	♑16
Feb	♑	♒23	♒	♒	♓3	♓	♈7	♈	♉10	♉	♊13	♊	♋16	♋	♌21	♌	♌	♍4	♍	♎14	♎	♎	♏2	♏	♐15	♐	♐	♑1			
Mar	♑	♒8	♒	♓11	♓	♈13	♈	♉15	♉	♊18	♊	♋23	♋	♋	♌4	♌	♍12	♍	♎22	♎	♎	♏10	♏	♐23	♐	♐	♑10	♑	♒18	♒	♓21
Apr	♓	♈22	♈	♉23	♉	♉	♊0	♊	♋4	♋	♌10	♌	♍18	♍	♍	♎5	♎	♏17	♏	♏	♐6	♐	♑18	♑	♑	♒3	♒	♓8	♓	♈9	
May	♈	♉9	♉	♊9	♊	♋11	♋	♌16	♌	♌	♍0	♍	♎11	♎	♏23	♏	♏	♐12	♐	♐	♑1	♑	♒10	♒	♓17	♓	♈19	♈	♉20	♉	♊19
Jun	♊	♋20	♋	♌23	♌	♌	♍6	♍	♎17	♎	♎	♏5	♏	♐18	♐	♐	♑6	♑	♒16	♒	♒	♓0	♓	♈4	♈	♉5	♉	♊6	♊	♋6	
Jul	♋	♌8	♌	♍14	♍	♎23	♎	♎	♏12	♏	♏	♐1	♐	♑12	♑	♒22	♒	♒	♓5	♓	♈10	♈	♉13	♉	♊15	♊	♋16	♋	♌18	♌	♍23
Aug	♍	♍	♎7	♎	♏19	♏	♏	♐8	♐	♑20	♑	♑	♒5	♒	♓11	♓	♈16	♈	♉19	♉	♊22	♊	♊	♋0	♋	♌3	♌	♍8	♍	♎16	♎
Sep	♎	♏3	♏	♐16	♐	♐	♑4	♑	♒13	♒	♓18	♓	♈22	♈	♈	♉1	♉	♊3	♊	♋7	♋	♌11	♌	♍17	♍	♍	♎0	♎	♏11	♏	
Oct	♏	♐0	♐	♑12	♑	♒22	♒	♒	♓4	♓	♈7	♈	♉8	♉	♊9	♊	♋12	♋	♌17	♌	♍23	♍	♍	♎8	♎	♏19	♏	♏	♐7	♐	♑20
Nov	♑	♑	♒7	♒	♓14	♓	♈17	♈	♉18	♉	♊18	♊	♋19	♋	♌22	♌	♌	♍5	♍	♎14	♎	♎	♏1	♏	♐14	♐	♐	♑3	♑	♒15	
Dec	♒	♓23	♓	♓	♈4	♈	♉5	♉	♊5	♊	♋4	♋	♌6	♌	♍11	♍	♎20	♎	♎	♏7	♏	♐20	♐	♐	♑9	♑	♒21	♒	♒	♓6	♓

1947	1	2	3	4	5	6	7	8	9	10	11	12	13	14	15	16	17	18	19	20	21	22	23	24	25	26	27	28	29	30	31
Jan	♈13	♈	♉16	♉	♊16	♊	♋15	♋	♌16	♌	♍19	♍	♍	♎2	♎	♏14	♏	♏	♐3	♐	♑15	♑	♑	♒3	♒	♓12	♓	♈19	♈	♈	♉0
Feb	♉	♊2	♊	♋2	♋	♌3	♌	♍5	♍	♎11	♎	♏21	♏	♏	♐10	♐	♑22	♑	♑	♒9	♒	♓18	♓	♓	♈0	♈	♉5	♉			
Mar	♊9	♊	♋11	♋	♌13	♌	♍15	♍	♎21	♎	♎	♏5	♏	♐18	♐	♐	♑6	♑	♒17	♒	♒	♓1	♓	♈7	♈	♉11	♉	♊14	♊	♋17	♋
Apr	♌20	♌	♌	♍0	♍	♎6	♎	♏14	♏	♏	♐2	♐	♑15	♑	♑	♒2	♒	♓10	♓	♈16	♈	♉18	♉	♊20	♊	♋23	♋	♋	♌2	♌	
May	♍7	♍	♎13	♎	♏22	♏	♏	♐10	♐	♑22	♑	♑	♒10	♒	♓20	♓	♓	♈2	♈	♉4	♉	♊5	♊	♋5	♋	♌8	♌	♍12	♍	♎19	♎
Jun	♎	♏5	♏	♐17	♐	♐	♑5	♑	♒18	♒	♒	♓4	♓	♈11	♈	♉14	♉	♊15	♊	♋15	♋	♌15	♌	♍18	♍	♍	♎1	♎	♏11	♏	
Jul	♐23	♐	♐	♑11	♑	♑	♒0	♒	♓11	♓	♈19	♈	♈	♉0	♉	♊2	♊	♋1	♋	♌1	♌	♍2	♍	♎7	♎	♏17	♏	♏	♐5	♐	♑18
Aug	♑	♑	♒6	♒	♓17	♓	♓	♈2	♈	♉8	♉	♊11	♊	♋12	♋	♌11	♌	♍12	♍	♎16	♎	♎	♏0	♏	♐11	♐	♐	♑0	♑	♒12	♒
Sep	♓22	♓	♓	♈7	♈	♉14	♉	♊18	♊	♋20	♋	♌21	♌	♍22	♍	♍	♎1	♎	♏8	♏	♐19	♐	♐	♑7	♑	♒19	♒	♒	♓6	♓	
Oct	♈13	♈	♉19	♉	♊23	♊	♊	♋3	♋	♌5	♌	♍7	♍	♎11	♎	♏17	♏	♏	♐3	♐	♑15	♑	♑	♒4	♒	♓14	♓	♈22	♈	♈	♉2
Nov	♉	♊5	♊	♋8	♋	♌11	♌	♍14	♍	♎19	♎	♎	♏2	♏	♐12	♐	♐	♑0	♑	♒12	♒	♓23	♓	♓	♈7	♈	♉12	♉	♊14	♊	
Dec	♋15	♋	♌16	♌	♍20	♍	♍	♎1	♎	♏9	♏	♐19	♐	♐	♑7	♑	♒20	♒	♒	♓8	♓	♈17	♈	♉23	♉	♉	♊0	♊	♋0	♋	♌0

1948	1	2	3	4	5	6	7	8	9	10	11	12	13	14	15	16	17	18	19	20	21	22	23	24	25	26	27	28	29	30	31
Jan	♌	♍2	♍	♎7	♎	♏15	♏	♏	♐2	♐	♑14	♑	♑	♒2	♒	♓15	♓	♓	♈1	♈	♉8	♉	♊12	♊	♋12	♋	♌11	♌	♍11	♍	♎14
Feb	♎	♏21	♏	♏	♐7	♐	♑20	♑	♑	♒8	♒	♓20	♓	♓	♈7	♈	♉16	♉	♊21	♊	♋22	♋	♌22	♌	♍22	♍	♎23	♎	♎		
Mar	♏4	♏	♐14	♐	♐	♑2	♑	♒15	♒	♒	♓2	♓	♈13	♈	♉22	♉	♉	♊4	♊	♋7	♋	♌8	♌	♍8	♍	♎10	♎	♏14	♏	♐22	♐
Apr	♐	♑9	♑	♒22	♒	♒	♓9	♓	♈20	♈	♈	♉3	♉	♊9	♊	♋13	♋	♌16	♌	♍17	♍	♎20	♎	♎	♏0	♏	♐7	♐	♑17	♑	
May	♑	♒5	♒	♓17	♓	♓	♈3	♈	♉11	♉	♊15	♊	♋18	♋	♌21	♌	♌	♍0	♍	♎3	♎	♏8	♏	♐16	♐	♐	♑2	♑	♒13	♒	♒
Jun	♓2	♓	♈12	♈	♉20	♉	♊23	♊	♊	♋1	♋	♌3	♌	♍5	♍	♎9	♎	♏15	♏	♐23	♐	♐	♑9	♑	♒21	♒	♒	♓10	♓	♈21	
Jul	♈	♈	♉5	♉	♊9	♊	♋10	♋	♌11	♌	♍12	♍	♎15	♎	♏21	♏	♏	♐5	♐	♑16	♑	♑	♒4	♒	♓16	♓	♓	♈5	♈	♉14	♉
Aug	♊19	♊	♋21	♋	♌20	♌	♍20	♍	♎22	♎	♎	♏3	♏	♐11	♐	♑22	♑	♑	♒10	♒	♓23	♓	♓	♈11	♈	♉21	♉	♉	♊4	♊	♋7
Sep	♋	♌7	♌	♍6	♍	♎7	♎	♏10	♏	♐17	♐	♐	♑4	♑	♒16	♒	♒	♓5	♓	♈17	♈	♈	♉3	♉	♊11	♊	♋15	♋	♌17	♌	
Oct	♍17	♍	♎17	♎	♏19	♏	♏	♐1	♐	♑11	♑	♒23	♒	♒	♓11	♓	♈23	♈	♈	♉9	♉	♊16	♊	♋22	♋	♋	♌1	♌	♍3	♍	♎4
Nov	♎	♏6	♏	♐11	♐	♑19	♑	♑	♒6	♒	♓19	♓	♓	♈7	♈	♉16	♉	♊22	♊	♊	♋3	♋	♌7	♌	♍10	♍	♎12	♎	♏15	♏	
Dec	♐20	♐	♐	♑4	♑	♒15	♒	♒	♓3	♓	♈15	♈	♈	♉1	♉	♊7	♊	♋10	♋	♌12	♌	♍15	♍	♎18	♎	♏23	♏	♏	♐5	♐	♑13

1949	1	2	3	4	5	6	7	8	9	10	11	12	13	14	15	16	17	18	19	20	21	22	23	24	25	26	27	28	29	30	31
Jan	♑	♒23	♒	♒	♓11	♓	♓	♈0	♈	♉10	♉	♊17	♊	♋19	♋	♌20	♌	♍21	♍	♍	♎0	♎	♏4	♏	♐11	♐	♑20	♑	♑	♒6	♒
Feb	♓19	♓	♓	♈8	♈	♉19	♉	♉	♊3	♊	♋6	♋	♌7	♌	♍6	♍	♎7	♎	♏10	♏	♐16	♐	♐	♑2	♑	♒13	♒	♒			
Mar	♓1	♓	♈14	♈	♈	♉2	♉	♊11	♊	♋16	♋	♌18	♌	♍17	♍	♎17	♎	♏18	♏	♐23	♐	♐	♑7	♑	♒19	♒	♒	♓7	♓	♈20	♈
Apr	♈	♉8	♉	♊18	♊	♊	♋1	♋	♌4	♌	♍4	♍	♎4	♎	♏4	♏	♐8	♐	♑14	♑	♑	♒1	♒	♓14	♓	♓	♈2	♈	♉14	♉	
May	♊23	♊	♊	♋6	♋	♌11	♌	♍13	♍	♎14	♎	♏15	♏	♐17	♐	♑23	♑	♑	♒8	♒	♓20	♓	♓	♈9	♈	♉21	♉	♉	♊6	♊	♋12
Jun	♋	♌17	♌	♍20	♍	♎22	♎	♎	♏0	♏	♐3	♐	♑8	♑	♒17	♒	♒	♓4	♓	♈17	♈	♈	♉5	♉	♊13	♊	♋19	♋	♌22	♌	
Jul	♌	♍1	♍	♎4	♎	♏7	♏	♐11	♐	♑17	♑	♑	♒1	♒	♓12	♓	♓	♈1	♈	♉13	♉	♊22	♊	♊	♋3	♋	♌6	♌	♍7	♍	♎10
Aug	♎	♏13	♏	♐18	♐	♐	♑0	♑	♒9	♒	♓20	♓	♓	♈9	♈	♉21	♉	♉	♊7	♊	♋13	♋	♌15	♌	♍16	♍	♎17	♎	♏19	♏	♐23
Sep	♐	♐	♑6	♑	♒16	♒	♒	♓3	♓	♈16	♈	♈	♉5	♉	♊15	♊	♋23	♋	♋	♌2	♌	♍2	♍	♎2	♎	♏2	♏	♐5	♐	♑12	
Oct	♑	♒21	♒	♒	♓9	♓	♈22	♈	♈	♉11	♉	♊22	♊	♊	♋7	♋	♌12	♌	♍13	♍	♎13	♎	♏13	♏	♐14	♐	♑19	♑	♑	♒3	♒
Nov	♓15	♓	♓	♈4	♈	♉17	♉	♉	♊4	♊	♋13	♋	♌19	♌	♍23	♍	♍	♎0	♎	♏0	♏	♐0	♐	♑4	♑	♒11	♒	♓22	♓	♓	
Dec	♈11	♈	♈	♉0	♉	♊10	♊	♋18	♋	♋	♌1	♌	♍6	♍	♎8	♎	♏10	♏	♐11	♐	♑14	♑	♒20	♒	♒	♓6	♓	♈19	♈	♈	♉7

1950	1	2	3	4	5	6	7	8	9	10	11	12	13	14	15	16	17	18	19	20	21	22	23	24	25	26	27	28	29	30	31
Jan	♉	♊18	♊	♊	♋1	♋	♌7	♌	♍11	♍	♎14	♎	♏17	♏	♐20	♐	♐	♑0	♑	♒5	♒	♓15	♓	♓	♈3	♈	♉16	♉	♉	♊2	♊
Feb	♋10	♋	♌14	♌	♍17	♍	♎20	♎	♏23	♏	♏	♐2	♐	♑7	♑	♒14	♒	♓23	♓	♓	♈11	♈	♈	♉0	♉	♊11	♊	♋20			
Mar	♋	♋	♌0	♌	♍2	♍	♎3	♎	♏5	♏	♐8	♐	♑13	♑	♒21	♒	♒	♓6	♓	♈18	♈	♈	♉7	♉	♊19	♊	♊	♋5	♋	♌11	♌
Apr	♍13	♍	♎13	♎	♏13	♏	♐14	♐	♑19	♑	♑	♒2	♒	♓12	♓	♓	♈1	♈	♉14	♉	♉	♊2	♊	♋13	♋	♌20	♌	♌	♍0	♍	
May	♎0	♏23	♏	♐23	♐	♐	♑2	♑	♒8	♒	♓18	♓	♓	♈7	♈	♉20	♉	♉	♊8	♊	♋19	♋	♋	♌3	♌	♍8	♍	♎10	♎	♏10	♏
Jun	♐10	♐	♑11	♑	♒16	♒	♒	♓1	♓	♈13	♈	♈	♉2	♉	♊14	♊	♊	♋0	♋	♌8	♌	♍15	♍	♎18	♎	♏20	♏	♐20	♐	♑21	
Jul	♑	♑	♒1	♒	♓9	♓	♈20	♈	♈	♉9	♉	♊21	♊	♊	♋7	♋	♌14	♌	♍20	♍	♍	♎0	♎	♏3	♏	♐5	♐	♑7	♑	♒11	♒
Aug	♓18	♓	♓	♈4	♈	♉16	♉	♉	♊4	♊	♋14	♋	♌21	♌	♌	♍2	♍	♎6	♎	♏8	♏	♐11	♐	♑15	♑	♒19	♒	♒	♓2	♓	♈12
Sep	♈	♈	♉1	♉	♊13	♊	♋23	♋	♋	♌6	♌	♍10	♍	♎13	♎	♏14	♏	♐17	♐	♑20	♑	♑	♒2	♒	♓10	♓	♈20	♈	♈	♉8	
Oct	♉	♊21	♊	♊	♋8	♋	♌16	♌	♍21	♍	♎22	♎	♏22	♏	♐23	♐	♐	♑2	♑	♒8	♒	♓16	♓	♓	♈3	♈	♉15	♉	♉	♊4	♊
Nov	♋16	♋	♋	♌1	♌	♍7	♍	♎9	♎	♏9	♏	♐8	♐	♑9	♑	♒14	♒	♓22	♓	♓	♈9	♈	♉21	♉	♉	♊10	♊	♋22	♋	♋	
Dec	♌9	♌	♍16	♍	♎19	♎	♏20	♏	♐19	♐	♑19	♑	♒22	♒	♒	♓4	♓	♈15	♈	♈	♉4	♉	♊16	♊	♊	♋4	♋	♌14	♌	♍22	♍

1951	1	2	3	4	5	6	7	8	9	10	11	12	13	14	15	16	17	18	19	20	21	22	23	24	25	26	27	28	29	30	31
Jan	♍	♎4	♎	♏6	♏	♐6	♐	♑6	♑	♒8	♒	♓13	♓	♈22	♈	♈	♉10	♉	♊23	♊	♊	♋10	♋	♌20	♌	♌	♍4	♍	♎10	♎	♏13
Feb	♏	♐15	♐	♑16	♑	♒18	♒	♓23	♓	♓	♈7	♈	♉18	♉	♉	♊7	♊	♋18	♋	♋	♌4	♌	♍10	♍	♎15	♎	♏19	♏			
Mar	♐22	♐	♐	♑0	♑	♒3	♒	♓8	♓	♈16	♈	♈	♉3	♉	♊15	♊	♊	♋3	♋	♌12	♌	♍19	♍	♎23	♎	♎	♏1	♏	♐3	♐	♑6
Apr	♑	♒10	♒	♓16	♓	♓	♈0	♈	♉11	♉	♊23	♊	♊	♋11	♋	♌22	♌	♌	♍5	♍	♎8	♎	♏9	♏	♐10	♐	♑12	♑	♒16	♒	
May	♓22	♓	♓	♈7	♈	♉18	♉	♉	♊6	♊	♋19	♋	♋	♌6	♌	♍14	♍	♎18	♎	♏19	♏	♐19	♐	♑19	♑	♒22	♒	♒	♓4	♓	♈13
Jun	♈	♈	♉0	♉	♊12	♊	♊	♋1	♋	♌13	♌	♍22	♍	♍	♎4	♎	♏6	♏	♐5	♐	♑5	♑	♒6	♒	♓10	♓	♈19	♈	♈	♉6	
Jul	♉	♊18	♊	♊	♋7	♋	♌19	♌	♌	♍5	♍	♎12	♎	♏15	♏	♐16	♐	♑15	♑	♒16	♒	♓19	♓	♓	♈2	♈	♉12	♉	♉	♊0	♊
Aug	♋13	♋	♋	♌0	♌	♍10	♍	♎18	♎	♏22	♏	♏	♐1	♐	♑1	♑	♒2	♒	♓5	♓	♈10	♈	♉20	♉	♉	♊7	♊	♋20	♋	♋	♌7
Sep	♌	♍16	♍	♎23	♎	♎	♏4	♏	♐7	♐	♑9	♑	♒11	♒	♓14	♓	♈20	♈	♈	♉4	♉	♊15	♊	♊	♋4	♋	♌15	♌	♌	♍0	
Oct	♍	♎6	♎	♏10	♏	♐12	♐	♑15	♑	♒19	♒	♓23	♓	♓	♈5	♈	♉13	♉	♉	♊0	♊	♋12	♋	♋	♌0	♌	♍9	♍	♎15	♎	♏18
Nov	♏	♐19	♐	♑21	♑	♑	♒0	♒	♓5	♓	♈12	♈	♉21	♉	♉	♊7	♊	♋20	♋	♋	♌9	♌	♍19	♍	♍	♎1	♎	♏4	♏	♐4	
Dec	♐	♑4	♑	♒6	♒	♓10	♓	♈18	♈	♈	♉3	♉	♊14	♊	♊	♋3	♋	♌16	♌	♌	♍3	♍	♎11	♎	♏15	♏	♐15	♐	♑14	♑	♒14

1952	1	2	3	4	5	6	7	8	9	10	11	12	13	14	15	16	17	18	19	20	21	22	23	24	25	26	27	28	29	30	31
Jan	♒	♓17	♓	♈23	♈	♈	♉9	♉	♊20	♊	♊	♋9	♋	♌22	♌	♌	♍10	♍	♎19	♎	♎	♏0	♏	♐2	♐	♑2	♑	♒1	♒	♓2	♓
Feb	♈7	♈	♉15	♉	♉	♊2	♊	♋15	♋	♋	♌4	♌	♍15	♍	♍	♎1	♎	♏7	♏	♐11	♐	♑12	♑	♒13	♒	♓13	♓	♈16	♈		
Mar	♉23	♉	♉	♊9	♊	♋22	♋	♋	♌11	♌	♍22	♍	♍	♎6	♎	♏13	♏	♐17	♐	♑20	♑	♒22	♒	♒	♓0	♓	♈3	♈	♉8	♉	♊18
Apr	♊	♊	♋6	♋	♌18	♌	♌	♍6	♍	♎13	♎	♏19	♏	♐23	♐	♐	♑2	♑	♒5	♒	♓8	♓	♈12	♈	♉18	♉	♉	♊2	♊	♋14	
May	♋	♋	♌3	♌	♍14	♍	♎22	♎	♎	♏3	♏	♐5	♐	♑7	♑	♒10	♒	♓14	♓	♈19	♈	♈	♉1	♉	♊10	♊	♋22	♋	♋	♌11	♌
Jun	♍23	♍	♍	♎7	♎	♏12	♏	♐14	♐	♑15	♑	♒16	♒	♓19	♓	♓	♈0	♈	♉8	♉	♊17	♊	♊	♋5	♋	♌18	♌	♌	♍6	♍	
Jul	♎16	♎	♏22	♏	♏	♐1	♐	♑1	♑	♒1	♒	♓2	♓	♈6	♈	♉13	♉	♊23	♊	♊	♋11	♋	♋	♌0	♌	♍13	♍	♍	♎0	♎	♏7
Aug	♏	♐11	♐	♑11	♑	♒11	♒	♓11	♓	♈13	♈	♉19	♉	♉	♊5	♊	♋17	♋	♋	♌6	♌	♍19	♍	♍	♎6	♎	♏14	♏	♐19	♐	♑21
Sep	♑	♒22	♒	♓21	♓	♈23	♈	♈	♉3	♉	♊12	♊	♋23	♋	♋	♌12	♌	♌	♍1	♍	♎11	♎	♏20	♏	♏	♐2	♐	♑5	♑	♒7	
Oct	♒	♓8	♓	♈9	♈	♉13	♉	♊20	♊	♊	♋7	♋	♌19	♌	♌	♍8	♍	♎18	♎	♎	♏1	♏	♐7	♐	♑11	♑	♒14	♒	♓17	♓	♈19
Nov	♈	♉22	♉	♉	♊5	♊	♋15	♋	♋	♌3	♌	♍16	♍	♍	♎2	♎	♏9	♏	♐13	♐	♑17	♑	♒20	♒	♓23	♓	♓	♈3	♈	♉7	
Dec	♉	♊14	♊	♋23	♋	♋	♌12	♌	♌	♍1	♍	♎11	♎	♏18	♏	♐22	♐	♐	♑0	♑	♒2	♒	♓4	♓	♈8	♈	♉14	♉	♊21	♊	♊

1953	1	2	3	4	5	6	7	8	9	10	11	12	13	14	15	16	17	18	19	20	21	22	23	24	25	26	27	28	29	30	31
Jan	♋7	♋	♌19	♌	♌	♍8	♍	♎20	♎	♎	♏4	♏	♐9	♐	♑10	♑	♒11	♒	♓11	♓	♈14	♈	♉19	♉	♉	♊4	♊	♋14	♋	♋	♌2
Feb	♌	♍15	♍	♍	♎4	♎	♏13	♏	♐19	♐	♑22	♑	♒22	♒	♓21	♓	♈22	♈	♈	♉2	♉	♊9	♊	♋20	♋	♋	♌9	♌			
Mar	♍21	♍	♍	♎10	♎	♏20	♏	♏	♐4	♐	♑8	♑	♒9	♒	♓8	♓	♈8	♈	♉10	♉	♊16	♊	♊	♋2	♋	♌15	♌	♌	♍4	♍	♎15
Apr	♎	♎	♏2	♏	♐10	♐	♑15	♑	♒18	♒	♓19	♓	♈19	♈	♉20	♉	♉	♊1	♊	♋10	♋	♌22	♌	♌	♍11	♍	♎22	♎	♎	♏8	
May	♏	♐15	♐	♑21	♑	♑	♒1	♒	♓3	♓	♈5	♈	♉6	♉	♊10	♊	♋18	♋	♋	♌5	♌	♍18	♍	♍	♎6	♎	♏15	♏	♐22	♐	♐
Jun	♑3	♑	♒6	♒	♓9	♓	♈12	♈	♉15	♉	♊19	♊	♊	♋3	♋	♌14	♌	♌	♍2	♍	♎14	♎	♎	♏0	♏	♐6	♐	♑10	♑	♒12	
Jul	♒	♓14	♓	♈17	♈	♉21	♉	♉	♊3	♊	♋11	♋	♌21	♌	♌	♍10	♍	♎22	♎	♎	♏9	♏	♐16	♐	♑19	♑	♒21	♒	♓21	♓	♈23
Aug	♈	♈	♉3	♉	♊9	♊	♋18	♋	♋	♌4	♌	♍17	♍	♍	♎6	♎	♏17	♏	♏	♐1	♐	♑6	♑	♒7	♒	♓7	♓	♈7	♈	♉9	♉
Sep	♊14	♊	♋23	♋	♋	♌11	♌	♍23	♍	♍	♎12	♎	♎	♏0	♏	♐9	♐	♑15	♑	♒18	♒	♓17	♓	♈17	♈	♉17	♉	♊21	♊	♊	
Oct	♋5	♋	♌17	♌	♌	♍5	♍	♎18	♎	♎	♏5	♏	♐16	♐	♑23	♑	♑	♒3	♒	♓4	♓	♈4	♈	♉4	♉	♊6	♊	♋12	♋	♌23	♌
Nov	♌	♍12	♍	♍	♎0	♎	♏11	♏	♐21	♐	♐	♑5	♑	♒10	♒	♓13	♓	♈14	♈	♉14	♉	♊16	♊	♋22	♋	♋	♌7	♌	♍19	♍	
Dec	♍	♎7	♎	♏18	♏	♏	♐3	♐	♑10	♑	♒15	♒	♓19	♓	♈22	♈	♈	♉0	♉	♊2	♊	♋7	♋	♌16	♌	♌	♍3	♍	♎16	♎	♎

1954	1	2	3	4	5	6	7	8	9	10	11	12	13	14	15	16	17	18	19	20	21	22	23	24	25	26	27	28	29	30	31
Jan	♏3	♏	♐12	♐	♑18	♑	♒22	♒	♒	♓0	♓	♈3	♈	♉6	♉	♊11	♊	♋16	♋	♋	♌1	♌	♍11	♍	♍	♎0	♎	♏12	♏	♐21	♐
Feb	♐	♑3	♑	♒6	♒	♓8	♓	♈9	♈	♉12	♉	♊16	♊	♋23	♋	♋	♌8	♌	♍19	♍	♍	♎7	♎	♏20	♏	♏	♐7	♐			
Mar	♑14	♑	♒17	♒	♓17	♓	♈17	♈	♉18	♉	♊22	♊	♊	♋5	♋	♌15	♌	♌	♍2	♍	♎14	♎	♎	♏3	♏	♐14	♐	♑23	♑	♑	♒3
Apr	♒	♓4	♓	♈4	♈	♉3	♉	♊5	♊	♋11	♋	♌20	♌	♌	♍8	♍	♎20	♎	♎	♏9	♏	♐20	♐	♐	♑6	♑	♒12	♒	♓15	♓	
May	♈15	♈	♉14	♉	♊15	♊	♋19	♋	♋	♌3	♌	♍14	♍	♍	♎3	♎	♏15	♏	♏	♐2	♐	♑12	♑	♒19	♒	♓23	♓	♓	♈0	♈	♉0
Jun	♉	♊1	♊	♋4	♋	♌11	♌	♍21	♍	♍	♎9	♎	♏22	♏	♏	♐9	♐	♑17	♑	♑	♒0	♒	♓5	♓	♈7	♈	♉9	♉	♊11	♊	
Jul	♋14	♋	♌20	♌	♌	♍5	♍	♎17	♎	♎	♏5	♏	♐16	♐	♐	♑1	♑	♒6	♒	♓10	♓	♈13	♈	♉16	♉	♊19	♊	♋23	♋	♋	♌5
Aug	♌	♍14	♍	♍	♎1	♎	♏13	♏	♏	♐1	♐	♑9	♑	♒14	♒	♓17	♓	♈19	♈	♉21	♉	♉	♊1	♊	♋6	♋	♌12	♌	♍22	♍	♍
Sep	♎9	♎	♏21	♏	♏	♐9	♐	♑19	♑	♑	♒0	♒	♓2	♓	♈2	♈	♉3	♉	♊6	♊	♋11	♋	♌19	♌	♌	♍4	♍	♎16	♎	♎	
Oct	♏4	♏	♐17	♐	♐	♑4	♑	♒10	♒	♓13	♓	♈12	♈	♉12	♉	♊13	♊	♋17	♋	♋	♌0	♌	♍10	♍	♎22	♎	♎	♏11	♏	♐23	♐
Nov	♐	♑11	♑	♒19	♒	♓23	♓	♓	♈0	♉23	♉	♊23	♊	♊	♋1	♋	♌7	♌	♍16	♍	♍	♎4	♎	♏17	♏	♏	♐5	♐	♑17	♑	
Dec	♑	♒2	♒	♓7	♓	♈10	♈	♉10	♉	♊10	♊	♋11	♋	♌15	♌	♍23	♍	♍	♎10	♎	♏23	♏	♏	♐12	♐	♑22	♑	♑	♒7	♒	♓14

1955	1	2	3	4	5	6	7	8	9	10	11	12	13	14	15	16	17	18	19	20	21	22	23	24	25	26	27	28	29	30	31
Jan	♓	♈18	♈	♉20	♉	♊20	♊	♋22	♋	♋	♌1	♌	♍8	♍	♎18	♎	♎	♏7	♏	♐19	♐	♐	♑6	♑	♒13	♒	♓19	♓	♈23	♈	♈
Feb	♉2	♉	♊5	♊	♋7	♋	♌11	♌	♍17	♍	♍	♎3	♎	♏15	♏	♏	♐3	♐	♑14	♑	♒22	♒	♒	♓2	♓	♈5	♈	♉8			
Mar	♉	♊11	♊	♋14	♋	♌19	♌	♌	♍2	♍	♎11	♎	♏23	♏	♏	♐12	♐	♑23	♑	♑	♒7	♒	♓11	♓	♈13	♈	♉14	♉	♊16	♊	♋20
Apr	♋	♋	♌2	♌	♍9	♍	♎19	♎	♎	♏6	♏	♐19	♐	♐	♑8	♑	♒17	♒	♓22	♓	♈23	♈	♉23	♉	♉	♊0	♊	♋2	♋	♌7	
May	♌	♍15	♍	♍	♎1	♎	♏13	♏	♏	♐2	♐	♑15	♑	♑	♒1	♒	♓7	♓	♈10	♈	♉10	♉	♊9	♊	♋10	♋	♌14	♌	♍21	♍	♍
Jun	♎7	♎	♏19	♏	♏	♐8	♐	♑21	♑	♑	♒7	♒	♓15	♓	♈19	♈	♉20	♉	♊20	♊	♋20	♋	♌22	♌	♌	♍4	♍	♎13	♎	♎	
Jul	♏1	♏	♐14	♐	♐	♑3	♑	♒13	♒	♓21	♓	♓	♈2	♈	♉5	♉	♊6	♊	♋6	♋	♌8	♌	♍12	♍	♎21	♎	♎	♏8	♏	♐21	♐
Aug	♐	♑9	♑	♒19	♒	♒	♓2	♓	♈8	♈	♉12	♉	♊14	♊	♋16	♋	♌18	♌	♍22	♍	♍	♎5	♎	♏16	♏	♏	♐5	♐	♑17	♑	♑
Sep	♒2	♒	♓9	♓	♈13	♈	♉17	♉	♊20	♊	♋23	♋	♋	♌2	♌	♍7	♍	♎14	♎	♎	♏0	♏	♐13	♐	♐	♑1	♑	♒11	♒	♓18	
Oct	♓	♈21	♈	♉23	♉	♉	♊1	♊	♋4	♋	♌9	♌	♍14	♍	♎22	♎	♎	♏8	♏	♐21	♐	♐	♑10	♑	♒20	♒	♒	♓3	♓	♈7	♈
Nov	♉8	♉	♊9	♊	♋10	♋	♌14	♌	♍20	♍	♍	♎5	♎	♏15	♏	♏	♐4	♐	♑17	♑	♑	♒5	♒	♓13	♓	♈18	♈	♉19	♉	♊19	
Dec	♊	♋19	♋	♌21	♌	♌	♍2	♍	♎10	♎	♏22	♏	♏	♐10	♐	♑23	♑	♑	♒11	♒	♓21	♓	♓	♈3	♈	♉6	♉	♊6	♊	♋5	♋

1956	1	2	3	4	5	6	7	8	9	10	11	12	13	14	15	16	17	18	19	20	21	22	23	24	25	26	27	28	29	30	31
Jan	♌6	♌	♍9	♍	♎16	♎	♎	♏3	♏	♐16	♐	♐	♑5	♑	♒17	♒	♒	♓3	♓	♈11	♈	♉15	♉	♊17	♊	♋17	♋	♌17	♌	♍19	♍
Feb	♍	♎0	♎	♏10	♏	♐23	♐	♐	♑12	♑	♒23	♒	♒	♓9	♓	♈16	♈	♉22	♉	♉	♊1	♊	♋3	♋	♌3	♌	♍5	♍	♎10		
Mar	♎	♏18	♏	♏	♐6	♐	♑19	♑	♑	♒7	♒	♓15	♓	♈22	♈	♈	♉3	♉	♊7	♊	♋10	♋	♌12	♌	♍15	♍	♎19	♎	♎	♏3	♏
Apr	♐15	♐	♐	♑3	♑	♒15	♒	♒	♓0	♓	♈6	♈	♉10	♉	♊12	♊	♋15	♋	♌18	♌	♍22	♍	♍	♎4	♎	♏12	♏	♐23	♐	♐	
May	♑11	♑	♒23	♒	♒	♓9	♓	♈15	♈	♉18	♉	♊20	♊	♋21	♋	♋	♌0	♌	♍4	♍	♎10	♎	♏19	♏	♏	♐6	♐	♑19	♑	♑	♒7
Jun	♒	♓18	♓	♓	♈1	♈	♉4	♉	♊5	♊	♋5	♋	♌6	♌	♍10	♍	♎16	♎	♎	♏1	♏	♐13	♐	♐	♑1	♑	♒14	♒	♒	♓1	
Jul	♓	♈10	♈	♉14	♉	♊16	♊	♋16	♋	♌15	♌	♍17	♍	♎22	♎	♎	♏7	♏	♐19	♐	♐	♑7	♑	♒20	♒	♒	♓7	♓	♈17	♈	♉23
Aug	♉	♉	♊2	♊	♋2	♋	♌2	♌	♍2	♍	♎6	♎	♏13	♏	♏	♐1	♐	♑14	♑	♑	♒2	♒	♓13	♓	♈22	♈	♈	♉5	♉	♊10	♊
Sep	♋12	♋	♌12	♌	♍13	♍	♎15	♎	♏21	♏	♏	♐8	♐	♑20	♑	♑	♒9	♒	♓19	♓	♓	♈4	♈	♉11	♉	♊16	♊	♋19	♋	♌21	
Oct	♌	♍22	♍	♍	♎1	♎	♏7	♏	♐16	♐	♐	♑4	♑	♒16	♒	♒	♓3	♓	♈11	♈	♉17	♉	♊21	♊	♊	♋0	♋	♌3	♌	♍6	♍
Nov	♎10	♎	♏16	♏	♏	♐1	♐	♑12	♑	♑	♒1	♒	♓12	♓	♈21	♈	♈	♉2	♉	♊5	♊	♋6	♋	♌9	♌	♍12	♍	♎17	♎	♎	
Dec	♏0	♏	♐9	♐	♑20	♑	♑	♒9	♒	♓21	♓	♓	♈6	♈	♉12	♉	♊14	♊	♋15	♋	♌15	♌	♍18	♍	♎22	♎	♎	♏6	♏	♐16	♐

1957	1	2	3	4	5	6	7	8	9	10	11	12	13	14	15	16	17	18	19	20	21	22	23	24	25	26	27	28	29	30	31
Jan	♐	♑3	♑	♒16	♒	♒	♓4	♓	♈15	♈	♉22	♉	♉	♊1	♊	♋2	♋	♌1	♌	♍1	♍	♎4	♎	♏11	♏	♐22	♐	♐	♑10	♑	♒22
Feb	♒	♒	♓11	♓	♈22	♈	♈	♉7	♉	♊12	♊	♋13	♋	♌12	♌	♍12	♍	♎13	♎	♏18	♏	♏	♐4	♐	♑16	♑	♑	♒4			
Mar	♒	♓16	♓	♓	♈4	♈	♉13	♉	♊20	♊	♋23	♋	♌23	♌	♍23	♍	♎23	♎	♎	♏3	♏	♐11	♐	♑22	♑	♑	♒11	♒	♓23	♓	♓
Apr	♈10	♈	♉19	♉	♉	♊1	♊	♋5	♋	♌8	♌	♍9	♍	♎10	♎	♏13	♏	♐20	♐	♐	♑6	♑	♒18	♒	♒	♓6	♓	♈17	♈	♈	
May	♉1	♉	♊7	♊	♋11	♋	♌14	♌	♍16	♍	♎19	♎	♏23	♏	♏	♐5	♐	♑15	♑	♑	♒2	♒	♓14	♓	♓	♈1	♈	♉9	♉	♊14	♊
Jun	♋17	♋	♌19	♌	♍22	♍	♍	♎1	♎	♏6	♏	♐13	♐	♑23	♑	♑	♒10	♒	♓23	♓	♓	♈10	♈	♉18	♉	♊23	♊	♊	♋1	♋	
Jul	♌2	♌	♍4	♍	♎7	♎	♏12	♏	♐20	♐	♐	♑6	♑	♒17	♒	♒	♓6	♓	♈18	♈	♈	♉4	♉	♊9	♊	♋11	♋	♌11	♌	♍11	♍
Aug	♎13	♎	♏18	♏	♏	♐2	♐	♑12	♑	♑	♒0	♒	♓12	♓	♓	♈1	♈	♉12	♉	♊18	♊	♋21	♋	♌21	♌	♍21	♍	♎21	♎	♎	♏0
Sep	♏	♐8	♐	♑18	♑	♑	♒6	♒	♓19	♓	♓	♈7	♈	♉18	♉	♉	♊2	♊	♋7	♋	♌8	♌	♍8	♍	♎7	♎	♏9	♏	♐15	♐	
Oct	♐	♑0	♑	♒12	♒	♒	♓1	♓	♈13	♈	♈	♉0	♉	♊8	♊	♋14	♋	♌17	♌	♍18	♍	♎18	♎	♏20	♏	♏	♐0	♐	♑8	♑	♒19
Nov	♒	♒	♓8	♓	♈20	♈	♈	♉6	♉	♊14	♊	♋19	♋	♌23	♌	♌	♍2	♍	♎4	♎	♏6	♏	♐10	♐	♑17	♑	♑	♒3	♒	♓16	
Dec	♓	♓	♈4	♈	♉14	♉	♊21	♊	♊	♋1	♋	♌4	♌	♍8	♍	♎11	♎	♏14	♏	♐19	♐	♐	♑2	♑	♒12	♒	♒	♓0	♓	♈13	♈

1958	1	2	3	4	5	6	7	8	9	10	11	12	13	14	15	16	17	18	19	20	21	22	23	24	25	26	27	28	29	30	31
Jan	♉23	♉	♉	♊6	♊	♋10	♋	♌11	♌	♍13	♍	♎16	♎	♏20	♏	♏	♐2	♐	♑10	♑	♒20	♒	♒	♓8	♓	♈21	♈	♈	♉8	♉	♊16
Feb	♊	♋20	♋	♌21	♌	♍21	♍	♎22	♎	♎	♏2	♏	♐8	♐	♑17	♑	♑	♒3	♒	♓15	♓	♓	♈4	♈	♉16	♉	♉	♊2			
Mar	♊	♋7	♋	♌8	♌	♍7	♍	♎7	♎	♏9	♏	♐14	♐	♑22	♑	♑	♒9	♒	♓21	♓	♓	♈10	♈	♉23	♉	♉	♊9	♊	♋16	♋	♌18
Apr	♌	♍19	♍	♎18	♎	♏18	♏	♐22	♐	♐	♑4	♑	♒15	♒	♒	♓3	♓	♈16	♈	♈	♉4	♉	♊15	♊	♋22	♋	♋	♌3	♌	♍5	
May	♍	♎5	♎	♏5	♏	♐7	♐	♑13	♑	♒22	♒	♒	♓10	♓	♈23	♈	♈	♉11	♉	♊20	♊	♊	♋4	♋	♌9	♌	♍12	♍	♎14	♎	♏15
Jun	♏	♐17	♐	♑22	♑	♑	♒6	♒	♓17	♓	♓	♈6	♈	♉18	♉	♉	♊3	♊	♋10	♋	♌14	♌	♍18	♍	♎21	♎	♏23	♏	♏	♐2	
Jul	♐	♑7	♑	♒15	♒	♒	♓1	♓	♈14	♈	♈	♉2	♉	♊11	♊	♋17	♋	♌21	♌	♍23	♍	♍	♎2	♎	♏5	♏	♐9	♐	♑15	♑	♒23
Aug	♒	♒	♓9	♓	♈22	♈	♈	♉10	♉	♊20	♊	♊	♋3	♋	♌6	♌	♍7	♍	♎8	♎	♏11	♏	♐15	♐	♑21	♑	♑	♒6	♒	♓17	♓
Sep	♓	♈5	♈	♉18	♉	♉	♊5	♊	♋12	♋	♌16	♌	♍17	♍	♎17	♎	♏17	♏	♐21	♐	♐	♑3	♑	♒12	♒	♓23	♓	♓	♈12	♈	
Oct	♈	♉1	♉	♊13	♊	♋21	♋	♋	♌2	♌	♍4	♍	♎3	♎	♏3	♏	♐4	♐	♑9	♑	♒18	♒	♒	♓5	♓	♈18	♈	♈	♉7	♉	♊19
Nov	♊	♊	♋4	♋	♌11	♌	♍14	♍	♎14	♎	♏14	♏	♐14	♐	♑17	♑	♑	♒0	♒	♓11	♓	♓	♈0	♈	♉13	♉	♉	♊0	♊	♋10	
Dec	♋	♌17	♌	♍22	♍	♍	♎0	♎	♏1	♏	♐1	♐	♑4	♑	♒9	♒	♓19	♓	♓	♈7	♈	♉20	♉	♉	♊7	♊	♋16	♋	♌22	♌	♌

1959	1	2	3	4	5	6	7	8	9	10	11	12	13	14	15	16	17	18	19	20	21	22	23	24	25	26	27	28	29	30	31
Jan	♍3	♍	♎7	♎	♏9	♏	♐11	♐	♑14	♑	♒19	♒	♒	♓4	♓	♈15	♈	♈	♉4	♉	♊15	♊	♊	♋0	♋	♌5	♌	♍9	♍	♎12	♎
Feb	♏15	♏	♐19	♐	♑22	♑	♑	♒4	♒	♓12	♓	♓	♈0	♈	♉13	♉	♉	♊0	♊	♋9	♋	♌14	♌	♍17	♍	♎19	♎	♏21			
Mar	♏	♏	♐0	♐	♑5	♑	♒11	♒	♓20	♓	♓	♈8	♈	♉20	♉	♉	♊9	♊	♋18	♋	♋	♌0	♌	♍3	♍	♎4	♎	♏4	♏	♐6	♐
Apr	♑10	♑	♒17	♒	♒	♓3	♓	♈15	♈	♈	♉3	♉	♊16	♊	♊	♋3	♋	♌10	♌	♍14	♍	♎14	♎	♏14	♏	♐14	♐	♑17	♑	♒23	
May	♒	♒	♓9	♓	♈21	♈	♈	♉10	♉	♊22	♊	♊	♋9	♋	♌18	♌	♍23	♍	♍	♎1	♎	♏1	♏	♐0	♐	♑1	♑	♒6	♒	♓15	♓
Jun	♓	♈3	♈	♉16	♉	♉	♊4	♊	♋15	♋	♋	♌0	♌	♍6	♍	♎10	♎	♏11	♏	♐11	♐	♑11	♑	♒15	♒	♓22	♓	♓	♈9	♈	
Jul	♉22	♉	♉	♊10	♊	♋21	♋	♋	♌5	♌	♍12	♍	♎16	♎	♏19	♏	♐20	♐	♑21	♑	♑	♒0	♒	♓7	♓	♈17	♈	♈	♉5	♉	♊18
Aug	♊	♊	♋4	♋	♌12	♌	♍18	♍	♎22	♎	♎	♏1	♏	♐4	♐	♑6	♑	♒10	♒	♓16	♓	♓	♈1	♈	♉13	♉	♉	♊2	♊	♋12	♋
Sep	♌20	♌	♌	♍1	♍	♎4	♎	♏6	♏	♐9	♐	♑13	♑	♒17	♒	♒	♓0	♓	♈10	♈	♉21	♉	♉	♊10	♊	♋21	♋	♋	♌5	♌	
Oct	♍10	♍	♎12	♎	♏13	♏	♐15	♐	♑18	♑	♒23	♒	♒	♓7	♓	♈17	♈	♈	♉5	♉	♊17	♊	♊	♋5	♋	♌15	♌	♍21	♍	♎23	♎
Nov	♏23	♏	♐23	♐	♐	♑0	♑	♒5	♒	♓13	♓	♈23	♈	♈	♉11	♉	♉	♊0	♊	♋12	♋	♌23	♌	♌	♍6	♍	♎10	♎	♏10	♏	
Dec	♐9	♐	♑9	♑	♒12	♒	♓19	♓	♓	♈5	♈	♉18	♉	♉	♊6	♊	♋18	♋	♋	♌5	♌	♍14	♍	♎19	♎	♏21	♏	♐21	♐	♑20	♑

1960	1	2	3	4	5	6	7	8	9	10	11	12	13	14	15	16	17	18	19	20	21	22	23	24	25	26	27	28	29	30	31
Jan	♒21	♒	♒	♓2	♓	♈12	♈	♈	♉0	♉	♊12	♊	♊	♋0	♋	♌11	♌	♍19	♍	♍	♎2	♎	♏5	♏	♐7	♐	♑7	♑	♒8	♒	♓12
Feb	♓	♈20	♈	♈	♉7	♉	♊20	♊	♊	♋7	♋	♌17	♌	♌	♍1	♍	♎7	♎	♏11	♏	♐14	♐	♑16	♑	♒18	♒	♓22	♓	♓		
Mar	♈5	♈	♉15	♉	♉	♊4	♊	♋16	♋	♋	♌2	♌	♍9	♍	♎14	♎	♏17	♏	♐19	♐	♑22	♑	♑	♒2	♒	♓7	♓	♈14	♈	♈	♉0
Apr	♉	♊12	♊	♊	♋0	♋	♌11	♌	♍18	♍	♎22	♎	♎	♏0	♏	♐1	♐	♑4	♑	♒8	♒	♓14	♓	♈22	♈	♈	♉8	♉	♊19	♊	
May	♊	♋8	♋	♌20	♌	♌	♍4	♍	♎8	♎	♏10	♏	♐10	♐	♑10	♑	♒13	♒	♓19	♓	♓	♈4	♈	♉14	♉	♉	♊2	♊	♋15	♋	♋
Jun	♌3	♌	♍13	♍	♎18	♎	♏20	♏	♐20	♐	♑19	♑	♒21	♒	♒	♓1	♓	♈9	♈	♉20	♉	♉	♊8	♊	♋21	♋	♋	♌9	♌	♍20	
Jul	♍	♍	♎3	♎	♏6	♏	♐6	♐	♑6	♑	♒6	♒	♓9	♓	♈16	♈	♈	♉2	♉	♊14	♊	♊	♋3	♋	♌15	♌	♌	♍1	♍	♎9	♎
Aug	♏14	♏	♐16	♐	♑16	♑	♒16	♒	♓18	♓	♓	♈0	♈	♉9	♉	♊21	♊	♊	♋9	♋	♌21	♌	♌	♍7	♍	♎15	♎	♏20	♏	♐23	♐
Sep	♐	♑1	♑	♒2	♒	♓4	♓	♈9	♈	♉17	♉	♉	♊4	♊	♋17	♋	♋	♌4	♌	♍14	♍	♎21	♎	♎	♏1	♏	♐5	♐	♑8	♑	
Oct	♒10	♒	♓14	♓	♈18	♈	♈	♉2	♉	♊12	♊	♊	♋1	♋	♌13	♌	♍23	♍	♍	♎5	♎	♏8	♏	♐11	♐	♑13	♑	♒16	♒	♓21	♓
Nov	♓	♈3	♈	♉10	♉	♊21	♊	♊	♋9	♋	♌22	♌	♌	♍8	♍	♎15	♎	♏18	♏	♐19	♐	♑20	♑	♒22	♒	♒	♓2	♓	♈9	♈	
Dec	♉18	♉	♉	♊4	♊	♋16	♋	♋	♌5	♌	♍17	♍	♍	♎1	♎	♏5	♏	♐5	♐	♑5	♑	♒5	♒	♓8	♓	♈14	♈	♈	♉0	♉	♊11

1961	1	2	3	4	5	6	7	8	9	10	11	12	13	14	15	16	17	18	19	20	21	22	23	24	25	26	27	28	29	30	31
Jan	♊	♋23	♋	♋	♌12	♌	♌	♍0	♍	♎9	♎	♏15	♏	♐16	♐	♑16	♑	♒15	♒	♓17	♓	♈21	♈	♈	♉5	♉	♊16	♊	♊	♋5	♋
Feb	♌18	♌	♌	♍6	♍	♎16	♎	♏23	♏	♏	♐2	♐	♑3	♑	♒3	♒	♓3	♓	♈6	♈	♉13	♉	♊23	♊	♊	♋11	♋	♋			
Mar	♌0	♌	♍12	♍	♎21	♎	♎	♏5	♏	♐9	♐	♑12	♑	♒13	♒	♓14	♓	♈16	♈	♉22	♉	♉	♊7	♊	♋19	♋	♋	♌7	♌	♍19	♍
Apr	♍	♎4	♎	♏10	♏	♐15	♐	♑18	♑	♒21	♒	♓23	♓	♓	♈2	♈	♉7	♉	♊15	♊	♊	♋3	♋	♌15	♌	♌	♍3	♍	♎12	♎	
May	♏17	♏	♐21	♐	♐	♑0	♑	♒3	♒	♓6	♓	♈10	♈	♉16	♉	♉	♊0	♊	♋11	♋	♋	♌0	♌	♍12	♍	♎21	♎	♎	♏2	♏	♐5
Jun	♐	♑6	♑	♒8	♒	♓11	♓	♈16	♈	♉23	♉	♉	♊7	♊	♋18	♋	♋	♌7	♌	♍20	♍	♍	♎6	♎	♏12	♏	♐15	♐	♑15	♑	
Jul	♒16	♒	♓17	♓	♈22	♈	♈	♉4	♉	♊14	♊	♊	♋1	♋	♌14	♌	♌	♍3	♍	♎14	♎	♏21	♏	♏	♐1	♐	♑2	♑	♒1	♒	♓1
Aug	♓	♈4	♈	♉10	♉	♊19	♊	♊	♋7	♋	♌20	♌	♌	♍9	♍	♎20	♎	♎	♏5	♏	♐10	♐	♑12	♑	♒12	♒	♓12	♓	♈13	♈	♉17
Sep	♉	♉	♊1	♊	♋13	♋	♋	♌2	♌	♍15	♍	♍	♎2	♎	♏11	♏	♐17	♐	♑21	♑	♒22	♒	♓22	♓	♈23	♈	♈	♉2	♉	♊9	
Oct	♊	♋20	♋	♋	♌9	♌	♍21	♍	♍	♎8	♎	♏16	♏	♐23	♐	♐	♑4	♑	♒7	♒	♓8	♓	♈10	♈	♉12	♉	♊18	♊	♊	♋4	♋
Nov	♌16	♌	♌	♍5	♍	♎16	♎	♏23	♏	♏	♐5	♐	♑9	♑	♒12	♒	♓15	♓	♈18	♈	♉22	♉	♉	♊3	♊	♋12	♋	♋	♌0	♌	
Dec	♍13	♍	♍	♎0	♎	♏8	♏	♐13	♐	♑15	♑	♒18	♒	♓21	♓	♓	♈0	♈	♉5	♉	♊12	♊	♋21	♋	♋	♌8	♌	♍22	♍	♍	♎9

1962	1	2	3	4	5	6	7	8	9	10	11	12	13	14	15	16	17	18	19	20	21	22	23	24	25	26	27	28	29	30	31
Jan	♎	♏18	♏	♐23	♐	♐	♑1	♑	♒1	♒	♓3	♓	♈6	♈	♉11	♉	♊19	♊	♊	♋4	♋	♌16	♌	♌	♍5	♍	♎17	♎	♎	♏3	♏
Feb	♐9	♐	♑12	♑	♒12	♒	♓12	♓	♈13	♈	♉17	♉	♉	♊0	♊	♋10	♋	♌22	♌	♌	♍11	♍	♍	♎0	♎	♏11	♏	♐18			
Mar	♐	♑22	♑	♒23	♒	♓22	♓	♈22	♈	♈	♉0	♉	♊6	♊	♋16	♋	♋	♌5	♌	♍18	♍	♍	♎6	♎	♏17	♏	♏	♐1	♐	♑7	♑
Apr	♒9	♒	♓9	♓	♈9	♈	♉10	♉	♊15	♊	♋23	♋	♋	♌11	♌	♌	♍0	♍	♎12	♎	♏22	♏	♏	♐7	♐	♑13	♑	♒17	♒	♓19	
May	♓	♈19	♈	♉21	♉	♉	♊0	♊	♋7	♋	♌18	♌	♌	♍7	♍	♎19	♎	♎	♏5	♏	♐13	♐	♑18	♑	♒23	♒	♒	♓2	♓	♈4	♈
Jun	♉6	♉	♊10	♊	♋16	♋	♋	♌3	♌	♍15	♍	♍	♎3	♎	♏13	♏	♐20	♐	♐	♑1	♑	♒4	♒	♓7	♓	♈10	♈	♉13	♉	♊18	
Jul	♊	♊	♋1	♋	♌11	♌	♍23	♍	♍	♎11	♎	♏22	♏	♏	♐5	♐	♑9	♑	♒12	♒	♓13	♓	♈15	♈	♉19	♉	♉	♊0	♊	♋8	♋
Aug	♌18	♌	♌	♍6	♍	♎19	♎	♎	♏6	♏	♐15	♐	♑19	♑	♒21	♒	♓21	♓	♈22	♈	♈	♉0	♉	♊6	♊	♋14	♋	♋	♌1	♌	♍13
Sep	♍	♍	♎2	♎	♏14	♏	♏	♐0	♐	♑5	♑	♒8	♒	♓8	♓	♈7	♈	♉8	♉	♊12	♊	♋20	♋	♋	♌7	♌	♍19	♍	♍	♎8	
Oct	♎	♏20	♏	♏	♐6	♐	♑14	♑	♒18	♒	♓19	♓	♈18	♈	♉18	♉	♊20	♊	♊	♋2	♋	♌13	♌	♌	♍1	♍	♎14	♎	♎	♏2	♏
Nov	♐12	♐	♑20	♑	♑	♒2	♒	♓4	♓	♈5	♈	♉5	♉	♊6	♊	♋11	♋	♌20	♌	♌	♍8	♍	♎21	♎	♎	♏8	♏	♐18	♐	♐	
Dec	♑2	♑	♒8	♒	♓11	♓	♈14	♈	♉15	♉	♊17	♊	♋21	♋	♋	♌5	♌	♍16	♍	♍	♎4	♎	♏16	♏	♏	♐1	♐	♑8	♑	♒13	♒

1963	1	2	3	4	5	6	7	8	9	10	11	12	13	14	15	16	17	18	19	20	21	22	23	24	25	26	27	28	29	30	31
Jan	♓17	♓	♈20	♈	♉23	♉	♉	♊2	♊	♋6	♋	♌14	♌	♌	♍0	♍	♎13	♎	♎	♏1	♏	♐10	♐	♑17	♑	♒21	♒	♓23	♓	♓	♈1
Feb	♈	♉4	♉	♊8	♊	♋14	♋	♌22	♌	♌	♍9	♍	♎21	♎	♎	♏9	♏	♐20	♐	♐	♑3	♑	♒7	♒	♓8	♓	♈8	♈			
Mar	♉10	♉	♊14	♊	♋20	♋	♋	♌5	♌	♍16	♍	♍	♎4	♎	♏16	♏	♏	♐4	♐	♑13	♑	♒17	♒	♓18	♓	♈18	♈	♉18	♉	♊20	♊
Apr	♊	♋2	♋	♌11	♌	♍22	♍	♍	♎10	♎	♏23	♏	♏	♐11	♐	♑21	♑	♑	♒3	♒	♓5	♓	♈5	♈	♉4	♉	♊5	♊	♋9	♋	
May	♌17	♌	♌	♍4	♍	♎16	♎	♎	♏5	♏	♐17	♐	♐	♑3	♑	♒10	♒	♓14	♓	♈15	♈	♉15	♉	♊15	♊	♋18	♋	♋	♌0	♌	♍10
Jun	♍	♎23	♎	♎	♏11	♏	♐23	♐	♐	♑8	♑	♒16	♒	♓21	♓	♈23	♈	♈	♉1	♉	♊1	♊	♋4	♋	♌9	♌	♍18	♍	♍	♎6	
Jul	♎	♏18	♏	♏	♐6	♐	♑15	♑	♒22	♒	♒	♓2	♓	♈6	♈	♉8	♉	♊10	♊	♋13	♋	♌18	♌	♌	♍3	♍	♎14	♎	♎	♏2	♏
Aug	♐14	♐	♑23	♑	♑	♒5	♒	♓8	♓	♈11	♈	♉14	♉	♊17	♊	♋21	♋	♋	♌3	♌	♍11	♍	♎22	♎	♎	♏10	♏	♐22	♐	♐	♑8
Sep	♑	♒14	♒	♓16	♓	♈18	♈	♉19	♉	♊22	♊	♊	♋3	♋	♌10	♌	♍19	♍	♍	♎5	♎	♏18	♏	♏	♐6	♐	♑17	♑	♑	♒0	
Oct	♒	♓2	♓	♈3	♈	♉3	♉	♊4	♊	♋8	♋	♌15	♌	♌	♍1	♍	♎12	♎	♎	♏0	♏	♐13	♐	♐	♑1	♑	♒9	♒	♓13	♓	♈14
Nov	♈	♉13	♉	♊13	♊	♋15	♋	♌21	♌	♌	♍7	♍	♎18	♎	♎	♏7	♏	♐19	♐	♐	♑7	♑	♒17	♒	♓23	♓	♓	♈1	♈	♉0	
Dec	♉	♊0	♊	♋1	♋	♌5	♌	♍13	♍	♍	♎0	♎	♏13	♏	♏	♐1	♐	♑13	♑	♒23	♒	♒	♓5	♓	♈9	♈	♉11	♉	♊11	♊	♋12

1964	1	2	3	4	5	6	7	8	9	10	11	12	13	14	15	16	17	18	19	20	21	22	23	24	25	26	27	28	29	30	31
Jan	♋	♌15	♌	♍21	♍	♍	♎7	♎	♏20	♏	♏	♐8	♐	♑20	♑	♑	♒4	♒	♓11	♓	♈16	♈	♉19	♉	♊20	♊	♋22	♋	♋	♌1	♌
Feb	♍7	♍	♎16	♎	♎	♏3	♏	♐16	♐	♐	♑3	♑	♒12	♒	♓17	♓	♈21	♈	♈	♉0	♉	♊3	♊	♋6	♋	♌10	♌	♍16	♍		
Mar	♍	♎0	♎	♏12	♏	♏	♐1	♐	♑12	♑	♒21	♒	♒	♓1	♓	♈4	♈	♉6	♉	♊8	♊	♋12	♋	♌17	♌	♌	♍0	♍	♎9	♎	♏20
Apr	♏	♏	♐9	♐	♑21	♑	♑	♒6	♒	♓11	♓	♈13	♈	♉14	♉	♊15	♊	♋18	♋	♌23	♌	♌	♍6	♍	♎15	♎	♎	♏3	♏	♐16	
May	♐	♐	♑4	♑	♒15	♒	♓21	♓	♓	♈0	♈	♉0	♉	♊0	♊	♋1	♋	♌5	♌	♍12	♍	♎21	♎	♎	♏9	♏	♐22	♐	♐	♑11	♑
Jun	♒22	♒	♒	♓6	♓	♈10	♈	♉11	♉	♊10	♊	♋10	♋	♌12	♌	♍18	♍	♍	♎3	♎	♏15	♏	♏	♐4	♐	♑17	♑	♑	♒4	♒	
Jul	♓12	♓	♈18	♈	♉20	♉	♊21	♊	♋21	♋	♌22	♌	♌	♍2	♍	♎10	♎	♏21	♏	♏	♐10	♐	♑23	♑	♑	♒10	♒	♓18	♓	♓	♈0
Aug	♈	♉4	♉	♊6	♊	♋7	♋	♌8	♌	♍12	♍	♎18	♎	♎	♏5	♏	♐18	♐	♐	♑6	♑	♒16	♒	♒	♓0	♓	♈5	♈	♉9	♉	♊13
Sep	♊	♋15	♋	♌17	♌	♍21	♍	♍	♎3	♎	♏13	♏	♏	♐2	♐	♑14	♑	♑	♒0	♒	♓8	♓	♈12	♈	♉15	♉	♊18	♊	♋21	♋	
Oct	♋	♌1	♌	♍5	♍	♎12	♎	♏21	♏	♏	♐10	♐	♑23	♑	♑	♒10	♒	♓17	♓	♈21	♈	♉23	♉	♉	♊0	♊	♋2	♋	♌6	♌	♍12
Nov	♍	♎19	♎	♎	♏5	♏	♐17	♐	♐	♑6	♑	♒18	♒	♒	♓3	♓	♈7	♈	♉9	♉	♊9	♊	♋9	♋	♌12	♌	♍17	♍	♍	♎1	
Dec	♎	♏12	♏	♏	♐0	♐	♑13	♑	♑	♒1	♒	♓11	♓	♈18	♈	♉20	♉	♊20	♊	♋19	♋	♌20	♌	♌	♍0	♍	♎7	♎	♏18	♏	♏

1965	1	2	3	4	5	6	7	8	9	10	11	12	13	14	15	16	17	18	19	20	21	22	23	24	25	26	27	28	29	30	31
Jan	♐6	♐	♑19	♑	♑	♒7	♒	♓18	♓	♓	♈2	♈	♉6	♉	♊7	♊	♋7	♋	♌7	♌	♍8	♍	♎14	♎	♎	♏0	♏	♐12	♐	♐	♑1
Feb	♑	♒13	♒	♒	♓0	♓	♈8	♈	♉14	♉	♊17	♊	♋18	♋	♌18	♌	♍19	♍	♎23	♎	♎	♏7	♏	♐19	♐	♐	♑8	♑			
Mar	♒20	♒	♒	♓6	♓	♈13	♈	♉19	♉	♊23	♊	♊	♋2	♋	♌3	♌	♍5	♍	♎9	♎	♏16	♏	♏	♐3	♐	♑16	♑	♑	♒4	♒	♓14
Apr	♓	♈20	♈	♈	♉1	♉	♊5	♊	♋8	♋	♌11	♌	♍14	♍	♎18	♎	♎	♏1	♏	♐12	♐	♐	♑0	♑	♒12	♒	♓22	♓	♓	♈5	
May	♈	♉9	♉	♊11	♊	♋13	♋	♌16	♌	♍20	♍	♍	♎1	♎	♏9	♏	♐20	♐	♐	♑8	♑	♒21	♒	♒	♓7	♓	♈15	♈	♉18	♉	♊20
Jun	♊	♋20	♋	♌22	♌	♌	♍1	♍	♎7	♎	♏16	♏	♏	♐3	♐	♑15	♑	♑	♒4	♒	♓15	♓	♓	♈0	♈	♉5	♉	♊6	♊	♋6	
Jul	♋	♌6	♌	♍8	♍	♎13	♎	♏21	♏	♏	♐9	♐	♑21	♑	♑	♒10	♒	♓22	♓	♓	♈7	♈	♉14	♉	♊16	♊	♋17	♋	♌16	♌	♍16
Aug	♍	♎20	♎	♎	♏3	♏	♐15	♐	♐	♑3	♑	♒16	♒	♒	♓3	♓	♈13	♈	♉21	♉	♉	♊1	♊	♋3	♋	♌3	♌	♍3	♍	♎5	♎
Sep	♏11	♏	♐21	♐	♐	♑10	♑	♒22	♒	♒	♓9	♓	♈19	♈	♈	♉3	♉	♊8	♊	♋11	♋	♌12	♌	♍13	♍	♎15	♎	♏20	♏	♏	
Oct	♐5	♐	♑17	♑	♑	♒6	♒	♓17	♓	♓	♈2	♈	♉8	♉	♊13	♊	♋17	♋	♌20	♌	♍22	♍	♍	♎1	♎	♏6	♏	♐14	♐	♐	♑1
Nov	♑	♒14	♒	♒	♓1	♓	♈10	♈	♉16	♉	♊20	♊	♋22	♋	♋	♌1	♌	♍4	♍	♎8	♎	♏14	♏	♐23	♐	♐	♑9	♑	♒22	♒	
Dec	♒	♓10	♓	♈19	♈	♈	♉2	♉	♊5	♊	♋6	♋	♌7	♌	♍10	♍	♎14	♎	♏21	♏	♏	♐6	♐	♑17	♑	♑	♒5	♒	♓18	♓	♓

1966	1	2	3	4	5	6	7	8	9	10	11	12	13	14	15	16	17	18	19	20	21	22	23	24	25	26	27	28	29	30	31
Jan	♈5	♈	♉12	♉	♊15	♊	♋16	♋	♌15	♌	♍16	♍	♎20	♎	♎	♏3	♏	♐12	♐	♐	♑0	♑	♒12	♒	♒	♓1	♓	♈12	♈	♉21	♉
Feb	♉	♊2	♊	♋3	♋	♌2	♌	♍2	♍	♎3	♎	♏9	♏	♐18	♐	♐	♑6	♑	♒18	♒	♒	♓7	♓	♈18	♈	♈	♉4	♉			
Mar	♊11	♊	♋14	♋	♌14	♌	♍13	♍	♎13	♎	♏17	♏	♏	♐1	♐	♑12	♑	♑	♒0	♒	♓13	♓	♓	♈0	♈	♉10	♉	♊17	♊	♋21	♋
Apr	♌23	♌	♌	♍0	♍	♎0	♎	♏3	♏	♐9	♐	♑19	♑	♑	♒7	♒	♓20	♓	♓	♈7	♈	♉16	♉	♊22	♊	♊	♋3	♋	♌6	♌	
May	♍8	♍	♎10	♎	♏13	♏	♐18	♐	♐	♑3	♑	♒15	♒	♒	♓3	♓	♈15	♈	♉23	♉	♉	♊5	♊	♋9	♋	♌12	♌	♍14	♍	♎17	♎
Jun	♏21	♏	♏	♐3	♐	♑12	♑	♒23	♒	♒	♓12	♓	♈23	♈	♈	♉8	♉	♊13	♊	♋16	♋	♌18	♌	♍20	♍	♎23	♎	♎	♏4	♏	
Jul	♐11	♐	♑20	♑	♑	♒7	♒	♓19	♓	♓	♈7	♈	♉17	♉	♊23	♊	♊	♋1	♋	♌2	♌	♍2	♍	♎5	♎	♏10	♏	♐17	♐	♐	♑3
Aug	♑	♒14	♒	♒	♓2	♓	♈15	♈	♈	♉2	♉	♊9	♊	♋11	♋	♌12	♌	♍11	♍	♎12	♎	♏15	♏	♐23	♐	♐	♑8	♑	♒20	♒	♒
Sep	♓8	♓	♈21	♈	♈	♉9	♉	♊17	♊	♋21	♋	♌22	♌	♍22	♍	♎21	♎	♏23	♏	♏	♐5	♐	♑14	♑	♑	♒2	♒	♓15	♓	♓	
Oct	♈3	♈	♉14	♉	♉	♊0	♊	♋5	♋	♌8	♌	♍9	♍	♎8	♎	♏9	♏	♐13	♐	♑21	♑	♑	♒9	♒	♓21	♓	♓	♈9	♈	♉20	♉
Nov	♉	♊5	♊	♋11	♋	♌15	♌	♍18	♍	♎19	♎	♏20	♏	♐23	♐	♐	♑6	♑	♒16	♒	♒	♓5	♓	♈17	♈	♈	♉4	♉	♊11	♊	
Dec	♋17	♋	♌21	♌	♌	♍0	♍	♎3	♎	♏5	♏	♐9	♐	♑16	♑	♑	♒1	♒	♓13	♓	♓	♈1	♈	♉12	♉	♊20	♊	♊	♋0	♋	♌3

1967	1	2	3	4	5	6	7	8	9	10	11	12	13	14	15	16	17	18	19	20	21	22	23	24	25	26	27	28	29	30	31
Jan	♌	♍5	♍	♎9	♎	♏12	♏	♐18	♐	♐	♑0	♑	♒9	♒	♓21	♓	♓	♈10	♈	♉21	♉	♉	♊6	♊	♋10	♋	♌11	♌	♍12	♍	♎14
Feb	♎	♏18	♏	♏	♐0	♐	♑7	♑	♒17	♒	♒	♓4	♓	♈17	♈	♈	♉6	♉	♊15	♊	♋20	♋	♌22	♌	♍22	♍	♎22	♎			
Mar	♎	♏0	♏	♐5	♐	♑13	♑	♒23	♒	♒	♓11	♓	♓	♈0	♈	♉13	♉	♊23	♊	♊	♋6	♋	♌9	♌	♍9	♍	♎8	♎	♏9	♏	♐12
Apr	♐	♑19	♑	♑	♒5	♒	♓17	♓	♓	♈6	♈	♉19	♉	♉	♊6	♊	♋14	♋	♌18	♌	♍20	♍	♎19	♎	♏19	♏	♐21	♐	♐	♑2	
May	♑	♒11	♒	♓23	♓	♓	♈12	♈	♈	♉1	♉	♊11	♊	♋19	♋	♋	♌1	♌	♍4	♍	♎5	♎	♏6	♏	♐7	♐	♑11	♑	♒19	♒	♒
Jun	♓6	♓	♈19	♈	♈	♉7	♉	♊17	♊	♊	♋1	♋	♌6	♌	♍10	♍	♎13	♎	♏15	♏	♐17	♐	♑21	♑	♑	♒4	♒	♓14	♓	♓	
Jul	♈3	♈	♉15	♉	♉	♊1	♊	♋8	♋	♌12	♌	♍16	♍	♎19	♎	♏22	♏	♏	♐1	♐	♑6	♑	♒12	♒	♓22	♓	♓	♈11	♈	♉23	♉
Aug	♉	♊10	♊	♋16	♋	♌20	♌	♍22	♍	♍	♎0	♎	♏3	♏	♐7	♐	♑13	♑	♒20	♒	♒	♓6	♓	♈18	♈	♈	♉7	♉	♊19	♊	♊
Sep	♋2	♋	♌6	♌	♍7	♍	♎7	♎	♏9	♏	♐12	♐	♑18	♑	♑	♒3	♒	♓13	♓	♓	♈1	♈	♉15	♉	♉	♊3	♊	♋11	♋	♌16	
Oct	♌	♍18	♍	♎17	♎	♏17	♏	♐19	♐	♐	♑0	♑	♒8	♒	♓19	♓	♓	♈8	♈	♉21	♉	♉	♊9	♊	♋19	♋	♋	♌1	♌	♍4	♍
Nov	♎5	♎	♏4	♏	♐4	♐	♑7	♑	♒14	♒	♒	♓1	♓	♈14	♈	♈	♉3	♉	♊15	♊	♊	♋1	♋	♌8	♌	♍13	♍	♎15	♎	♏15	
Dec	♏	♐15	♐	♑17	♑	♒22	♒	♒	♓8	♓	♈21	♈	♈	♉10	♉	♊21	♊	♊	♋6	♋	♌14	♌	♍20	♍	♎23	♎	♎	♏1	♏	♐2	♐

1968	1	2	3	4	5	6	7	8	9	10	11	12	13	14	15	16	17	18	19	20	21	22	23	24	25	26	27	28	29	30	31
Jan	♑4	♑	♒8	♒	♓16	♓	♓	♈4	♈	♉17	♉	♉	♊5	♊	♋14	♋	♌20	♌	♌	♍1	♍	♎5	♎	♏8	♏	♐10	♐	♑13	♑	♒18	♒
Feb	♒	♓1	♓	♈13	♈	♈	♉1	♉	♊13	♊	♋22	♋	♋	♌4	♌	♍8	♍	♎10	♎	♏13	♏	♐16	♐	♑21	♑	♑	♒2	♒	♓10		
Mar	♓	♈21	♈	♈	♉10	♉	♊22	♊	♊	♋8	♋	♌14	♌	♍17	♍	♎18	♎	♏19	♏	♐22	♐	♐	♑2	♑	♒9	♒	♓17	♓	♓	♈4	♈
Apr	♉17	♉	♉	♊6	♊	♋16	♋	♋	♌0	♌	♍4	♍	♎4	♎	♏4	♏	♐5	♐	♑8	♑	♒14	♒	♓23	♓	♓	♈11	♈	♉23	♉	♉	
May	♊12	♊	♊	♋0	♋	♌9	♌	♍14	♍	♎15	♎	♏15	♏	♐14	♐	♑16	♑	♒20	♒	♒	♓5	♓	♈17	♈	♈	♉5	♉	♊18	♊	♊	♋6
Jun	♋	♌15	♌	♍22	♍	♍	♎1	♎	♏2	♏	♐1	♐	♑1	♑	♒5	♒	♓12	♓	♈23	♈	♈	♉12	♉	♉	♊0	♊	♋11	♋	♌21	♌	
Jul	♌	♍4	♍	♎8	♎	♏11	♏	♐11	♐	♑12	♑	♒14	♒	♓20	♓	♓	♈6	♈	♉18	♉	♉	♊7	♊	♋18	♋	♋	♌3	♌	♍9	♍	♎14
Aug	♎	♏17	♏	♐20	♐	♑21	♑	♑	♒0	♒	♓5	♓	♈14	♈	♈	♉2	♉	♊15	♊	♊	♋2	♋	♌10	♌	♍16	♍	♎20	♎	♏23	♏	♏
Sep	♐2	♐	♑5	♑	♒8	♒	♓14	♓	♈23	♈	♈	♉10	♉	♊23	♊	♊	♋10	♋	♌19	♌	♌	♍0	♍	♎3	♎	♏5	♏	♐7	♐	♑10	
Oct	♑	♒15	♒	♓22	♓	♓	♈7	♈	♉18	♉	♉	♊7	♊	♋19	♋	♋	♌4	♌	♍10	♍	♎13	♎	♏13	♏	♐14	♐	♑16	♑	♒20	♒	♒
Nov	♓4	♓	♈14	♈	♈	♉1	♉	♊14	♊	♊	♋2	♋	♌13	♌	♍20	♍	♍	♎0	♎	♏0	♐23	♐	♐	♑0	♑	♒3	♒	♓9	♓	♈19	
Dec	♈	♈	♉8	♉	♊20	♊	♊	♋8	♋	♌20	♌	♌	♍5	♍	♎10	♎	♏11	♏	♐11	♐	♑10	♑	♒11	♒	♓16	♓	♓	♈1	♈	♉14	♉

1969	1	2	3	4	5	6	7	8	9	10	11	12	13	14	15	16	17	18	19	20	21	22	23	24	25	26	27	28	29	30	31
Jan	♉	♊2	♊	♋14	♋	♋	♌1	♌	♍11	♍	♎18	♎	♏21	♏	♐22	♐	♑21	♑	♒22	♒	♒	♓1	♓	♈9	♈	♉20	♉	♉	♊9	♊	♋21
Feb	♋	♋	♌8	♌	♍16	♍	♎23	♎	♎	♏4	♏	♐6	♐	♑7	♑	♒9	♒	♓12	♓	♈18	♈	♈	♉4	♉	♊16	♊	♊	♋5			
Mar	♋	♌15	♌	♍23	♍	♍	♎5	♎	♏9	♏	♐12	♐	♑15	♑	♒17	♒	♓21	♓	♓	♈4	♈	♉13	♉	♉	♊1	♊	♋13	♋	♋	♌0	♌
Apr	♍8	♍	♎13	♎	♏15	♏	♐18	♐	♑20	♑	♑	♒0	♒	♓5	♓	♈12	♈	♉21	♉	♉	♊9	♊	♋21	♋	♋	♌9	♌	♍17	♍	♎22	
May	♎	♎	♏0	♏	♐1	♐	♑2	♑	♒5	♒	♓11	♓	♈18	♈	♈	♉4	♉	♊16	♊	♊	♋4	♋	♌17	♌	♌	♍2	♍	♎8	♎	♏10	♏
Jun	♐10	♐	♑10	♑	♒12	♒	♓16	♓	♓	♈0	♈	♉10	♉	♊22	♊	♊	♋11	♋	♌23	♌	♌	♍10	♍	♎17	♎	♏21	♏	♐21	♐	♑20	
Jul	♑	♒20	♒	♓23	♓	♓	♈6	♈	♉16	♉	♉	♊4	♊	♋17	♋	♋	♌5	♌	♍16	♍	♍	♎1	♎	♏5	♏	♐7	♐	♑7	♑	♒6	♒
Aug	♓8	♓	♈13	♈	♉22	♉	♉	♊10	♊	♋23	♋	♋	♌11	♌	♍22	♍	♍	♎6	♎	♏12	♏	♐15	♐	♑17	♑	♒17	♒	♓18	♓	♈22	♈
Sep	♈	♉6	♉	♊17	♊	♊	♋6	♋	♌18	♌	♌	♍4	♍	♎12	♎	♏18	♏	♐22	♐	♐	♑0	♑	♒2	♒	♓4	♓	♈8	♈	♉15	♉	
Oct	♉	♊1	♊	♋14	♋	♋	♌2	♌	♍12	♍	♎19	♎	♎	♏0	♏	♐3	♐	♑6	♑	♒9	♒	♓12	♓	♈17	♈	♈	♉0	♉	♊10	♊	♋22
Nov	♋	♋	♌10	♌	♍21	♍	♍	♎4	♎	♏8	♏	♐10	♐	♑11	♑	♒14	♒	♓18	♓	♓	♈0	♈	♉8	♉	♊18	♊	♊	♋5	♋	♌18	
Dec	♌	♌	♍6	♍	♎14	♎	♏18	♏	♐19	♐	♑19	♑	♒20	♒	♒	♓0	♓	♈6	♈	♉14	♉	♉	♊1	♊	♋12	♋	♋	♌1	♌	♍14	♍

1970	1	2	3	4	5	6	7	8	9	10	11	12	13	14	15	16	17	18	19	20	21	22	23	24	25	26	27	28	29	30	31
Jan	♍	♎0	♎	♏5	♏	♐6	♐	♑6	♑	♒6	♒	♓7	♓	♈12	♈	♉20	♉	♉	♊7	♊	♋19	♋	♋	♌8	♌	♍20	♍	♍	♎7	♎	♏14
Feb	♏	♐17	♐	♑17	♑	♒17	♒	♓17	♓	♈20	♈	♈	♉2	♉	♊13	♊	♊	♋1	♋	♌14	♌	♌	♍2	♍	♎12	♎	♏20	♏			
Mar	♏	♐1	♐	♑3	♑	♒4	♒	♓4	♓	♈6	♈	♉11	♉	♊20	♊	♊	♋8	♋	♌21	♌	♌	♍9	♍	♎18	♎	♎	♏2	♏	♐7	♐	♑11
Apr	♑	♒13	♒	♓14	♓	♈16	♈	♉21	♉	♉	♊4	♊	♋15	♋	♋	♌4	♌	♍16	♍	♍	♎2	♎	♏8	♏	♐13	♐	♑16	♑	♒19	♒	
May	♓22	♓	♓	♈1	♈	♉6	♉	♊13	♊	♊	♋0	♋	♌12	♌	♌	♍1	♍	♎10	♎	♏16	♏	♐20	♐	♑22	♑	♑	♒0	♒	♓4	♓	♈8
Jun	♈	♉14	♉	♊21	♊	♊	♋8	♋	♌20	♌	♌	♍9	♍	♎19	♎	♎	♏2	♏	♐5	♐	♑6	♑	♒7	♒	♓9	♓	♈13	♈	♉20	♉	
Jul	♉	♊4	♊	♋15	♋	♋	♌3	♌	♍16	♍	♍	♎4	♎	♏11	♏	♐15	♐	♑16	♑	♒16	♒	♓16	♓	♈19	♈	♈	♉1	♉	♊10	♊	♋21
Aug	♋	♋	♌10	♌	♍23	♍	♍	♎11	♎	♏20	♏	♏	♐1	♐	♑2	♑	♒2	♒	♓2	♓	♈3	♈	♉8	♉	♊16	♊	♊	♋3	♋	♌16	♌
Sep	♌	♍5	♍	♎17	♎	♎	♏2	♏	♐9	♐	♑12	♑	♒13	♒	♓13	♓	♈13	♈	♉16	♉	♊23	♊	♊	♋9	♋	♌22	♌	♌	♍11	♍	
Oct	♎22	♎	♎	♏8	♏	♐15	♐	♑20	♑	♒22	♒	♓23	♓	♓	♈0	♈	♉2	♉	♊7	♊	♋17	♋	♋	♌5	♌	♍18	♍	♍	♎5	♎	♏14
Nov	♏	♐20	♐	♐	♑1	♑	♒5	♒	♓7	♓	♈9	♈	♉12	♉	♊17	♊	♊	♋1	♋	♌13	♌	♌	♍2	♍	♎13	♎	♏22	♏	♏	♐3	
Dec	♐	♑7	♑	♒10	♒	♓13	♓	♈17	♈	♉21	♉	♉	♊2	♊	♋10	♋	♌21	♌	♌	♍10	♍	♎22	♎	♎	♏7	♏	♐12	♐	♑15	♑	♒17

1971	1	2	3	4	5	6	7	8	9	10	11	12	13	14	15	16	17	18	19	20	21	22	23	24	25	26	27	28	29	30	31
Jan	♒	♓19	♓	♈22	♈	♈	♉3	♉	♊9	♊	♋18	♋	♋	♌5	♌	♍18	♍	♍	♎7	♎	♏17	♏	♐23	♐	♐	♑1	♑	♒2	♒	♓2	♓
Feb	♈4	♈	♉8	♉	♊15	♊	♊	♋1	♋	♌12	♌	♌	♍1	♍	♎14	♎	♎	♏1	♏	♐9	♐	♑12	♑	♒13	♒	♓13	♓	♈13			
Mar	♈	♉15	♉	♊21	♊	♊	♋6	♋	♌19	♌	♌	♍7	♍	♎20	♎	♎	♏7	♏	♐16	♐	♑22	♑	♑	♒0	♒	♓0	♈23	♈	♈	♉0	♉
Apr	♊4	♊	♋13	♋	♋	♌1	♌	♍14	♍	♍	♎2	♎	♏13	♏	♐22	♐	♐	♑5	♑	♒9	♒	♓10	♓	♈10	♈	♉11	♉	♊14	♊	♋21	
May	♋	♋	♌7	♌	♍20	♍	♍	♎9	♎	♏19	♏	♏	♐4	♐	♑10	♑	♒15	♒	♓18	♓	♈19	♈	♉21	♉	♊23	♊	♊	♋6	♋	♌15	♌
Jun	♌	♍4	♍	♎16	♎	♎	♏3	♏	♐11	♐	♑16	♑	♒20	♒	♓23	♓	♓	♈2	♈	♉5	♉	♊8	♊	♋14	♋	♋	♌0	♌	♍12	♍	
Jul	♍	♎0	♎	♏11	♏	♐19	♐	♐	♑0	♑	♒3	♒	♓5	♓	♈8	♈	♉11	♉	♊16	♊	♋22	♋	♋	♌8	♌	♍20	♍	♍	♎8	♎	♏20
Aug	♏	♏	♐4	♐	♑9	♑	♒11	♒	♓12	♓	♈14	♈	♉16	♉	♊21	♊	♊	♋5	♋	♌15	♌	♌	♍3	♍	♎15	♎	♎	♏4	♏	♐13	♐
Sep	♑19	♑	♒22	♒	♓22	♓	♈22	♈	♉23	♉	♉	♊3	♊	♋11	♋	♌21	♌	♌	♍9	♍	♎22	♎	♎	♏10	♏	♐21	♐	♐	♑5	♑	
Oct	♒8	♒	♓9	♓	♈8	♈	♉8	♉	♊10	♊	♋16	♋	♋	♌3	♌	♍15	♍	♍	♎4	♎	♏16	♏	♏	♐3	♐	♑12	♑	♒17	♒	♓19	♓
Nov	♈19	♈	♉19	♉	♊20	♊	♊	♋0	♋	♌9	♌	♍21	♍	♍	♎10	♎	♏22	♏	♏	♐8	♐	♑17	♑	♑	♒0	♒	♓4	♓	♈5	♈	
Dec	♉5	♉	♊6	♊	♋10	♋	♌18	♌	♌	♍5	♍	♎17	♎	♎	♏5	♏	♐15	♐	♑23	♑	♑	♒5	♒	♓9	♓	♈12	♈	♉14	♉	♊16	♊

1972	1	2	3	4	5	6	7	8	9	10	11	12	13	14	15	16	17	18	19	20	21	22	23	24	25	26	27	28	29	30	31
Jan	♋20	♋	♋	♌3	♌	♍13	♍	♍	♎1	♎	♏13	♏	♏	♐0	♐	♑7	♑	♒12	♒	♓15	♓	♈18	♈	♉21	♉	♉	♊0	♊	♋5	♋	♌12
Feb	♌	♍22	♍	♍	♎10	♎	♏22	♏	♏	♐9	♐	♑16	♑	♒21	♒	♓22	♓	♓	♈0	♈	♉2	♉	♊6	♊	♋12	♋	♌20	♌	♌		
Mar	♍6	♍	♎17	♎	♎	♏6	♏	♐18	♐	♐	♑2	♑	♒7	♒	♓8	♓	♈8	♈	♉9	♉	♊12	♊	♋17	♋	♋	♌2	♌	♍12	♍	♍	♎0
Apr	♎	♏13	♏	♏	♐1	♐	♑11	♑	♒17	♒	♓19	♓	♈19	♈	♉18	♉	♊19	♊	♋23	♋	♋	♌7	♌	♍18	♍	♍	♎6	♎	♏19	♏	
May	♏	♐7	♐	♑18	♑	♑	♒1	♒	♓5	♓	♈6	♈	♉5	♉	♊5	♊	♋8	♋	♌14	♌	♌	♍0	♍	♎12	♎	♎	♏1	♏	♐13	♐	♑23
Jun	♑	♑	♒8	♒	♓13	♓	♈15	♈	♉16	♉	♊16	♊	♋17	♋	♌23	♌	♌	♍7	♍	♎19	♎	♎	♏8	♏	♐19	♐	♐	♑5	♑	♒13	
Jul	♒	♓18	♓	♈22	♈	♈	♉0	♉	♊1	♊	♋3	♋	♌8	♌	♍16	♍	♍	♎3	♎	♏15	♏	♏	♐3	♐	♑13	♑	♒19	♒	♒	♓0	♓
Aug	♈3	♈	♉6	♉	♊9	♊	♋12	♋	♌17	♌	♌	♍1	♍	♎11	♎	♏23	♏	♏	♐11	♐	♑21	♑	♑	♒4	♒	♓7	♓	♈9	♈	♉11	♉
Sep	♊15	♊	♋19	♋	♋	♌1	♌	♍9	♍	♎19	♎	♎	♏7	♏	♐20	♐	♐	♑6	♑	♒13	♒	♓17	♓	♈17	♈	♉18	♉	♊20	♊	♊	
Oct	♋0	♋	♌7	♌	♍16	♍	♍	♎2	♎	♏14	♏	♏	♐3	♐	♑15	♑	♒23	♒	♒	♓3	♓	♈4	♈	♉3	♉	♊4	♊	♋6	♋	♌12	♌
Nov	♍21	♍	♍	♎8	♎	♏20	♏	♏	♐9	♐	♑22	♑	♑	♒7	♒	♓13	♓	♈15	♈	♉15	♉	♊14	♊	♋15	♋	♌19	♌	♌	♍3	♍	
Dec	♎14	♎	♎	♏3	♏	♐15	♐	♐	♑3	♑	♒14	♒	♓21	♓	♓	♈1	♈	♉2	♉	♊1	♊	♋1	♋	♌4	♌	♍10	♍	♎21	♎	♎	♏9

1973	1	2	3	4	5	6	7	8	9	10	11	12	13	14	15	16	17	18	19	20	21	22	23	24	25	26	27	28	29	30	31
Jan	♏	♐22	♐	♐	♑10	♑	♒19	♒	♒	♓3	♓	♈8	♈	♉11	♉	♊12	♊	♋12	♋	♌15	♌	♍20	♍	♍	♎5	♎	♏16	♏	♏	♐5	♐
Feb	♑17	♑	♑	♒2	♒	♓8	♓	♈13	♈	♉17	♉	♊19	♊	♋22	♋	♋	♌1	♌	♍6	♍	♎13	♎	♎	♏0	♏	♐13	♐	♐			
Mar	♑1	♑	♒10	♒	♓16	♓	♈19	♈	♉22	♉	♉	♊1	♊	♋4	♋	♌9	♌	♍14	♍	♎22	♎	♎	♏9	♏	♐21	♐	♐	♑10	♑	♒19	♒
Apr	♒	♓1	♓	♈4	♈	♉5	♉	♊7	♊	♋10	♋	♌15	♌	♍21	♍	♍	♎6	♎	♏16	♏	♏	♐5	♐	♑18	♑	♑	♒4	♒	♓11	♓	
May	♈14	♈	♉14	♉	♊15	♊	♋16	♋	♌20	♌	♌	♍3	♍	♎12	♎	♏23	♏	♏	♐12	♐	♐	♑1	♑	♒12	♒	♓20	♓	♓	♈0	♈	♉1
Jun	♉	♊1	♊	♋1	♋	♌3	♌	♍9	♍	♎18	♎	♎	♏5	♏	♐18	♐	♐	♑7	♑	♒18	♒	♒	♓3	♓	♈9	♈	♉11	♉	♊11	♊	
Jul	♋11	♋	♌12	♌	♍16	♍	♍	♎0	♎	♏11	♏	♏	♐0	♐	♑13	♑	♑	♒0	♒	♓9	♓	♈16	♈	♉20	♉	♊21	♊	♋21	♋	♌22	♌
Aug	♌	♍1	♍	♎8	♎	♏18	♏	♏	♐7	♐	♑19	♑	♑	♒6	♒	♓15	♓	♈21	♈	♈	♉2	♉	♊5	♊	♋7	♋	♌8	♌	♍11	♍	♎17
Sep	♎	♎	♏2	♏	♐14	♐	♐	♑3	♑	♒14	♒	♓22	♓	♓	♈3	♈	♉7	♉	♊10	♊	♋13	♋	♌16	♌	♍20	♍	♍	♎2	♎	♏11	
Oct	♏	♐22	♐	♐	♑11	♑	♒23	♒	♒	♓6	♓	♈11	♈	♉14	♉	♊16	♊	♋19	♋	♌22	♌	♌	♍3	♍	♎10	♎	♏19	♏	♏	♐6	♐
Nov	♑19	♑	♑	♒7	♒	♓16	♓	♈21	♈	♉23	♉	♉	♊0	♊	♋1	♋	♌4	♌	♍9	♍	♎16	♎	♎	♏2	♏	♐14	♐	♐	♑3	♑	
Dec	♒15	♒	♒	♓1	♓	♈7	♈	♉10	♉	♊10	♊	♋10	♋	♌11	♌	♍15	♍	♎22	♎	♎	♏8	♏	♐20	♐	♐	♑9	♑	♒22	♒	♒	♓9

1974	1	2	3	4	5	6	7	8	9	10	11	12	13	14	15	16	17	18	19	20	21	22	23	24	25	26	27	28	29	30	31
Jan	♓	♈17	♈	♉21	♉	♊22	♊	♋21	♋	♌21	♌	♍23	♍	♍	♎4	♎	♏14	♏	♏	♐2	♐	♑15	♑	♑	♒4	♒	♓15	♓	♈23	♈	♈
Feb	♉5	♉	♊8	♊	♋8	♋	♌8	♌	♍9	♍	♎13	♎	♏21	♏	♏	♐8	♐	♑22	♑	♑	♒10	♒	♓20	♓	♓	♈5	♈	♉11			
Mar	♉	♊16	♊	♋18	♋	♌18	♌	♍19	♍	♎23	♎	♎	♏5	♏	♐16	♐	♐	♑5	♑	♒17	♒	♒	♓3	♓	♈11	♈	♉17	♉	♊21	♊	♊
Apr	♋0	♋	♌3	♌	♍5	♍	♎8	♎	♏15	♏	♏	♐1	♐	♑13	♑	♑	♒1	♒	♓12	♓	♈19	♈	♈	♉0	♉	♊3	♊	♋5	♋	♌8	
May	♌	♍12	♍	♎16	♎	♏23	♏	♏	♐9	♐	♑21	♑	♑	♒10	♒	♓20	♓	♓	♈4	♈	♉8	♉	♊11	♊	♋12	♋	♌14	♌	♍17	♍	♎23
Jun	♎	♎	♏6	♏	♐16	♐	♐	♑4	♑	♒17	♒	♒	♓5	♓	♈13	♈	♉18	♉	♊20	♊	♋21	♋	♌21	♌	♍23	♍	♍	♎4	♎	♏12	
Jul	♏	♐23	♐	♐	♑11	♑	♑	♒0	♒	♓12	♓	♈22	♈	♈	♉4	♉	♊7	♊	♋7	♋	♌6	♌	♍7	♍	♎11	♎	♏18	♏	♏	♐5	♐
Aug	♑17	♑	♑	♒6	♒	♓18	♓	♓	♈4	♈	♉12	♉	♊16	♊	♋17	♋	♌17	♌	♍17	♍	♎19	♎	♎	♏1	♏	♐11	♐	♑23	♑	♑	♒12
Sep	♒	♒	♓0	♓	♈10	♈	♉18	♉	♉	♊0	♊	♋3	♋	♌3	♌	♍3	♍	♎5	♎	♏9	♏	♐18	♐	♐	♑6	♑	♒19	♒	♒	♓6	
Oct	♓	♈16	♈	♈	♉0	♉	♊5	♊	♋9	♋	♌12	♌	♍13	♍	♎15	♎	♏19	♏	♏	♐3	♐	♑14	♑	♑	♒2	♒	♓14	♓	♈23	♈	♈
Nov	♉6	♉	♊11	♊	♋15	♋	♌18	♌	♍21	♍	♍	♎0	♎	♏4	♏	♐12	♐	♑22	♑	♑	♒11	♒	♓23	♓	♓	♈9	♈	♉15	♉	♊19	
Dec	♊	♋21	♋	♌23	♌	♌	♍2	♍	♎6	♎	♏12	♏	♐20	♐	♐	♑7	♑	♒19	♒	♒	♓7	♓	♈18	♈	♈	♉1	♉	♊5	♊	♋6	♋

1975	1	2	3	4	5	6	7	8	9	10	11	12	13	14	15	16	17	18	19	20	21	22	23	24	25	26	27	28	29	30	31
Jan	♌6	♌	♍8	♍	♎12	♎	♏18	♏	♏	♐3	♐	♑14	♑	♑	♒2	♒	♓14	♓	♓	♈2	♈	♉11	♉	♊16	♊	♋17	♋	♌16	♌	♍16	♍
Feb	♎18	♎	♎	♏0	♏	♐9	♐	♑20	♑	♑	♒8	♒	♓21	♓	♓	♈9	♈	♉19	♉	♉	♊2	♊	♋4	♋	♌4	♌	♍3	♍			
Mar	♎3	♎	♏7	♏	♐15	♐	♐	♑2	♑	♒14	♒	♒	♓3	♓	♈15	♈	♈	♉1	♉	♊9	♊	♋13	♋	♌14	♌	♍14	♍	♎14	♎	♏16	♏
Apr	♐22	♐	♐	♑8	♑	♒21	♒	♒	♓9	♓	♈21	♈	♈	♉7	♉	♊14	♊	♋19	♋	♌22	♌	♌	♍0	♍	♎0	♎	♏3	♏	♐8	♐	
May	♑16	♑	♑	♒4	♒	♓16	♓	♓	♈4	♈	♉13	♉	♊20	♊	♊	♋1	♋	♌4	♌	♍7	♍	♎9	♎	♏12	♏	♐17	♐	♐	♑1	♑	♒12
Jun	♒	♒	♓0	♓	♈12	♈	♉21	♉	♉	♊4	♊	♋7	♋	♌10	♌	♍12	♍	♎15	♎	♏20	♏	♏	♐1	♐	♑10	♑	♒20	♒	♒	♓8	
Jul	♓	♈20	♈	♈	♉6	♉	♊13	♊	♋16	♋	♌17	♌	♍18	♍	♎21	♎	♎	♏1	♏	♐8	♐	♑17	♑	♑	♒4	♒	♓16	♓	♓	♈4	♈
Aug	♉15	♉	♊22	♊	♊	♋2	♋	♌2	♌	♍2	♍	♎3	♎	♏7	♏	♐14	♐	♑23	♑	♑	♒10	♒	♓22	♓	♓	♈11	♈	♉23	♉	♉	♊7
Sep	♊	♋12	♋	♌13	♌	♍12	♍	♎12	♎	♏14	♏	♐19	♐	♐	♑5	♑	♒16	♒	♒	♓4	♓	♈17	♈	♈	♉5	♉	♊15	♊	♋21	♋	
Oct	♌23	♌	♍23	♍	♎22	♎	♏23	♏	♏	♐3	♐	♑11	♑	♒22	♒	♒	♓11	♓	♈23	♈	♈	♉11	♉	♊20	♊	♊	♋3	♋	♌7	♌	♍9
Nov	♍	♎9	♎	♏10	♏	♐13	♐	♑19	♑	♑	♒5	♒	♓18	♓	♓	♈6	♈	♉17	♉	♉	♊2	♊	♋9	♋	♌13	♌	♍17	♍	♎19	♎	
Dec	♏20	♏	♐23	♐	♐	♑5	♑	♒14	♒	♒	♓1	♓	♈14	♈	♈	♉1	♉	♊10	♊	♋15	♋	♌19	♌	♍22	♍	♍	♎1	♎	♏4	♏	♐8

1976	1	2	3	4	5	6	7	8	9	10	11	12	13	14	15	16	17	18	19	20	21	22	23	24	25	26	27	28	29	30	31
Jan	♐	♑14	♑	♒23	♒	♒	♓10	♓	♈22	♈	♈	♉10	♉	♊19	♊	♊	♋0	♋	♌2	♌	♍4	♍	♎6	♎	♏10	♏	♐15	♐	♑22	♑	♑
Feb	♒7	♒	♓18	♓	♓	♈7	♈	♉19	♉	♉	♊5	♊	♋10	♋	♌12	♌	♍12	♍	♎13	♎	♏16	♏	♐21	♐	♐	♑4	♑	♒14	♒		
Mar	♒	♓1	♓	♈14	♈	♈	♉3	♉	♊13	♊	♋20	♋	♌23	♌	♍23	♍	♎22	♎	♏23	♏	♏	♐3	♐	♑10	♑	♒19	♒	♒	♓7	♓	♈20
Apr	♈	♈	♉9	♉	♊20	♊	♊	♋5	♋	♌9	♌	♍10	♍	♎10	♎	♏9	♏	♐11	♐	♑16	♑	♑	♒1	♒	♓13	♓	♓	♈2	♈	♉15	
May	♉	♉	♊2	♊	♋11	♋	♌17	♌	♍20	♍	♎20	♎	♏20	♏	♐21	♐	♐	♑1	♑	♒8	♒	♓19	♓	♓	♈8	♈	♉21	♉	♉	♊8	♊
Jun	♋16	♋	♌22	♌	♌	♍3	♍	♎5	♎	♏6	♏	♐7	♐	♑11	♑	♒17	♒	♒	♓3	♓	♈16	♈	♈	♉4	♉	♊15	♊	♋23	♋	♋	
Jul	♌4	♌	♍8	♍	♎11	♎	♏14	♏	♐16	♐	♑20	♑	♑	♒2	♒	♓11	♓	♓	♈0	♈	♉12	♉	♊23	♊	♊	♋6	♋	♌11	♌	♍14	♍
Aug	♎16	♎	♏19	♏	♐23	♐	♐	♑4	♑	♒10	♒	♓20	♓	♓	♈7	♈	♉20	♉	♉	♊8	♊	♋15	♋	♌20	♌	♍22	♍	♎23	♎	♎	♏1
Sep	♏	♐5	♐	♑10	♑	♒17	♒	♒	♓3	♓	♈15	♈	♈	♉4	♉	♊16	♊	♊	♋1	♋	♌6	♌	♍8	♍	♎8	♎	♏8	♏	♐10	♐	
Oct	♑15	♑	♒23	♒	♒	♓10	♓	♈22	♈	♈	♉11	♉	♊23	♊	♊	♋9	♋	♌16	♌	♍18	♍	♎19	♎	♏18	♏	♐19	♐	♑22	♑	♑	♒5
Nov	♒	♓15	♓	♓	♈4	♈	♉17	♉	♉	♊5	♊	♋16	♋	♋	♌0	♌	♍4	♍	♎6	♎	♏5	♏	♐5	♐	♑7	♑	♒12	♒	♓22	♓	
Dec	♓	♈10	♈	♉23	♉	♉	♊11	♊	♋21	♋	♋	♌6	♌	♍12	♍	♎15	♎	♏16	♏	♐16	♐	♑17	♑	♒21	♒	♒	♓5	♓	♈17	♈	♈

1977	1	2	3	4	5	6	7	8	9	10	11	12	13	14	15	16	17	18	19	20	21	22	23	24	25	26	27	28	29	30	31
Jan	♉6	♉	♊18	♊	♊	♋4	♋	♌11	♌	♍17	♍	♎21	♎	♎	♏0	♏	♐2	♐	♑4	♑	♒7	♒	♓14	♓	♓	♈1	♈	♉14	♉	♉	♊2
Feb	♊	♋12	♋	♌18	♌	♍23	♍	♍	♎2	♎	♏6	♏	♐9	♐	♑12	♑	♒17	♒	♒	♓0	♓	♈10	♈	♉22	♉	♉	♊11	♊			
Mar	♋21	♋	♋	♌3	♌	♍7	♍	♎9	♎	♏11	♏	♐14	♐	♑18	♑	♑	♒0	♒	♓8	♓	♈18	♈	♈	♉6	♉	♊19	♊	♊	♋6	♋	♌13
Apr	♌	♍17	♍	♎19	♎	♏19	♏	♐20	♐	♐	♑0	♑	♒5	♒	♓14	♓	♓	♈1	♈	♉13	♉	♉	♊2	♊	♋14	♋	♌23	♌	♌	♍4	
May	♍	♎5	♎	♏5	♏	♐5	♐	♑7	♑	♒11	♒	♓19	♓	♓	♈7	♈	♉19	♉	♉	♊8	♊	♋20	♋	♋	♌6	♌	♍13	♍	♎16	♎	♏16
Jun	♏	♐15	♐	♑16	♑	♒19	♒	♒	♓2	♓	♈12	♈	♈	♉1	♉	♊14	♊	♊	♋2	♋	♌12	♌	♍19	♍	♍	♎0	♎	♏2	♏	♐2	
Jul	♐	♑2	♑	♒4	♒	♓9	♓	♈19	♈	♈	♉8	♉	♊20	♊	♊	♋8	♋	♌17	♌	♌	♍1	♍	♎6	♎	♏10	♏	♐11	♐	♑12	♑	♒14
Aug	♒	♓19	♓	♓	♈3	♈	♉15	♉	♉	♊4	♊	♋15	♋	♋	♌0	♌	♍7	♍	♎12	♎	♏15	♏	♐18	♐	♑20	♑	♒23	♒	♒	♓4	♓
Sep	♈12	♈	♉23	♉	♉	♊12	♊	♋23	♋	♋	♌8	♌	♍14	♍	♎18	♎	♏21	♏	♏	♐0	♐	♑3	♑	♒7	♒	♓12	♓	♈20	♈	♈	
Oct	♉7	♉	♊20	♊	♊	♋8	♋	♌17	♌	♌	♍0	♍	♎3	♎	♏4	♏	♐6	♐	♑8	♑	♒12	♒	♓19	♓	♓	♈4	♈	♉15	♉	♉	♊3
Nov	♊	♋16	♋	♋	♌3	♌	♍10	♍	♎14	♎	♏14	♏	♐14	♐	♑15	♑	♒18	♒	♒	♓1	♓	♈10	♈	♉22	♉	♉	♊10	♊	♋22	♋	
Dec	♋	♌10	♌	♍19	♍	♍	♎0	♎	♏1	♏	♐1	♐	♑0	♑	♒2	♒	♓7	♓	♈16	♈	♈	♉4	♉	♊16	♊	♊	♋4	♋	♌16	♌	♌

1978	1	2	3	4	5	6	7	8	9	10	11	12	13	14	15	16	17	18	19	20	21	22	23	24	25	26	27	28	29	30	31
Jan	♍2	♍	♎9	♎	♏12	♏	♐12	♐	♑11	♑	♒12	♒	♓15	♓	♈23	♈	♈	♉10	♉	♊22	♊	♊	♋11	♋	♌22	♌	♌	♍7	♍	♎15	♎
Feb	♏20	♏	♐22	♐	♑22	♑	♒23	♒	♒	♓1	♓	♈7	♈	♉17	♉	♉	♊5	♊	♋18	♋	♋	♌5	♌	♍14	♍	♎20	♎	♎			
Mar	♏1	♏	♐5	♐	♑7	♑	♒9	♒	♓11	♓	♈17	♈	♈	♉2	♉	♊13	♊	♊	♋2	♋	♌13	♌	♍21	♍	♍	♎3	♎	♏7	♏	♐10	♐
Apr	♑13	♑	♒16	♒	♓20	♓	♓	♈2	♈	♉11	♉	♊22	♊	♊	♋10	♋	♌22	♌	♌	♍7	♍	♎12	♎	♏15	♏	♐16	♐	♑18	♑	♒21	
May	♒	♒	♓2	♓	♈9	♈	♉18	♉	♉	♊5	♊	♋18	♋	♋	♌6	♌	♍16	♍	♎22	♎	♎	♏0	♏	♐1	♐	♑1	♑	♒3	♒	♓8	♓
Jun	♈15	♈	♈	♉1	♉	♊12	♊	♊	♋0	♋	♌13	♌	♌	♍0	♍	♎8	♎	♏11	♏	♐11	♐	♑11	♑	♒11	♒	♓14	♓	♈21	♈	♈	
Jul	♉6	♉	♊18	♊	♊	♋7	♋	♌19	♌	♌	♍7	♍	♎16	♎	♏20	♏	♐22	♐	♑21	♑	♒21	♒	♓22	♓	♓	♈3	♈	♉12	♉	♉	♊0
Aug	♊	♋13	♋	♋	♌1	♌	♍12	♍	♎22	♎	♎	♏4	♏	♐7	♐	♑8	♑	♒7	♒	♓8	♓	♈12	♈	♉20	♉	♉	♊7	♊	♋19	♋	♋
Sep	♌7	♌	♍18	♍	♍	♎3	♎	♏10	♏	♐14	♐	♑16	♑	♒17	♒	♓19	♓	♈22	♈	♈	♉4	♉	♊14	♊	♊	♋2	♋	♌15	♌	♌	
Oct	♍2	♍	♎10	♎	♏15	♏	♐19	♐	♑22	♑	♑	♒1	♒	♓4	♓	♈7	♈	♉14	♉	♊23	♊	♊	♋10	♋	♌23	♌	♌	♍10	♍	♎18	♎
Nov	♏23	♏	♏	♐1	♐	♑4	♑	♒7	♒	♓10	♓	♈16	♈	♉22	♉	♉	♊7	♊	♋19	♋	♋	♌7	♌	♍19	♍	♍	♎4	♎	♏8	♏	
Dec	♐10	♐	♑11	♑	♒12	♒	♓16	♓	♈22	♈	♈	♉5	♉	♊15	♊	♊	♋2	♋	♌15	♌	♌	♍3	♍	♎13	♎	♏19	♏	♐20	♐	♑20	♑

1979	1	2	3	4	5	6	7	8	9	10	11	12	13	14	15	16	17	18	19	20	21	22	23	24	25	26	27	28	29	30	31
Jan	♒20	♒	♓22	♓	♓	♈3	♈	♉11	♉	♊21	♊	♊	♋9	♋	♌21	♌	♌	♍10	♍	♎21	♎	♎	♏4	♏	♐7	♐	♑8	♑	♒7	♒	♓7
Feb	♓	♈10	♈	♉17	♉	♉	♊3	♊	♋15	♋	♋	♌4	♌	♍16	♍	♍	♎3	♎	♏12	♏	♐17	♐	♑18	♑	♒18	♒	♓18	♓			
Mar	♈20	♈	♈	♉1	♉	♊9	♊	♋21	♋	♋	♌10	♌	♍22	♍	♍	♎9	♎	♏17	♏	♐23	♐	♐	♑3	♑	♒4	♒	♓5	♓	♈6	♈	♉10
Apr	♉	♊18	♊	♊	♋4	♋	♌17	♌	♌	♍6	♍	♎16	♎	♏23	♏	♏	♐5	♐	♑9	♑	♒12	♒	♓14	♓	♈16	♈	♉20	♉	♉	♊3	
May	♊	♋13	♋	♋	♌1	♌	♍14	♍	♍	♎0	♎	♏7	♏	♐11	♐	♑14	♑	♒17	♒	♓20	♓	♓	♈0	♈	♉4	♉	♊11	♊	♋21	♋	♋
Jun	♌9	♌	♍22	♍	♍	♎8	♎	♏15	♏	♐19	♐	♑21	♑	♒23	♒	♒	♓1	♓	♈5	♈	♉11	♉	♊19	♊	♊	♋4	♋	♌17	♌	♌	
Jul	♍6	♍	♎17	♎	♎	♏1	♏	♐5	♐	♑6	♑	♒7	♒	♓8	♓	♈11	♈	♉17	♉	♉	♊1	♊	♋11	♋	♌23	♌	♌	♍13	♍	♍	♎1
Aug	♎	♏10	♏	♐15	♐	♑17	♑	♒17	♒	♓16	♓	♈18	♈	♉22	♉	♉	♊6	♊	♋17	♋	♋	♌6	♌	♍19	♍	♍	♎7	♎	♏17	♏	♏
Sep	♐0	♐	♑3	♑	♒3	♒	♓3	♓	♈3	♈	♉6	♉	♊13	♊	♋23	♋	♋	♌12	♌	♌	♍1	♍	♎13	♎	♏23	♏	♏	♐7	♐	♑11	
Oct	♑	♒13	♒	♓14	♓	♈14	♈	♉16	♉	♊21	♊	♊	♋6	♋	♌18	♌	♌	♍7	♍	♎19	♎	♎	♏5	♏	♐12	♐	♑18	♑	♒21	♒	♓23
Nov	♓	♓	♈0	♈	♉2	♉	♊6	♊	♋14	♋	♋	♌2	♌	♍15	♍	♍	♎3	♎	♏12	♏	♐18	♐	♑23	♑	♑	♒3	♒	♓6	♓	♈9	
Dec	♈	♉11	♉	♊16	♊	♋23	♋	♋	♌10	♌	♍23	♍	♍	♎11	♎	♏20	♏	♏	♐2	♐	♑6	♑	♒8	♒	♓11	♓	♈15	♈	♉19	♉	♉

1980	1	2	3	4	5	6	7	8	9	10	11	12	13	14	15	16	17	18	19	20	21	22	23	24	25	26	27	28	29	30	31
Jan	♊0	♊	♋8	♋	♌18	♌	♌	♍7	♍	♎20	♎	♎	♏6	♏	♐12	♐	♑15	♑	♒17	♒	♓18	♓	♈20	♈	♈	♉0	♉	♊7	♊	♋15	♋
Feb	♋	♌2	♌	♍15	♍	♍	♎3	♎	♏15	♏	♐22	♐	♐	♑2	♑	♒3	♒	♓3	♓	♈3	♈	♉6	♉	♊12	♊	♋21	♋	♋	♌9		
Mar	♌	♍21	♍	♍	♎10	♎	♏22	♏	♏	♐7	♐	♑12	♑	♒14	♒	♓14	♓	♈13	♈	♉14	♉	♊19	♊	♊	♋3	♋	♌14	♌	♌	♍3	♍
Apr	♎16	♎	♎	♏4	♏	♐13	♐	♑20	♑	♑	♒0	♒	♓1	♓	♈0	♈	♉1	♉	♊3	♊	♋10	♋	♌21	♌	♌	♍10	♍	♎22	♎	♎	
May	♏9	♏	♐19	♐	♐	♑2	♑	♒7	♒	♓10	♓	♈11	♈	♉11	♉	♊13	♊	♋19	♋	♋	♌4	♌	♍17	♍	♍	♎5	♎	♏16	♏	♏	♐1
Jun	♐	♑8	♑	♒13	♒	♓16	♓	♈18	♈	♉20	♉	♊23	♊	♊	♋4	♋	♌13	♌	♌	♍1	♍	♎13	♎	♎	♏0	♏	♐9	♐	♑14	♑	
Jul	♒18	♒	♓21	♓	♓	♈0	♈	♉3	♉	♊7	♊	♋13	♋	♌21	♌	♌	♍9	♍	♎21	♎	♎	♏9	♏	♐18	♐	♑23	♑	♑	♒2	♒	♓4
Aug	♓	♈6	♈	♉9	♉	♊13	♊	♋20	♋	♋	♌5	♌	♍16	♍	♍	♎5	♎	♏17	♏	♏	♐3	♐	♑9	♑	♒12	♒	♓12	♓	♈13	♈	♉14
Sep	♉	♊19	♊	♊	♋2	♋	♌11	♌	♍23	♍	♍	♎12	♎	♎	♏0	♏	♐11	♐	♑19	♑	♒22	♒	♓23	♓	♈22	♈	♉22	♉	♉	♊1	
Oct	♊	♋7	♋	♌17	♌	♌	♍5	♍	♎18	♎	♎	♏6	♏	♐18	♐	♐	♑3	♑	♒8	♒	♓10	♓	♈9	♈	♉9	♉	♊10	♊	♋14	♋	♌23
Nov	♌	♌	♍11	♍	♍	♎0	♎	♏12	♏	♐23	♐	♐	♑9	♑	♒16	♒	♓19	♓	♈20	♈	♉20	♉	♊20	♊	♋23	♋	♋	♌7	♌	♍18	
Dec	♍	♍	♎7	♎	♏19	♏	♏	♐5	♐	♑14	♑	♒21	♒	♒	♓2	♓	♈5	♈	♉6	♉	♊7	♊	♋10	♋	♌16	♌	♌	♍2	♍	♎14	♎

1981	1	2	3	4	5	6	7	8	9	10	11	12	13	14	15	16	17	18	19	20	21	22	23	24	25	26	27	28	29	30	31
Jan	♎	♏2	♏	♐13	♐	♑21	♑	♑	♒3	♒	♓7	♓	♈10	♈	♉13	♉	♊16	♊	♋19	♋	♋	♌2	♌	♍11	♍	♎22	♎	♎	♏11	♏	♐22
Feb	♐	♐	♑6	♑	♒11	♒	♓14	♓	♈16	♈	♉19	♉	♊22	♊	♊	♋3	♋	♌10	♌	♍19	♍	♍	♎7	♎	♏19	♏	♏	♐7			
Mar	♐	♑16	♑	♒21	♒	♓23	♓	♈23	♈	♈	♉1	♉	♊4	♊	♋9	♋	♌17	♌	♌	♍3	♍	♎14	♎	♎	♏2	♏	♐15	♐	♐	♑1	♑
Apr	♒7	♒	♓9	♓	♈9	♈	♉9	♉	♊10	♊	♋15	♋	♌22	♌	♌	♍9	♍	♎20	♎	♎	♏9	♏	♐21	♐	♐	♑8	♑	♒16	♒	♓20	
May	♓	♈20	♈	♉20	♉	♊19	♊	♋22	♋	♋	♌4	♌	♍14	♍	♍	♎2	♎	♏15	♏	♏	♐3	♐	♑14	♑	♒23	♒	♒	♓4	♓	♈6	♈
Jun	♉6	♉	♊6	♊	♋7	♋	♌12	♌	♍21	♍	♍	♎9	♎	♏21	♏	♏	♐9	♐	♑20	♑	♑	♒4	♒	♓11	♓	♈14	♈	♉16	♉	♊16	
Jul	♊	♋17	♋	♌21	♌	♌	♍5	♍	♎16	♎	♎	♏4	♏	♐16	♐	♐	♑3	♑	♒10	♒	♓16	♓	♈20	♈	♉23	♉	♉	♊1	♊	♋3	♋
Aug	♌7	♌	♍14	♍	♍	♎0	♎	♏12	♏	♏	♐0	♐	♑10	♑	♒18	♒	♓22	♓	♓	♈1	♈	♉4	♉	♊7	♊	♋11	♋	♌15	♌	♍22	♍
Sep	♍	♎8	♎	♏20	♏	♏	♐8	♐	♑19	♑	♑	♒3	♒	♓7	♓	♈9	♈	♉10	♉	♊12	♊	♋16	♋	♌22	♌	♌	♍6	♍	♎16	♎	
Oct	♎	♏3	♏	♐16	♐	♐	♑4	♑	♒13	♒	♓17	♓	♈18	♈	♉18	♉	♊19	♊	♋22	♋	♋	♌4	♌	♍12	♍	♎23	♎	♎	♏10	♏	♐23
Nov	♐	♐	♑12	♑	♒22	♒	♒	♓3	♓	♈5	♈	♉5	♉	♊4	♊	♋5	♋	♌10	♌	♍18	♍	♍	♎4	♎	♏17	♏	♏	♐5	♐	♑18	
Dec	♑	♑	♒5	♒	♓12	♓	♈16	♈	♉16	♉	♊15	♊	♋15	♋	♌18	♌	♌	♍0	♍	♎10	♎	♏23	♏	♏	♐11	♐	♐	♑0	♑	♒10	♒

1982	1	2	3	4	5	6	7	8	9	10	11	12	13	14	15	16	17	18	19	20	21	22	23	24	25	26	27	28	29	30	31
Jan	♓19	♓	♓	♈0	♈	♉2	♉	♊2	♊	♋2	♋	♌4	♌	♍9	♍	♎18	♎	♎	♏5	♏	♐18	♐	♐	♑6	♑	♒16	♒	♒	♓0	♓	♈5
Feb	♈	♉9	♉	♊11	♊	♋13	♋	♌15	♌	♍19	♍	♍	♎2	♎	♏13	♏	♏	♐2	♐	♑14	♑	♑	♒0	♒	♓6	♓	♈11	♈			
Mar	♉15	♉	♊18	♊	♋21	♋	♋	♌0	♌	♍4	♍	♎12	♎	♏22	♏	♏	♐10	♐	♑23	♑	♑	♒9	♒	♓15	♓	♈18	♈	♉21	♉	♊23	♊
Apr	♊	♋2	♋	♌6	♌	♍12	♍	♎20	♎	♎	♏6	♏	♐18	♐	♐	♑7	♑	♒18	♒	♒	♓1	♓	♈4	♈	♉5	♉	♊6	♊	♋8	♋	
May	♌12	♌	♍18	♍	♍	♎3	♎	♏13	♏	♏	♐1	♐	♑14	♑	♑	♒2	♒	♓10	♓	♈14	♈	♉15	♉	♊15	♊	♋15	♋	♌18	♌	♌	♍0
Jun	♍	♎8	♎	♏19	♏	♏	♐8	♐	♑21	♑	♑	♒9	♒	♓18	♓	♓	♈0	♈	♉2	♉	♊2	♊	♋1	♋	♌2	♌	♍6	♍	♎14	♎	
Jul	♎	♏1	♏	♐14	♐	♐	♑3	♑	♒15	♒	♒	♓0	♓	♈7	♈	♉11	♉	♊12	♊	♋12	♋	♌12	♌	♍15	♍	♎21	♎	♎	♏7	♏	♐20
Aug	♐	♐	♑9	♑	♒21	♒	♒	♓6	♓	♈13	♈	♉18	♉	♊21	♊	♋22	♋	♌23	♌	♌	♍1	♍	♎6	♎	♏15	♏	♏	♐3	♐	♑16	♑
Sep	♑	♒3	♒	♓12	♓	♈19	♈	♉23	♉	♉	♊3	♊	♋6	♋	♌8	♌	♍10	♍	♎15	♎	♎	♏0	♏	♐11	♐	♐	♑0	♑	♒12	♒	
Oct	♓20	♓	♓	♈2	♈	♉5	♉	♊8	♊	♋11	♋	♌15	♌	♍19	♍	♍	♎0	♎	♏8	♏	♐19	♐	♐	♑8	♑	♒20	♒	♒	♓5	♓	♈11
Nov	♈	♉13	♉	♊15	♊	♋17	♋	♌20	♌	♌	♍1	♍	♎7	♎	♏16	♏	♏	♐3	♐	♑16	♑	♑	♒5	♒	♓15	♓	♈21	♈	♈	♉0	
Dec	♉	♊0	♊	♋1	♋	♌2	♌	♍6	♍	♎13	♎	♏22	♏	♏	♐10	♐	♑23	♑	♑	♒12	♒	♓23	♓	♓	♈7	♈	♉11	♉	♊12	♊	♋11

1983	1	2	3	4	5	6	7	8	9	10	11	12	13	14	15	16	17	18	19	20	21	22	23	24	25	26	27	28	29	30	31
Jan	♋	♌11	♌	♍13	♍	♎19	♎	♎	♏4	♏	♐16	♐	♐	♑5	♑	♒18	♒	♒	♓5	♓	♈15	♈	♉20	♉	♊23	♊	♋22	♋	♌22	♌	♍23
Feb	♍	♍	♎2	♎	♏10	♏	♐22	♐	♐	♑11	♑	♑	♒0	♒	♓11	♓	♈20	♈	♈	♉3	♉	♊7	♊	♋9	♋	♌9	♌	♍9			
Mar	♍	♎12	♎	♏19	♏	♏	♐5	♐	♑18	♑	♑	♒7	♒	♓17	♓	♓	♈2	♈	♉8	♉	♊13	♊	♋17	♋	♌18	♌	♍20	♍	♎22	♎	♎
Apr	♏4	♏	♐13	♐	♐	♑2	♑	♒14	♒	♒	♓1	♓	♈9	♈	♉15	♉	♊19	♊	♋22	♋	♋	♌1	♌	♍4	♍	♎7	♎	♏13	♏	♐22	
May	♐	♐	♑10	♑	♒22	♒	♒	♓10	♓	♈18	♈	♉23	♉	♉	♊2	♊	♋4	♋	♌6	♌	♍10	♍	♎14	♎	♏21	♏	♏	♐6	♐	♑18	♑
Jun	♑	♒6	♒	♓18	♓	♓	♈3	♈	♉8	♉	♊11	♊	♋11	♋	♌13	♌	♍15	♍	♎20	♎	♎	♏3	♏	♐13	♐	♐	♑1	♑	♒14	♒	
Jul	♒	♓2	♓	♈12	♈	♉18	♉	♊21	♊	♋21	♋	♌21	♌	♍22	♍	♍	♎2	♎	♏9	♏	♐19	♐	♐	♑7	♑	♒20	♒	♒	♓8	♓	♈19
Aug	♈	♈	♉3	♉	♊7	♊	♋8	♋	♌7	♌	♍7	♍	♎9	♎	♏15	♏	♏	♐1	♐	♑13	♑	♑	♒2	♒	♓14	♓	♓	♈1	♈	♉10	♉
Sep	♊15	♊	♋18	♋	♌18	♌	♍18	♍	♎19	♎	♏23	♏	♏	♐8	♐	♑19	♑	♑	♒8	♒	♓20	♓	♓	♈6	♈	♉15	♉	♊22	♊	♊	
Oct	♋2	♋	♌3	♌	♍4	♍	♎5	♎	♏8	♏	♐16	♐	♐	♑3	♑	♒15	♒	♒	♓3	♓	♈13	♈	♉21	♉	♉	♊3	♊	♋7	♋	♌10	♌
Nov	♍13	♍	♎15	♎	♏18	♏	♏	♐1	♐	♑11	♑	♒23	♒	♒	♓12	♓	♈22	♈	♈	♉5	♉	♊10	♊	♋13	♋	♌16	♌	♍19	♍	♎22	
Dec	♎	♎	♏3	♏	♐10	♐	♑20	♑	♑	♒8	♒	♓20	♓	♓	♈7	♈	♉15	♉	♊19	♊	♋21	♋	♌22	♌	♌	♍0	♍	♎4	♎	♏10	♏

1984	1	2	3	4	5	6	7	8	9	10	11	12	13	14	15	16	17	18	19	20	21	22	23	24	25	26	27	28	29	30	31
Jan	♐18	♐	♐	♑4	♑	♒15	♒	♒	♓4	♓	♈16	♈	♈	♉1	♉	♊6	♊	♋7	♋	♌7	♌	♍7	♍	♎10	♎	♏15	♏	♐23	♐	♐	♑10
Feb	♑	♒22	♒	♒	♓11	♓	♈23	♈	♈	♉9	♉	♊16	♊	♋18	♋	♌18	♌	♍17	♍	♎18	♎	♏21	♏	♏	♐5	♐	♑16	♑	♑		
Mar	♒4	♒	♓17	♓	♓	♈5	♈	♉16	♉	♉	♊0	♊	♋4	♋	♌5	♌	♍4	♍	♎4	♎	♏6	♏	♐12	♐	♑22	♑	♑	♒10	♒	♓23	♓
Apr	♓	♈11	♈	♉21	♉	♉	♊6	♊	♋12	♋	♌14	♌	♍15	♍	♎15	♎	♏16	♏	♐21	♐	♐	♑6	♑	♒17	♒	♒	♓6	♓	♈18	♈	
May	♈	♉4	♉	♊11	♊	♋17	♋	♌21	♌	♍23	♍	♍	♎0	♎	♏2	♏	♐7	♐	♑14	♑	♑	♒1	♒	♓13	♓	♓	♈1	♈	♉11	♉	♊18
Jun	♊	♋23	♋	♋	♌2	♌	♍5	♍	♎8	♎	♏11	♏	♐16	♐	♑23	♑	♑	♒9	♒	♓21	♓	♓	♈9	♈	♉20	♉	♉	♊3	♊	♋6	
Jul	♋	♌8	♌	♍10	♍	♎13	♎	♏17	♏	♐23	♐	♐	♑7	♑	♒17	♒	♒	♓5	♓	♈18	♈	♈	♉5	♉	♊12	♊	♋16	♋	♌17	♌	♍17
Aug	♍	♎19	♎	♏23	♏	♏	♐5	♐	♑14	♑	♑	♒0	♒	♓12	♓	♓	♈1	♈	♉13	♉	♊21	♊	♊	♋2	♋	♌3	♌	♍2	♍	♎3	♎
Sep	♏5	♏	♐11	♐	♑19	♑	♑	♒6	♒	♓18	♓	♓	♈7	♈	♉19	♉	♉	♊5	♊	♋11	♋	♌14	♌	♍13	♍	♎13	♎	♏13	♏	♐17	
Oct	♐	♐	♑1	♑	♒12	♒	♒	♓1	♓	♈13	♈	♈	♉1	♉	♊12	♊	♋19	♋	♌23	♌	♌	♍0	♍	♎0	♎	♏0	♏	♐2	♐	♑9	♑
Nov	♒19	♒	♒	♓7	♓	♈20	♈	♈	♉7	♉	♊17	♊	♊	♋1	♋	♌6	♌	♍9	♍	♎10	♎	♏11	♏	♐13	♐	♑18	♑	♑	♒3	♒	
Dec	♓14	♓	♓	♈3	♈	♉15	♉	♉	♊0	♊	♋6	♋	♌11	♌	♍15	♍	♎17	♎	♏20	♏	♐23	♐	♐	♑4	♑	♒12	♒	♓23	♓	♓	♈11

1985	1	2	3	4	5	6	7	8	9	10	11	12	13	14	15	16	17	18	19	20	21	22	23	24	25	26	27	28	29	30	31
Jan	♈	♉23	♉	♉	♊8	♊	♋14	♋	♌17	♌	♍20	♍	♎23	♎	♎	♏2	♏	♐7	♐	♑13	♑	♒20	♒	♒	♓7	♓	♈19	♈	♈	♉8	♉
Feb	♊18	♊	♊	♋0	♋	♌2	♌	♍3	♍	♎5	♎	♏8	♏	♐13	♐	♑19	♑	♑	♒4	♒	♓15	♓	♓	♈3	♈	♉16	♉	♉			
Mar	♊3	♊	♋10	♋	♌13	♌	♍13	♍	♎13	♎	♏14	♏	♐18	♐	♐	♑1	♑	♒10	♒	♓21	♓	♓	♈10	♈	♉23	♉	♉	♊11	♊	♋19	♋
Apr	♌23	♌	♌	♍0	♍	♎0	♏23	♏	♏	♐1	♐	♑7	♑	♒16	♒	♒	♓3	♓	♈16	♈	♈	♉5	♉	♊17	♊	♊	♋2	♋	♌8	♌	
May	♍10	♍	♎11	♎	♏10	♏	♐11	♐	♑15	♑	♒22	♒	♒	♓9	♓	♈22	♈	♈	♉11	♉	♊22	♊	♊	♋8	♋	♌14	♌	♍18	♍	♎20	♎
Jun	♏21	♏	♐21	♐	♐	♑0	♑	♒6	♒	♓16	♓	♓	♈5	♈	♉18	♉	♉	♊5	♊	♋13	♋	♌20	♌	♌	♍0	♍	♎3	♎	♏5	♏	
Jul	♐7	♐	♑10	♑	♒15	♒	♒	♓0	♓	♈12	♈	♈	♉1	♉	♊12	♊	♋20	♋	♋	♌2	♌	♍6	♍	♎9	♎	♏12	♏	♐15	♐	♑19	♑
Aug	♑	♒0	♒	♓9	♓	♈20	♈	♈	♉9	♉	♊21	♊	♊	♋5	♋	♌10	♌	♍13	♍	♎15	♎	♏17	♏	♐21	♐	♐	♑2	♑	♒8	♒	♓17
Sep	♓	♓	♈4	♈	♉17	♉	♉	♊5	♊	♋14	♋	♌20	♌	♍22	♍	♎23	♎	♎	♏0	♏	♐2	♐	♑7	♑	♒14	♒	♒	♓0	♓	♈11	
Oct	♈	♈	♉0	♉	♊13	♊	♋23	♋	♋	♌6	♌	♍8	♍	♎9	♎	♏8	♏	♐9	♐	♑13	♑	♒20	♒	♒	♓6	♓	♈18	♈	♈	♉7	♉
Nov	♊19	♊	♊	♋6	♋	♌15	♌	♍19	♍	♎20	♎	♏19	♏	♐19	♐	♑21	♑	♑	♒2	♒	♓12	♓	♓	♈0	♈	♉13	♉	♉	♊1	♊	
Dec	♋12	♋	♌21	♌	♌	♍3	♍	♎6	♎	♏7	♏	♐6	♐	♑7	♑	♒11	♒	♓19	♓	♓	♈6	♈	♉19	♉	♉	♊8	♊	♋18	♋	♋	♌3

1986	1	2	3	4	5	6	7	8	9	10	11	12	13	14	15	16	17	18	19	20	21	22	23	24	25	26	27	28	29	30	31
Jan	♌	♍9	♍	♎13	♎	♏16	♏	♐17	♐	♑18	♑	♒21	♒	♒	♓4	♓	♈14	♈	♈	♉3	♉	♊15	♊	♊	♋1	♋	♌9	♌	♍15	♍	♎19
Feb	♎	♏22	♏	♏	♐1	♐	♑3	♑	♒7	♒	♓13	♓	♈23	♈	♈	♉11	♉	♉	♊0	♊	♋10	♋	♌17	♌	♍22	♍	♍	♎1			
Mar	♎	♏4	♏	♐7	♐	♑10	♑	♒15	♒	♓22	♓	♓	♈7	♈	♉19	♉	♉	♊8	♊	♋19	♋	♋	♌3	♌	♍7	♍	♎9	♎	♏10	♏	♐12
Apr	♐	♑16	♑	♒21	♒	♒	♓5	♓	♈15	♈	♈	♉3	♉	♊15	♊	♊	♋3	♋	♌12	♌	♍18	♍	♎19	♎	♏20	♏	♐20	♐	♑22	♑	
May	♑	♒3	♒	♓10	♓	♈21	♈	♈	♉9	♉	♊22	♊	♊	♋10	♋	♌20	♌	♌	♍3	♍	♎6	♎	♏6	♏	♐6	♐	♑6	♑	♒9	♒	♓16
Jun	♓	♓	♈3	♈	♉15	♉	♉	♊4	♊	♋16	♋	♋	♌3	♌	♍11	♍	♎15	♎	♏17	♏	♐16	♐	♑16	♑	♒18	♒	♓23	♓	♓	♈9	
Jul	♈	♉21	♉	♉	♊10	♊	♋22	♋	♋	♌8	♌	♍17	♍	♎22	♎	♎	♏1	♏	♐2	♐	♑3	♑	♒4	♒	♓8	♓	♈16	♈	♈	♉4	♉
Aug	♊17	♊	♊	♋5	♋	♌14	♌	♍22	♍	♍	♎4	♎	♏8	♏	♐10	♐	♑12	♑	♒14	♒	♓18	♓	♓	♈1	♈	♉12	♉	♉	♊0	♊	♋12
Sep	♋	♌22	♌	♌	♍5	♍	♎10	♎	♏13	♏	♐16	♐	♑19	♑	♒22	♒	♒	♓3	♓	♈10	♈	♉20	♉	♉	♊9	♊	♋21	♋	♋	♌7	
Oct	♌	♍13	♍	♎17	♎	♏20	♏	♐22	♐	♐	♑0	♑	♒4	♒	♓10	♓	♈18	♈	♈	♉4	♉	♊16	♊	♊	♋5	♋	♌16	♌	♍23	♍	♍
Nov	♎3	♎	♏5	♏	♐5	♐	♑6	♑	♒10	♒	♓16	♓	♓	♈1	♈	♉11	♉	♊23	♊	♊	♋12	♋	♋	♌0	♌	♍9	♍	♎14	♎	♏15	
Dec	♏	♐15	♐	♑15	♑	♒16	♒	♓22	♓	♓	♈6	♈	♉18	♉	♉	♊6	♊	♋18	♋	♋	♌6	♌	♍17	♍	♍	♎0	♎	♏2	♏	♐2	♐

1987	1	2	3	4	5	6	7	8	9	10	11	12	13	14	15	16	17	18	19	20	21	22	23	24	25	26	27	28	29	30	31
Jan	♑1	♑	♒2	♒	♓5	♓	♈12	♈	♈	♉0	♉	♊12	♊	♊	♋0	♋	♌12	♌	♍23	♍	♍	♎7	♎	♏11	♏	♐13	♐	♑13	♑	♒13	♒
Feb	♓15	♓	♈20	♈	♈	♉6	♉	♊19	♊	♊	♋7	♋	♌19	♌	♌	♍4	♍	♎12	♎	♏18	♏	♐21	♐	♑22	♑	♒23	♒	♒			
Mar	♓1	♓	♈6	♈	♉15	♉	♉	♊2	♊	♋15	♋	♋	♌2	♌	♍11	♍	♎18	♎	♏23	♏	♏	♐3	♐	♑5	♑	♒8	♒	♓11	♓	♈16	♈
Apr	♈	♉0	♉	♊11	♊	♋23	♋	♋	♌11	♌	♍20	♍	♍	♎2	♎	♏6	♏	♐8	♐	♑11	♑	♒14	♒	♓18	♓	♓	♈0	♈	♉8	♉	
May	♊19	♊	♊	♋7	♋	♌19	♌	♌	♍5	♍	♎12	♎	♏15	♏	♐16	♐	♑17	♑	♒19	♒	♒	♓0	♓	♈6	♈	♉15	♉	♉	♊2	♊	♋14
Jun	♋	♋	♌3	♌	♍14	♍	♎21	♎	♎	♏1	♏	♐2	♐	♑1	♑	♒2	♒	♓5	♓	♈12	♈	♉21	♉	♉	♊8	♊	♋20	♋	♋	♌9	
Jul	♌	♍21	♍	♍	♎6	♎	♏11	♏	♐12	♐	♑11	♑	♒11	♒	♓13	♓	♈18	♈	♈	♉3	♉	♊14	♊	♊	♋3	♋	♌15	♌	♌	♍3	♍
Aug	♎13	♎	♏19	♏	♐22	♐	♑22	♑	♒22	♒	♓22	♓	♓	♈2	♈	♉9	♉	♊20	♊	♊	♋9	♋	♌21	♌	♌	♍9	♍	♎18	♎	♎	♏2
Sep	♏	♐6	♐	♑8	♑	♒8	♒	♓9	♓	♈11	♈	♉18	♉	♉	♊3	♊	♋15	♋	♋	♌4	♌	♍15	♍	♍	♎0	♎	♏7	♏	♐12	♐	
Oct	♑15	♑	♒17	♒	♓19	♓	♈21	♈	♈	♉3	♉	♊12	♊	♋23	♋	♋	♌12	♌	♍23	♍	♍	♎8	♎	♏13	♏	♐17	♐	♑20	♑	♒23	♒
Nov	♒	♓2	♓	♈6	♈	♉12	♉	♊20	♊	♊	♋8	♋	♌20	♌	♌	♍8	♍	♎17	♎	♏22	♏	♏	♐1	♐	♑2	♑	♒4	♒	♓8	♓	
Dec	♈13	♈	♉20	♉	♉	♊5	♊	♋15	♋	♋	♌4	♌	♍17	♍	♍	♎3	♎	♏8	♏	♐10	♐	♑11	♑	♒11	♒	♓14	♓	♈19	♈	♈	♉2

1988	1	2	3	4	5	6	7	8	9	10	11	12	13	14	15	16	17	18	19	20	21	22	23	24	25	26	27	28	29	30	31
Jan	♉	♊12	♊	♋23	♋	♋	♌11	♌	♌	♍0	♍	♎11	♎	♏18	♏	♐21	♐	♑22	♑	♒21	♒	♓22	♓	♓	♈1	♈	♉8	♉	♊17	♊	♊
Feb	♋5	♋	♌17	♌	♌	♍6	♍	♎18	♎	♎	♏3	♏	♐7	♐	♑9	♑	♒8	♒	♓8	♓	♈9	♈	♉14	♉	♊23	♊	♊	♋11	♋		
Mar	♋	♌0	♌	♍12	♍	♍	♎0	♎	♏9	♏	♐15	♐	♑18	♑	♒19	♒	♓19	♓	♈20	♈	♈	♉0	♉	♊7	♊	♋18	♋	♋	♌6	♌	♍19
Apr	♍	♍	♎6	♎	♏14	♏	♐21	♐	♐	♑1	♑	♒4	♒	♓5	♓	♈6	♈	♉10	♉	♊16	♊	♊	♋1	♋	♌14	♌	♌	♍3	♍	♎13	
May	♎	♏21	♏	♏	♐2	♐	♑6	♑	♒10	♒	♓12	♓	♈15	♈	♉19	♉	♉	♊1	♊	♋10	♋	♌22	♌	♌	♍11	♍	♎22	♎	♎	♏5	♏
Jun	♐10	♐	♑13	♑	♒15	♒	♓18	♓	♈22	♈	♈	♉2	♉	♊9	♊	♋18	♋	♋	♌6	♌	♍19	♍	♍	♎6	♎	♏15	♏	♐19	♐	♑21	
Jul	♑	♒22	♒	♒	♓0	♓	♈3	♈	♉8	♉	♊16	♊	♊	♋1	♋	♌13	♌	♌	♍2	♍	♎14	♎	♎	♏0	♏	♐5	♐	♑7	♑	♒7	♒
Aug	♓7	♓	♈9	♈	♉14	♉	♊21	♊	♊	♋7	♋	♌19	♌	♌	♍8	♍	♎21	♎	♎	♏8	♏	♐14	♐	♑17	♑	♒18	♒	♓17	♓	♈17	♈
Sep	♉20	♉	♉	♊3	♊	♋13	♋	♋	♌1	♌	♍15	♍	♍	♎3	♎	♏14	♏	♐22	♐	♐	♑3	♑	♒4	♒	♓4	♓	♈4	♈	♉5	♉	
Oct	♊10	♊	♋19	♋	♋	♌8	♌	♍21	♍	♍	♎9	♎	♏19	♏	♏	♐4	♐	♑10	♑	♒13	♒	♓14	♓	♈15	♈	♉16	♉	♊20	♊	♊	♋3
Nov	♋	♌15	♌	♌	♍4	♍	♎16	♎	♎	♏2	♏	♐9	♐	♑15	♑	♒19	♒	♓22	♓	♓	♈0	♈	♉2	♉	♊6	♊	♋12	♋	♌23	♌	
Dec	♌	♍12	♍	♍	♎0	♎	♏10	♏	♐16	♐	♑21	♑	♑	♒1	♒	♓4	♓	♈7	♈	♉10	♉	♊15	♊	♋22	♋	♋	♌7	♌	♍20	♍	♍

1989	1	2	3	4	5	6	7	8	9	10	11	12	13	14	15	16	17	18	19	20	21	22	23	24	25	26	27	28	29	30	31
Jan	♎9	♎	♏19	♏	♏	♐2	♐	♑5	♑	♒8	♒	♓9	♓	♈12	♈	♉16	♉	♊22	♊	♊	♋6	♋	♌16	♌	♌	♍4	♍	♎17	♎	♎	♏4
Feb	♏	♐12	♐	♑16	♑	♒17	♒	♓18	♓	♈19	♈	♉22	♉	♉	♊4	♊	♋12	♋	♌23	♌	♌	♍11	♍	♍	♎0	♎	♏12	♏			
Mar	♐21	♐	♐	♑2	♑	♒4	♒	♓4	♓	♈4	♈	♉5	♉	♊9	♊	♋17	♋	♋	♌5	♌	♍17	♍	♍	♎6	♎	♏18	♏	♏	♐4	♐	♑11
Apr	♑	♒15	♒	♓15	♓	♈15	♈	♉15	♉	♊17	♊	♊	♋0	♋	♌11	♌	♍23	♍	♍	♎12	♎	♎	♏0	♏	♐10	♐	♑18	♑	♒23	♒	
May	♒	♓1	♓	♈1	♈	♉1	♉	♊3	♊	♋8	♋	♌18	♌	♌	♍6	♍	♎19	♎	♎	♏6	♏	♐16	♐	♑23	♑	♑	♒5	♒	♓8	♓	♈10
Jun	♈	♉11	♉	♊13	♊	♋18	♋	♋	♌2	♌	♍13	♍	♍	♎2	♎	♏14	♏	♐23	♐	♐	♑5	♑	♒10	♒	♓14	♓	♈17	♈	♉19	♉	
Jul	♊22	♊	♊	♋3	♋	♌10	♌	♍22	♍	♍	♎10	♎	♏22	♏	♏	♐7	♐	♑13	♑	♒17	♒	♓20	♓	♈22	♈	♈	♉1	♉	♊5	♊	♋11
Aug	♋	♌19	♌	♌	♍5	♍	♎18	♎	♎	♏6	♏	♐16	♐	♑23	♑	♑	♒2	♒	♓3	♓	♈4	♈	♉6	♉	♊11	♊	♋17	♋	♋	♌2	♌
Sep	♍13	♍	♍	♎1	♎	♏14	♏	♏	♐1	♐	♑8	♑	♒12	♒	♓13	♓	♈13	♈	♉13	♉	♊16	♊	♋22	♋	♋	♌8	♌	♍19	♍	♍	
Oct	♎8	♎	♏20	♏	♏	♐8	♐	♑17	♑	♒22	♒	♒	♓0	♓	♈0	♉23	♉	♉	♊0	♊	♋5	♋	♌13	♌	♌	♍1	♍	♎14	♎	♎	♏2
Nov	♏	♐14	♐	♐	♑0	♑	♒7	♒	♓10	♓	♈11	♈	♉10	♉	♊10	♊	♋13	♋	♌20	♌	♌	♍7	♍	♎20	♎	♎	♏8	♏	♐20	♐	
Dec	♐	♑5	♑	♒13	♒	♓18	♓	♈20	♈	♉21	♉	♊21	♊	♋23	♋	♋	♌5	♌	♍15	♍	♍	♎3	♎	♏16	♏	♏	♐3	♐	♑11	♑	♒18

1990	1	2	3	4	5	6	7	8	9	10	11	12	13	14	15	16	17	18	19	20	21	22	23	24	25	26	27	28	29	30	31
Jan	♒	♓23	♓	♓	♈3	♈	♉5	♉	♊7	♊	♋10	♋	♌15	♌	♌	♍0	♍	♎11	♎	♎	♏0	♏	♐11	♐	♑19	♑	♑	♒1	♒	♓5	♓
Feb	♈8	♈	♉11	♉	♊14	♊	♋18	♋	♋	♌0	♌	♍9	♍	♎20	♎	♎	♏8	♏	♐20	♐	♐	♑5	♑	♒10	♒	♓13	♓	♈15			
Mar	♈	♉17	♉	♊20	♊	♊	♋1	♋	♌8	♌	♍16	♍	♍	♎3	♎	♏16	♏	♏	♐4	♐	♑14	♑	♒21	♒	♓23	♓	♓	♈0	♈	♉0	♉
Apr	♊2	♊	♋6	♋	♌13	♌	♍23	♍	♍	♎10	♎	♏22	♏	♏	♐11	♐	♑22	♑	♑	♒6	♒	♓10	♓	♈11	♈	♉10	♉	♊10	♊	♋13	
May	♋	♌19	♌	♌	♍5	♍	♎16	♎	♎	♏5	♏	♐17	♐	♐	♑5	♑	♒14	♒	♓19	♓	♈21	♈	♉21	♉	♊20	♊	♋21	♋	♋	♌2	♌
Jun	♍11	♍	♎22	♎	♎	♏11	♏	♐23	♐	♐	♑10	♑	♒20	♒	♒	♓2	♓	♈6	♈	♉7	♉	♊7	♊	♋7	♋	♌11	♌	♍18	♍	♍	
Jul	♎5	♎	♏17	♏	♏	♐6	♐	♑17	♑	♑	♒1	♒	♓8	♓	♈12	♈	♉15	♉	♊16	♊	♋17	♋	♌21	♌	♌	♍3	♍	♎13	♎	♎	♏1
Aug	♏	♐13	♐	♐	♑0	♑	♒8	♒	♓14	♓	♈18	♈	♉21	♉	♊23	♊	♊	♋2	♋	♌6	♌	♍12	♍	♎21	♎	♎	♏9	♏	♐21	♐	♐
Sep	♑8	♑	♒16	♒	♓21	♓	♓	♈0	♈	♉2	♉	♊5	♊	♋8	♋	♌13	♌	♍20	♍	♍	♎5	♎	♏17	♏	♏	♐5	♐	♑17	♑	♑	
Oct	♒2	♒	♓7	♓	♈8	♈	♉9	♉	♊11	♊	♋14	♋	♌19	♌	♌	♍3	♍	♎13	♎	♎	♏0	♏	♐13	♐	♐	♑1	♑	♒11	♒	♓17	♓
Nov	♈19	♈	♉19	♉	♊19	♊	♋20	♋	♋	♌1	♌	♍9	♍	♎19	♎	♎	♏6	♏	♐19	♐	♐	♑8	♑	♒19	♒	♒	♓3	♓	♈6	♈	
Dec	♉6	♉	♊5	♊	♋5	♋	♌8	♌	♍15	♍	♍	♎1	♎	♏13	♏	♏	♐1	♐	♑14	♑	♑	♒1	♒	♓10	♓	♈15	♈	♉17	♉	♊17	♊

1991	1	2	3	4	5	6	7	8	9	10	11	12	13	14	15	16	17	18	19	20	21	22	23	24	25	26	27	28	29	30	31
Jan	♋16	♋	♌18	♌	♍22	♍	♍	♎7	♎	♏19	♏	♏	♐8	♐	♑20	♑	♑	♒7	♒	♓15	♓	♈22	♈	♈	♉1	♉	♊3	♊	♋3	♋	♌5
Feb	♌	♍8	♍	♎15	♎	♎	♏2	♏	♐15	♐	♐	♑3	♑	♒14	♒	♓21	♓	♓	♈3	♈	♉7	♉	♊10	♊	♋12	♋	♌15	♌			
Mar	♍18	♍	♍	♎1	♎	♏11	♏	♐23	♐	♐	♑11	♑	♒22	♒	♒	♓5	♓	♈9	♈	♉13	♉	♊15	♊	♋19	♋	♌22	♌	♌	♍3	♍	♎10
Apr	♎	♏19	♏	♏	♐7	♐	♑20	♑	♑	♒7	♒	♓14	♓	♈18	♈	♉20	♉	♊21	♊	♊	♋0	♋	♌4	♌	♍10	♍	♎17	♎	♎	♏3	
May	♏	♐15	♐	♐	♑4	♑	♒16	♒	♒	♓0	♓	♈4	♈	♉5	♉	♊6	♊	♋7	♋	♌10	♌	♍15	♍	♎23	♎	♎	♏9	♏	♐21	♐	♐
Jun	♑10	♑	♒23	♒	♒	♓8	♓	♈14	♈	♉16	♉	♊16	♊	♋16	♋	♌17	♌	♍21	♍	♍	♎5	♎	♏15	♏	♏	♐4	♐	♑17	♑	♑	
Jul	♒5	♒	♓15	♓	♈22	♈	♈	♉2	♉	♊3	♊	♋2	♋	♌2	♌	♍5	♍	♎11	♎	♏21	♏	♏	♐10	♐	♑23	♑	♑	♒11	♒	♓21	♓
Aug	♓	♈5	♈	♉10	♉	♊12	♊	♋13	♋	♌13	♌	♍15	♍	♎20	♎	♎	♏4	♏	♐16	♐	♐	♑5	♑	♒17	♒	♒	♓3	♓	♈10	♈	♉16
Sep	♉	♊19	♊	♋21	♋	♌23	♌	♌	♍1	♍	♎5	♎	♏13	♏	♏	♐0	♐	♑13	♑	♑	♒1	♒	♓10	♓	♈16	♈	♉21	♉	♉	♊1	
Oct	♊	♋4	♋	♌7	♌	♍10	♍	♎14	♎	♏21	♏	♏	♐8	♐	♑21	♑	♑	♒9	♒	♓19	♓	♓	♈1	♈	♉4	♉	♊7	♊	♋9	♋	♌12
Nov	♌	♍17	♍	♎22	♎	♎	♏6	♏	♐16	♐	♐	♑5	♑	♒18	♒	♒	♓4	♓	♈11	♈	♉14	♉	♊15	♊	♋16	♋	♌18	♌	♍22	♍	
Dec	♍	♎4	♎	♏13	♏	♏	♐0	♐	♑12	♑	♑	♒1	♒	♓13	♓	♈21	♈	♈	♉1	♉	♊1	♊	♋1	♋	♌2	♌	♍4	♍	♎10	♎	♏19

1992	1	2	3	4	5	6	7	8	9	10	11	12	13	14	15	16	17	18	19	20	21	22	23	24	25	26	27	28	29	30	31
Jan	♏	♏	♐6	♐	♑19	♑	♑	♒8	♒	♓20	♓	♓	♈5	♈	♉11	♉	♊13	♊	♋13	♋	♌12	♌	♍13	♍	♎17	♎	♎	♏1	♏	♐12	♐
Feb	♐	♑1	♑	♒14	♒	♒	♓1	♓	♈11	♈	♉19	♉	♊23	♊	♊	♋0	♌23	♌	♍23	♍	♍	♎2	♎	♏8	♏	♐18	♐	♐	♑7		
Mar	♑	♒20	♒	♒	♓7	♓	♈17	♈	♈	♉0	♉	♊6	♊	♋8	♋	♌10	♌	♍10	♍	♎12	♎	♏17	♏	♏	♐2	♐	♑15	♑	♑	♒3	♒
Apr	♓15	♓	♈23	♈	♈	♉6	♉	♊11	♊	♋15	♋	♌17	♌	♍19	♍	♎22	♎	♎	♏3	♏	♐11	♐	♑23	♑	♑	♒11	♒	♓23	♓	♓	
May	♈7	♈	♉13	♉	♊17	♊	♋20	♋	♌23	♌	♌	♍2	♍	♎6	♎	♏11	♏	♐20	♐	♐	♑7	♑	♒19	♒	♒	♓7	♓	♈16	♈	♉22	♉
Jun	♉	♊1	♊	♋3	♋	♌4	♌	♍7	♍	♎12	♎	♏18	♏	♏	♐3	♐	♑14	♑	♑	♒3	♒	♓15	♓	♓	♈1	♈	♉8	♉	♊11	♊	
Jul	♋12	♋	♌12	♌	♍13	♍	♎17	♎	♎	♏0	♏	♐9	♐	♑21	♑	♑	♒10	♒	♓22	♓	♓	♈9	♈	♉17	♉	♊21	♊	♋22	♋	♌22	♌
Aug	♍22	♍	♍	♎0	♎	♏6	♏	♐15	♐	♐	♑3	♑	♒16	♒	♒	♓4	♓	♈16	♈	♈	♉1	♉	♊6	♊	♋9	♋	♌8	♌	♍8	♍	♎9
Sep	♎	♏13	♏	♐21	♐	♐	♑9	♑	♒22	♒	♒	♓10	♓	♈21	♈	♈	♉7	♉	♊13	♊	♋17	♋	♌19	♌	♍19	♍	♎19	♎	♏22	♏	
Oct	♏	♐5	♐	♑16	♑	♑	♒5	♒	♓17	♓	♓	♈3	♈	♉12	♉	♊19	♊	♊	♋0	♋	♌3	♌	♍4	♍	♎5	♎	♏8	♏	♐14	♐	♐
Nov	♑0	♑	♒12	♒	♒	♓0	♓	♈11	♈	♉19	♉	♉	♊1	♊	♋5	♋	♌8	♌	♍11	♍	♎14	♎	♏18	♏	♏	♐0	♐	♑9	♑	♒20	
Dec	♒	♒	♓9	♓	♈20	♈	♈	♉4	♉	♊9	♊	♋12	♋	♌14	♌	♍16	♍	♎20	♎	♎	♏1	♏	♐8	♐	♑17	♑	♑	♒5	♒	♓17	♓

1993	1	2	3	4	5	6	7	8	9	10	11	12	13	14	15	16	17	18	19	20	21	22	23	24	25	26	27	28	29	30	31
Jan	♓	♈5	♈	♉14	♉	♊19	♊	♋21	♋	♌22	♌	♍23	♍	♍	♎1	♎	♏7	♏	♐14	♐	♐	♑0	♑	♒12	♒	♒	♓0	♓	♈13	♈	♉23
Feb	♉	♉	♊6	♊	♋8	♋	♌8	♌	♍8	♍	♎8	♎	♏12	♏	♐20	♐	♐	♑6	♑	♒18	♒	♒	♓7	♓	♈19	♈	♈	♉7			
Mar	♉	♊15	♊	♋19	♋	♌19	♌	♍18	♍	♎18	♎	♏20	♏	♏	♐2	♐	♑12	♑	♑	♒0	♒	♓13	♓	♓	♈1	♈	♉12	♉	♊21	♊	♊
Apr	♋3	♋	♌5	♌	♍5	♍	♎5	♎	♏6	♏	♐10	♐	♑19	♑	♑	♒7	♒	♓19	♓	♓	♈7	♈	♉18	♉	♉	♊3	♊	♋9	♋	♌13	
May	♌	♍15	♍	♎15	♎	♏17	♏	♐20	♐	♐	♑3	♑	♒14	♒	♒	♓2	♓	♈14	♈	♈	♉1	♉	♊9	♊	♋15	♋	♌19	♌	♍21	♍	♍
Jun	♎0	♎	♏2	♏	♐6	♐	♑12	♑	♒22	♒	♒	♓10	♓	♈22	♈	♈	♉9	♉	♊17	♊	♋21	♋	♋	♌0	♌	♍3	♍	♎6	♎	♏9	
Jul	♏	♐14	♐	♑21	♑	♑	♒6	♒	♓18	♓	♓	♈7	♈	♉18	♉	♉	♊2	♊	♋6	♋	♌8	♌	♍9	♍	♎11	♎	♏15	♏	♐20	♐	♐
Aug	♑4	♑	♒14	♒	♒	♓2	♓	♈14	♈	♈	♉2	♉	♊11	♊	♋16	♋	♌17	♌	♍17	♍	♎18	♎	♏20	♏	♏	♐2	♐	♑10	♑	♒21	♒
Sep	♒	♓8	♓	♈21	♈	♈	♉9	♉	♊20	♊	♊	♋2	♋	♌4	♌	♍4	♍	♎3	♎	♏4	♏	♐8	♐	♑16	♑	♑	♒2	♒	♓14	♓	
Oct	♓	♈3	♈	♉15	♉	♉	♊2	♊	♋10	♋	♌14	♌	♍14	♍	♎14	♎	♏14	♏	♐16	♐	♑22	♑	♑	♒8	♒	♓21	♓	♓	♈9	♈	♉21
Nov	♉	♉	♊8	♊	♋16	♋	♌22	♌	♌	♍0	♍	♎1	♎	♏1	♏	♐2	♐	♑7	♑	♒16	♒	♒	♓3	♓	♈16	♈	♈	♉4	♉	♊14	
Dec	♊	♋22	♋	♋	♌3	♌	♍7	♍	♎9	♎	♏11	♏	♐13	♐	♑17	♑	♑	♒1	♒	♓11	♓	♓	♈0	♈	♉12	♉	♊22	♊	♊	♋4	♋

1994	1	2	3	4	5	6	7	8	9	10	11	12	13	14	15	16	17	18	19	20	21	22	23	24	25	26	27	28	29	30	31
Jan	♌9	♌	♍12	♍	♎16	♎	♏19	♏	♐22	♐	♐	♑3	♑	♒10	♒	♓20	♓	♓	♈8	♈	♉21	♉	♉	♊7	♊	♋13	♋	♌17	♌	♍19	♍
Feb	♎21	♎	♎	♏0	♏	♐5	♐	♑10	♑	♒18	♒	♒	♓4	♓	♈16	♈	♈	♉5	♉	♊16	♊	♋23	♋	♋	♌3	♌	♍4	♍			
Mar	♎4	♎	♏6	♏	♐10	♐	♑16	♑	♑	♒1	♒	♓11	♓	♈23	♈	♈	♉12	♉	♉	♊0	♊	♋9	♋	♌13	♌	♍14	♍	♎14	♎	♏14	♏
Apr	♐16	♐	♑22	♑	♑	♒6	♒	♓17	♓	♓	♈6	♈	♉19	♉	♉	♊7	♊	♋17	♋	♌23	♌	♌	♍1	♍	♎1	♎	♏0	♏	♐1	♐	
May	♑5	♑	♒12	♒	♓23	♓	♓	♈12	♈	♈	♉1	♉	♊13	♊	♋23	♋	♋	♌6	♌	♍10	♍	♎11	♎	♏11	♏	♐12	♐	♑14	♑	♒20	♒
Jun	♒	♓6	♓	♈18	♈	♈	♉7	♉	♊19	♊	♊	♋4	♋	♌12	♌	♍17	♍	♎20	♎	♏21	♏	♐22	♐	♐	♑0	♑	♒5	♒	♓13	♓	
Jul	♓	♈1	♈	♉14	♉	♉	♊2	♊	♋11	♋	♌17	♌	♍22	♍	♍	♎2	♎	♏4	♏	♐6	♐	♑9	♑	♒14	♒	♓22	♓	♓	♈9	♈	♉22
Aug	♉	♉	♊10	♊	♋19	♋	♋	♌0	♌	♍4	♍	♎7	♎	♏10	♏	♐13	♐	♑17	♑	♒23	♒	♒	♓6	♓	♈17	♈	♈	♉6	♉	♊18	♊
Sep	♊	♋4	♋	♌9	♌	♍12	♍	♎14	♎	♏15	♏	♐18	♐	♑23	♑	♑	♒5	♒	♓14	♓	♓	♈1	♈	♉14	♉	♉	♊2	♊	♋13	♋	
Oct	♌19	♌	♍22	♍	♎23	♎	♏23	♏	♏	♐1	♐	♑4	♑	♒11	♒	♓20	♓	♓	♈8	♈	♉20	♉	♉	♊9	♊	♋21	♋	♋	♌5	♌	♍9
Nov	♍	♎10	♎	♏10	♏	♐9	♐	♑11	♑	♒17	♒	♒	♓2	♓	♈14	♈	♈	♉3	♉	♊15	♊	♊	♋3	♋	♌12	♌	♍18	♍	♎21	♎	
Dec	♏21	♏	♐20	♐	♑21	♑	♑	♒1	♒	♓8	♓	♈20	♈	♈	♉9	♉	♊22	♊	♊	♋9	♋	♌18	♌	♌	♍1	♍	♎5	♎	♏7	♏	♐7

1995	1	2	3	4	5	6	7	8	9	10	11	12	13	14	15	16	17	18	19	20	21	22	23	24	25	26	27	28	29	30	31
Jan	♐	♑8	♑	♒10	♒	♓17	♓	♓	♈3	♈	♉16	♉	♉	♊5	♊	♋15	♋	♋	♌0	♌	♍6	♍	♎11	♎	♏15	♏	♐17	♐	♑18	♑	♒21
Feb	♒	♒	♓2	♓	♈11	♈	♈	♉0	♉	♊12	♊	♋23	♋	♋	♌7	♌	♍13	♍	♎17	♎	♏20	♏	♐23	♐	♐	♑2	♑	♒6			
Mar	♒	♓11	♓	♈20	♈	♈	♉8	♉	♊21	♊	♊	♋8	♋	♌16	♌	♍21	♍	♍	♎0	♎	♏2	♏	♐4	♐	♑8	♑	♒13	♒	♓19	♓	♓
Apr	♈4	♈	♉16	♉	♉	♊5	♊	♋17	♋	♋	♌2	♌	♍7	♍	♎10	♎	♏10	♏	♐11	♐	♑13	♑	♒18	♒	♒	♓1	♓	♈11	♈	♉23	
May	♉	♉	♊12	♊	♊	♋0	♋	♌10	♌	♍17	♍	♎20	♎	♏21	♏	♐20	♐	♑21	♑	♑	♒0	♒	♓7	♓	♈17	♈	♈	♉5	♉	♊18	♊
Jun	♊	♋6	♋	♌17	♌	♌	♍2	♍	♎6	♎	♏7	♏	♐7	♐	♑6	♑	♒8	♒	♓13	♓	♈23	♈	♈	♉11	♉	♉	♊0	♊	♋12	♋	
Jul	♌23	♌	♌	♍8	♍	♎14	♎	♏17	♏	♐17	♐	♑17	♑	♒18	♒	♓22	♓	♓	♈6	♈	♉17	♉	♉	♊6	♊	♋18	♋	♋	♌5	♌	♍13
Aug	♍	♎20	♎	♎	♏0	♏	♐2	♐	♑3	♑	♒4	♒	♓7	♓	♈14	♈	♈	♉1	♉	♊13	♊	♊	♋1	♋	♌12	♌	♍19	♍	♍	♎1	♎
Sep	♏6	♏	♐9	♐	♑11	♑	♒13	♒	♓17	♓	♈23	♈	♈	♉9	♉	♊21	♊	♊	♋9	♋	♌20	♌	♌	♍3	♍	♎8	♎	♏11	♏	♐14	
Oct	♐	♑17	♑	♒20	♒	♒	♓1	♓	♈8	♈	♉18	♉	♉	♊5	♊	♋18	♋	♋	♌5	♌	♍13	♍	♎17	♎	♏19	♏	♐20	♐	♑22	♑	♑
Nov	♒2	♒	♓8	♓	♈15	♈	♈	♉1	♉	♊13	♊	♊	♋2	♋	♌13	♌	♍22	♍	♍	♎4	♎	♏5	♏	♐5	♐	♑6	♑	♒8	♒	♓13	
Dec	♓	♈21	♈	♈	♉8	♉	♊20	♊	♊	♋8	♋	♌21	♌	♌	♍7	♍	♎14	♎	♏17	♏	♐16	♐	♑16	♑	♒16	♒	♓19	♓	♓	♈3	♈

1996	1	2	3	4	5	6	7	8	9	10	11	12	13	14	15	16	17	18	19	20	21	22	23	24	25	26	27	28	29	30	31
Jan	♉14	♉	♉	♊2	♊	♋14	♋	♋	♌3	♌	♍14	♍	♎22	♎	♎	♏2	♏	♐4	♐	♑3	♑	♒3	♒	♓4	♓	♈10	♈	♉20	♉	♉	♊8
Feb	♊	♋21	♋	♋	♌9	♌	♍19	♍	♍	♎4	♎	♏10	♏	♐13	♐	♑14	♑	♒14	♒	♓15	♓	♈19	♈	♈	♉4	♉	♊15	♊	♊		
Mar	♋4	♋	♌16	♌	♌	♍1	♍	♎9	♎	♏15	♏	♐19	♐	♑22	♑	♒23	♒	♒	♓1	♓	♈5	♈	♉13	♉	♊23	♊	♊	♋12	♋	♌23	♌
Apr	♌	♍9	♍	♎16	♎	♏21	♏	♏	♐0	♐	♑3	♑	♒6	♒	♓9	♓	♈14	♈	♉22	♉	♉	♊8	♊	♋20	♋	♋	♌8	♌	♍18	♍	
May	♍	♎1	♎	♏5	♏	♐7	♐	♑9	♑	♒12	♒	♓16	♓	♈22	♈	♈	♉5	♉	♊16	♊	♊	♋3	♋	♌16	♌	♌	♍3	♍	♎11	♎	♏15
Jun	♏	♐16	♐	♑16	♑	♒18	♒	♓21	♓	♓	♈3	♈	♉12	♉	♊22	♊	♊	♋10	♋	♌23	♌	♌	♍11	♍	♎20	♎	♎	♏1	♏	♐2	
Jul	♐	♑2	♑	♒2	♒	♓4	♓	♈9	♈	♉17	♉	♉	♊4	♊	♋16	♋	♋	♌5	♌	♍17	♍	♍	♎4	♎	♏10	♏	♐13	♐	♑13	♑	♒12
Aug	♒	♓12	♓	♈16	♈	♉23	♉	♉	♊10	♊	♋22	♋	♋	♌11	♌	♍23	♍	♍	♎10	♎	♏17	♏	♐21	♐	♑23	♑	♒23	♒	♓23	♓	♓
Sep	♈1	♈	♉7	♉	♊17	♊	♊	♋5	♋	♌17	♌	♌	♍5	♍	♎15	♎	♏23	♏	♏	♐4	♐	♑7	♑	♒8	♒	♓9	♓	♈11	♈	♉16	
Oct	♉	♉	♊1	♊	♋12	♋	♋	♌1	♌	♍12	♍	♎22	♎	♎	♏5	♏	♐9	♐	♑13	♑	♒16	♒	♓18	♓	♈21	♈	♈	♉2	♉	♊10	♊
Nov	♋20	♋	♋	♌9	♌	♍21	♍	♍	♎6	♎	♏12	♏	♐16	♐	♑18	♑	♒21	♒	♒	♓0	♓	♈5	♈	♉11	♉	♊18	♊	♊	♋5	♋	
Dec	♌17	♌	♌	♍6	♍	♎16	♎	♏22	♏	♏	♐1	♐	♑2	♑	♒3	♒	♓6	♓	♈11	♈	♉17	♉	♉	♊2	♊	♋12	♋	♋	♌1	♌	♍14

1997	1	2	3	4	5	6	7	8	9	10	11	12	13	14	15	16	17	18	19	20	21	22	23	24	25	26	27	28	29	30	31
Jan	♍	♍	♎1	♎	♏8	♏	♐11	♐	♑12	♑	♒11	♒	♓12	♓	♈16	♈	♉23	♉	♉	♊8	♊	♋19	♋	♋	♌7	♌	♍20	♍	♍	♎8	♎
Feb	♏17	♏	♐22	♐	♑23	♑	♒22	♒	♓22	♓	♓	♈0	♈	♉5	♉	♊14	♊	♊	♋1	♋	♌14	♌	♌	♍2	♍	♎14	♎	♎			
Mar	♏0	♏	♐6	♐	♑9	♑	♒10	♒	♓9	♓	♈10	♈	♉13	♉	♊20	♊	♊	♋7	♋	♌20	♌	♌	♍9	♍	♎20	♎	♎	♏6	♏	♐13	♐
Apr	♑17	♑	♒19	♒	♓20	♓	♈21	♈	♉23	♉	♉	♊5	♊	♋15	♋	♋	♌3	♌	♍16	♍	♍	♎3	♎	♏12	♏	♐18	♐	♑23	♑	♑	
May	♒2	♒	♓4	♓	♈6	♈	♉9	♉	♊14	♊	♋23	♋	♋	♌11	♌	♍23	♍	♍	♎11	♎	♏19	♏	♏	♐1	♐	♑4	♑	♒7	♒	♓10	♓
Jun	♈14	♈	♉17	♉	♊23	♊	♊	♋7	♋	♌19	♌	♌	♍8	♍	♎19	♎	♎	♏4	♏	♐9	♐	♑12	♑	♒13	♒	♓16	♓	♈19	♈	♈	
Jul	♉0	♉	♊7	♊	♋15	♋	♋	♌2	♌	♍15	♍	♍	♎4	♎	♏13	♏	♐19	♐	♑21	♑	♒22	♒	♓22	♓	♓	♈1	♈	♉5	♉	♊12	♊
Aug	♋22	♋	♋	♌9	♌	♍22	♍	♍	♎11	♎	♏22	♏	♏	♐4	♐	♑7	♑	♒8	♒	♓7	♓	♈8	♈	♉11	♉	♊18	♊	♊	♋4	♋	♌15
Sep	♌	♌	♍4	♍	♎17	♎	♎	♏5	♏	♐13	♐	♑17	♑	♒19	♒	♓18	♓	♈18	♈	♉20	♉	♉	♊1	♊	♋9	♋	♌21	♌	♌	♍10	
Oct	♍	♎23	♎	♎	♏10	♏	♐19	♐	♐	♑1	♑	♒4	♒	♓5	♓	♈5	♈	♉6	♉	♊9	♊	♋17	♋	♋	♌4	♌	♍17	♍	♍	♎6	♎
Nov	♏16	♏	♏	♐1	♐	♑7	♑	♒12	♒	♓14	♓	♈15	♈	♉16	♉	♊19	♊	♊	♋1	♋	♌12	♌	♌	♍0	♍	♎13	♎	♏23	♏	♏	
Dec	♐7	♐	♑13	♑	♒17	♒	♓20	♓	♈23	♈	♈	♉2	♉	♊5	♊	♋11	♋	♌20	♌	♌	♍9	♍	♎21	♎	♎	♏8	♏	♐15	♐	♑20	♑

1998	1	2	3	4	5	6	7	8	9	10	11	12	13	14	15	16	17	18	19	20	21	22	23	24	25	26	27	28	29	30	31
Jan	♒23	♒	♒	♓2	♓	♈5	♈	♉9	♉	♊13	♊	♋20	♋	♋	♌5	♌	♍17	♍	♍	♎6	♎	♏17	♏	♏	♐1	♐	♑6	♑	♒8	♒	♓9
Feb	♓	♈10	♈	♉14	♉	♊19	♊	♊	♋3	♋	♌12	♌	♌	♍0	♍	♎13	♎	♎	♏1	♏	♐11	♐	♑16	♑	♒18	♒	♓18	♓			
Mar	♈18	♈	♉20	♉	♉	♊1	♊	♋8	♋	♌19	♌	♌	♍7	♍	♎20	♎	♎	♏8	♏	♐19	♐	♐	♑2	♑	♒5	♒	♓5	♓	♈5	♈	♉5
Apr	♉	♊8	♊	♋14	♋	♋	♌1	♌	♍13	♍	♍	♎2	♎	♏14	♏	♏	♐1	♐	♑9	♑	♒14	♒	♓16	♓	♈16	♈	♉16	♉	♊17	♊	
May	♋22	♋	♋	♌7	♌	♍19	♍	♍	♎8	♎	♏20	♏	♏	♐6	♐	♑15	♑	♒21	♒	♒	♓0	♓	♈2	♈	♉2	♉	♊3	♊	♋7	♋	♌15
Jun	♌	♌	♍2	♍	♎15	♎	♎	♏3	♏	♐13	♐	♑20	♑	♑	♒2	♒	♓6	♓	♈9	♈	♉11	♉	♊13	♊	♋17	♋	♋	♌0	♌	♍10	
Jul	♍	♎23	♎	♎	♏11	♏	♐21	♐	♐	♑4	♑	♒8	♒	♓12	♓	♈15	♈	♉17	♉	♊21	♊	♊	♋1	♋	♌8	♌	♍19	♍	♍	♎7	♎
Aug	♏19	♏	♏	♐5	♐	♑12	♑	♒16	♒	♓18	♓	♈20	♈	♉23	♉	♉	♊3	♊	♋8	♋	♌16	♌	♌	♍2	♍	♎15	♎	♎	♏3	♏	♐14
Sep	♐	♑22	♑	♑	♒2	♒	♓3	♓	♈4	♈	♉5	♉	♊8	♊	♋14	♋	♌22	♌	♌	♍9	♍	♎21	♎	♎	♏10	♏	♐22	♐	♐	♑7	
Oct	♑	♒12	♒	♓14	♓	♈14	♈	♉13	♉	♊15	♊	♋20	♋	♋	♌4	♌	♍15	♍	♍	♎4	♎	♏16	♏	♏	♐4	♐	♑15	♑	♒22	♒	♒
Nov	♓1	♓	♈1	♈	♉0	♉	♊0	♊	♋3	♋	♌10	♌	♍21	♍	♍	♎10	♎	♏22	♏	♏	♐10	♐	♑20	♑	♑	♒5	♒	♓10	♓	♈11	
Dec	♈	♉11	♉	♊11	♊	♋13	♋	♌18	♌	♌	♍4	♍	♎16	♎	♎	♏5	♏	♐16	♐	♐	♑2	♑	♒10	♒	♓16	♓	♈19	♈	♉21	♉	♊22

1999	1	2	3	4	5	6	7	8	9	10	11	12	13	14	15	16	17	18	19	20	21	22	23	24	25	26	27	28	29	30	31
Jan	♊	♋23	♋	♋	♌4	♌	♍12	♍	♍	♎0	♎	♏12	♏	♏	♐0	♐	♑9	♑	♒16	♒	♓21	♓	♓	♈1	♈	♉4	♉	♊6	♊	♋9	♋
Feb	♌14	♌	♍22	♍	♍	♎8	♎	♏21	♏	♏	♐8	♐	♑18	♑	♑	♒0	♒	♓4	♓	♈7	♈	♉9	♉	♊12	♊	♋16	♋	♌22			
Mar	♌	♌	♍6	♍	♎17	♎	♎	♏5	♏	♐17	♐	♐	♑3	♑	♒10	♒	♓13	♓	♈15	♈	♉15	♉	♊18	♊	♋22	♋	♋	♌5	♌	♍13	♍
Apr	♍	♎0	♎	♏12	♏	♏	♐1	♐	♑12	♑	♒20	♒	♒	♓0	♓	♈1	♈	♉0	♉	♊1	♊	♋4	♋	♌10	♌	♍19	♍	♍	♎7	♎	
May	♏19	♏	♏	♐7	♐	♑19	♑	♑	♒5	♒	♓10	♓	♈11	♈	♉11	♉	♊10	♊	♋12	♋	♌16	♌	♌	♍1	♍	♎12	♎	♎	♏1	♏	♐13
Jun	♐	♐	♑1	♑	♒11	♒	♓18	♓	♈21	♈	♉22	♉	♊21	♊	♋21	♋	♋	♌1	♌	♍8	♍	♎19	♎	♎	♏7	♏	♐19	♐	♐	♑7	
Jul	♑	♒17	♒	♒	♓0	♓	♈4	♈	♉6	♉	♊7	♊	♋8	♋	♌10	♌	♍16	♍	♍	♎2	♎	♏14	♏	♏	♐2	♐	♑14	♑	♒23	♒	♒
Aug	♓5	♓	♈10	♈	♉13	♉	♊15	♊	♋17	♋	♌20	♌	♌	♍2	♍	♎10	♎	♏22	♏	♏	♐10	♐	♑21	♑	♑	♒6	♒	♓12	♓	♈16	♈
Sep	♉19	♉	♊21	♊	♊	♋0	♋	♌5	♌	♍10	♍	♎19	♎	♎	♏6	♏	♐18	♐	♐	♑6	♑	♒15	♒	♓21	♓	♈23	♈	♈	♉1	♉	
Oct	♊3	♊	♋6	♋	♌11	♌	♍18	♍	♍	♎3	♎	♏13	♏	♏	♐2	♐	♑15	♑	♑	♒1	♒	♓7	♓	♈9	♈	♉9	♉	♊10	♊	♋12	♋
Nov	♌16	♌	♌	♍0	♍	♎9	♎	♏20	♏	♏	♐9	♐	♑22	♑	♑	♒9	♒	♓17	♓	♈20	♈	♉20	♉	♊19	♊	♋20	♋	♌23	♌	♌	
Dec	♍5	♍	♎15	♎	♎	♏3	♏	♐15	♐	♐	♑4	♑	♒16	♒	♒	♓1	♓	♈6	♈	♉7	♉	♊7	♊	♋6	♋	♌8	♌	♍12	♍	♎21	♎

2000	1	2	3	4	5	6	7	8	9	10	11	12	13	14	15	16	17	18	19	20	21	22	23	24	25	26	27	28	29	30	31
Jan	♎	♏9	♏	♐21	♐	♐	♑10	♑	♒22	♒	♒	♓7	♓	♈13	♈	♉17	♉	♊18	♊	♋18	♋	♌18	♌	♍22	♍	♍	♎5	♎	♏15	♏	♏
Feb	♐4	♐	♑17	♑	♑	♒4	♒	♓12	♓	♈19	♈	♈	♉0	♉	♊2	♊	♋4	♋	♌5	♌	♍8	♍	♎14	♎	♏23	♏	♏	♐12	♐		
Mar	♐	♑0	♑	♒11	♒	♓19	♓	♓	♈1	♈	♉5	♉	♊8	♊	♋11	♋	♌14	♌	♍18	♍	♎23	♎	♎	♏8	♏	♐20	♐	♐	♑9	♑	♒20
Apr	♒	♒	♓4	♓	♈9	♈	♉11	♉	♊13	♊	♋16	♋	♌20	♌	♌	♍1	♍	♎8	♎	♏16	♏	♏	♐4	♐	♑17	♑	♑	♒5	♒	♓13	
May	♓	♈18	♈	♉20	♉	♊21	♊	♋22	♋	♋	♌1	♌	♍7	♍	♎14	♎	♎	♏0	♏	♐11	♐	♐	♑0	♑	♒13	♒	♓22	♓	♓	♈4	♈
Jun	♉6	♉	♊6	♊	♋6	♋	♌8	♌	♍12	♍	♎20	♎	♎	♏6	♏	♐17	♐	♐	♑6	♑	♒19	♒	♒	♓6	♓	♈13	♈	♉16	♉	♊17	
Jul	♊	♋16	♋	♌17	♌	♍19	♍	♍	♎2	♎	♏11	♏	♐23	♐	♐	♑12	♑	♑	♒1	♒	♓12	♓	♈20	♈	♈	♉1	♉	♊3	♊	♋3	♋
Aug	♌3	♌	♍5	♍	♎9	♎	♏18	♏	♏	♐6	♐	♑19	♑	♑	♒7	♒	♓18	♓	♓	♈2	♈	♉8	♉	♊11	♊	♋13	♋	♌13	♌	♍15	♍
Sep	♎18	♎	♎	♏2	♏	♐13	♐	♐	♑2	♑	♒14	♒	♒	♓0	♓	♈8	♈	♉13	♉	♊17	♊	♋20	♋	♌22	♌	♌	♍0	♍	♎4	♎	
Oct	♏11	♏	♐21	♐	♐	♑10	♑	♒22	♒	♒	♓8	♓	♈15	♈	♉19	♉	♊23	♊	♊	♋2	♋	♌5	♌	♍8	♍	♎13	♎	♏20	♏	♏	♐5
Nov	♐	♑18	♑	♑	♒7	♒	♓17	♓	♓	♈0	♈	♉4	♉	♊6	♊	♋7	♋	♌10	♌	♍14	♍	♎20	♎	♎	♏3	♏	♐13	♐	♐	♑2	
Dec	♑	♒15	♒	♒	♓2	♓	♈10	♈	♉14	♉	♊16	♊	♋16	♋	♌17	♌	♍20	♍	♍	♎1	♎	♏10	♏	♐20	♐	♐	♑8	♑	♒22	♒	♒

2001	1	2	3	4	5	6	7	8	9	10	11	12	13	14	15	16	17	18	19	20	21	22	23	24	25	26	27	28	29	30	31
Jan	♓10	♓	♈19	♈	♈	♉1	♉	♊3	♊	♋3	♋	♌2	♌	♍3	♍	♎7	♎	♏15	♏	♏	♐2	♐	♑15	♑	♑	♒4	♒	♓16	♓	♓	♈2
Feb	♈	♉10	♉	♊13	♊	♋14	♋	♌13	♌	♍13	♍	♎16	♎	♏22	♏	♏	♐8	♐	♑21	♑	♑	♒10	♒	♓22	♓	♓	♈8	♈			
Mar	♉16	♉	♊21	♊	♊	♋0	♋	♌0	♌	♍0	♍	♎2	♎	♏6	♏	♐15	♐	♐	♑4	♑	♒17	♒	♒	♓4	♓	♈14	♈	♉21	♉	♉	♊3
Apr	♊	♋7	♋	♌9	♌	♍10	♍	♎12	♎	♏16	♏	♏	♐0	♐	♑11	♑	♑	♒0	♒	♓12	♓	♈21	♈	♈	♉4	♉	♊9	♊	♋12	♋	
May	♌15	♌	♍18	♍	♎21	♎	♎	♏1	♏	♐9	♐	♑20	♑	♑	♒8	♒	♓20	♓	♓	♈6	♈	♉12	♉	♊16	♊	♋18	♋	♌21	♌	♌	♍0
Jun	♍	♎4	♎	♏9	♏	♐17	♐	♐	♑4	♑	♒16	♒	♒	♓4	♓	♈15	♈	♉21	♉	♉	♊1	♊	♋2	♋	♌3	♌	♍5	♍	♎9	♎	
Jul	♏15	♏	♏	♐0	♐	♑11	♑	♒23	♒	♒	♓12	♓	♈23	♈	♈	♉7	♉	♊11	♊	♋12	♋	♌12	♌	♍13	♍	♎15	♎	♏21	♏	♏	♐6
Aug	♐	♑17	♑	♑	♒6	♒	♓18	♓	♓	♈6	♈	♉15	♉	♊21	♊	♋23	♋	♌23	♌	♍22	♍	♎23	♎	♎	♏3	♏	♐12	♐	♑23	♑	♑
Sep	♒12	♒	♒	♓0	♓	♈12	♈	♉22	♉	♉	♊5	♊	♋8	♋	♌9	♌	♍9	♍	♎9	♎	♏12	♏	♐19	♐	♐	♑5	♑	♒18	♒	♒	
Oct	♓6	♓	♈18	♈	♈	♉3	♉	♊11	♊	♋16	♋	♌18	♌	♍19	♍	♎20	♎	♏22	♏	♏	♐3	♐	♑13	♑	♑	♒1	♒	♓14	♓	♓	♈1
Nov	♈	♉9	♉	♊16	♊	♋21	♋	♋	♌1	♌	♍3	♍	♎5	♎	♏8	♏	♐13	♐	♑22	♑	♑	♒9	♒	♓22	♓	♓	♈9	♈	♉17	♉	
Dec	♊23	♊	♊	♋3	♋	♌6	♌	♍9	♍	♎12	♎	♏16	♏	♐22	♐	♐	♑6	♑	♒18	♒	♒	♓6	♓	♈18	♈	♈	♉3	♉	♊9	♊	♋11

2002	1	2	3	4	5	6	7	8	9	10	11	12	13	14	15	16	17	18	19	20	21	22	23	24	25	26	27	28	29	30	31
Jan	♋	♌13	♌	♍15	♍	♎18	♎	♏22	♏	♏	♐5	♐	♑14	♑	♑	♒1	♒	♓14	♓	♓	♈2	♈	♉13	♉	♊19	♊	♋22	♋	♌22	♌	♍22
Feb	♍	♍	♎0	♎	♏4	♏	♐11	♐	♑21	♑	♑	♒8	♒	♓21	♓	♓	♈9	♈	♉21	♉	♉	♊5	♊	♋9	♋	♌9	♌	♍9			
Mar	♍	♎8	♎	♏11	♏	♐17	♐	♐	♑2	♑	♒14	♒	♒	♓3	♓	♈15	♈	♈	♉3	♉	♊12	♊	♋18	♋	♌20	♌	♍20	♍	♎19	♎	♏20
Apr	♏	♏	♐0	♐	♑9	♑	♒20	♒	♒	♓9	♓	♈21	♈	♈	♉9	♉	♊18	♊	♊	♋1	♋	♌5	♌	♍6	♍	♎6	♎	♏7	♏	♐10	
May	♐	♑17	♑	♑	♒3	♒	♓15	♓	♓	♈4	♈	♉15	♉	♉	♊0	♊	♋6	♋	♌11	♌	♍14	♍	♎15	♎	♏17	♏	♐20	♐	♐	♑2	♑
Jun	♒11	♒	♓23	♓	♓	♈11	♈	♉22	♉	♉	♊7	♊	♋12	♋	♌16	♌	♍19	♍	♎22	♎	♎	♏1	♏	♐5	♐	♑11	♑	♒20	♒	♒	
Jul	♓7	♓	♈19	♈	♈	♉7	♉	♊15	♊	♋20	♋	♌23	♌	♌	♍1	♍	♎3	♎	♏7	♏	♐12	♐	♑19	♑	♑	♒4	♒	♓15	♓	♓	♈3
Aug	♈	♉15	♉	♉	♊0	♊	♋6	♋	♌8	♌	♍8	♍	♎9	♎	♏12	♏	♐18	♐	♐	♑1	♑	♒11	♒	♓22	♓	♓	♈11	♈	♉23	♉	♉
Sep	♊9	♊	♋16	♋	♌18	♌	♍18	♍	♎18	♎	♏19	♏	♐23	♐	♐	♑7	♑	♒17	♒	♒	♓4	♓	♈17	♈	♈	♉6	♉	♊17	♊	♊	
Oct	♋1	♋	♌4	♌	♍5	♍	♎4	♎	♏4	♏	♐6	♐	♑13	♑	♒23	♒	♒	♓10	♓	♈23	♈	♈	♉11	♉	♊23	♊	♊	♋8	♋	♌13	♌
Nov	♍15	♍	♎15	♎	♏15	♏	♐16	♐	♑21	♑	♑	♒5	♒	♓17	♓	♓	♈6	♈	♉18	♉	♉	♊5	♊	♋13	♋	♌19	♌	♍23	♍	♍	
Dec	♎1	♎	♏2	♏	♐3	♐	♑7	♑	♒14	♒	♒	♓0	♓	♈13	♈	♈	♉1	♉	♊12	♊	♋19	♋	♋	♌1	♌	♍5	♍	♎8	♎	♏10	♏

2003	1	2	3	4	5	6	7	8	9	10	11	12	13	14	15	16	17	18	19	20	21	22	23	24	25	26	27	28	29	30	31
Jan	♐13	♐	♑17	♑	♒23	♒	♒	♓9	♓	♈21	♈	♈	♉9	♉	♊20	♊	♊	♋3	♋	♌8	♌	♍11	♍	♎13	♎	♏17	♏	♐20	♐	♐	♑1
Feb	♑	♒8	♒	♓17	♓	♓	♈5	♈	♉18	♉	♉	♊5	♊	♋13	♋	♌17	♌	♍18	♍	♎20	♎	♏22	♏	♏	♐2	♐	♑8	♑			
Mar	♒15	♒	♒	♓1	♓	♈13	♈	♈	♉2	♉	♊14	♊	♋23	♋	♋	♌3	♌	♍4	♍	♎4	♎	♏5	♏	♐8	♐	♑13	♑	♒21	♒	♒	♓8
Apr	♓	♈19	♈	♈	♉8	♉	♊21	♊	♊	♋7	♋	♌13	♌	♍15	♍	♎15	♎	♏15	♏	♐16	♐	♑19	♑	♑	♒3	♒	♓13	♓	♓	♈2	
May	♈	♉15	♉	♉	♊3	♊	♋14	♋	♌21	♌	♌	♍1	♍	♎2	♎	♏2	♏	♐2	♐	♑4	♑	♒10	♒	♓19	♓	♓	♈8	♈	♉21	♉	♉
Jun	♊9	♊	♋19	♋	♋	♌3	♌	♍9	♍	♎11	♎	♏12	♏	♐12	♐	♑14	♑	♒18	♒	♒	♓3	♓	♈14	♈	♈	♉3	♉	♊16	♊	♊	
Jul	♋1	♋	♌9	♌	♍14	♍	♎18	♎	♏20	♏	♐22	♐	♐	♑0	♑	♒4	♒	♓11	♓	♈22	♈	♈	♉11	♉	♊23	♊	♊	♋9	♋	♌15	♌
Aug	♍20	♍	♎23	♎	♎	♏2	♏	♐5	♐	♑8	♑	♒13	♒	♓20	♓	♓	♈6	♈	♉19	♉	♉	♊7	♊	♋17	♋	♌23	♌	♌	♍3	♍	♎5
Sep	♎	♏8	♏	♐11	♐	♑15	♑	♒20	♒	♒	♓4	♓	♈14	♈	♈	♉3	♉	♊16	♊	♊	♋2	♋	♌9	♌	♍12	♍	♎14	♎	♏14	♏	
Oct	♐16	♐	♑20	♑	♑	♒3	♒	♓11	♓	♈21	♈	♈	♉10	♉	♊23	♊	♊	♋11	♋	♌19	♌	♍23	♍	♍	♎0	♎	♏0	♏	♐0	♐	♑2
Nov	♑	♒8	♒	♓17	♓	♓	♈4	♈	♉16	♉	♉	♊5	♊	♋17	♋	♋	♌3	♌	♍9	♍	♎11	♎	♏11	♏	♐10	♐	♑11	♑	♒15	♒	
Dec	♓23	♓	♓	♈10	♈	♉23	♉	♉	♊11	♊	♋23	♋	♋	♌9	♌	♍17	♍	♎21	♎	♏22	♏	♐22	♐	♑22	♑	♑	♒0	♒	♓6	♓	♈16

2004	1	2	3	4	5	6	7	8	9	10	11	12	13	14	15	16	17	18	19	20	21	22	23	24	25	26	27	28	29	30	31
Jan	♈	♈	♉5	♉	♊18	♊	♊	♋5	♋	♌15	♌	♍22	♍	♍	♎4	♎	♏7	♏	♐8	♐	♑9	♑	♒11	♒	♓15	♓	♓	♈0	♈	♉12	♉
Feb	♉	♊1	♊	♋13	♋	♌21	♌	♌	♍4	♍	♎9	♎	♏13	♏	♐16	♐	♑18	♑	♒20	♒	♒	♓1	♓	♈9	♈	♉21	♉	♉	♊9		
Mar	♊	♋21	♋	♋	♌6	♌	♍11	♍	♎15	♎	♏18	♏	♐21	♐	♐	♑0	♑	♒4	♒	♓10	♓	♈18	♈	♈	♉5	♉	♊18	♊	♊	♋6	♋
Apr	♌15	♌	♍21	♍	♍	♎0	♎	♏1	♏	♐3	♐	♑6	♑	♒10	♒	♓17	♓	♓	♈1	♈	♉13	♉	♉	♊1	♊	♋14	♋	♋	♌0	♌	
May	♍7	♍	♎10	♎	♏11	♏	♐11	♐	♑12	♑	♒16	♒	♓22	♓	♓	♈8	♈	♉19	♉	♉	♊8	♊	♋20	♋	♋	♌8	♌	♍16	♍	♎20	♎
Jun	♏22	♏	♐21	♐	♑21	♑	♒23	♒	♒	♓4	♓	♈13	♈	♈	♉1	♉	♊14	♊	♊	♋2	♋	♌14	♌	♍23	♍	♍	♎5	♎	♏8	♏	
Jul	♐8	♐	♑7	♑	♒8	♒	♓12	♓	♈20	♈	♈	♉7	♉	♊20	♊	♊	♋8	♋	♌19	♌	♌	♍5	♍	♎12	♎	♏16	♏	♐17	♐	♑18	♑
Aug	♒18	♒	♓21	♓	♓	♈3	♈	♉14	♉	♉	♊3	♊	♋15	♋	♋	♌2	♌	♍10	♍	♎17	♎	♏22	♏	♏	♐1	♐	♑3	♑	♒4	♒	♓7
Sep	♓	♈12	♈	♉22	♉	♉	♊10	♊	♋22	♋	♋	♌9	♌	♍17	♍	♎23	♎	♎	♏3	♏	♐7	♐	♑9	♑	♒12	♒	♓16	♓	♈22	♈	
Oct	♈	♉7	♉	♊18	♊	♊	♋7	♋	♌18	♌	♌	♍2	♍	♎7	♎	♏10	♏	♐12	♐	♑15	♑	♒18	♒	♓23	♓	♓	♈6	♈	♉15	♉	♉
Nov	♊2	♊	♋15	♋	♋	♌3	♌	♍12	♍	♎17	♎	♏20	♏	♐20	♐	♑21	♑	♑	♒0	♒	♓5	♓	♈12	♈	♉22	♉	♉	♊10	♊	♋22	
Dec	♋	♋	♌10	♌	♍21	♍	♍	♎4	♎	♏6	♏	♐7	♐	♑6	♑	♒7	♒	♓10	♓	♈18	♈	♈	♉4	♉	♊16	♊	♊	♋4	♋	♌17	♌

2005	1	2	3	4	5	6	7	8	9	10	11	12	13	14	15	16	17	18	19	20	21	22	23	24	25	26	27	28	29	30	31
Jan	♌	♍4	♍	♎13	♎	♏17	♏	♐18	♐	♑17	♑	♒17	♒	♓18	♓	♓	♈0	♈	♉10	♉	♊22	♊	♊	♋11	♋	♌23	♌	♌	♍10	♍	♎19
Feb	♎	♎	♏1	♏	♐4	♐	♑4	♑	♒4	♒	♓5	♓	♈9	♈	♉17	♉	♉	♊5	♊	♋17	♋	♋	♌5	♌	♍16	♍	♍	♎1			
Mar	♎	♏7	♏	♐11	♐	♑13	♑	♒14	♒	♓15	♓	♈19	♈	♈	♉2	♉	♊12	♊	♊	♋0	♋	♌13	♌	♍23	♍	♍	♎7	♎	♏13	♏	♐17
Apr	♐	♑20	♑	♒22	♒	♒	♓1	♓	♈4	♈	♉11	♉	♊21	♊	♊	♋9	♋	♌21	♌	♌	♍7	♍	♎15	♎	♏20	♏	♐23	♐	♐	♑1	
May	♑	♒4	♒	♓8	♓	♈13	♈	♉20	♉	♉	♊5	♊	♋17	♋	♋	♌5	♌	♍16	♍	♍	♎0	♎	♏5	♏	♐7	♐	♑8	♑	♒10	♒	♓13
Jun	♓	♈19	♈	♈	♉3	♉	♊12	♊	♊	♋0	♋	♌13	♌	♌	♍1	♍	♎10	♎	♏15	♏	♐17	♐	♑17	♑	♒17	♒	♓19	♓	♓	♈0	
Jul	♈	♉8	♉	♊19	♊	♊	♋6	♋	♌19	♌	♌	♍8	♍	♎18	♎	♎	♏0	♏	♐3	♐	♑3	♑	♒2	♒	♓3	♓	♈7	♈	♉14	♉	♉
Aug	♊0	♊	♋12	♋	♋	♌1	♌	♍13	♍	♍	♎0	♎	♏8	♏	♐12	♐	♑13	♑	♒13	♒	♓13	♓	♈15	♈	♉21	♉	♉	♊6	♊	♋18	♋
Sep	♋	♌7	♌	♍19	♍	♍	♎6	♎	♏14	♏	♐20	♐	♑23	♑	♒23	♒	♓23	♓	♓	♈1	♈	♉6	♉	♊14	♊	♊	♋1	♋	♌14	♌	
Oct	♌	♍2	♍	♎12	♎	♏20	♏	♏	♐2	♐	♑5	♑	♒8	♒	♓9	♓	♈11	♈	♉15	♉	♊23	♊	♊	♋9	♋	♌22	♌	♌	♍10	♍	♎20
Nov	♎	♎	♏3	♏	♐7	♐	♑11	♑	♒14	♒	♓17	♓	♈20	♈	♈	♉1	♉	♊8	♊	♋18	♋	♋	♌6	♌	♍18	♍	♍	♎5	♎	♏11	
Dec	♏	♐15	♐	♑17	♑	♒19	♒	♓22	♓	♓	♈3	♈	♉8	♉	♊16	♊	♊	♋2	♋	♌14	♌	♌	♍3	♍	♎14	♎	♏22	♏	♏	♐1	♐

2006	1	2	3	4	5	6	7	8	9	10	11	12	13	14	15	16	17	18	19	20	21	22	23	24	25	26	27	28	29	30	31
Jan	♑2	♑	♒2	♒	♓4	♓	♈8	♈	♉14	♉	♊23	♊	♊	♋9	♋	♌21	♌	♌	♍10	♍	♎22	♎	♎	♏7	♏	♐12	♐	♑13	♑	♒13	♒
Feb	♓12	♓	♈14	♈	♉20	♉	♉	♊4	♊	♋15	♋	♋	♌3	♌	♍16	♍	♍	♎5	♎	♏15	♏	♐21	♐	♐	♑0	♑	♒0	♓23			
Mar	♓	♓	♈0	♈	♉3	♉	♊10	♊	♋21	♋	♋	♌10	♌	♍22	♍	♍	♎11	♎	♏21	♏	♏	♐4	♐	♑9	♑	♒10	♒	♓10	♓	♈11	♈
Apr	♉13	♉	♊18	♊	♊	♋4	♋	♌16	♌	♌	♍5	♍	♎17	♎	♎	♏2	♏	♐10	♐	♑15	♑	♒18	♒	♓20	♓	♈21	♈	♉23	♉	♉	
May	♊4	♊	♋12	♋	♌23	♌	♌	♍12	♍	♍	♎0	♎	♏9	♏	♐16	♐	♑20	♑	♑	♒0	♒	♓3	♓	♈5	♈	♉8	♉	♊13	♊	♋21	♋
Jun	♋	♌8	♌	♍20	♍	♍	♎8	♎	♏18	♏	♐23	♐	♐	♑3	♑	♒5	♒	♓8	♓	♈11	♈	♉16	♉	♊21	♊	♊	♋5	♋	♌16	♌	
Jul	♌	♍4	♍	♎17	♎	♎	♏3	♏	♐9	♐	♑11	♑	♒13	♒	♓14	♓	♈17	♈	♉21	♉	♉	♊4	♊	♋12	♋	♌23	♌	♌	♍12	♍	♍
Aug	♎1	♎	♏11	♏	♐18	♐	♑21	♑	♒22	♒	♓22	♓	♈23	♈	♈	♉3	♉	♊9	♊	♋18	♋	♋	♌5	♌	♍18	♍	♍	♎7	♎	♏19	♏
Sep	♏	♐3	♐	♑8	♑	♒9	♒	♓8	♓	♈8	♈	♉10	♉	♊15	♊	♊	♋0	♋	♌11	♌	♌	♍0	♍	♎13	♎	♎	♏1	♏	♐10	♐	
Oct	♑16	♑	♒19	♒	♓20	♓	♈19	♈	♉20	♉	♊23	♊	♊	♋6	♋	♌17	♌	♌	♍7	♍	♎19	♎	♎	♏7	♏	♐16	♐	♑23	♑	♑	♒3
Nov	♒	♓5	♓	♈6	♈	♉6	♉	♊9	♊	♋15	♋	♋	♌1	♌	♍13	♍	♍	♎2	♎	♏13	♏	♐22	♐	♐	♑4	♑	♒9	♒	♓13	♓	
Dec	♈15	♈	♉17	♉	♊19	♊	♊	♋0	♋	♌9	♌	♍21	♍	♍	♎10	♎	♏21	♏	♏	♐5	♐	♑11	♑	♒15	♒	♓18	♓	♈21	♈	♈	♉0

2007	1	2	3	4	5	6	7	8	9	10	11	12	13	14	15	16	17	18	19	20	21	22	23	24	25	26	27	28	29	30	31
Jan	♉	♊4	♊	♋10	♋	♌18	♌	♌	♍6	♍	♎18	♎	♎	♏6	♏	♐14	♐	♑19	♑	♒22	♒	♒	♓0	♓	♈3	♈	♉6	♉	♊11	♊	♋17
Feb	♋	♋	♌2	♌	♍14	♍	♍	♎2	♎	♏15	♏	♏	♐0	♐	♑6	♑	♒8	♒	♓9	♓	♈10	♈	♉12	♉	♊16	♊	♊	♋0			
Mar	♋	♌9	♌	♍21	♍	♍	♎10	♎	♏22	♏	♏	♐9	♐	♑16	♑	♒19	♒	♓20	♓	♈19	♈	♉20	♉	♊23	♊	♊	♋5	♋	♌15	♌	♌
Apr	♍3	♍	♎16	♎	♎	♏4	♏	♐16	♐	♐	♑0	♑	♒5	♒	♓6	♓	♈6	♈	♉6	♉	♊7	♊	♋12	♋	♌21	♌	♌	♍9	♍	♎22	
May	♎	♎	♏10	♏	♐21	♐	♐	♑6	♑	♒13	♒	♓16	♓	♈17	♈	♉16	♉	♊17	♊	♋21	♋	♋	♌4	♌	♍16	♍	♍	♎5	♎	♏17	♏
Jun	♏	♐3	♐	♑12	♑	♒18	♒	♓23	♓	♓	♈1	♈	♉2	♉	♊3	♊	♋6	♋	♌13	♌	♍23	♍	♍	♎12	♎	♎	♏0	♏	♐10	♐	
Jul	♑18	♑	♑	♒0	♒	♓4	♓	♈7	♈	♉10	♉	♊12	♊	♋15	♋	♌22	♌	♌	♍8	♍	♎20	♎	♎	♏8	♏	♐18	♐	♐	♑2	♑	♒7
Aug	♒	♓10	♓	♈13	♈	♉15	♉	♊19	♊	♋23	♋	♋	♌6	♌	♍16	♍	♍	♎4	♎	♏16	♏	♏	♐3	♐	♑11	♑	♒16	♒	♓18	♓	♈19
Sep	♈	♉21	♉	♉	♊0	♊	♋5	♋	♌13	♌	♍23	♍	♍	♎11	♎	♎	♏0	♏	♐12	♐	♑21	♑	♑	♒2	♒	♓4	♓	♈4	♈	♉4	
Oct	♉	♊6	♊	♋11	♋	♌19	♌	♌	♍6	♍	♎18	♎	♎	♏6	♏	♐19	♐	♐	♑5	♑	♒12	♒	♓15	♓	♈15	♈	♉14	♉	♊14	♊	♋17
Nov	♋	♋	♌1	♌	♍11	♍	♍	♎0	♎	♏12	♏	♏	♐0	♐	♑11	♑	♒20	♒	♒	♓1	♓	♈2	♈	♉2	♉	♊1	♊	♋3	♋	♌8	
Dec	♌	♍17	♍	♍	♎6	♎	♏19	♏	♏	♐6	♐	♑17	♑	♑	♒2	♒	♓8	♓	♈11	♈	♉12	♉	♊12	♊	♋13	♋	♌17	♌	♌	♍1	♍

2008	1	2	3	4	5	6	7	8	9	10	11	12	13	14	15	16	17	18	19	20	21	22	23	24	25	26	27	28	29	30	31
Jan	♎13	♎	♎	♏2	♏	♐13	♐	♑23	♑	♑	♒7	♒	♓13	♓	♈17	♈	♉20	♉	♊22	♊	♊	♋0	♋	♌3	♌	♍11	♍	♎21	♎	♎	♏9
Feb	♏	♐21	♐	♐	♑7	♑	♒15	♒	♓19	♓	♈23	♈	♈	♉2	♉	♊5	♊	♋8	♋	♌13	♌	♍20	♍	♍	♎6	♎	♏18	♏	♏		
Mar	♐6	♐	♑16	♑	♑	♒0	♒	♓4	♓	♈6	♈	♉7	♉	♊10	♊	♋14	♋	♌20	♌	♌	♍4	♍	♎14	♎	♎	♏1	♏	♐14	♐	♐	♑1
Apr	♑	♒10	♒	♓14	♓	♈15	♈	♉15	♉	♊16	♊	♋19	♋	♋	♌1	♌	♍10	♍	♎21	♎	♎	♏8	♏	♐21	♐	♐	♑9	♑	♒19	♒	
May	♒	♓0	♓	♈2	♈	♉1	♉	♊1	♊	♋2	♋	♌7	♌	♍16	♍	♍	♎3	♎	♏15	♏	♏	♐3	♐	♑15	♑	♑	♒2	♒	♓9	♓	♈12
Jun	♈	♉12	♉	♊11	♊	♋12	♋	♌15	♌	♍22	♍	♍	♎8	♎	♏21	♏	♏	♐9	♐	♑21	♑	♑	♒8	♒	♓15	♓	♈20	♈	♉22	♉	
Jul	♊22	♊	♋22	♋	♋	♌0	♌	♍6	♍	♎15	♎	♎	♏3	♏	♐16	♐	♐	♑3	♑	♒13	♒	♓21	♓	♓	♈2	♈	♉5	♉	♊7	♊	♋8
Aug	♋	♌10	♌	♍15	♍	♎23	♎	♎	♏11	♏	♐23	♐	♐	♑11	♑	♒20	♒	♒	♓3	♓	♈8	♈	♉11	♉	♊14	♊	♋16	♋	♌19	♌	♌
Sep	♍0	♍	♎8	♎	♏19	♏	♏	♐7	♐	♑19	♑	♑	♒5	♒	♓11	♓	♈14	♈	♉17	♉	♊19	♊	♋22	♋	♋	♌3	♌	♍9	♍	♎16	
Oct	♎	♎	♏3	♏	♐15	♐	♐	♑4	♑	♒14	♒	♓20	♓	♈23	♈	♈	♉0	♉	♊1	♊	♋4	♋	♌8	♌	♍15	♍	♍	♎0	♎	♏10	♏
Nov	♐22	♐	♐	♑11	♑	♒23	♒	♒	♓6	♓	♈10	♈	♉10	♉	♊10	♊	♋11	♋	♌14	♌	♍20	♍	♍	♎6	♎	♏17	♏	♏	♐5	♐	
Dec	♑18	♑	♑	♒6	♒	♓15	♓	♈20	♈	♉22	♉	♊21	♊	♋20	♋	♌22	♌	♌	♍3	♍	♎11	♎	♏23	♏	♏	♐11	♐	♐	♑0	♑	♒12

2009	1	2	3	4	5	6	7	8	9	10	11	12	13	14	15	16	17	18	19	20	21	22	23	24	25	26	27	28	29	30	31
Jan	♒	♓22	♓	♓	♈5	♈	♉8	♉	♊8	♊	♋8	♋	♌8	♌	♍11	♍	♎18	♎	♎	♏5	♏	♐18	♐	♐	♑6	♑	♒18	♒	♒	♓4	♓
Feb	♈11	♈	♉16	♉	♊18	♊	♋18	♋	♌19	♌	♍22	♍	♍	♎3	♎	♏12	♏	♏	♐1	♐	♑13	♑	♑	♒1	♒	♓10	♓	♈16			
Mar	♈	♉21	♉	♉	♊1	♊	♋3	♋	♌5	♌	♍8	♍	♎13	♎	♏21	♏	♏	♐9	♐	♑21	♑	♑	♒9	♒	♓18	♓	♈23	♈	♈	♉3	♉
Apr	♊6	♊	♋9	♋	♌12	♌	♍16	♍	♎22	♎	♎	♏6	♏	♐17	♐	♐	♑6	♑	♒18	♒	♒	♓3	♓	♈8	♈	♉11	♉	♊12	♊	♋14	
May	♋	♌18	♌	♍23	♍	♍	♎5	♎	♏14	♏	♏	♐1	♐	♑13	♑	♑	♒2	♒	♓12	♓	♈18	♈	♉20	♉	♊21	♊	♋21	♋	♌23	♌	♌
Jun	♍4	♍	♎11	♎	♏20	♏	♏	♐7	♐	♑20	♑	♑	♒9	♒	♓20	♓	♓	♈3	♈	♉7	♉	♊7	♊	♋7	♋	♌7	♌	♍10	♍	♎17	
Jul	♎	♎	♏2	♏	♐13	♐	♐	♑2	♑	♒15	♒	♒	♓3	♓	♈11	♈	♉16	♉	♊18	♊	♋17	♋	♌17	♌	♍19	♍	♎23	♎	♎	♏8	♏
Aug	♐19	♐	♐	♑8	♑	♒21	♒	♒	♓8	♓	♈17	♈	♉23	♉	♉	♊3	♊	♋4	♋	♌4	♌	♍5	♍	♎8	♎	♏15	♏	♏	♐2	♐	♑15
Sep	♑	♑	♒4	♒	♓14	♓	♈23	♈	♈	♉5	♉	♊10	♊	♋12	♋	♌14	♌	♍15	♍	♎18	♎	♎	♏0	♏	♐10	♐	♑22	♑	♑	♒11	
Oct	♒	♓22	♓	♓	♈5	♈	♉11	♉	♊15	♊	♋18	♋	♌21	♌	♌	♍0	♍	♎3	♎	♏9	♏	♐18	♐	♐	♑6	♑	♒19	♒	♒	♓6	♓
Nov	♈14	♈	♉18	♉	♊21	♊	♊	♋0	♋	♌3	♌	♍6	♍	♎11	♎	♏18	♏	♏	♐3	♐	♑15	♑	♑	♒4	♒	♓15	♓	♈23	♈	♈	
Dec	♉4	♉	♊6	♊	♋7	♋	♌8	♌	♍12	♍	♎17	♎	♎	♏1	♏	♐10	♐	♑22	♑	♑	♒11	♒	♓23	♓	♓	♈9	♈	♉15	♉	♊17	♊

2010	1	2	3	4	5	6	7	8	9	10	11	12	13	14	15	16	17	18	19	20	21	22	23	24	25	26	27	28	29	30	31
Jan	♋17	♋	♌17	♌	♍18	♍	♎23	♎	♎	♏6	♏	♐17	♐	♐	♑5	♑	♒18	♒	♒	♓6	♓	♈17	♈	♈	♉0	♉	♊4	♊	♋4	♋	♌3
Feb	♌	♍3	♍	♎6	♎	♏12	♏	♐22	♐	♐	♑11	♑	♑	♒0	♒	♓12	♓	♈23	♈	♈	♉8	♉	♊13	♊	♋15	♋	♌15	♌			
Mar	♍14	♍	♎15	♎	♏20	♏	♏	♐5	♐	♑17	♑	♑	♒6	♒	♓18	♓	♓	♈5	♈	♉13	♉	♊19	♊	♋23	♋	♋	♌1	♌	♍1	♍	♎2
Apr	♎	♏6	♏	♐13	♐	♐	♑0	♑	♒13	♒	♒	♓1	♓	♈11	♈	♉19	♉	♉	♊1	♊	♋5	♋	♌8	♌	♍10	♍	♎12	♎	♏15	♏	
May	♐22	♐	♐	♑8	♑	♒21	♒	♒	♓9	♓	♈19	♈	♈	♉2	♉	♊7	♊	♋10	♋	♌13	♌	♍16	♍	♎19	♎	♎	♏0	♏	♐7	♐	♑17
Jun	♑	♑	♒5	♒	♓17	♓	♓	♈4	♈	♉11	♉	♊15	♊	♋17	♋	♌19	♌	♍21	♍	♍	♎1	♎	♏7	♏	♐14	♐	♐	♑0	♑	♒13	
Jul	♒	♒	♓1	♓	♈12	♈	♉21	♉	♉	♊1	♊	♋3	♋	♌3	♌	♍4	♍	♎7	♎	♏12	♏	♐21	♐	♐	♑7	♑	♒19	♒	♒	♓8	♓
Aug	♈20	♈	♈	♉5	♉	♊11	♊	♋13	♋	♌13	♌	♍13	♍	♎14	♎	♏18	♏	♏	♐2	♐	♑13	♑	♑	♒2	♒	♓14	♓	♓	♈2	♈	♉13
Sep	♉	♊20	♊	♋23	♋	♋	♌0	♍23	♍	♎23	♎	♎	♏2	♏	♐8	♐	♑19	♑	♑	♒8	♒	♓20	♓	♓	♈8	♈	♉18	♉	♉	♊2	
Oct	♊	♋8	♋	♌10	♌	♍10	♍	♎10	♎	♏11	♏	♐17	♐	♐	♑2	♑	♒14	♒	♒	♓3	♓	♈14	♈	♈	♉0	♉	♊8	♊	♋14	♋	♌17
Nov	♌	♍19	♍	♎20	♎	♏22	♏	♏	♐2	♐	♑10	♑	♒22	♒	♒	♓10	♓	♈22	♈	♈	♉7	♉	♊14	♊	♋19	♋	♌23	♌	♌	♍2	
Dec	♍	♎4	♎	♏7	♏	♐12	♐	♑20	♑	♑	♒6	♒	♓19	♓	♓	♈7	♈	♉16	♉	♊22	♊	♊	♋2	♋	♌5	♌	♍7	♍	♎10	♎	♏14

Index

air signs *see* Aquarius Moon; Gemini Moon; Libra Moon
Aquarius Moon 134-45
  top tips 141-3
  troubleshooting 143-5
Aquarius Moon interactions
  Aquarius Moon 226
  Aries Moon 166-7
  Cancer Moon 194
  Capricorn Moon 224-5
  Gemini Moon 185-6
  Leo Moon 201-2
  Libra Moon 213
  Pisces Moon 227–8
  Sagittarius Moon 221
  Scorpio Moon 217-8
  Taurus Moon 176-7
  Virgo Moon 208
archetypes 14, 231
  see also symbolism
Aries Moon 14-25
  top tips 22
  troubleshooting 23-5
Aries Moon interactions
  Aquarius Moon 166-7
  Aries Moon 158-9
  Cancer Moon 161
  Capricorn Moon 166
  Gemini Moon 160–1
  Leo Moon 161-2
  Libra Moon 163-4
  Pisces Moon 167-8
  Sagittarius Moon 165
  Scorpio Moon 164–5
  Taurus Moon 159–60
  Virgo Moon 162-3
Ascendant (rising sign) 4, 231
astrological archetypes 14, 231
  see also symbolism
astrological tables 233-63

calculations, Moon sign 233-4
Cancer Moon 48-60
  top tips 57-8
  troubleshooting 58-60
Cancer Moon interactions
  Aquarius Moon 194
  Aries Moon 161
  Cancer Moon 187-8
  Capricorn Moon 193-4
  Gemini Moon 179-180
  Leo Moon 188
  Libra Moon 190-91
  Pisces Moon 195
  Sagittarius Moon 192-3
  Scorpio Moon 191-2
  Taurus Moon 171-2
  Virgo Moon 189–90
Capricorn Moon 122-33
  top tips 129-31

troubleshooting 131-33
Capricorn Moon interactions
Aquarius Moon 224-5
Aries Moon 166
Cancer Moon 193-4
Capricorn Moon 223-4
Gemini Moon 184-5
Leo Moon 200-1
Libra Moon 213
Pisces Moon 225–6
Sagittarius Moon 221
Scorpio Moon 217-18
Taurus Moon 175-6
Virgo Moon 207-8

earth signs *see* Capricorn Moon; Taurus Moon; Virgo Moon

fire signs *see* Aries Moon; Leo Moon; Sagittarius Moon

Gemini Moon 36-47
top tips 43-4
troubleshooting 45-7
Gemini Moon interactions
Aquarius Moon 185-6
Aries Moon 160–61
Cancer Moon 179-80
Capricorn Moon 184-5
Gemini Moon 178-9
Leo Moon 180–81
Libra Moon 182
Pisces Moon 186-7
Sagittarius Moon 184
Scorpio Moon 183
Taurus Moon 169-70
Virgo Moon 181
glyphs 235

Leo Moon 61-72
top tips 69-70
troubleshooting 70-2
Leo Moon interactions
Aquarius Moon 201-2
Aries Moon 161-2
Cancer Moon 188–9
Capricorn Moon 200-1
Gemini Moon 180–81
Leo Moon 196
Libra Moon 198
Pisces Moon 202-3
Sagittarius Moon 200
Scorpio Moon 199
Taurus Moon 171
Virgo Moon 197
Libra Moon 87-97
top tips 94-5
troubleshooting 95-7
Libra Moon interactions
Aquarius Moon 213–4
Aries Moon 163-4
Cancer Moon 190–91
Capricorn Moon 213
Gemini Moon 182
Leo Moon 198
Libra Moon 210
Pisces Moon 214
Sagittarius Moon 212
Scorpio Moon 211
Taurus Moon 173
Virgo Moon 204
love 8

Moon
Moon sign calculations & tables 233-62
properties & symbolism xv-xvii, xx-xxii, 1-2, 4-5
Vedic (moon-sign) astrology xiii, xiv, xvii, xix-xx, 2, 3, 8-11

see also specific moon signs (eg Aries Moon)

Pisces Moon 146-56
top tips 153-5
troubleshooting 155-6
Pisces Moon interactions
Aquarius Moon 227–8
Aries Moon 167-8
Cancer Moon 195
Capricorn Moon 225–6
Gemini Moon 186-7
Leo Moon 202-3
Libra Moon 214–5
Pisces Moon 228–9
Sagittarius Moon 223
Scorpio Moon 219
Taurus Moon 177-8
Virgo Moon 209

relationships xix-xx, 6-11, 157-8
see also specific moon signs (eg Aries Moon) and specific moon sign interactions (eg Aries Moon interactions)
rising sign (Ascendant) 4, 231

Sagittarius Moon 111-21
top tips 118-19
troubleshooting 119-21
Sagittarius Moon interactions
Aquarius Moon 222
Aries Moon 165
Cancer Moon 192–3
Capricorn Moon 220
Gemini Moon 184
Leo Moon 199
Libra Moon 212
Pisces Moon 223
Sagittarius Moon 220
Scorpio Moon 216-17
Taurus Moon 174-5
Virgo Moon 206-7
Scorpio Moon 98-110
top tips 106-7
troubleshooting 108-10
Scorpio Moon interactions
Aquarius Moon 218
Aries Moon 164–5
Cancer Moon 191-2
Capricorn Moon 217-8
Gemini Moon 183
Leo Moon 199
Libra Moon 211-12
Pisces Moon 219
Sagittarius Moon 216-7
Scorpio Moon 215-6
Taurus Moon 174
Virgo Moon 205–6
seduction top tips
Aquarius Moon 141-43
Aries Moon 22-3
Cancer Moon 57-8
Capricorn Moon 129-30
Gemini Moon 43-5
Leo Moon 69-70
Libra Moon 94-5
Pisces Moon 153-5
Sagittarius Moon 118-19
Scorpio Moon 106-7
Taurus Moon 32-3
Virgo Moon 82-3
Sun
properties & symbolism xv-xvii, xx-xii
Sun signs & Sun-sign astrology xiii, xvii-xix, 4, 231
symbolism 13-15, 231-2
Aquarius Moon 134
Aries Moon 15

Cancer Moon 48
Capricorn Moon 122
Gemini Moon 37
Leo Moon 61
Libra Moon 87
Moon xv-xvii, xx-xxii, 1-2, 4-5
Pisces Moon 145
Sagittarius Moon 111
Scorpio Moon 98
Sun xv-xvi, xx-xxii
Taurus Moon 26
Virgo Moon 73

Taurus Moon 26-35
top tips 32-3
troubleshooting 33-5
Taurus Moon interactions
Aquarius Moon 176-7
Aries Moon 159–60
Cancer Moon 170-71
Capricorn Moon 175-6
Gemini Moon 169-70
Leo Moon 171–2
Libra Moon 173
Pisces Moon 177-8
Sagittarius Moon 174-5
Scorpio Moon 174
Taurus Moon 168-9
Virgo Moon 172–3
time zones table 235

Vedas xiv-xv, xvii
Vedic (moon sign) astrology xiii, xiv, xvii, xix-xx, 2, 3, 8-11
see also specific moon signs (eg Aries Moon)
Virgo Moon 73-86
top tips 82-3
troubleshooting 83-6
Virgo Moon interactions
Aquarius Moon 208
Aries Moon 162-3
Cancer Moon 189–90
Capricorn Moon 207-8
Gemini Moon 181
Leo Moon 197
Libra Moon 204–5
Pisces Moon 209
Sagittarius Moon 206-7
Scorpio Moon 205-6
Taurus Moon 172
Virgo Moon 203–4

water signs *see* Cancer Moon; Pisces Moon; Scorpio Moon

zodiac archetypes 14, 231
see also symbolism